Artistic Integration in Gothic Buildings

In this collaborative work seventeen international scholars use contemporary methodologies to explore the ways in which we understand Gothic church buildings today. *Artistic Integration in Gothic Buildings* discusses major monuments that have traditionally stood at the core of medieval art-historical studies: the cathedrals of Durham, Wells, Chartres, Reims, Poitiers, Strasbourg, and Naumburg, the abbey of Saint-Denis, and the Sainte-Chapelle in Paris. The contributors approach the subject from different specialties and methodologies within the field of art history, as well as from the disciplines of history, liturgical studies, and theology.

Willibald Sauerländer's overview acknowledges that, since the early nineteenth century, scholars have studied monuments that no longer perform their original functions. Once the settings for complex and diversified rituals with religious, social, and political dimensions, these great cages of stone, filled with images in metal, paint, glass, stone, and textiles, have been adapted over the centuries to ever-changing historical, cultural, and religious contexts. Artistic intentions as well as the nature of the audience for these structures have shifted continuously over time. This volume addresses the development of scholarship on the Gothic church, reviewing the variable, but largely exclusive, agendas from the early nineteenth century to the present, including those of Viollet-le-Duc, Lefèvre-Pontalis, Mâle, Sedlmayr, von Simson, Panofsky, Grodecki, and Bony. *Artistic Integration in Gothic Buildings* reassesses the traditional canon through a new pluralism of approaches and presents the Gothic church as an intricate and complex living monument that has been evolving over more than eight centuries.

VIRGINIA CHIEFFO RAGUIN teaches in the Department of Visual Arts, College of the Holy Cross.

KATHRYN BRUSH teaches in the Department of Visual Arts, University of Western Ontario.

PETER DRAPER teaches in the Department of History of Art at Birkbeck College, University of London.

D1066316

Artistic Integration in Gothic Buildings

Edited by

Virginia Chieffo Raguin
Kathryn Brush
Peter Draper

UNIVERSITY OF TORONTO PRESS
Toronto Buffalo London

© University of Toronto Press Incorporated 1995
Toronto Buffalo London
Printed in Canada

ISBN 0-8020-0457-1 (cloth)
ISBN 0-8020-7477-4 (paper)

Printed on acid-free paper

Canadian Cataloguing in Publication Data

Main entry under title:

Artistic integration in Gothic buildings

Rev. papers presented at the conference "Artistic
integration in early Gothic churches" held at York
University, Toronto, on Apr. 7–9, 1989.
ISBN 0-8020-0457-1 (bound) ISBN 0-8020-7477-4 (pbk.)

1. Church architecture – Europe – Congresses.
2. Architecture, Gothic – Europe – Congresses.
I. Raguin, Virginia Chieffo, 1941–   . II. Brush,
Kathryn.   III. Draper, Peter.

NA5453.A77 1995   726'.5'0940902   C95-930403-7

University of Toronto Press acknowledges the financial assistance to its
publishing program of the Canada Council and the Ontario Arts Council.

Contents

Contents   vii

Foreword

Michael M. Sheehan CSB

If Raoul Glaber of the eleventh century had lived in Germany in the first generation after the Second World War, and if he had observed the hundreds of new churches that rose from the ruins, he might well have written that "it was as if the whole earth, having cast off the old by shaking itself, were clothing itself everywhere with the white robe of the church." Those churches, delayed fruit of much reflection and experimentation during the twenty years before the war, were not only statements of sophisticated contemporary architecture and engineering, but also involved careful consideration of the pastoral needs of the parish and the liturgical and private use of the sacred spaces that were created. The churches embraced iconographic programs that mirrored and supported the beliefs of the congregation, and forms of embellishment that stated the role of the new structures within the local society. In some dioceses at least, administrators, well aware of the sacred clutter that can so quickly disfigure religious edifices, established regulations that protected the synthesis that had been created, allowing additions and renewal only under the most careful supervision. Thus, were a scholar at the end of this century to examine the churches that resulted from this careful process, it would likely be possible to come to a satisfactory understanding of the complex motives that lay behind their creation, the development of their plans, even the sequence of their realization.

The religious monuments that survive from the Middle Ages – a much more distant past – still exercise a powerful attraction: even the new, Post-Modern architecture of the 1990s has chosen to mime their forms once more. It is clear enough to the medievalist, and to others less informed, that these buildings encompass rich combinations of architecture, iconographic programs expressed in different media, and – much more elusive – aspects of the medieval vision of life and its ultimate purpose. For the student of the history of ideas, the medieval period was a time of major synthesis, the age of the *summa*, be it theology, philosophy, or law. This may help to explain why the scholarly desire to seek the principles of integration which may or may not be stated in the immense and very complex architectural compositions that survive among us has proved to be irresistible. Yet it is clear that, more than any other medieval buildings, the great churches have enjoyed – and suffered – long lives of continued use. Over the centuries they have conformed to the shifting purposes and tastes of the communities that occupied them: repair, differing needs for space, liturgical change, and redirected pastoral emphasis have led to building and rebuilding, decoration and redecoration, statement and restatement of iconographic programs. To penetrate the accretions of the centuries and arrive at the principles of integration at the time of foundation, or at any crucial moment in the history of these buildings, has been attempted many times but has proven to be no easy task. And lurking in the background has been the troubling question touching the epistemology of the historiographical process: to what extent, if at all, can the purposes of a distant past be understood by us who live in a somewhat different world. For all their seeming transparency, the great medieval churches stand before us in majestic silence, silence that the research of the last decade tended to enhance rather than diminish.

The York University Colloquium set out to re-examine these matters once more, to seek to penetrate the silence that shrouds the great medieval churches by moving back through the documents that remain to us – and the monuments themselves, palimpsests though they be, are the principal record – to suggest, if possible, the degree of integration that lay behind them at their foundation or at moments when they underwent major adjustments. Some of the results follow, results that are very informative indeed.

Preface

The Editors

The essays collected in this volume would never have been brought together were it not for the dedication shown by Richard Schneider to the organization of the conference "Artistic Integration in Early Gothic Churches" held at York University, in Toronto, on 7–9 April, 1989. Richard expended an extraordinary amount of energy seeking out scholars interested in this issue and developing, even before the conference, a healthy dialogue among participants. He envisioned a conference in which scholars would not simply reconfirm already-held positions, but engage each other, and their specialties, in a productive re-examination of the interrelationship of social, political, artistic, and religious dimensions of the Gothic building. To this end, he sought out scholars not only from very different specialties in the fields of art history, but also from the fields of history, liturgy, and theology. The countries represented by the participants include Canada, the United States, Germany, Switzerland, and Great Britain. All of us owe him a special debt of gratitude.

This volume was put together by an editorial committee consisting of Peter Draper, Kathryn Brush, and Virginia Raguin (coordinator). The essays that began as conference papers have been altered substantially. They present the specific points of view of each author, the context of previous scholarship on similar questions, and the interrelated concepts articulated by other essays within the volume. Our desire to keep a compassionate dialogue, not only with one another but also with past scholarship, is reflected in the structure of the volume as a whole. Ideas of artistic integration have, we hope, been debated with passion and energy, and, if from multiple points of view, at least with civility.

A number of the papers discuss major monuments that have traditionally stood at the core of medieval art-historical studies: the cathedrals of Durham, Wells, Chartres, Reims, Poitiers, Strasbourg, and Naumburg; the abbey of Saint-Denis; and the Sainte-Chapelle in Paris. Although not all the contributors to this volume raise the same questions in relation to each monument, collectively they engage in these essays a wide variety of current scholarly directions. Each essay on a specific monument addresses it as a physical presence and as a product of a complex set of circumstances. At times the authors attempt to examine how these issues inevitably change through time, according to the perspective of the affected classes, patrons, and the re-evaluated priorities of the users of the monument. The fabric of the building is not separated from liturgy or decoration; neither are subsequent transformations (accretions) divorced from the monument's purported meaning. The essays do not parallel each other, but each represents a considered approach – that is, to work from the monument out to broader questions of reception and social context. This collection attempts to broaden the scope of our inquiry, but to remain true to a belief that buildings can be "read" in diverse ways and to suggest insights into the values of the societies that built and used them.

Along with the studies of selected monuments, this collection includes a number of more theoretical studies of the historiography of modern scholarship; the classification of periods, styles, and concepts; and the development of separate disciplines that often have impeded larger, more synthetic studies of the Gothic building. Several papers focus on the issue of liturgy in its broadest definition, as the use of the building by those owning and operating it. Several authors probe the function of the monument beyond its primary users to the larger sociohistorical setting within medieval history. Thus we see a dialogue among seeing, describing, and interpreting and the mechanics of other interpretive acts beyond the "visual" or the "art" of art history.

In speaking for all the contributors, the editors hope that these collected essays will serve as a basis for discussion by our colleagues. Most fervent, however, is our hope that our work will be of service to the general reader and to undergraduate students beginning their study of so rich and rewarding a subject. Particular thanks should be given to Willibald Sauerländer, Madeline Caviness, and Brigitte Bedos-Rezak for their perceptive essays discussing to the texts collected here.

The editors wish to thank Birkbeck College, University of London; the Research and Publications Fund of the College of the Holy Cross; the Faculty of Arts and Foundation Western, University of Western Ontario; the Research Foundation of the City University of New York; and the Pontifical Institute of Mediaeval Studies for generous subsidies which helped make publication possible.

Artistic Integration in Gothic Buildings

Integration: A Closed or Open Proposal?

Willibald Sauerländer

Sauerländer's overview of the essays contained in Artistic Integration in Gothic Buildings *acknowledges that, even since the early nineteenth century, scholars have been confronted with monuments that no longer perform their original functions. The moment of the creation of these great cages of stone, filled with images in metal, stone – paint, glass, and textiles – has passed, as surely as have Villon's "snows of yesteryear." Once the settings for complex and heterogeneous rituals of religious, social, and political dimensions, the buildings now stand in a completely different time frame and are experienced by a completely different audience. Sauerländer addresses the hermeneutics of the development of scholarship concerning the Gothic building through an overview of the variable, but largely exclusive, agendas from the early nineteenth century to the present, the worlds of Viollet-le-Duc, Lefèvre-Pontalis, Mâle, Sedlmayr, von Simson, Panofsky, Grodecki, and Bony. He voices for the contributors to this volume the conclusion that there is no way back to the real Gothic cathedral or the real twelfth-century audience. He distinguishes, however, three modes of discourse concerning the theme of integration within the fifteen separate essays: integration by time, integration by performance, and integration by context. He welcomes the result of this collection of essays, which he sees as manifesting a new pluralism of approaches rather than a focused reading of the Gothic cathedral according to a uniform set of principles.*

In the first years of this century, when the separation of church and state was an issue of political dispute in France, socialist deputies in the French parliament went so far as to demand the secularization of all church buildings. Marcel Proust's response eloquently defended the ecclesiastical status of the great French cathedrals. The novelist warned that the cathedrals, once despoiled of their liturgical functions, would soon become the object of a new kind of aesthetic élitism. "Let us imagine that with Catholicism extinguished for centuries, the customs of the faith disappear ... The cathedrals remain, however, ... despoiled and silent ... Artists are inspired to create moments of theatre based on the mysterious events that once took place ... Sacred drama is played and the cathedral sings once again ... This resurrection of Catholic ceremonies achieves the historical, social, physical, and musical beauty that only Wagner approached by his evocation of these themes in *Parsifal*. Bus loads of snobs travel to the holy place (whether Amiens, Chartres, Bourges, Laon, Reims, Beauvais, Rouen, or Paris) and once each year they are able to experience the emotions they had looked for in Bayreuth, ... enjoying a work of art in the setting that had been constructed for it alone."[1]

Proust's poignant text reveals the fundamental dilemma that all studies of Gothic cathedrals have faced since the days of Willis, Vitet, or Kugler. The early art historians conducted retrospective investigations in the face of a phenomenon which, again citing Proust, one might call "the death of the cathedrals."[2] The subjects were ecclesiastical buildings that had lost their original function, their old rites and customs, their liturgical furniture, their shrines and reliquaries, and, above all, their audience. Bare remnants from disintegrated and expropriated ensembles confronted the researcher. The sterile specialization of nineteenth-century studies of Gothic art and architecture, which separated the building from its decoration, the pillar from the statue attached to it, or the stained-glass window from the choir-stall, was the unavoidable and fatal consequence of the disintegration of the monuments themselves.

The technical and empirical bias in past art-historical research, however, reflected characteristic patterns in nineteenth-century scholarship as a whole. The separation of the study of architecture from histories of painting and sculpture paralleled the separation in the nineteenth-century academic curriculum between architecture and engineering, on the one side, and the "fine arts" of painting and sculpture, on the other side. Interest in and the study of Gothic architecture had not been initiated by art historians but by historic-revival architects who looked on Gothic buildings as models for their own projects. Viollet-le-Duc emerges as one of the better-known examples of a general movement that encouraged practitioners to become historians of period styles.[3] Even an art historian from the end of the nineteenth century such as Georg Dehio, who had never been an architect, began his massive volumes filled with plans and elevations of Romanesque and Gothic churches as model-books for historic-revival architects.[4] The architects' concerns prioritized problems of technique, engineering, and patterns of design of Gothic building. With the rise of the modern movement in architecture around 1900, the historicist interest from architects came to an end. The technical approach to the problems of Gothic architecture, however, continued to shape art-historical studies through the time of Marcel Aubert and Henri Focillon. One need only review the extensive debate on the origin, the function, and the importance of the rib-vault in past scholarly literature.[5]

This specialization in architectural studies was no more exaggerated than that in another branch of nineteenth-century science, the self-styled *archéologie médiévale*.[6] This study had nothing to do with the archaeology of medieval sites as this field has developed in the last two or three decades. The *archéologie médiévale* of the past had taken root in the atmosphere established by the Ecole des Chartes and it remained a very French-centred enterprise. The Ecole had been founded in 1821, and its chair of medieval archaeology created in 1846. Like the paleographers and historians of the Ecole, the *archéologists* approached ecclesiastical monuments as historical documents. Mouldings and joints had to be read and deciphered like charts. Lefèvre-Pontalis, one of the leading *archéologists*, was, characteristically enough, professor of medieval archaeology at the Ecole des Chartes and director of the Société Française d'Archéologie. He delineated the program of medieval archaeological science in his seminal essay "Comment doit-on rédiger la monographie d'une église?" as the following: (1) Determine the campaign of construction; (2) Dismember the edifice; (3) Connect the church to a specific school.

Setting the dominant tone of architectural discourse for decades, Lefèvre-Pontalis articulated the importance of plotting chronological sequences through a study of moulding profiles, elements that he believed to be the most precise evidence of building changes in the Middle Ages.[7] This doctrine, although formulated as late as 1906, is indebted to the unquestioned positivism of the tradition of Auguste

Comte. The method applied by the medieval archaeologist is the same as that used in zoology, botany, or mineralogy. The characteristics of the object, in this instance the mouldings of a Gothic church, were unambiguous, and their significance unequivocal. The scientist had only to examine and to classify these identification marks to determine the categories of genera and species, or, if one were addressing a medieval building, date and school. The scientist/ archaeologist could also decide the place of the object in the evolution of the species. In the case of the Gothic church, this would be translated as dating and reading the sequence of building campaigns in relationship to other buildings of the same type. The botanist observes the shapes of flowers and leaves; the archaeologist the forms of the mouldings. The mouldings are the archaeologist's chronometer.

As early as 1880, the writer Gustave Flaubert denounced this scholarly belief in the rigidity of architectural characteristics. In his novel *Bouvard et Pécuchet*, to a large degree a satire ridiculing the positivism of Comte, a character exclaims, "But the style of a monument does not always coincide with the date one supposes. The rounded arch is still prevalent in Provence in the thirteenth century. The pointed arch is perhaps of an earlier origin, and yet scholars debate the antiquity of the Romanesque over the Gothic style." Bouvard and Pécuchet, the two would-be scientists and the grotesque heroes of Flaubert's story, observe that "this lack of certitude vexes them."[8] But who would dare to deny that, until quite recently, most of us have remained like Bouvard and Pécuchet? Most of our studies of Early and High Gothic architecture have been dominated by the positivistic belief in a linear chronology readable as schema of unambiguous characteristics and identification marks.

One could probably trace the historical origins of specialized research in other branches of Gothic art with similar results. Among the pioneers of the study of Gothic stained-glass windows were scholars such as Bégule in France, and Geiges and Oidtmann in Germany, whose main profession was the production of historical-revival stained-glass windows.[9] The extreme specialization of the study of Gothic sculpture as separated from its original architectural context is analysed perceptively by Kathryn Brush in this volume. This specialization corresponded to the interests of museums and collectors, and also to the need of nineteenth-century restorers and manufacturers for convenient models for their production of historicist statues.

These interests have been obsolete almost nearly a century now. But the aftermath of this artificial segregation of the different branches of Gothic art has continued. It has shaped our scholarly mentalities, our books, and even our curricula. As late as 1990, art-historical medievalists tend to split into specialists for architecture, sculpture, stained glass, and decorative arts. Beat Brenk's review of the scholarship on the Sainte-Chapelle reveals how debilitating the situation remains. Even nowadays "the death of the cathedrals" is reflected in the positivistic disintegration of the research on Gothic cathedrals.

One might expect that at least the study of iconography, from its beginnings, embraced all the different branches of the figurative arts in the Gothic period. In a deeper sense, however, research on Christian iconography has been no less affected by the process of historical disintegration than has the study of architecture or of sculpture. The cathedral's rich imagery of portals, choir screens, altars, stained-glass windows, shrines, and statues had been connected with the liturgy. Local cults and customs had been born of a local topography full of memories, remembrances, and meanings, addressing a manifold audience which lived within the physical matrix of commemorative feasts, saints' biographies, reliquaries, and images in the churches. The audience passed the statues of the martyrs Potentianus and Modesta on their way to the Puits des Saints Forts at Chartres. They viewed images of the translation of the relics of Saint Firmin on the west façade of Amiens before they entered the cathedral to visit the saint's shrine in the choir. The study of Christian iconography as it was established around 1830, however, was a systematic registration of images which had lost their original function and their audience. From Cahier to Auber, Crosnier, and Barbier de Montault, many of the leading specialists of Christian iconography in France were learned Catholic priests who wanted to resuscitate the pious images of medieval cathedrals as a sort of visual catechism in the service of the Catholic revival.[10] In 1898, Emile Mâle began his series of books on religious art in France in the climate of the vehement dispute between anticlericalism and "renouveau catholique." He exhorted his French reader to abandon the idea of trying to see in "our" ancient artists independent, restless souls, ever ready to shake off the yoke of the church.[11] Mâle's book is an admirable iconographic study; it is also a Catholic-revival confession of faith. The students of the iconography of the cathedrals became but another kind of specialists – namely, in the classification and identification of pious images. They were interested in signs, attributes, hagiography, and typology, but not in the function of images, and not at all in their audience.

And yet there has always been – since the iconoclasm of the French Revolution and since the death of the church of the "Ancien Régime" – a nostalgic yearning for the lost integrated cathedral. It is voiced very early in Chateaubriand's *Génie du christianisme*, finds its echo in Victor Hugo's *The Hunchback of Notre-Dame* (*Notre-Dame de Paris*), and returns at the end of the nineteenth century in the languorous sentimentalism of Huysmans's *La cathédrale*. There is even an American echo of this nostalgia in Henry Adams's *Mont-Saint-Michel and Chartres*, which appeared in 1904, six years after Huysmans's work. All of these were literary voices from outside the academy. The dream of the integrated cathedral, however, did not remain extraneous to art-historical and historical scholarship. In the aftermath of the Second World War, when the experience of profound inhumanity had aroused the desire for a new spirituality, Hans Sedlmayr and Otto von Simson wrote their books *Die Entstehung der Kathedrale* and *The Gothic Cathedral: Origins of Gothic Architecture and the Medieval Concept of Order*, respectively, with the explicit intention of summing up and transcending the perspectives of specialized research. Sedlmayr clearly articulated this goal in his preface, stating that the cathedral was erected through cooperative work and that only through such work could its goal of the awakening of the spirit be realized. He outlined his program: "The results of separate studies for a century now come together to produce a new complete image, so that we can describe the *whole* cathedral, not simply its architecture."[12] Von Simson's argument is surprisingly similar: "The scholarship of a century has yielded penetrating insights into the aesthetic and constructive aspects of Gothic architecture. Yet neither the just definition nor the sensitive appreciation of style and design can quite explain the cathedrals. What experience did these great sanctuaries inspire in those who worshiped in them?"[13] The two books are different from each other, but both aimed at a new holistic understanding of the cathedral through a reintegration of its disintegrated parts. Characteristically, neither book fared well with specialists, who ignored the larger issues and criticized specific details.[14] Largely unexplored, however, was the more fundamental issue of whether these holistic visions of the cathedral were more the expression of a crisis in twentieth-century spirituality than a genuine historical insight.[15] This is precisely the question that remains with us today. More recently, the distinguished

French historian Georges Duby published *Le temps des cathédrales,* which has been more or less passed over in silence by art historians.[16]

The specialists may have good reasons for this attitude. But it remains an odd situation: generalists and specialists neglecting and, in some instances, even distrusting each other's scholarship. Moreover, specialized research on the architecture, sculpture, stained glass, furniture, and the treasures of the Gothic cathedrals have remained, for the most part, immune to the astonishing renewal of medieval studies in such neighbouring field as literature and history. It is only in recent years, and often by outsiders such as Wolfgang Kemp or by younger scholars such as Michael Camille, that the insights of recent literary studies have begun to be applied to Gothic imagery.[17] In our volume, Virginia Raguin's discussion of the stained-glass windows of the cathedral at Poitiers takes this new approach. This belated reception of modern methods has had disturbing practical consequences. One of them is a loss of status and audience for medieval art history over the last ten years. One might call this another case of disintegration.

There appears, then, much justification for the desire to reintegrate the specialized and separated studies of Gothic architecture, sculpture, stained glass, and so on. But history teaches us also that there is no easy way back to the "whole" of the cathedral, if we want to avoid creating another Post-Modern dream. There are also compelling reasons against an unreflective rush to the holistic cathedral, and also against an ill-considered borrowing of fashionable methods from other fields. Even in a reintegrated cathedral the scholar must always contend with Flaubert's biting sentence "Le bon dieu est dans le détail" (God is in the detail).

II

Any discussion of the discourse set out in the essays in this volume must start from one fundamental hermeneutical premise: there is no way back to the *real* Gothic cathedral, to the *real* twelfth-century audience, to any kind of medieval wholeness, if ever such a thing existed. As Madeline Caviness rightly says, our present, "Post-Modern" yearning for integration brings us not one inch closer to Suger, Chartres, or Reims than Chateaubriand, Viollet-le-Duc, or Panofsky had been. This yearning reflects only our own desire to look on the cathedrals in a different light. It is ironic, but refreshing, to observe that the result of the dialogue in these essays is less a new integration than a new pluralism of surprisingly diverse approaches. This is the most interesting and the most promising aspect of the experiment we have undertaken. Very different kinds of possible integrations were proposed. I will describe three, marking each, quite deliberately, with a question mark.

Integration in Time?

In the period of early twentieth-century modernism, our predecessors saw Early Gothic architecture and art as a type of twelfth-century avant-garde. The building of the façade and the choir at Saint-Denis was celebrated as the birth of a new style, and Suger was praised as the patron, or even the inventor, of a medieval modernism. "It was as if the President of the United States were to have had the White House rebuilt by Frank Lloyd Wright," to quote Panofsky.[18] This view has been questioned since the appearance in 1962 of Renato Poggioli's *Teoria dell'arte d'avanguardia*.[19] The notion of a permanent stylistic innovation of modern art is no longer accepted as a given. This erosion of the concept of the avant-garde was not unnoticed by medieval scholarship. Saint-Denis has ceased to be viewed as a tribute to change or newness, and the rebuilding of the façade and the choir of the old abbey church in the twelfth century has become connected with a quite different concept of time which one might call, following Fernand Braudel, "la longue durée."[20] Eric Fernie and William Clark remind us in this volume of the written, and even visual, evidence that, in a twelfth-century perspective, the façade and the choir at Saint-Denis were not intended to be seen as daring innovations but as renewals, monuments enhancing a *renovatio* of the early, pre-Carolingian tradition of the churches of Paris.[21] These ideas are a welcome and reasonable revision of earlier opinions which saw Suger's achievements at Saint-Denis as a sort of anti-Romanesque revolution in style.[22] The rebuilding of the façade and of the choir at Saint-Denis in the time of Abbot Suger is now viewed as integrated into the meaningful continuity of the history of the great royal abbey since the early Middle Ages. And yet this diachronic perspective could easily become a no less dangerous trap than the earlier vision of Saint-Denis as a revolutionary building. The trap which I have in mind is perhaps best described by a sigh of the "curé" of Saint-Denis which I overheard in the late 1950s. Looking down in the trenches of

Formigé's excavations, he lamented, "If they keep this up, they will be rebuilding the Merovingian church for us." The intention of Suger, of the chapter of the cathedral at Notre-Dame, or of the abbots of Saint-Germain-des-Prés may well have been to achieve nothing more than a renewal of their early medieval churches. The result of their retrospective efforts was, nevertheless, a form of architecture and sculpture which had never been seen before. This dialectic between possible intention and evident result seems to me to lie at the heart of the hermeneutic crux of our present discourse on Gothic. To limit or unilaterally focus our attention to what we suppose might have been the intention of the patrons eight hundred years ago will produce only a new form of disintegration. With Brigitte Bedos-Rezak and Bernard McGinn, I would argue that we have to be aware of the complex and dialectic relation between the intention, which in our case might have been *renovatio*, and the result, which evidently became *innovatio*. Such an awareness might permit us a more complex, a more pluralistic understanding of the situation at Saint-Denis around 1140 than our predecessors could have. We have more questions, and our answers are, one hopes, less sure. And we should operate with an open concept of time transcending the bias of either the synchronic or the diachronic perspective.

Integration of Performance?

For a long time architectural historians have looked on cathedrals as monuments of pure architecture, as a shell of stone enclosing a mysterious space, a sacred void. As late as 1983, Jean Bony, probably the most sensitive historian of medieval architecture of his generation, did not hesitate to write: "It is rather difficult now to be immediately conscious of that width and of that continuity of space ... because of the early sixteenth-century choir screen, which manages to destroy the interior unity of the choir at Chartres."[23] Ecclesiastical furniture is regarded as a barrier against that aesthetic experience of continuous space, which was, since the days of the nineteenth-century Romantics, the great fascination for any modern beholder entering a Gothic cathedral. "Learning from Las Vegas,' to use Venturi's well-known and ironic slogan, we have, over the last ten or fifteen years, begun to remember that the old cathedrals were once places of social communication, assembling an audience or even simultaneously different audiences around rites and images, costumes and reliquaries. We try to reconstruct the performances which once took place in the nowadays largely empty and nearly dead cathedrals. We believe we have understood that the numerous images in the cathedrals were more than a series of iconographic puzzles. They were distributed on portals and pillars, altars and choir screens, tombs and holy sepulchres; they appeared on windows and walls. Their distribution corresponded to a local topography of multidimensional traditions. The reconstruction of the sacred performances which once took place in the cathedrals presupposes – or must go together with – a reconstruction of the original setting of the stage where such performances took place.

Beat Brenk has come close to a solution to the problem presented by this delicate task in his study of certain new aspects of the architectural and iconographic program of the Sainte-Chapelle in Paris. But the Sainte-Chapelle is an exceptional building with hardly more than a single function, the veneration of a royal relic. To reconstruct the original furnishings of a large cathedral is a much more complex undertaking. Peter Kurmann and Brigitte Kurmann-Schwarz remind us that the distribution of the monumental statues on the south transept at Chartres reflects the distribution of the patron saints in the chapels of the ambulatory of the cathedral. The imagery of the portals of a cathedral is not an abstract representation of sacred history, but a site-specific guide inviting the faithful to visit designated sacred places in the interior of the cathedral.

Another means of reconstructing the original setting of the interior of the cathedral is not mentioned in this volume – namely, the study of all the later written and visual sources representing the interior of the cathedrals before the wave of iconoclastic destruction and liturgical purification begun in the sixteenth century. Contemporary documents dating from the thirteenth through fifteenth centuries, and still of some use from the seventeenth and eighteenth centuries, describe the living cathedral, with its ancient furnishings and sometimes even its specific audiences on great feast days. Such documents reveal the building's growth in meaning through the accumulation of new cults and customs.[24] The complexity of the stage setting in a large cathedral reflects different, even competitive traditions, cults, obligations, and interests. Not a holistic unity would emerge from such a study, but rather a diachronic image of the cathedral with always new additions, changes, and enrichments. Madeline Caviness's recent study of the abbeys of Braine and Saint-Remi at Reims describes two important Early Gothic buildings in this perspective.[25]

The performance in the cathedral was mainly, if not exclusively, liturgical. It is probably fair to assume that the liturgical needs were integral to the planning process of any large cathedral. Arnold Klukas has shown in a very convincing way the demands for liturgical expansion and renewal which led to the erection of the new retro-choir, the Chapel of the Nine Altars at the cathedral at Durham. Roger Reynolds reminds us of the complexity of liturgical problems and how difficult it is to cope with them as long as so many of the relevant texts remain unpublished. Two German cathedrals have recently been the object of relatively careful if not complete liturgical studies by the art historian Renate Kroos. The result indicates that, at Bamberg, we see continuity; for Cologne, we see change. The building program of the thirteenth-century cathedral at Bamberg was evidently dictated by extant liturgical tradition. The liturgical topography of the preceding Early Romanesque building, which had been erected after the foundation of the see in 1107, remained operative, a clear case of *renovatio*. The new Gothic cathedral at Cologne, however, was begun in 1248 and shows a totally new building program, one which displays a clear self-reflective unity and a radical break with the preceding early medieval buildings. The plan of the new building at Cologne aroused the resistance of conservative members of the chapter, and no effort was spared to transfer all the liturgical customs from the old cathedral, with its double choir, to the new Gothic building, with its ambulatory and radiating chapels.[26] Liturgical tradition and architectural innovation are combined. In France information is often scant concerning the ground-plans of the early medieval or Romanesque buildings preceding the Gothic cathedrals; it remains an open question to what degree a new building reflects the liturgical topography of its predecessor. In cases like Laon or Sens, one wonders if this was also the case. Sometimes – Laon is an example, among others – the erection of a Gothic cathedral was the grounds for the redaction of a new ordinary. In other cases liturgical traditions interfered heavily with the unity of the plan of a new Gothic cathedral. The integration of Notre-Dame-la-Ronde into the new cathedral at Metz was a compromise between liturgical and ecclesiastical traditions. The result is an architectural oddity. The integration of liturgy into our reading and mapping of Gothic cathedrals is certainly overdue. The building without the performance is but a piece of abstract architectural styling. Yet liturgy in medieval churches was no less complex and unsystematic than the distribution of the ecclesiastical furniture. The regularity of Gothic design creates the illusion of a unity, even uniformity, which belies the complexity of the different liturgical functions.[27]

Integration of Context?

It was not by chance, that "art in context" was developed as a new methodological perspective in the aftermath of the social and the intellectual crisis which began in the 1960s. Neither Branner's book on Bourges of 1962, nor my own *Gothic Sculpture in France*, which appeared ten years later, nor even Jean Bony's *French Gothic Architecture of the 12th and 13th Centuries*, published in 1983, paid much attention to the problems of the social, economic, ideological, and political context surrounding "les chantiers des cathédrales."[28] Barbara Abou-El-Haj discusses in this volume the difficult problems of a social, political, and ideological contextualization of the cathedrals. The integration of context is certainly the most difficult and delicate task for the art historian, because it cannot be based on the visual and physical evidence of the monuments themselves but presupposes a perspective from the outside, seeing the cathedrals as extraneous events in an urban, agricultural, feudal environment. And yet this integration of context is probably of even greater importance than the integration of time and performance. There are many reasons to assume that the outside context affected the shape and the program of the cathedrals more profoundly than we previously thought. Although their results are still limited and not uncontested, recent studies of the economic and political context of Chartres or Reims have demonstrated that the idea of the cathedral as the spiritual image of a political and social consensus is doomed. All too often the erection of these gigantic ecclesiastical buildings was accompanied by bitter conflicts with the communes and occasionally also with the nobility. Another important field of conflict around the cathedrals not mentioned in our volume is that of religious conflict, or heresy. The erection of the great Gothic cathedrals and the extermination of the Cathars in the south of France were not only contemporaneous but interconnected events.[29] The most difficult but also the most fascinating question is how these conflicts may have affected the images and forms of Early and High Gothic cathedrals. Are the gigantic proportions of Chartres, Reims, or Beauvais visual statements of an embattled church confronting conflicts and threats? Does the glazing of Chartres reflect recent political events such as the crusades against the Albigensians, the ambitions of the royal house and of the dukes of Britanny, and other more local interests, or is the program an image of consensus and order in medieval Christian society?[30] These are questions which may be difficult to answer. But these questions show that the perspective from the outside – the integration of context – brings us back right into the centre of the cathedral itself, however not into a holistic cathedral.

I will try to sum up: for someone of my generation, who was brought up in the years after the Second World War with the nostalgic idea of the Gothic cathedral as the spiritual image of social, political, and ideological consensus, the Post-Modern perspective of integration looks very ambivalent. If integration is taken to mean, once more, that all the different parts and images of the Gothic cathedral corresponded to a medieval concept of order, then one can only say that such a holistic assumption is not confirmed by the study of the different cathedrals, of their program, of their performance, and of their context. The essays collected in this volume show this consistently. If integration means, however, that our studies of Early and High Gothic cathedrals should embrace new aspects, fresh questions, and neglected dimensions, it is not only more than welcome, but overdue. In other words, integration will be productive only if it makes our discourse on the Gothic cathedrals broader and more enlightened, if it opens doors and leaves the old dream of the holistic cathedral alone.

NOTES

1 Proust's essay appeared in *Le Figaro* on 16 August 1904. It has been reprinted in Marcel Proust, *Pastiches et mélanges* (Paris, 1919), pp. 198–9. Editors' note: It is of significance in this context that Proust was the author of a French translation, with commentary, of *The Bible of Amiens*, Ruskin's study of the cathedral of Amiens as carrier of Christian faith [*La Bible d'Amiens* (Paris, 1904)].

2 This was the title of Proust's essay. For the "dead" cathedral in a somewhat different context, see Willibald Sauerländer, "La cathédrale et la révolution," *L'art et les révolutions. Actes du XXVIIe Congrès international de l'histoire de l'art* (Strasbourg, 1990), pp. 67–106.

3 For the bibliography on Viollet-le-Duc, see *Viollet-le-Duc* [exh. cat., Galer-

ies Nationales du Grand Palais] (Paris, 1980). See also M. Steinhauser, "Gotik und Moderne," in *Die alte Stadt: Denkmal oder Lebensraum*, ed. C. Meckseper and H. Siebenmorgen, pp. 27–66 (Göttingen, 1985).

4 See the preface to the first fascicle of Georg Dehio and G. von Bezold, *Die kirchliche Baukunst des Abendlandes* (Stuttgart, 1884).

5 See Marcel Aubert, "Les plus anciennes croisées d'ogives, leur rôle dans la construction," *Bulletin monumental* 93 (1934), 5–67 and 137–237.

6 See Marcel Aubert, "Les études d'archéologie du moyen âge en France 1834–1934," *Congrès archéologique* 97 (1934), 211–57.

7 E. Lefèvre-Pontalis, "Comment doit-on rédiger la monographie d'une église?" *Bulletin monumental* 70 (1906), 452–82.

8 Gustave Flaubert, *Bouvard et Pécuchet* in *Oeuvre posthume*, introduction and notes by E. Maynal [Classiques Garnier] (Paris, n.d.), p. 124.

9 Lucien Bégule, *Les vitraux du moyen âge et de la renaissance dans la région lyonnaise et spécialement dans l'ancien diocèse de Lyon* (Lyon, 1911). Bégule was also a maker of stained-glass windows. Geiges restored and published the stained glass of the cathedral at Freiburg-im-Breisgau. See Fritz Geiges, *Der mittelalterliche Fensterschmuck des Freiburger Münsters* (Freiburg, 1931). Heinrich Oidtmann was the head of a large firm producing stained glass and published on glass in the Rhineland: *Die Glasmalerei*, 2 vols. (Cologne, 1892–8) and *Die rheinischen Glasmalereien vom 12. bis zum 16. Jahrhundert*, 2 vols. (Düsseldorf, 1912 and 1929). See, further, Virginia Raguin, "Revivals, Revivalists, and Architectural Stained Glass," *The Journal of the Society of Architectural Historians* 49 (1990), 310–39.

10 A brief mention of a few individuals will have to suffice. Charles Cahier and Arthur Martin, who published, among other things, four volumes of *Mélanges d'archéologie, d'histoire et de littérature* (Paris), which appeared from 1847 to 1856, were Jesuits. Auber, the author of *Histoire et théorie de symbolisme religieux*, 4 vols. (Paris, 1884), and *Histoire de la cathédrale de Poitiers*, 2 vols. (Poitiers, 1848–9), mentioned in Raguin's essay in this volume, was a member of the diocesan clergy. Crosnier, who published an *Iconographie chrétienne*, 2d ed. (Tours, 1876), became bishop of Nevers. Barbier de Montault, the author of *Traité pratique de la construction, de l'ameublement et de la décoration des églises selon les régles canoniques et les traditions romaines*, 2 vols. (Paris, 1878), was a "Cameriere" at the Vatican.

11 "Il faut ... renoncer à faire de nos vieux artistes du moyen âge des esprits indépendants, inquiets, toujours prêts à secouer le joug de l'église": Emile Mâle, *L'art religieux du XIIIe siècle en France*, 5th ed. (Paris, 1923), p. 399. Mâle's work has enjoyed continued popularity. See the paperback transla-

tion of this seminal text, *The Gothic Image: Religious Art in France of the Thir-teenth Century*, trans. Dora Nussey (New York, 1958).

12 Hans Sedlmayr, *Die Entstehung der Kathedrale* (Zurich, 1950), p. 9.

13 Otto von Simson, *The Gothic Cathedral: Origins of Gothic Architecture and the Medieval Concept of Order* (New York, 1956; Harper Torchbook, 1964), pp. xiv–xv.

14 See Louis Grodecki, "L'interpretation de l'art gothique: Hans Sedlmayr, *Die Entstehung der Kathedrale*," *Critique* 8/65 (1952), 847–57; Sumner Mc-Knight Crosby review of Otto von Simson, *The Gothic Cathedral, Art Bulletin* 42 (1960), 149–60. Exchange of responses by von Simson and Crosby, ibid., 316–21.

15 See, however, Martin Gosebruch on Sedlmayr, *Die Entstehung der Kathedrale. Göttingische Gelehrte Anzeigen* 211 (1954), 309 ff., and more recently Paul Crossley, "Medieval Architecture and Meaning: The Limits of Iconography," *The Burlington Magazine* 130 (1988), 116–21.

16 Georges Duby, *Le temps des cathédrales. L'Art et la société 980–1420* (Paris, 1976); trans. Eleanor Levieux and Barbara Thompson as *The Age of the Cathedrals: Art and Society 980–1420* (Chicago, 1981).

17 See, for example, Wolfgang Kemp, *Sermo Corporeus. Die Erzählung der mittelalterlichen Glasfenster* (Munich, 1987), and Michael Camille, "Seeing and Reading: Some Visual Implications of Medieval Literacy and Illiteracy," *Art History* 7 (1985), 26–49.

18 Erwin Panofsky, *Abbot Suger on the Abbey Church of Saint-Denis and Its Art Treasures* (Princeton, 1946), p. 27.

19 O. Poggioli, *Teoria dell'arte d'avanguardia* (Bologna, 1962); P. Burger, *Theorie der Avantgarde* (Frankfurt, 1974); and Ernst Gombrich, *Kunst and Fortschritt* (Cologne, 1978).

20 Fernand Braudel, *Ecrits sur l'histoire* (Paris, 1969), p. 41.

21 I have also expressed similar views. See Willibald Sauerländer, "Abwegige Gedanken über französische Architektur und 'the Renaissance of the Twelfth Century,'" *Etudes d'art médiéval offertes à Louis Grodecki* (Paris, 1981), pp. 167–83; idem., "'Première architecture gothique' or 'Renaissance of the Twelfth Century'? Changing Perspectives of Evaluation in Architectural History," *Sewanee Mediaeval Colloquium Occasional Papers* 2 (1985), 25–43; idem., *Das Jahrhundert der grossen Kathedralen* (Munich, 1989), p. 22.

22 The term "anti-roman" was coined by Louis Grodecki. See Louis Grodecki, *Le Moyen Âge retrouvé*, vol. 1 in *De l'an mil à l'an 1200* (Paris, 1986), p. 12. Grodecki's vision of the anti-Romanesque character of Suger's achievement at Saint-Denis remains, in my opinion, still a highly valuable contribution.

23 Jean Bony, *French Gothic Architecture of the 12th and 13th Centuries* (Berkeley, 1983), pp. 222–3.

24 See Willibald Sauerländer, "Gedanken über das Nachleben des gotischen Kirchenraumes im Spiegel der Malerei," *Münchner Jahrbuch der bildenden Kunst* (1994, forthcoming); see, for the rise of the laity and its incursion into sacred space, Corine Schlief, *Donatio et Memoria: Stifter, Stiftungen and Motivationen an Beispielen aus der Lorenzkirche in Nürnberg* (Munich, 1990).

25 Madeline Caviness, *The Sumptuous Arts of the Royal Abbeys of St Remi and Braine* (Princeton, 1990).

26 Renate Kroos, "Liturgische Quellen zum Bamberger Dom," *Zeitschrift für Kunstgeschichte* 39 (1976), 105–47; idem, "Liturgische Quellen zum Kölner Domchor," *Kölner Domblatt* 44/45 (1979), 35–203.

27 Editors' note: Arnold Klukas proposed a teleological integration of the building in commenting on the session "Medieval Functionalism: Ritual and Architecture," 78th Annual Meeting of the College Art Association of America, New York, February 1990. He suggested that the upper, architecturally unified, portions of the cathedral may have functioned to evoke the unity of the Heavenly Jerusalem against the architectural divisions of the floor level that reflected social divisions of a stratified earthly society.

28 Robert Branner, *La cathédrale de Bourges et sa place dans l'architecture gothique* (Paris, 1962), trans. and ed. Shirley Prager Branner, *The Cathedral of Bourges and Its Place in Gothic Architecture* (New York and Cambridge, 1989); Willibald Sauerländer, *Gotische Skulptur in Frankreich 1140–1270* (Munich, 1970), trans. Janet Sondheimer, *Gothic Sculpture in France 1140–1270* (London and New York, 1972).

29 For these issues see Sauerländer, *Kathedralen*, pp. 2, 157, 417.

30 See Françoise Perrot, "Le vitrail, la croisade et la Champagne: Réflection sur les fenêtres hautes du choeur de la cathédrale de Chartres," in *Les Champenois et la Croisade* [*Actes des quatrièmes journées rémoises, 27–28 Nov. 1987*], ed. Y. Bellenger and D. Quéruel, pp. 109–28 (Paris, 1989); and, recently, Beat Brenk, "Bildprogrammatik und Geschichtsverständnis der Kapetinger im Querhaus der Kathedrale von Chartres," *Arte medievale*, 2d ser., 5/2 (1991), 71–96.

2

Integration or Segregation among Disciplines? The Historiography of Gothic Sculpture as Case-Study

Kathryn Brush

Brush's essay addresses the historical prejudice of scholarship, demonstrating why the art-historical subspecialities of architecture, sculpture, and stained glass do not, as yet, converse fruitfully with one another. In order to understand this state of our scholarship, Brush comments specifically on the historiography of Gothic sculpture. During the nineteenth century, Gothic sculpture came to be viewed as having a "history" that was distinct from the sculpture of other periods, such as the Greek, or classical era. Beyond attempting to distinguish Gothic sculpture apart from past contexts, scholars also began to view Gothic carvings as independent of the environment of the architecture that housed them.

Referring to the writings of early art historians such as Kügler, Schnaase, and Lübke, as well as to the development of technical and empirical classification systems, Brush investigates the ways in which an autonomous history of Gothic sculpture took shape. In addition, she traces the development of research resources such as photographic corpora which served to introduce the works under study to a broader public. Photographic reproductions, however, had the effect of distancing the scholar from the contexts in which the works were originally meant to be seen and enabled him or her to pass judgment and classify works, often without firsthand experience of the medieval site. Like photographic reproductions, the museums of plaster casts founded in the second half of the late nineteenth century fostered a kind of self-referentiality that was measurable and knowable in closed, purely visual systems without needing recourse to historical explanations. Extra-academic factors, for example, the physical dislodgement of medieval sculpture follow-

ing the French Revolution and Napoleonic occupations, and the art market, which was linked to the context of the now collectible object, contributed to the fashioning of "Gothic sculpture" as a specialized area of study. Further, nationalist political agendas of the late nineteenth century helped to inform the writing of separate "national" histories of Gothic sculpture.

In this essay I wish to consider the issue of "integration" in relation to the modern formation and development of medieval scholarship. Remarkably few synthetic or integrative views of Gothic have been proposed by medievalist scholars during the past hundred years. These would include the iconographical *summae* of Emile Mâle and the phenomenologically oriented vision of the Gothic cathedral put forward by Hans Sedlmayr.[1] To these comprehensive explanatory systems, we could add those of Erwin Panofsky and Otto von Simson, who envisioned the Gothic cathedral as a kind of *Gesamtkunstwerk* generated by philosophical and theological thought of the twelfth and thirteenth centuries, and in a certain sense, equatable with it.[2] Yet all of these attempts to construct holistic explanations of Gothic represent exceptions rather than the rule. As we debate the issue of "medieval integration" from our late twentieth-century perspective, should we not be considering more closely *why* synthetic approaches have, for the most part, been neglected by the majority of medievalists?

In the following pages I will argue that views of Gothic incorporating a wide range of material, ideological, and methodological considerations have been, to a large degree, precluded by the disciplinary and subdisciplinary specialization which has characterized humanities scholarship since the nineteenth century. It was during the last century that many of the hermeneutical tools and distinctive orientations of modern disciplines, such as art history, liturgical studies, and history, were first established. In order to obtain some idea of how, when, and why modern discourse on the Middle Ages has taken the segregative shape(s) it has, I have chosen here to isolate the nineteenth-century historiography of Gothic sculpture as a test case. The increasingly autonomous "history" of Gothic sculpture prevented a full consideration of sculpture within the context of the monument as a whole – architecture, sculpture, painting, glass, etc. – either by historians of architecture or by historians of sculpture. I will attempt to assess the ways in which Gothic sculpture came to be studied as a separate entity, or subdiscipline within art history, which by its very nature did not favour integrative analysis.[3]

The founding perspectives on Gothic sculpture have received very little critical analysis to date; therefore, my remarks here are exploratory. Yet I suspect that even this preliminary historiography of Gothic sculpture is reflective of broader trends in the developmental histories of medievalist disciplines in general. I will first examine strictly academic factors which appear to have contributed importantly to the formulation of "Gothic sculpture" as an independent area of inquiry within the discipline of art history. Then, I will consider stimuli from the extra-academic sphere. The remarks which follow are concerned in particular with German scholarship, as it was largely as a result of the ground-breaking writings of German-speaking scholars that medieval art history, with its subspecialty of Gothic sculpture, emerged as a "scientific" discipline in the years between 1850 and 1900.

With a few notable exceptions, the study of Gothic sculpture did not become a tangible issue for important scholarly discussion until the second half of the nineteenth century. Before that, "Gothic sculpture" was not defined as a scholarly concept or as a category of aesthetic objects in the sense that we employ the term today. It seems very important to consider briefly why this was so, particularly since we know that enormous enthusiasm for Gothic architecture had been awakened at the beginning of the nineteenth century. Indeed, while Romantic writings, such as the young Goethe's *Von deutscher Baukunst* of 1772 and Chateaubriand's *Génie du christianisme* of 1802, exhibit a new-found, almost reverential appreciation of Gothic structures, they contain little or no mention of the sculpture which, so evidently to us, was an integral part of their fabric. The primacy assigned architecture in this era within both academic and literary circles may help to explain why monuments of Gothic sculpture were regarded by most as little more than "medieval embroideries" or "ornamental embellishment."[4] But it is even more likely that the lack of scholarly and popular interest in Gothic sculpture until well into the nineteenth century was conditioned to a very large degree by the enduring influence of Johann Joachim Winckelmann's (1717–1768) championing of the aesthetic norms of Greek antiquity, and of Greek sculpture in particular.

Winckelmann's writings, such as *Gedanken über die Nachahmung der*

griechischen Werke in der Malerei und Bildhauerkunst (1755) and
Geschichte der Kunst des Altertums (1764), had a formative impact on
the development of the disciplines of archaeology and art history, and
on German intellectual thought generally. For the historiography of
Gothic sculpture it is important to recall that increased travel to and
study of sites in Greece and Asia Minor in this period, as well as the
large-scale importation of monuments of antique sculpture into Western Europe both before and after 1800, also helped to encourage and
sustain a predominantly classicizing sculptural taste.[5] Clearly, these
circumstances resonated with the long-standing classical orientation
of the academies of art, and of European educational institutions in
general. It is hardly surprising, then, that the relatively few scholarly
commentaries on medieval sculpture written during the first half of
the nineteenth century were often informed by the language and
associated negative value judgments derived from established "normative" descriptions of antique statuary.

In 1822, for instance, the lawyer and antiquarian Karl Peter Lepsius
(1772–1853) published the first detailed discussion of the thirteenth-
century sculpture in the west choir of Naumburg cathedral.[6] Lepsius's descriptions of the life-sized founder figures reveals that he
alternately praised and criticized the sculptures according to the
degree to which their pose, drapery treatment, and psychology
reflected and/or deviated from that of their classical forbears.[7]
Although Lepsius's aesthetic prejudices were grounded in the pre-
vailing ideals of his day, it is highly significant that his account of the
Naumburg sculptures was far from disparaging, for he drew attention to their value as cultural and historical documents of the medieval past.[8] His remarks bore the clear imprint of the Romantic
rediscovery of the Middle Ages, as influenced by the writings of
Goethe, Herder, Wackenroder, Schlegel, Schiller, and others. Yet,
while Gothic architecture served as a major rallying point for the
medievalist and nationalist rhetoric manifested in these years in Germany as well as in France and England, monumental sculpture
tended to be largely ignored. It seems ultimately to have been the
cumulative force of the Romantic re-evaluation of the Middle Ages
that prompted some antiquarians and scholars, such as Lepsius, to
initiate discourse on the historical significance of Gothic statuary
despite its aesthetic non-conformity with classical ideals.

Besides passing references to Gothic sculpture in studies of medieval architecture, other, more systematic discussions began to appear

with increasing frequency in comprehensive analyses of the general history of art and of medieval *Kunst-* and *Kulturlandschaften*, which were first developed in the early nineteenth century. This new genre of scholarly study responded in part to the Romantic conviction that particular cultures and temperaments were specifically and informatively shaped by local geographic and environmental conditions. However, the early art-historical chronicles must also be understood in relation to the very important debates, especially in the 1820s and 1830s, over the nature of "history" generally and its specific relevance for the present. Although this is not the place to address the diverse philosophical positions informing the development of the modern scholarly discipline of history, it is important to note that, from the early nineteenth century onward, significant changes in the conception of historical writing took place and these had understandably far-reaching implications for the development of art history. In turning away from the abstract theorizing of earlier centuries, the discipline of history became increasingly document-based and more objective in outlook. Recently, Hayden White, Peter Paret, and others have drawn attention to the novelistic character of the act of arranging documented events of history into a significant narrative sequence or pattern.[9] Yet, the ground-breaking texts for the history of art follow this method of writing history. Among them are Franz Kugler's (1808–1858) *Handbuch der Kunstgeschichte* of 1842 and his *Pommersche Kunstgeschichte* of 1840, and Wilhelm Lübke's (1826–1893) *Die mittelalterliche Kunst in Westfalen* of 1853.[10] In all of these books, the art historian positioned himself to trace and interpret major developmental sequences between artistic monuments of different eras, cultures, and/or geopolitical regions.

Kugler's innovative *Handbuch* represented the first intellectually rigorous attempt to construct a history of art that would establish a meaningful sequence of artistic developments from prehistoric to modern times. The handbook went through five editions until 1872, and accordingly had enormous influence on both well-educated and general audiences in Germany and elsewhere.[11] Each of the two chapters treating art of the Middle Ages was divided into two subsections under the rubrics "architecture" and "graphic and plastic arts" (*bildende Kunst*). In each chapter, architecture received by far the lengthiest treatment.[12] From the outset, Kugler acknowledged the paucity of information regarding medieval sculpture, noting that it was virtually *terra incognita* at the time.[13] It is also interesting that, early on in his text, Kugler remarked upon the close alliance between architecture and sculpture in the Gothic period, but then proceeded to accord them separate treatment.[14] Likely Kugler's hierarchical, medium-based treatment of the arts reflected the traditional hierarchical schemes established earlier by the academies, as well as a general nineteenth-century tendency to separate and systematize the various disciplines and fields of human endeavour according to classificatory methods derived from the natural sciences. Noteworthy, too, is the fact that, within the text, Kugler further subdivided his discussion of sculpture into smaller groups differentiated by scale and material, although it is unclear (still to us today) whether, or to what degree, these abstract modern categories correspond to any truly medieval awareness of distinctions. In their language and formulation, Kugler's descriptions of Gothic sculpture bore unmistakable vestiges of his classical schooling.[15] But in spite of these period traits of language and organization, Kugler wove together in the *Handbuch* one of the first pictures of the *Entwickelungsgang* (development) of medieval art and architecture, and documented it in a more rigorous and objective manner than had ever been the case before.

Similar observations relating to medium obtain in Kugler's and Lübke's examinations of the geographically and historically defined *Kunstlandschaften* (cultural provinces) of Pomerania and Westphalia. In these books, Gothic monuments of sculpture are mentioned and admired, often with reference to the descriptive vocabulary normally employed for classical statuary.[16] Once again, works of sculpture receive marginal treatment in relation to architecture and are not treated as integral parts of it.[17]

To these pioneering texts predating the professionalization of art history, we could also add the multivolume *Geschichte der bildenden Künste*, published by Carl Schnaase (1798–1875) in the years between 1843 and 1864.[18] Like Kugler's handbook, Schnaase's treatment of medieval sculpture was embedded within a general history of art, of which a remarkable five volumes were dedicated to the Middle Ages.[19] His theoretical premises differed somewhat from those of Kugler and Lübke. Schnaase was not as concerned with establishing chronological lines of development or with empirically based methods of classification, as he was with elucidating the monuments within the historical, intellectual, and social ambience of the periods that sponsored them.[20] Thus his discussions of the monuments of a specific era were preceded by a historical overview. Schnaase's treatments of the monuments were ordered by medium (architecture occupied the first place), and were then further partitioned by geography, scale, and material. It is highly significant that Schnaase's efforts to locate works within their respective historical contexts led him to challenge prevailing aesthetic norms and argue the impossibility of judging medieval sculpture with criteria borrowed from the study of antique statuary.[21]

Another important forum for discussion of Gothic sculpture in the first half of the nineteenth century was the area of inquiry known as Christian archaeology. The equation of Christian virtue with medieval art had first been made in the writings of the Romantics, such as Wackenroder and Schlegel. In the following decades, Gothic came to be projected by many as the perfect Christian style – a style, it was believed, embodying the spirit of a great age of faith. The study of Christian archaeology was regarded by many (especially those in ecclesiastical spheres) as being virtually synonymous with the history of medieval religious art. From our late twentieth-century vantage point, these investigations appear to have been rather unfocused, even diffuse in nature, as they embraced a wide range of subjects, such as church architecture, liturgical furnishings, and ecclesiastical vestments, as well as historical studies of the development of the liturgy and church music.

Some of the most prominent journals dedicated to Christian archaeology which emerged in the course of the 1840s and 1850s were the *Annales archéologiques* in France; *The Ecclesiologist* in England; and the *Kölner Domblatt*, the *Organ für christliche Kunst*, and the *Zeitschrift für christliche Archäologie und Kunst* in Germany.[22] Most of these journals published short articles and notices on individual works or groups of Gothic sculpture in which the works themselves were treated largely as medieval religious "artefacts" divorced from their original architectural and historical milieu. Significantly, considerable stress was placed on their iconography and/or theological meaning.[23] It is likely that such discussions were in some way programmed to resist the desanctification and/or aestheticization that had inevitably begun to accompany academic art-historical study of religious sculpture. Since these "Christian" notices on monumental sculpture were randomly interspersed in the journals between accounts of baptismal fonts, chalices, pavement tiles, or church bells, it is clear that the perspective represented by the Christian archaeologists was segregative rather than synthetic.

Often such archaeologically oriented studies were linked to the planning or completion of ecclesiastical building projects in a neo-Gothic style. Perhaps one of the most striking examples in this regard is Cologne cathedral, completed between 1842 and 1880. Peter Bloch, who has studied medievalizing tendencies in nineteenth-century German sculpture, has remarked that the neo-Gothic revival was never so potent in sculpture as in architecture. In his examination of the revivalist sculpture of the archdiocese of Cologne, he noted that many of the works, pre-eminently among them the sculpture of the cathedral workshop, incorporated a mix of stylistic features borrowed from diverse historical eras, including classical antiquity and the Renaissance.[24] Alternatively, stylistic elements drawn from different periods of the Middle Ages were freely combined within a single work. According to Bloch, greater archaeological accuracy was not achieved until the later decades of the century, by which time considerably more knowledge about medieval sculpture had accrued. In this connection it is interesting to recall that Viollet-le-Duc's restorations of Gothic sculptural programs during the 1850s and 1860s were often more creative than archaeologically exact.[25]

In scholarship of the first half of the nineteenth century, the intimate relationship of Gothic architecture and sculpture was frequently remarked upon. Yet works of sculpture were treated in a manner that divorced them from their original architectural setting and, in turn, from any kind of holistic or interactive understanding of medieval church design. Ultimately, Gothic sculpture came to acquire an independent history that was distinct from that of Gothic architecture, as well as from that of Greek sculpture.[26] It seems that much of the responsibility for the creation of a separate history of Gothic sculpture would go to the later work of some of the scholars already mentioned, and especially to the next generation of German-speaking art historians, who built upon the achievements of their predecessors to produce some of the first specialized histories of medieval art and of individual media in the years between 1860 and 1900.

I would argue that one of the most influential books for the development of the subdiscipline of Gothic sculpture, and for other period histories of sculpture, was Wilhelm Lübke's *Geschichte der Plastik von den ältesten Zeiten bis auf die Gegenwart*, first published in 1863 and reissued in an expanded edition in 1871.[27] In this book, Lübke attempted for the first time to construct a "total" history of sculpture from the ancient Near Eastern civilizations to modern times. Fortunately for us, Lübke outlined his primary motivations for writing a specialized history of the medium of sculpture in the foreword to the first edition of his book.[28] He began his commentary by asserting that more precise knowledge about a separate branch of art could be gained by separating it from the totality of the history of art. Not only would this "segregation" permit a more exacting interrogation of problems central and particular to a given medium, argued Lübke, but it would also afford at the same time fresh insights into the overall picture of the history of art. As he saw it, the medium of sculpture was especially in need of specialized historical treatment. According to Lübke, sculpture of the Middle Ages had long been accorded a subordinate place within art-historical scholarship in comparison with medieval architecture and painting owing to the tenacious belief that sculpture, in particular, had achieved an absolute perfection in antiquity.[29] Both in the introduction and in the main text, Lübke announced his intention to overcome this fundamental dichotomy by demonstrating that much new territory could be won for the history of art through study of the northern schools of medieval sculpture.[30]

Although I cannot address individual details of Lübke's treatment of separate eras and monuments in this short essay, it is interesting to note that he saw his investigation as unifying the empirical or formal observations of Kugler with the historical and contextual concerns of Schnaase.[31] Taking his classificatory cues from the earlier models, Lübke organized the diverse "books" in his study, including the 200-page account of medieval sculpture, into chapters further subdivided by era and geography, and then by scale and material. Significantly, Lübke's text was accompanied by numerous wood engravings, which enabled the works of sculpture to become accessible to a wider audience with a certain degree of visual immediacy.[32] I might speculate that these visual accompaniments to the written text may also have had the effect, in one way or another, of validating the notion of there being an "autonomous" history of sculpture as the works were shown isolated from their context. Furthermore, the practice of illustrating the works of sculpture in a manner that detached them from their original architectural settings militated against the formation of an integrated view of Gothic church planning.

The institutionalization of art history as an academic subject at the university, as well as the information explosion which accompanied this development, also fostered the formation of progressively more specialized areas of study, such as "medieval sculpture" and "Gothic sculpture." Indeed the fashioning of art history as a serious academic discipline in Germany and Austria in the 1880s and 1890s seems to have buttressed earlier trends towards the construction of comprehensive histories of art and, perhaps more important, the progressive subdivision of this larger vision into independent and largely non-conversant specialist histories of different media and periods. A list of prominent specialist medieval histories produced during this period would include Wilhelm Bode's *Geschichte der deutschen Plastik* of 1885, Franz von Reber's *Kunstgeschichte des Mittelalters* of 1886, and Wilhelm Vöge's epic history of French Gothic sculpture published in 1894 as *Die Anfänge des monumentalen Stiles im Mittelalter*.[33] Vöge's highly influential book represented the first systematic attempt to document the genesis of the Gothic style in northern French sculpture and to provide it with an onward genealogy. Specialized histories such as these quickly spawned a number of monographic studies of sculpture at individual sites in Germany and France. By the end of the century, "Gothic sculpture" was well on the way to being established as an autonomous area of art-historical study. A broader inspection would likely show that this scholarly isolation of Gothic sculpture bore certain procedural analogies to the formulation of other medieval (and non-medieval) specialist histories, such as those of stained glass and painting.

I would also like to suggest that the kind of intellectual partitioning which led to autonomous histories of different media and individual sites was paralleled on a broader theoretical level in the last decades of the nineteenth century. The experiments in art-historical theory and method conducted in Germany and Austria in the 1880s and 1890s indicate that the formalization of art history as a new, scientific discipline was accompanied by a persistent, almost aggressive tendency favouring segregation not only between media, but also between methodologies. Put very briefly, the fledgling discipline in part justified its autonomous existence and defined its identity within the academic establishment in terms of its separateness and divergence from more established disciplines, such as archaeology and history. We have already seen that, in many instances, the architects of the new subject felt the need to demonstrate its "scientific" qualities by adopting methods akin to those of the natural sciences. While it is difficult to sum up a complex, self-aggrandizing strategy in a few sentences, it seems that the self-proclaimed autonomy of the modern discipline in turn sponsored, methodologically speaking, the development of arbitrary, self-contained philological systems. In their extreme forms at least, these appear to have displaced the objects of art-historical investigation even farther from their original historical and cultural ambience than the distance of centuries necessitated.

In this regard, it is instructive to contemplate briefly the hermeneutical construct of *Stil*, or style, which became a remarkably important tool of art-historical investigation at the end of the century.[34] Refined as an instrument of connoisseurship by Giovanni Morelli (1816–1891) and others, the exacting and systematic science of stylistic analysis soon came to be regarded by many art historians as an end in itself. The informative power accorded "style" as a self-sufficient interpretative system had important consequences for the study of Gothic sculpture. In the absence of documents, it allowed "histories" to be written, which, in their abstract tracings of perceived internal developments, often had the effect of disengaging the works almost totally from their original geographic, social, and cultural context.[35] Once formulated as an investigative tool of the science of art history in the 1880s and 1890s, stylistic analysis came to provide an authoritative research paradigm for much subsequent scholarship on Gothic sculpture.

In this connection, it is important to suggest that photography may have, in a certain sense, complemented and reinforced this clinical, formally oriented mode of studying Gothic sculpture. Here I am referring to the increasing number of visual *corpora* of medieval sculpture published in the last decades of the century in both France and Germany.[36] While photographic reproductions served to introduce the works to a wider public, they also had the effect of distancing the scholar from the context in which the works were originally meant to be seen, and also enabled him or her to pass judgment and classify them, often without firsthand experience of the medieval site.[37] Furthermore, the photographic anthology posited entirely new series of relationships between works of sculpture of different eras, regions, and scale in a manner having very little correspondence with the conditions of the Middle Ages. It seems very likely, too, that photographic contrivances, such as close-ups and truncated views, had the effect of alienating the sculptures not only from the study of other media, but also from the viewer's kinesthetic experience of the time and space unity of their placement.

As indicated earlier in this essay, I do not believe that the development of "Gothic sculpture" as an independent art history specialty can be explained solely with reference to happenings in the scholarly sphere. I would like now to put forward briefly several hypotheses regarding extra-academic factors that I believe contributed significantly to the impetus towards species segregation (in a Darwinian sense) in the nineteenth century.

First of all, it is important to consider what might be termed the "literal isolation" of Gothic sculpture vis-à-vis its original physical and cultic context that occurred in the wake of the French Revolution and the Napoleonic occupations of much of Europe. The physical dislodgement of sculpture resulting from the dissolution or destruction of monasteries and other medieval religious foundations permitted individual pieces not only to be studied apart from their architectural setting but, even more important perhaps, to be studied exclusively for the first time as "art," as opposed to "cult object" or "folklore." This literal isolation of Gothic sculpture, which enabled it to enter randomly into newly founded public museums purified of its cultic and miraculous aspects, must have supported in one way or another the development of an independent scientific history of sculpture.[38] We need only acknowledge, for instance, that it was an influx of German medieval sculpture into the Department of Christian Art in the Berlin museums which prompted Wilhelm Bode later in the century to construct the first history of German sculpture, the above-cited *Geschichte der deutschen Plastik* of 1885.[39]

A further observation, derived from and dependent on my last, has to do with the art market in the nineteenth century. Clearly, the physical separation of much Gothic sculpture from its original cultic environment created a new and unprecedented market situation. While we would certainly have to consider issues of taste, as well as collecting patterns in different cities or regions of Europe, might we not find that – when viewed from the perspective of the art market – there were obvious commercial advantages to be gained from the study of Gothic sculpture as a separate commodity divorced from its original context and function?

I would also argue that the isolated study of Gothic sculpture was fostered in the second half of the century by the establishment of major public collections of plaster casts of medieval sculpture, such as the Musée de Sculpture Comparée in Paris, and the large cast collection at the South Kensington Museum.[40] Designed to serve a general pedagogical function, the cast collections facilitated in a fashion comparable to photography the independent study of medieval sculpture. While the plaster casts had certain advantages over photographic reproductions in terms of their scale and three-dimensionality, they, like the photographic *corpora*, informed a kind of self-referentiality that was measurable and knowable in closed, purely visual systems without needing recourse to historical explanations. Not only were the assemblages of casts aesthetically distanced from the original works owing to differences in materials, but they were also physically removed from the medieval settings of the originals. In this way, the display and selection of plaster copies inaugurated, and in many instances actually produced, novel and unexpected relationships between medieval works of sculpture at some physical and aesthetic distance from the originals. I should point out here that the study of sculpture as a separate entity through the medium of casts also served certain nationalistic agendas, for in terms of selection and presentation such apparently neutral didactic ensembles in fact provided much room for politically tuned visual comparisons.[41]

In this regard, I have one final query that pertains to what might be seen as a culminating aspect of segregation, the emergence of separate written "national" histories of Gothic sculpture at the end of the nineteenth century. To what degree was this development forced by modern political circumstances? Especially following the Franco-Prussian War of 1870–1, the literature on medieval monuments produced by French and German scholars evinced a desire not only to secure respective national patrimonies but also to underscore formal and temperamental distinctions between "French Gothic sculpture" and "German Gothic sculpture."[42] Future studies will need to investigate the degree to which a psycho-political dynamic informed the language used to articulate these overtly nationalistic histories of medieval sculpture, which, because of their modern political point of origin, gave rise to discourse that bears little, if any, relation to historical realities of the Middle Ages.

This brief commentary on the nineteenth-century historiography of Gothic sculpture indicates in a preliminary fashion some of the historical circumstances, ideological positions, and methodologies which contributed to the formulation of "Gothic sculpture" as a scholarly subdiscipline by the years around 1900. Within the cadre of the present integrative undertaking, it seems important to draw attention to the roots of the traditional segregative configuration of medieval art-historical scholarship and to begin to account for them, as this disciplinary and subdisciplinary segmentation and specialization continue to influence our *modus operandi* as scholars in many fields in the late twentieth century. At the risk of generalizing too broadly, it seems that in addressing the issue of "artistic integration" in Gothic churches, we are in fact confronting an issue of infinite complexity, having multiple definitions, connotations, and layers of meaning. "Integration" can involve making interactive sense of historical, liturgical, and artistic fragments from the Middle Ages, as Beat Brenk, Peter Kurmann and Brigitte Kurmann-Schwarz, Virginia Raguin, and others attempt to do in diverse ways in this volume. At the same time, I would suggest that it insists on a certain coming to terms with the considerable methodological challenges posed by both past and present functionings of the random ideologies of our modern humanities disciplines.[43]

NOTES

This essay draws on research for my forthcoming book *The Shaping of Art History: Wilhelm Vöge, Adolph Goldschmidt, and the Study of Medieval Art* (Cambridge University Press).

1 Emile Mâle's first comprehensive iconographically based interpretation of the Gothic cathedral was presented in his *L'art religieux en France au XIIIe siècle* (Paris, 1898). It appeared half a century before Hans Sedlmayr's *Die Entstehung der Kathedrale* (Zurich, 1950), which, as Paul Crossley has recently asserted, "led gothic architecture into the realm of associative fantasy." For a recent assessment of the *Strukturforschung* of Sedlmayr and the modernist aesthetics underlying his interpretation of the Gothic cathedral, see P. Crossley, "Medieval Architecture and Meaning: The Limits of Iconography," *The Burlington Magazine* 130 (1988), 116–21 quote p. 118. Willibald Sauerländer has commented on modern interpretations of Gothic structures (including Sedlmayr's) in "'Première architecture gothique' or 'Renaissance of the Twelfth Century'? Changing Perspectives of Evaluation in Architectural History," *Sewanee Mediaeval Colloquium Occasional Papers* 2 (1985), 25–43. See also the essays by Bernard McGinn, Roger Reynolds, Brigitte Bedos-Rezak, and Willibald Sauerländer in this volume.

2 Erwin Panofsky, *Gothic Architecture and Scholasticism* (New York, 1957); Otto von Simson, *The Gothic Cathedral: Origins of Gothic Architecture and the Medieval Concept of Order* (New York, 1956). Crossley, in "Medieval Archi-

tecture and Meaning," situates the unitary theological explanations of Panofsky and von Simson within a long tradition of idealist cultural history. In the present volume, Barbara Abou-El-Haj, Brigitte Bedos-Rezak, Peter Kurmann and Brigitte Kurmann-Schwarz, and Willibald Sauerländer consider critically the "integrated" views of Gothic put forward by Panofsky and von Simson. For a discussion of the term *Gesamtkunstwerk*, see the Kurmann and Kurmann-Schwarz essay, note 2.

3 In this essay I am concerned primarily with monumental stone sculpture (twelfth to fourteenth centuries) in an architectural context.

4 In Victor Hugo's celebrated medievalizing novel *Notre-Dame de Paris* (*The Hunchback of Notre-Dame*) of 1831, for instance, the cathedral serves both as the main subject of the novel and as a picturesque backdrop for the unfolding of the narrative. While clearly the cathedral sculpture had been extensively damaged during the French Revolution, it is remarkable that Hugo made little detailed reference to it, apart from brief mentions of statues of saints and the "romantic" gargoyles.

5 Adolf Michaelis, in *Die archäologischen Entdeckungen des neunzehnten Jahrhunderts* (Leipzig, 1906), provides a useful summary of the major archaeological discoveries during this period and documents the entry of many classical sculptures into European public collections.

6 Karl Peter Lepsius, "Ueber das Alterthum und die Stifter des Domes zu Naumburg und deren Statuen im westlichen Chor desselben," in *Mittheilungen aus dem Gebiet historisch-antiquarischer Forschungen* 1 (Naumburg, 1822). Lepsius's study was republished several times, including in a book of his collected essays entitled *Kleine Schriften. Beiträge zur thüringisch-sächsischen Geschichte und deutschen Kunst- und Alterthumskunde*, vol. 1 (Magdeburg, 1854), pp. 1–35. My citations are from the 1854 publication.

7 Lepsius, *Kleine Schriften*, pp. 9–13; for instance, p. 10: "With regard to the overall character and workmanship [of these figures] it cannot be denied that they were for the most part carved in a splendid style and display relatively correct proportions. The facial features are not without expression ... and despite the fact that the artist did not succeed in mastering ideal forms, it is clear that he made efforts to do so." Lepsius's description of the figure of Regelindis, (p. 12) is particularly revealing: "The fine, sensitively worked head of Regelindis would be far more appealing if her laughing expression displayed greater moderation. Her pose has a certain grace, and she is almost too slender ... In order to convey the delicate and graceful character of this statue in its entirety, it should have been depicted from the side." All translations from the German texts are my own.

8 Lepsius, in ibid., p. 3, termed the Naumburg sculptures "remarkable documents of old German art" that belonged to the "incunabula of German stone sculpture." Here he followed the formulations of Johann Dominik Fiorillo in his *Geschichte der zeichnenden Künste in Deutschland und den Vereinigten Niederlanden*, vol. 1 (Hanover, 1815), p. 466.

9 Hayden White, *Metahistory: The Historical Imagination in Nineteenth-Century Europe* (Baltimore and London, 1973); idem, *The Content of the Form: Narrative Discourse and Historical Representation* (Baltimore and London, 1987); Peter Paret, *Art as History: Episodes in the Culture and Politics of Nineteenth-Century Germany* (Princeton, 1988).

10 Franz Kugler, *Handbuch der Kunstgeschichte* (Stuttgart, 1842); idem, *Pommersche Kunstgeschichte nach den erhaltenen Monumenten dargestellt* (Stettin, 1840); Wilhelm Lübke, *Die mittelalterliche Kunst in Westfalen nach den vorhandenen Denkmälern dargestellt* (Leipzig, 1853). Lübke's first book was inspired by the writings of Kugler and Carl Schnaase (1798–1875) and was dedicated jointly to them. See the accounts of Kugler and Schnaase by Wilhelm Waetzoldt in *Deutsche Kunsthistoriker*, Vol. 2: *Von Passavant bis Justi* (Leipzig, 1924), pp. 70–92 (Schnaase) and pp. 143–72 (Kugler). For a brief summary of Lübke's career, with bibliography, see the notice by Thomas Lersch in *Neue Deutsche Biographie*, vol. 15 (Berlin, 1987), pp. 444–6.

11 The second edition, which contained additions by Jacob Burckhardt (1818–1897), was published in Stuttgart in 1848. The third edition was expanded to three volumes (Stuttgart, 1856–9) and was the first edition with illustrations in the text. The fourth and fifth editions (Stuttgart, 1861 and 1872, respectively) were revised by Wilhelm Lübke. My citations are from the second edition of 1848.

12 Chapter 13, entitled "Art of the Romanesque Style," was subdivided into "Architecture" (70 pages) and "Plastic and Graphic Arts" (30 pages), while chapter 14, "Art of the German Style," was similarly organized, with 60 pages devoted to architecture and 40 pages to all other media. This is not the place to go into the lengthy terminological debates in the first half of the nineteenth century regarding the various forms of nomenclature for what we now term "Gothic," and which Kugler referred to as the "Germanic style." Kugler employed the term "Gothic" in his *Handbuch* from the third edition onwards. It is important to point out that Kugler discussed a number of works of sculpture which would now be termed "Gothic" under the rubric of "Romanesque."

13 For instance, Kugler, *Handbuch*, p. 604: "We have only fragmentary knowledge of art executed in the Germanic [i.e., Gothic] style"; p. 609: "In

addition, we cannot yet make any comprehensive judgments on German sculpture executed in the Germanic [Gothic] style."

14 For instance, *Handbuch*, p. 603: "As noted earlier, the Germanic style [in sculpture] developed in consonance with the architecture to which it is intimately connected."

15 For instance, in his discussion of the life-sized founder figures in the west choir of Naumburg cathedral, *Handbuch*, p. 615: "Remembrances of antiquity have been favourably resolved in the overall character of the style, and they linger most noticeably in the curiously large scale of the project; a very noble and dignified taste can be frequently noted in the drapery. The handling of the gestures, the variety in the description of individual figures, and the dramatic character of the reliefs reveal an artist endowed with a lively and excited spirit. However, [these works] lack an acute feeling for nature. This deficiency is all the more disturbing, since the merits outlined above would give cause for a greater appreciation of these sculptures."

16 See, for instance, the description of the jamb statues on the south portal of the minster in Münster, Lübke, *Die mittelalterliche Kunst*, p. 133: "Here we see great richness, variety in the poses, lively and graceful movements and a sensitive treatment of the space. The style of the figures is determined by their splendid, if somewhat rigid stance, and by their ceremonial dignity ... In the heads one notes a marked degree of individuality despite the severity of their conception. At times, the drapery, which manifests rich and changing patterns, nearly approaches antique standards of beauty. Like antique works, these figures, enveloped in their drapery, aim to make the viewer speculate on the form of the body below." See also Kugler's description of the stucco group of the Holy Kinship in the church of Saint Nicholas in Stralsund in his *Pommersche Kunstgeschichte*, p. 178: "The figures retain a certain stiffness in their bearing and the proportions are not entirely natural. Yet there is a sense of nobility in the arrangement of the drapery and the rather broad faces are strangely gentle in expression."

17 Lübke, in *Die mittelalterliche Kunst*, for example, p. 48, remarked upon the intimate ties between architecture and the plastic and graphic arts ("They were the younger sisters of architecture, whose fixed and immutable laws lent the varied and largely accidental nature of the plastic and graphic arts the gravity and regularity of architectonic structuring. Therefore the developmental process of medieval architecture, with its various phases, is reflected faithfully in the workings of the plastic and graphic arts; in this way, these follow step by step the examples set by the older sister")

but then proceeded to divide his book into two sections devoted to "architecture" and "graphic and plastic arts." The latter was further subdivided by medium into two subsections – namely, "painting" and "sculpture." It is interesting that Lübke's discussion of Westphalian architecture occupied approximately 250 pages of his book, while only 60 pages were dedicated to his treatment of sculpture, which included works in stone, wood, and ivory, as well as liturgical vessels.

18 Carl Schnaase, *Geschichte der bildenden Künste*, 7 vols. (Düsseldorf, 1843–64). A second edition was published in Düsseldorf between 1866 and 1879. For a contemporary review of the importance of the histories of art written by Kugler and Schnaase, see W. Lübke, "Die heutige Kunst und die Kunstwissenschaft" in *Zeitschrift für bildende Kunst* 1 (1866), 3–13.

19 Schnaase's five-volume discussion of medieval art (volumes 3–7 of the *Geschichte der bildenden Künste*) covered the centuries from the Early Christian period to the late Middle Ages in both northern and southern Europe. Volumes 4 (*Das eigentliche Mittelalter*) and 5 (*Entstehung und Ausbildung des gothischen Styls*) are of particular interest here.

20 Schnaase outlined his methodological approach in the foreword to volume 4 of his *Geschichte der bildenden Künste*, which was at the same time the second volume of his history of medieval art (*Das eigentliche Mittelalter*) published in the first edition of 1854, pp. v–x.

21 Schnaase, *Das eigentliche Mittelalter*, pp. 530–1: "Although we no longer refer to the Middle Ages with disdain, we still continue to judge the works of this era according to the standards of the art of antiquity. Hence, we value only those features of the works which display a rather successful retention of antique motifs, or which are reminiscent of them. If we could accustom ourselves to directing our eyes more closely to the novel and nascent elements in the works, to assuming the attitudes of the time, and to making ourselves more receptive to an understanding of the original intentions, the works of this era would appear to us less displeasing and unsatisfactory. We would not consider the incomplete depiction of the natural world to be an obstacle, but instead would understand and value the relative approximation of it."

22 *Annales archéologiques* (Paris, 1844–72); *The Ecclesiologist* (Cambridge and London, 1842–68); *Kölner Domblatt: Amtliche Mittheilungen des Central-Dombau-Vereins, mit Beiträgen historischen, kunstgeschichtlichen und technischen Inhalts* (Cologne, 1845–85/92); *Organ für christliche Kunst. Organ des Christlichen Kunstvereins für Deutschland* (Cologne, 1851–73); *Zeitschrift für christliche Archäologie und Kunst* (Leipzig, 1856–8). For an informative account of the propagandistic agendas of these journals, and of the links

between their editors and contributors, see Georg Germann, *Gothic Revival in Europe and Britain: Sources, Influences and Ideas*, trans. Gerald Onn (London, 1972), ch. 3, pp. 99–165. Countless books dealing with Christian archaeology also appeared at this time. See, for instance, Adolphe-Napoléon Didron, *Manuel d'iconographie chrétienne* (Paris, 1845), and Heinrich Otte, *Grundzüge der kirchlichen Kunst-Archäologie des deutschen Mittelalters* (Leipzig, 1855).

23 In Didron's *Annales archéologiques*, for example, works of Gothic sculpture were routinely mentioned under the rubric "iconographie des cathédrales." See, for instance, vol. 9 (1849), 99–110, for a discussion of sculpture from Chartres cathedral illustrating the theme of the Second Day of Creation.

24 Peter Bloch, "Kölner Skulpturen des 19. Jahrhunderts," *Wallraf-Richartz-Jahrbuch* 29 (1967), 243–90; idem, "Sculptures néo-gothiques en Allemagne," *Revue de l'art* 21 (1973), 70–9.

25 Also interesting is Viollet-le-Duc's lengthy article on "sculpture" in his *Dictionnaire raisonné de l'architecture*, vol. 8 (Paris, 1866), pp. 97–279, in which he discussed the medium without extensive reference to architectural contexts. The same is true of the wood engravings that accompany the text. In his *Dictionnaire raisonné du mobilier français*, 6 vols. (Paris, 1858–75), individual works of Gothic sculpture received treatment under headings such as "manteau," "robe," and "toilette." For a recent assessment of Viollet-le-Duc's portrayal of Gothic jamb figures as medieval "genre figures," see Willibald Sauerländer, "Kleider machen Leute: Vergessenes aus Viollet-le-Ducs 'Dictionnaire du mobilier français,'" *Arte medievale* 1 (1983), 221–40. For his restorations of medieval sculpture, see "Viollet-le-Duc et la restauration de la sculpture" in the exhibition catalogue *Viollet-le-Duc* [Galeries Nationales du Grand Palais] (Paris, 1980), pp. 144–73.

26 See my earlier comments. For a relatively early comprehensive history of Greek sculpture, see Johannes Overbeck, *Geschichte der griechischen Plastik*, 2 vols. (Leipzig, 1857–8). In my forthcoming book I also discuss the late nineteenth-century study of medieval sculpture in relation to investigations of Italian Renaissance sculpture carried out in the same years.

27 Wilhelm Lübke, *Geschichte der Plastik von den ältesten Zeiten bis auf die Gegenwart* (Leipzig, 1863; 2d ed., 1871).

28 The foreword to the first edition is reprinted in the second edition of 1871, pp. v–vii.

29 Ibid., p. v.

30 Ibid., p. vii. Elsewhere in the text – for instance, pp. 7, 345 – Lübke echoed

Schnaase in stating that medieval sculpture should not be measured with the yardstick of antiquity.

31 Ibid., p. vi.

32 The first edition had 231 illustrations, and the second 377.

33 Wilhelm Bode, *Geschichte der deutschen Plastik* (Berlin, 1885). Bode's monograph on German sculpture, which was illustrated with wood engravings, appeared as the second volume in a series devoted to the history of German art. Four other scholars wrote specialist histories dealing with other "independent" branches of the arts. These were Robert Dohme, *Geschichte der deutschen Baukunst* (Berlin, 1887); Hubert Janitschek, *Geschichte der deutschen Malerei* (Berlin, 1890); Karl Friedrich Lützow, *Geschichte des deutschen Kupferstiches und Holzschnittes* (Berlin, 1891) and Jakob von Falke's *Geschichte des deutschen Kunstgewerbes* (Berlin, 1888). Franz von Reber's *Kunstgeschichte des Mittelalters* (Leipzig, 1886) includes the discussions "Die Plastik der romanischen Epoche" (pp. 391–426) and "Die Plastik der gothischen Periode" (pp. 531–78). Wilhelm Vöge, in *Die Anfänge des monumentalen Stiles im Mittelalter. Eine Untersuchung über die erste Blütezeit französischer Plastik* (Strasbourg, 1894), analyses both the sources for and influences of the Early Gothic sculptural ensemble on the west façade of Chartres cathedral. For this book, see my article "Wilhelm Vöge and the Role of Human Agency in the Making of Medieval Sculpture: Reflections on an Art Historical Pioneer," *Konsthistorisk Tidskrift* 62 (1993), 69–83.

34 The concept of style in art history is analysed historiographically by Willibald Sauerländer in "From Stilus to Style: Reflections on the Fate of a Notion," *Art History* 6 (1983), 253–70.

35 In this volume, see Peter Draper's discussion of the limitations of stylistic histories for understanding the character and the manner of the building of Wells cathedral.

36 For instance, A. de Baudot, *La sculpture française au moyen âge et à la renaissance* (Paris, 1884); Georg Dehio and F. Winter, *Kunstgeschichte in Bildern. Systematische Darstellung der Entwicklung der bildenden Kunst vom klassischen Altertum bis zum Ende des 18. Jahrhunderts*, vol. 2: *Das Mittelalter* (Leipzig, 1902); Paul Vitry and Gaston Brière, *Documents de sculpture française du moyen âge* (Paris, 1904).

37 See the related comments made by Heinrich Dilly concerning the impact of photographic reproductions and the magic lantern on the teaching and documentary methods of the discipline of art history at the end of the nineteenth century in "Lichtbildprojektion - Prothese der Kunstbetrachtung," *Kunstwissenschaft und Kunstvermittlung*, ed. Irene Below, pp. 153–72

(Giessen, 1975). For an important recent examination of photography as a fundamental piece of the historiography and methodology of art history, see the series of four articles by Anthony Hamber, "The Photography of the Visual Arts, 1839–1880," *Visual Resources* 5/4 (1989), 289–310 (Part I); 6/1 (1989), 19–41 (Part II); 6/2 (1989), 165–79 (Part III); 6/3 (1990), 219–41 (Part IV).

38 In this connection, it is relevant to recall the random assemblage of fragments of architecture, sculpture, and stained glass that formed the core of Alexandre Lenoir's Musée des Monuments Français set up in the monastery of the Petits-Augustins in Paris following the French Revolution. See his *Description historique et chronologique des monumens de sculpture réunis au Musée des monuments français*, 6 ed. (Paris, 1802, but issued in multiple editions). The installations were recorded visually in *Vues pittoresques et perspectives des salles du Musée des monumens français, et des principaux ouvrages d'architecture, de sculpture et de peinture sur verre qu'elles renferment: Gravés au burin, en vingt estampes par MM. J.B. Réville et J. Lavallée, d'après les dessins de M. Vauzelle ...* (Paris, 1816). I would also like to draw attention to the article by Joanna Ziegler, "The Medieval Virgin as Object: Art or Anthropology?" *Historical Reflections/Réflexions historiques* 16 (1989), 251–64, in which Ziegler discusses the "museumification" of Virgin statues in the nineteenth century, and the ways in which this denied the ritual context. See also the important collection of essays in *Das kunst- und kulturgeschichtliche Museum im 19. Jahrhundert*, ed. Bernward Deneke and Rainer Kahsnitz (Munich, 1977). Susan Crane, Department of History, University of Chicago, is currently completing a dissertation entitled "Collecting and Historical Consciousness: The Emergence of New Forms for Collective Memory in Early 19th-Century Germany" in which she is investigating the new institutions and practices created in Germany for the purpose of assembling historical objects and artefacts. Topics examined in this thesis include the foundation of local historical associations and their archival and museum collections between 1819 and 1851, as well as the Prussian-directed inventorizing of architectural ruins. I wish to thank Susan Crane for providing me with this information.

39 See Wilhelm Bode, *Mein Leben*, 2 vols. (Berlin, 1930), esp. vol. 1, pp. 190–1, and vol. 2, pp. 17–18.

40 The South Kensington Museum was founded in 1852, while the Musée de Sculpture Comparée was opened to the public in 1882. One of the earliest catalogues of the South Kensington Museum which includes discussion of the plaster cast collection is *A Guide to the Art Collections of the South Kensington Museum illustrated with plans and wood engravings* (London,

1871). For the Musée de Sculpture Comparée, see *Catalogue des sculptures. Appartenant aux divers centres d'art et aux diverses époques, exposées dans les galeries du Trocadéro* (Paris, 1883).

41 The introduction to the catalogue of the Paris collection, esp. pp. v–vi, makes it very clear that the cast collection was conceived as a glorious celebration of French national art, and that the comparative (foreign) material would illustrate the wide sphere of French artistic influence.

42 This issue is addressed in my forthcoming book. See also my article "Gothic Sculpture as a Locus for the Polemics of National Identity" in *Concepts of National Identity in the Middle Ages*, ed. Simon Forde, Lesley Johnson, and Alan V. Murray (University of Leeds, Centre for Mediaeval Studies, forthcoming).

43 See the related comments in the essays by Bernard McGinn, Roger Reynolds, Brigitte Bedos-Rezak, and Willibald Sauerländer in this volume.

3

From Admirable Tabernacle to the House of God: Some Theological Reflections on Medieval Architectural Integration

Bernard McGinn

McGinn probes the issue of "integration" of Gothic buildings by examining the possible relevance of an Augustinian aesthetic to this period. Augustine (354–430), bishop of Hippo, was one of the seminal thinkers of the Middle Ages. To Augustine, the locus, *the physical space of the church, brought believers together to share in sacramental and liturgical acts, and made sensible, in however limited a way, the promised bliss of God's presence in eternity. McGinn explains key words describing the physical* locus *of prayer, in particular the injunction that the building must be "admirable," and, like Caviness, delves into the richness of language to try to fathom meaning. Like Bedos-Rezak and Sauerländer, he is concerned with the problematic issue of the goals and means of our analysis, specifically concerning the intentions of the creators and the impact of a building on those who used it. Can we distinguish between renovation (an updating of tradition) and innovation (something that is a true departure)?*

Reflecting on the pluralism of approaches by art historians in this volume, McGinn points to a similar tendency among contemporary theologians to recognize a diversity of aesthetics in the Middle Ages. He sees a central place, however, for Augustine, especially his concept of beauty as reflecting harmonia, *the fitting order established by God. McGinn argues that Augustine saw beauty as a kind of sign given by one intelligent mind to another in order to convey a message. The humanly constructed beauty of a church building is meant to form an "admirable tabernacle" which will lead to God. With this basic assumption, he reviews recent literature concerning the "intentions" variously ascribed to Suger for the reconstruction of Saint-*

Denis. His analysis therefore complements the essays of Fernie and Clark, but develops a perspective from Augustinian aesthetics, seeing Suger's sense of beauty grounded in the necessity of the transition from material to spiritual beauty. He does not see Suger as an isolated example, however, but urges continued exploration of "applied theology" in medieval art.

In his sermon commenting on Psalm 41, Augustine analyses the psalm's teaching on how we may attain a foretaste of heaven in this life (what today some would describe as mystical experience): "When I was 'pouring out my soul above myself in order to attain my God' (v. 5a), how did I accomplish this? 'I entered into the place of the tabernacle' (v. 5b). Outside the place of the tabernacle, I will seek God erroneously. 'I entered into the place of the admirable tabernacle, even unto the house of God' (v. 5c). Admire many things in the tabernacle ... for God's tabernacle on earth is the faithful ... Ascending the tabernacle, he [i.e., David] arrived at the house of God."[1] Like all the early Christian Fathers, Augustine insisted not only that the Church was necessary for salvation, but that even the ecstatic experiences that give some hint of what heavenly joy will be like are always ecclesial – it is only in and through the Church that such experiences are possible.[2]

In this passage, Augustine views the Church in its fundamental reality as the faithful who make up the body of Christ. But this *tabernaculum admirabile* of believers has a "place," a locus, where it becomes manifest and where it shares in the sacramental and liturgical actions that grant Christ's mystical body continued vitality. That place is the actual church building.

I do not think it out of harmony with Augustine's thought (though it goes beyond anything he said in explicit fashion) to claim that, from an Augustinian perspective, the church building is essentially a *tabernaculum admirabile* whose function is to give access to the *domus Dei* of heaven. Two conclusions are implied in this view. First, the church building should be *admirabile* – worthy of wonder – both in itself and as the locus for what takes place within it. Second, the relation between the tabernacle and the heavenly house should be "written into" the fabric in such a way that it can be discerned by the faithful, or at least explained to them by the clergy. Just as the text of Scripture uses both literal and figurative signs to teach a single message, that of charity,[3] so too the many components of a medieval church, from the perspective of an Augustinian theological aesthetic, are meant to harmonize as an "admirable tabernacle" that gives access to the "house of God." These components are beautiful and integrated if they fulfil this function; they are ugly and out of joint if they do not.

I realize that this brief suggestion about a possible Augustinian aesthetic of the church building would need many pages, perhaps even volumes, to justify. It may also seem that such a general theological program could have at best only a distant relation to the actual building of medieval churches. (I admit that it is impossible to prove that any medieval master builder had anything like it consciously in mind.) But, contrary to Tertullian's famous remark, I think that Athens does have something to do with Jerusalem, that is, that art history and theology can learn from each other. Indeed, art historians in general have been more willing to explore these relations, while the historical theologians have often neglected non-textual resources and evidence. My "Augustinian" suggestion will have served a purpose if it helps to open the dialogue between art historians and theologians who seek to gain a more complete understanding of the dynamics of medieval culture.

In searching for an interpretive link of some sort between medieval churches and the world which created them, art historians have often looked to theology and the history of theology as a source of inspiration which could "reveal the purposes" of the cathedral-builders, but not always with success. In fact, the kind of abstract, purely descriptive art history so prevalent in recent decades can be seen in part, as, an abreaction to the rather heavy-handed invocation of theological ideas found in the classic works of Emile Mâle and many of his successors, such as Günter Bandmann, Hans Sedlmayr, Erwin Panofsky, and Otto von Simson.[4] Therefore, it is important in a volume whose intention is to debate appropriate methodologies for an "integrated" view of Gothic churches to have a close critical look at these traditional attempts to wed architectural history. More important, this dialogue challenges the historical theologian to say whether he or she can provide the art-historical investigator with a set of tools for a more complete – and more proper? – grasp of the meaning of these buildings.[5]

Trying to be precise about this issue is a real challenge for a theologian, who rarely – it must be admitted with a measure of embarrassment – attempts to analyse concrete works of art. I often envy the art historians: they get to deal with such concrete and tangible things.

One might also be tempted to think that the objects of their studies are therefore more open to convincing explanations of meaning and function. But the disagreements among art historians do not seem to be appreciably less than those of historians of thought, despite the tangibility of what they investigate. So perhaps a theologian can provide insight into what I take to be some of the crucial issues raised in the attempt to construct a more integrated approach to the study of Gothic cathedrals. These issues seem to revolve around a cluster of words beginning with "i" – integration, intention, innovation, and influence. Let me begin with brief reflections on each.

All of the essays – and the rationale of the original colloquium itself – address, or at least imply, these four notions. While we do not need to give hard-and-fast definitions of these concepts, we at least need to think about what we mean when we use them. For instance, art historians and historians in general need to have a set of categories in mind in order to identify what will count for real integration, as well as for what kinds of integration we might wish to talk about, and on what grounds we wish to talk about them. The Augustinian perspective that I am suggesting here would argue that a theological integration in terms of the relation of the *tabernaculum admirabile* to the *domus Dei* should not be forgotten as we try to assess the issue of how medieval Gothic cathedrals may or may not be conceived of as integrated monuments. Augustine's thought is not a magic key for all medieval conceptions of integration, but the bishop of Hippo was the single most influential figure in Western thought for a millennium, and he should be taken seriously.

Similarly, what do we mean when we talk about "intention"? Is it the intention of a patron, planner, or builder, or the intention that others add to an original monument or text? In the past generation, theology has been revolutionized by hermeneutical studies, especially by the insistence that the "intention" of any text involves not only what the original author(s) may have meant (should that be recoverable), but also the meanings that accrue to the text over history which give it intention in a broader and more complex sense. Something analogous to this may apply to buildings, especially buildings like Gothic cathedrals, which were constructed (and used) over centuries. As Paul Crossley reminds us, one of the central methodological problems of many previous attempts to relate theology and architecture in the Middle Ages lay "ultimately in the whole notion of a period of architecture conveying a single and precise significance."[6] But the admission of multiple meanings, what Richard Krautheimer once referred to as "multi-think,"[7] or a multitude of connotations, some part of an original plan, others accrued by use and alteration, is still, I believe, something worth investigating.

From this perspective, for example, the "intention" of Saint-Denis is not only what Suger and the actual group of people responsible for the early twelfth-century construction of the church thought they were doing, but it must also take into account what later generations of users and rebuilders thought about the first work, and what they added to it. This approach is represented, I believe, in a number of the essays in this book.[8]

Another issue which arises in many of these essays is the idea of "innovation," a concept that always implies some relation to what medieval authors described as *renovatio*.[9] When does the attempt at a *renovatio* become a real innovation, or perhaps even a revolution? What criteria do we use to determine this? Of course, this is not a question restricted to art history. One of the most important influences on medieval aesthetics was that of the mysterious author who wrote under the name of Dionysius, Paul's Athenian convert. Today, historians tend to view this Dionysius (ca. 500) as a great innovator in Christian theology, and yet his own appeal was to tradition, since he put himself forward as a representative of what he learned at the feet of the apostles and was accepted on these grounds. Is this merely because of the gullibility of centuries of naïve Christians who had no understanding of modern historical-critical method, or is something else involved too, perhaps a rather different sense of what constitutes renovation (an updating of tradition) as against innovation (something that is a real departure)?[10]

Finally, there is the question of what we mean by "influence," both in the history of thought and in art history. Art historians might have a right to expect that the history of thought should have worked out adequate categories for what constitutes a "real" influence, but in practice this is not so clear. One can find both hard-nosed definitions of influence which say that only if we can prove that a particular author read another can we call the latter an influence; one can also find views - which, I admit, are often problematic – which accept much broader conceptions of influence, down to vague notions of a *Zeitgeist* in which ideas float in the air to be inhaled by anyone in the vicinity.[11] Can we find a middle ground between hard and often positivistic ideas of influence and the appeal to any categories that may enable us to talk about "influence," even if we cannot actually demonstrate that a certain text was read at a certain moment by a later author? *Mutatis mutandis*, the problem is relevant in art history, whether speaking of the "influence" of one building on another, or even more of the subject I will now turn to, the "influence" of texts and ideas on artistic monuments.

From a theological point of view, I would like to suggest a consideration of some themes drawn from the Augustinian perspective outlined above which may be helpful in thinking about integration, intention, innovation, and influence in medieval architectural history. These themes are heuristic devices designed to open up questions rather than provide easy answers. They will not necessarily reveal integrations, but they may help us to specify what kinds of integrations we are looking for.

The first theme is broad and somewhat theoretical: what can medieval understandings of *theologia* in general, especially the role of beauty as a transcendental theological term, tell us about artistic, and especially architectural, integration in the Middle Ages? The others involve particular aspects of Christian theology, especially those dealing with God's relation to creation – what the Greeks called *oikonomia* and the Latins *providentia*, and what moderns often describe as salvation history. We might speak of them as applied theology.

Theology and Medieval Art

Many of the great art historians whose names come up in these essays, for instance, Mâle, Panofsky, and von Simson, have been interested in the relation between art works and *theologia* in a general sense as a way to draw parallels between the disciplines or to show how theology "inspired," "influenced," perhaps even "caused," certain works of art. Their conclusions are well known and have been subject to much criticism, though their status as courageous pioneers always needs to be recognized. However we evaluate their success, it is evident that they often tended to operate from a broad perspective which sought to find general analogies between art and theology. They also at times seem to presuppose, if not always to argue for, a single medieval aesthetic. All too often we find their interpretations make entertaining reading, but are either too general or too arbitrary to be convincing. Today, we tend to resist any unidirectional emphasis on how far the theological ideas of a single learned patron can really provide the "explanation" of any work of art, let alone one as complex as a Gothic cathedral.

It seems to me that contemporary history of medieval theology supports this tendency found among the art historians, and also has some contributions to make that have thus far not been fully appreciated. First, I would stress the growing awareness of the diversity of theological aesthetics in the Middle Ages. When we ask about the relation between *theologia* and art, we need to remain attentive to the different understandings of theology and its divisions, as well as to the variety of ways of conceiving of the beautiful and its function in the process of salvation.

Recent work has emphasized that there was not one, but several traditions of "theological aesthetics" in the Middle Ages.[12] Much more work needs to be done on the identification and study of these traditions – Augustinian, Dionysian, Franciscan, Thomistic, etc. - before we will be in a position to approach general issues in the relations between *theologia* and medieval art. (This does not, of course, prevent us from making particular forays, in both the general and the applied fields, as noted below.)

In older studies of medieval aesthetics, there was often an overconcentration on the Dionysian aesthetic tradition. This is not to deny the great significance of Dionysian aesthetic centred on the notion of *theophania*, or divine manifestation, but it needs to be put into perspective as one tradition among others. Not every invocation of *Lichtmetaphysik* (the "metaphysics of light") encountered in texts or argued for in terms of a particular monument needs to be Dionysian.[13] There is also confusion about just where Dionysian influence is most often found. From the time in which the Dionysian corpus was translated by John Scottus Eriugena in the ninth century, it was picked up by a number of important writers, but contrary to what one often reads, Dionysianism was far more a scholastic than a monastic phenomenon.[14] The great Dionysian of the twelfth century is the canon, Hugh of St Victor, and the major spread of Dionysianism came through the adoption of the glossed *Corpus Dionysiacum* in the University of Paris in the thirteenth century and its subsequent study by the Rhineland Dominicans, spearheaded by Albert the Great. In other words, the assumption that a specifically Dionysian aesthetic was at work in any monastic building or artefact needs concrete proof and cannot be assumed as part of a general theological legacy.

It is Augustine and Augustinian aesthetics which are much more likely to be found in a monastic milieu.[15] There is an important role for light in Augustine's thoughts on beauty, but rather than *theophania* I would argue that *harmonia*, the fitting order (*ordo*) established by God, is the central theme. As against other treatments of Augustine's aesthetics,[16] however, I think that the bishop's views cannot be fully grasped unless we understand their hermeneutical character – beauty is a kind of *signum*, a sign given by one intelligent mind to another in order to convey a message. The humanly constructed beauty of a church building is meant to form an "admirable tabernacle" which will lead to God.

Allow me to illustrate the issue of Dionysianism and Augustinianism by a consideration of the well-known case of Suger and the building of Saint-Denis. Erwin Panofsky's account of Suger's Dionysianism, first published in 1946, is among the best-known works of medieval art history.[17] But a number of scholars have pointed out how shaky Panofsky's claims actually are, and recently Peter Kidson has ably summarized the opposition in a devastating attack.[18] Kidson's excellent critique of Panofsky's appeal to the Dionysian tradition as the only meaningful reading of Suger's intentions also dismisses the credo that Suger "needed a philosophy to defend his taste in art, and that his works of art were actually inspired by such doctrines."[19] One can agree with this without necessarily thinking that Suger's "philosophy" (actually his theology) has no relation to his part in the building of Saint-Denis. Indeed, Kidson replaces Panofsky's overwhelming emphasis on *theoria* with a completely pragmatic and down-to-earth, perhaps even somewhat contemptuous, notion that what Suger has to say about "light" is a stock-in-trade commonplace, an "emasculated reflection" of Augustine, coming from everyday sermonizing.[20] Perhaps there is more to both Augustine and Suger than that.

Suger, to be sure, knew something of the Dionysian corpus and felt a real devotion to the great patron of his house. But he was steeped in Augustine's thought, and especially his hermeneutics. Grover Zinn has ably argued that what Dionysianism there is in Suger is actually very close to that we find in Hugh of St Victor and his pupil Richard – a Dionysianism that can be best characterized as "Augustinianized."[21] Everywhere, Suger follows the characteristic Augustinian method of theologizing by taking words from ordinary language – such as "bright" – and revealing their meaning by a rhetoric of *repeti-*

tio while building the plane of meaning up from the mundane to the eschatological.[22] Suger had grasped the inner meaning of the Augustinian theory of signs and applied it to the beautiful objects he commissioned for his church, as the last line of the poem he had inscribed on the golden altar frontal in the upper choir indicates – *Significata magis significante placent* (The things signified please more than that which signifies).[23] Indeed, a passage from chapter 5 of the *De consecratione*, which is a brief meditation on Ephesians 2: 19–22, could be taken as a perfect summary of how the "admirable tabernacle" of the faithful who form Christ's Body, as set forth and made concrete in the church building, leads on to the heavenly home:

"Now therefore you are no more strangers and foreigners," says he [Paul], "but fellow citizens with the saints and of the household of God; and are built upon the foundation of the apostles and prophets, Jesus Christ himself being the chief cornerstone" which joins one wall to the other, "in whom the whole building" – whether spiritual or material – "grows into one holy temple in the Lord." "In whom we, too," are taught "to be builded together for an habitation of God through the Holy Spirit" by ourselves in a spiritual way, the more loftily and fitly we strive to build in a material way.[24]

Similarly, Suger's climactic view of his achievement is replete with the sense of *harmonia* characteristic of Augustinians: "Thus, when with wise counsel and under the dictation of the Holy Ghost Whose unction instructs us in all things, that which we proposed to carry out had been designed with perspicacious order ..."[25]

If Kidson had given more attention to the deep Augustinian dimension in Suger's thought, it is doubtful that he would have insisted that the abbot's aesthetic is grounded in the "physical beauty of the building" and is read "through the senses."[26] Rather, Suger's sense of beauty is grounded in the necessity of the transition from material to spiritual beauty, as he puts it in a passage that has both Dionysian and Augustinian dimensions: "Thus, when ... worthy meditation has induced me to reflect, transferring that which is material to that which is immaterial, on the diversity of the sacred virtues, then it seems to me that I see myself dwelling ... in some strange region of the universe which neither exists entirely in the slime of the earth nor entirely in the purity of Heaven; and that, by the grace of God, I can be transported from this inferior to that higher world in an anagogical manner."[27] We, then, recognize in Suger essentially an

Augustinian aesthetic, though with some interesting Dionysian high-lights.[28] This is not to claim that Suger was in any way an eminent theologian, though he had at least as much grasp of current theological trends as the average ecclesiastical leader of our own century.

It is important not to be simple-minded. I do not mean to suggest a unidirectional sense of influence of theological speculation upon building campaigns or programs; naïvety of this sort is no longer per-missible, either to art historians or to historical theologians. It is sim-ple practical wisdom to realize - using the kind of common sense which Kidson and a number of contributors to this volume encourage – that Suger placed his spiritual, liturgical, and pastoral needs in the lap of his master of the works, and in return expected to receive archi-tectural solutions to his problems.[29] His accumulation of money was to pay not only for costly materials, but also for hiring global exper-tise.[30] Nor am I ignoring the frequent warning – voiced in this vol-ume by Barbara Abou-El-Haj and Brigitte Bedos-Rezak – that Suger's text is a *post hoc* self-justification, an *apologia* for a massive and gaudy work of socio-economic engineering and political aggrandizement, so that the text cannot describe for us the *meaning* of Saint-Denis as a mere equation with Suger's stated intentions. All that the present essay wishes to claim is that, when trying to grasp Saint-Denis in an "integrated" (or "holistic") understanding of its historical signifi-cance, it behoves us to take the theological dimension of Suger's lan-guage very seriously, because *theologia* in a general sense was all-pervasive in his world-view, both *ante hoc* and *post hoc*.

If this last, most fundamental idea is to be taken seriously, it will certainly modify the art-historical discussion of the meaning or his-torical significance of monumental churches. Sometimes it is omis-sions which will have to be filled in: in this volume, Arnold Klukas has offered an important analysis of the evolution of stages of style and form at Durham in response to changing liturgical and ecclesio-logical needs, but he did not investigate the possibility that, since the chapter at Durham was a convent of black monks (Benedictines), their theological *Weltanschauung* may well have coloured the surface appearances he describes in ways hitherto unexplored. Again, Roger Reynolds has properly issued a strong call for more precise liturgical investigation when analysing the formal structures of churches, but would this research not be all the richer if informed by a history of liturgical theology in the era of the edifice?[31] At other times, it is errors of commission which will have to be rectified: Panofsky's

Gothic Architecture and Scholasticism is a failure because he operates from a mere analogy between two modes of *modern* descriptions of form, in the one case, art historians' description of the form of a building; in the other, idea historians' descriptions of the form of argument in technical scholasticism.[32] The fatal flaw is that he did not seek out the operative world-view and history of values of the people who built the cathedrals.

En revanche, the historical theologian must be prepared to embrace a world of theological activity much greater than the pages of texts, commentaries, formal treatises, and sermons with which he or she is so comfortable, and in which the theological ideas are so explicit. If the critical claim I have made in this essay is true – namely, that a theological mentality was all-pervasive in the world of the cathedral-builders and that it informed their sensibilities and hence their design commissions – I, or any historical theologian, must be prepared to examine monumental buildings in search of signs of theology, whether conscious or unconscious. But how little theological work of this sort is to be found!

Applied Theology and Medieval Art

These grand theological theories, and the possibility that they can be related to actual monuments, offer only one side of the question of a collaboration between art history and historical theology. What comes out in most of the essays in this book has much more to do with what I have called "applied theology," that is, particular applications of distinct theological doctrines to specific monuments. In contrast to the influences and analogies that relate to *theologia* as such, and to theological conceptions of beauty as a transcendental principle, in applied theology one asks to what extent a particular doctrine may have helped shape a monument or some aspect of it. Let me give two brief illustrations, which come from various essays in this volume.

First, there is the way in which specific details of *Heilsgeschichte*, salvation history as exegetically interpreted, are displayed in various monuments and to what ends. There is a good example of this in Beat Brenk's essay, which depends on certain models of sacred kingship as a basis for its interpretation of the Sainte-Chapelle. The relation between iconographic programs and scriptural exegesis is a complex one, broader and more nuanced than the older concept of simple "typology" which characterized the approach of Emile Mâle, who at times really did seem to think that programmers simply read literary and theological texts and then illustrated their ideas. The result of this approach was a kind of iconography-as-theology detached from notions of either historical or architectural context.

The "integrative" notion of the building as an entity, incorporating design, style, execution, and iconography in one meaningful whole, marks a great improvement in the application of *Heilsgeschichte* to the reading of churches as historical witnesses, as is seen in this volume in all the essays which deal with churches that have large iconographic programs, for example, Chartres, Poitiers, and Saint-Denis. William Clark even tries to treat purely architectonic decor – the "Merovingian" Corinthian capitals – as being potential typological bearers of meaning. Virginia Raguin sees a kind of *harmonia* at Poitiers linking both secular and sacred narrative through common aesthetic structures. Surely, it is the ubiquitousness of this form of theological awareness in the Early Gothic era that makes this an effective argument.

Because medieval supervisors of great building campaigns, like Suger, had a theological formation, they understood that what was operating in a "reading" of their church was not a simplistic dictionary of types but rather a language, most often based on the Augustinian theory of signs, which permitted every element of the building, both figural and architectural, and even decorative, to be interpreted in reference to a higher meaning.[33] By quoting Augustine in the inscription on his bronze doors, Suger indicated how his building was to be read: not with the senses, but with the higher understanding which would perceive the physical doors as the "door of Paradise ... The things signified please more than that which signifies." Indeed, as both Fernie and Clark have argued in their essays here, Suger's architectural project was itself a gloss on history, an idea rooted in the Augustinian exegetical method which was the soul of monastic scriptural contemplation.[34]

A second area involves the whole notion of "sacramental theology" in its broadest sense, including liturgy, which creates both a general and a functional integration of every church: these buildings were not meant just for observation, but for practice. They were *loca*, places where the liturgy was celebrated and sacraments received, all of which can influence programs and designs. As this topic is discussed in this volume at length by Reynolds and Klukas, I need not dwell on it further here, but it offers another example of "applied theology" which entered into the daily experience of just about everyone in the Middle Ages.

These areas, and many others of applied theology, need to be opened up for further investigation and discussion. Such cooperative research on particular doctrines must continue to be illuminated by ongoing consideration of the relation between general theological aesthetics, in all its varieties, and medieval art and architecture. Such a program would seem utopian without the evidence of a volume such as this. I am not sure that the answers are here, but it strikes me that the right questions are beginning to be addressed. Even if that should not prove to be the case, there can be no doubt that a new conversation has begun.

NOTES

This essay is based upon oral remarks originally delivered at the colloquium upon which this volume is based. I wish to thank all those who responded to me at that time and helped contribute to this expanded written form. Special thanks are due to Richard Schneider, who transcribed the taped remarks and made numerous suggestions for developing the themes.

1 Augustine, *Enarratio in psalmum* XLI.9, *Patrologia Latina*, 36: 469–70.

2 For an analysis of Augustine's mysticism showing its fundamentally ecclesial nature, see Bernard McGinn, *The Foundations of Mysticism*, Vol. 1: *The Presence of God: A History of Western Christian Mysticism* (New York, 1991), ch. 7.

3 This is the main theme of Augustine's hermeneutics as laid out in the *De doctrina christiana*, books 1 and 2, but found throughout his exegesis.

4 See the critique of the latter four by Paul Crossley, "Medieval Architecture and Meaning: The Limits of Iconography," *The Burlington Magazine* 130 (1988), 116–21. See also the essays of Kathryn Brush and Willibald Sauerländer in this volume.

5 As was emphasized in an intervention at the Toronto colloquium by Brian Whittaker, the distinction which is being suggested in these remarks is not unlike that stated by Kant, between *Zweck* and *Zweckmässigkeit*, that is, between the judgment our rational faculty makes about a thing – such as a Gothic church – by referring it to our concept of that thing, and our direct aesthetic appreciation of the thing without reference to concepts. It is

extremely important to remember that, in the Middle Ages, aesthetics was an aspect of theology, and that medieval viewers would find the notion of a "pure" aesthetic appreciation absolutely foreign and faulty. For medieval thinkers, beauty (*pulchrum*) was a transcendental predicate, so that all beauty below was analogical and teleological (see, e.g., Augustine, *De civitate Dei* 5.11). In this sense, it is doubtful whether medieval monuments should be spoken of as "works of art," at least not in the modern sense of that term.

6 Crossley, "Medieval Architecture," 120.

7 Richard Krautheimer, "Postscript" to "Introduction to an 'Iconography of Medieval Architecture,'" in his *Studies in Early Christian, Medieval, and Renaissance Art* (New York, 1969), p. 149.

8 The appeal to hermeneutic reinterpretation through new use is at the heart of the methodologies employed in the essays of Arnold Klukas, Eric Fernie, and William Clark, even if they do not make technical reference to theology in their arguments.

9 For instance, I find this issue central to the reflections on Chartres, Saint-Denis, and Durham in the essays of Kurmann and Kurmann-Schwarz, Fernie, and Klukas.

10 The most perceptive recent theological study of Dionysius (as against a purely historical-critical one) argues for a renovative rather than an innovative interpretation. See Hans Urs von Balthasar, *The Glory of the Lord. A Theological Aesthetic. II. Studies in Theological Style: Clerical Styles* (New York, 1984), pp. 144–210.

11 On the inherent problems of the argument from the *Zeitgeist*, see Ernst Gombrich, *In Search of Cultural History* (Oxford, 1969).

12 This is not always sufficiently evident in older works, like Edgar de Bruyn, *The Esthetics of the Middle Ages* (New York, 1969), the English abridgment of the original three-volume work of 1946. More recent work on medieval aesthetics includes the important studies of Umberto Eco, *The Aesthetics of Thomas Aquinas*, 2d ed. (Cambridge, MA, 1988); and *Art and Beauty in the Middle Ages* (New Haven, 1986).

13 Among the studies of *Lichtmetaphysik*, nothing has surpassed the old work of Clemens Baeumcker, *Witelo, Ein Philosoph und Naturforscher des XIII. Jahrhunderts* [*Beiträge zur Geschichte der Philosophie des Mittelalters* 3.2] (Münster, 1900), pp. 358–422.

14 See Bernard McGinn, "Pseudo-Dionysius and the Early Cistercians," in *One Yet Two: Monastic Tradition East and West*, ed. M. Basil Pennington (Kalamazoo, MI, 1976), pp. 200–41.

15 This volume deals with buildings primarily of the twelfth and early thir-

teenth centuries, so I have confined my main discussion to the most pre-vailing theological modes of that era. There are other very powerful and convincing forms of theological aesthetic found later in the thirteenth cen-tury in the work of both Aquinas and Bonaventure, especially in Bonaventure's notion of exemplarism, encapsulated in the word *expressio* and all that it means for him. Theologians are beginning to deal with this material, and it would be creative to see a happy collaboration between theologians and the kind of art history represented by the essays of this colloquium.

16 Among these, see von Balthasar, *The Glory of the Lord. II. Clerical Styles*, pp. 95–143, an account I find problematic as a result of its concentration on early works of Augustine; and Robert J. O'Connell, *Art and the Christian Intelligence in Saint Augustine* (Cambridge, MA, 1978).

17 I will cite from the second edition, Erwin Panofsky, *Abbot Suger on the Abbey Church of St.-Denis and its Art Treasures*, ed. Gerda Panofsky-Soergel (Princeton, 1979).

18 Peter Kidson, "Panofsky, Suger, and St. Denis," *Journal of the Warburg and Courtauld Institutes* 50 (1987), 1–17.

19 Ibid., 5. On this subject, see most recently Conrad Rudolph, *Artistic Change at St-Denis: Abbot Suger's Program and the Early Twelfth-Century Controversy Over Art* (Princeton, 1990).

20 Kidson, "Panofsky," 7.

21 Grover A. Zinn, "Suger, Theology, and the Pseudo-Dionysian Tradition," in *Abbot Suger and Saint-Denis*, ed. Paula Lieber Gerson, pp. 33–40 (New York, 1986).

22 For an illustration, see the *De administratione* XXVIII: "Claret enim claris quod clare concopulatur / Et quod perfundit lux nova, claret opus / Nobile, quod constat auctum sub tempore nostro ..." Cited in Panofsky, *Abbot Suger*, p. 50.

23 Panofsky, *Abbot Suger*, p. 54 (my translation, since I often find Panofsky's misleading).

24 Ibid., 104, for Latin text, and p. 105 for the translation, which I have adapted slightly here.

25 Suger, *De consecr.* IV, in Panofsky, *Abbot Suger*, pp. 100–1. *Ordo* is, of course, Augustine's constant key word for describing the harmonious beauty of God's creation. When Suger, in the sentence immediately preceding the one quoted here, emphasizes the use of geometry and instruments of measure, he is equally expressing a favourite Augustinian theology of *ordo* going back to Wisdom 11: 21.

26 Kidson, "Panofsky," 7.

27 Suger, *De admin.* XXXIII, cited in Panofsky, *Abbot Suger*, pp. 62–5. On seeing the immaterial reality within the material, see the discussion of *De doctrina christiana* below.

28 The distinction between the Augustinian and the Dionysian modes in the
twelfth century has been studied by M.-D. Chenu in "The Symbolist Mentality," in his *Nature, Man and Society in the Twelfth Century*, trans. J. Taylor
and L.K. Little (Chicago, 1968), esp. pp. 124–8.

29 Kidson, "Panofsky," 11.

30 Suger, *De admin.* XXIV, cited in Panofsky, *Abbot Suger*, pp. 42–3.

31 There is a large body of liturgical-commentary texts for the era investigated by this volume; Durandus is only the climax of a long century and a
half of development.

32 On Panofsky, see Crossley, "Medieval Architecture," pp. 119–20.

33 Again, the fundamental text here is Augustine's *De doctrina christiana*, on
which there is a large literature. Particularly important for his theory of
signs are the essays of R.A. Markus and B. Darrell Jackson in *Augustine: A
Collection of Critical Essays*, ed. R.A. Markus (Garden City, 1972), pp. 59–
147.

34 This emphasis on the predominance of exegetical theology should offer a
caution to readers who insist on a highly philosophical and abstract
theology to explain the significance of medieval churches. The critique
implied here of Otto von Simson's *The Gothic Cathedral* (New York, 1962) is
clear.

4

Liturgy and the Monument

Roger E. Reynolds

Liturgy plays an essential role in determining the use and significance of medieval religious edifices. Reynolds presents a cursive yet comprehensive overview of the ways in which liturgical functions may determine specific parameters of buildings and affect their subsequent modifications. Buildings, after all, reflect the needs of their builders and users. Reynolds sees a reciprocal relationship between the forms of the buildings and the actions taking place within them, suggesting that liturgical practice was often designed to conform to existing buildings. Basing his convictions on study of medieval liturgical books, he suggests that the patrons had formulated clear intentions about the purpose of building, and that later readers can retrieve those intentions from our reading of the text.

Medieval society, as is often stated, was divided between those who worked (peasants), those who fought (the nobility), and those who prayed (the religious orders). The liturgy, therefore must be seen as possessing a central social function, a function reflected in these buildings. This structural division of society is discussed again in the essays of Bedos-Rezak and Abou-El-Haj, although from the perspective of the vast majority of the population that was excluded from the class "that prayed."

Reynolds is clear about the difficulties facing scholars, especially art historians not specifically trained in the evaluation of liturgical issues. The author posits the value of the collaborative work as a vital element of integrated study. He stresses, however, that liturgical function must be addressed for a comprehensive evaluation of the dimensions of an edifice.

Before we probe the integrating function of liturgy, we may address the role of our institutes as encouraging or impeding scholarly integration. The pressing issue of bridging the disciplines as we think of artistic integration has been at the heart of the founding of Toronto's Institute of Mediaeval Studies. One of the founders of Toronto's institute was Etienne Gilson, a distinguished philosopher. Early in his career he had seen that, to appreciate medieval philosophy correctly, one had to understand the culture of the Middle Ages globally, and to that end he realized the need for a multidisciplinary institute. He tried to establish such an institute at Paris but was rebuffed and advised to remain a philosopher. He then went to the United States, where, at Harvard, among other potential sites, he suggested the same, with the same result. Finally he came to Canada, where his vision was caught in Toronto by the Basilian Fathers, with whom Gilson founded such an institute with no departmental lines. Later in the 1930s, a petition was sent to Rome for a Pontifical Charter, which at that time encompassed only philosophical and theological institutes. It would have been simple for Rome to have pigeon-holed the institute as a pontifical philosophical institute. But Gilson and his colleagues persisted in asking for exactly what they wanted. And hence, more than half-century ago, the Pontifical Institute was chartered to devote itself to the investigation of the whole of medieval culture. And indeed, the recent papal constitution, *Sapientia Christiana*, has recognized medieval studies as a discipline in itself.[1]

A second story follows from this and deals with one of the best-known teachers of the Pontifical Institute, Father Leonard Boyle. He is most familiar to scholars of art history for his archaeological work at San Clemente. To his co-workers at the Vatican, however, he is a librarian. To others here in Toronto, he is a palaeographer, a diplomatist, a Thomistic philosopher, a canonist, a hagiographer, and a specialist in medieval pastoral manuals. A decade ago, when I arrived at the Pontifical Institute, I wondered just who the real Father Boyle was, and so at lunch one day I asked him if he were the institute's palaeographer. With his mischievous twinkle he replied with a firm "no." After a few more negative responses to my probes – canonist? theologian? church historian? – I asked him in exasperation what he thought he was. He replied in a straightforward manner – "a medievalist, pure and simple." Since that time, I have often asked Father Boyle if he has changed his mind or his identity, and as of a month before the conference entitled "Artistic Integration in Early Gothic

Churches" his answer has remained unchanged. That is, he continues to embody the ideal set out by Gilson sixty years ago in the founding of the Institute of Mediaeval Studies. Father Boyle is concerned with the whole of medieval culture and refuses to be compartmentalized into a single discipline or specialization.

Because most of us teach or have taught as members of traditional university departments, it is not surprising that we often limit ourselves in art history as well as in other disciplines. I would suggest, however, that despite these constraints, we must follow the lead of both Gilson and Boyle and commit ourselves as medievalists. In that way, the bridges that have been encouraged by this collection of essays can be constructed. And, I would suggest, that it is in this way that we can appreciate most fully and understand the artistic integration of the ecclesiastical monuments we study.

Almost all the essays in this volume address in some way the intention of the creators of Gothic monuments, and almost all claim that intention is "difficult" to discern, or even unknowable. As a liturgical scholar, I take as a first premise the precision of such texts as medieval pontificals, with their exact directions and prayers for the dedication or consecration of a church. Those who prayed these prayers hard on the construction of the church may have been hypocritical or simply using well-worn traditional prayers directed at certain audiences or containing certain *topoi*, but those who prayed nevertheless offered these prayers frequently, with great pomp and ceremony, before God, royalty, nobility, and the people of diocese and parish. These prayers clearly expressed intentions underlying the construction of a building: (1) that it act as God's house, (2) that it honour a saint or saints whose relics were entombed in the altar, (3) that priests would offer sacrifice of praise (*hic quoque sacerdotes sacrificia laudis offerant*), (4) that the faithful would pay their vows (*hic fideles populi vota persolvant*), and (5) that sins would be forgiven and the faithful repair their faults (*hic peccatorum onera solvantur fidelesque lapsi reparentur*).[2] In short, while from these prayers of dedication it is clear that these buildings were constructed with several intentions in mind, one was always liturgical.

Before dealing with the problem of how this irreducible liturgical purpose affected architectural design, one must ask, compellingly, what is, or what was, liturgy? Was it worship to be performed publicly? That is, was a person saying his or her prayers privately in a side chapel or oratory performing a liturgical act? Many liturgists would say no. Was the veneration of saints in itself a liturgical act? That is, were the multiple chapels built in the great pilgrimage churches intended for liturgical ceremony or simply to contain lucrative relics appealing to private spiritual devotion? Further, is a calendar with its numerous saints and feasts necessarily liturgical? In short, are all of the actions taking place in a church that are commonly associated with liturgy really liturgical?

Moreover, for the purpose of our joint inquiry one might well ask if liturgy is or was an art form; that is, should liturgy even be included in discussions of "artistic integration"? Although several essays in this volume classify liturgy as a "function," liturgy is and clearly was an art form. Certainly, it is universally agreed that liturgical music is an art form.[3] Further, the dramatic aspects of the liturgy might be classed as artistic, such as the postures of the celebrants, hand movements, and the like.[4] Then, there are the actual mini-dramas such as the *Quem Queritis* plays, the veneration of the cross on Good Friday, and other performances of this type. And finally there is a magnificent art form in the drama of processions: the stational processions in Rome, Marian processions, Palm Sunday processions, baptismal processions, offertory processions, Gospel processions, processions of translation or exposition of relics, processions for the major and minor litanies, "lustration" processions, "pilgrimage" processions, monastic processions, and Corpus Christi processions, to name a few.[5] In short, the performance of liturgy emphatically is an art form and hence deserves to be embraced in our discussion of artistic integration in the creation of Early Gothic buildings, all the more so because all the actions just outlined require organization of space, sight-line, raised daises, and other elements of architectural design.

Despite what seems to be a general acknowledgment of the importance of liturgical factors in the construction of the Gothic churches and despite a consensus that liturgy should be considered an element of artistic integration, it is often difficult to link liturgical use with specific architectural forms. Arnold Klukas, as a most welcome exception, has integrated liturgical use into the very heart of his discussion of the architectural changes affecting the cathedral of Durham over time. Peter Draper has mentioned the retention of the Lady chapel and Anglo-Saxon font in the cathedral at Wells and the placement of the effigies of Saxon bishops. One would encourage further research relating these structural and figural elements to possible liturgical consideration. Draper also stresses that the clarity and regularity of the plan of the cathedral is fully in keeping with the liturgy and ordered religious life of a community of canons. We need in general to know much more about how this clarity and regularity might have been different from that reflecting the liturgy and ordered religious life of a community of monks. Would the cathedral have been designed differently for a monastic clergy?

To cite another case, Eric Fernie and William Clark observe Suger's respect for the standing building at Saint-Denis; given Suger's well-known concern for liturgical performance and liturgical paraphernalia, is it possible that his respect for the standing building was related to liturgical concerns? But evidence for this must be adduced.

Despite the lack of precise documentation expressed here regarding the persuasiveness of argument from liturgy presented in this volume, I believe there is a definite relationship between liturgical practice and our magnificent monuments. It is highly probable that there were considerations given to liturgical function in the building and decoration of any church simply because churches were intended, at least in part, for liturgical practice, as the dedication prayers indicate.

For which ceremonies were architectural and decorative considerations relevant? There are the obvious ones such as Mass, the Office, and baptism. Builders must provide such things as an altar for Mass, means of access for the people taking communion, protection for the sacred space around the altar, and so forth. For the Office, a choir and perhaps a nearby bell tower are necessary.[6] If one wants to attract spectators to grand performances of the Office (and Mass?) one must provide spectator access, for example, in an ambulatory.[7] Finally, for baptism a baptistery, or at least a font placed in the church, is necessary. Clearly the architectural and decorative contexts for these liturgical practices were designed with the ceremony in mind. But beyond these obvious points of functional contact between liturgical practice and architecture, there remains the largely unstudied question of how much liturgical concerns controlled decorative or design schemes.

There are a number of other areas in which liturgy impinges on architecture. First are the needs of processions, such as the obvious requirements of space, openness, and provision for crowds, be they large or small.[8] But beyond this, to be effective means of communication, processions must have a "stage" and appropriate "props," a point that Willibald Sauerländer also raises in this volume.[9] For the early Middle Ages, one thinks, for example, of the "processional" basilica of San Apollinare Nuovo in Ravenna with its mosaic "prop" of virgins, martyrs, and saints reflecting the actual processions of clergy and people below, or of the triumphal arches in the great Roman basilicas. So, in the construction and decoration of Early Gothic churches, one finds similar phenomena of staging props for processions, such as those cited by Sauerländer for the coronation rites in the cathedral of Reims.

Another area in which liturgy, architectural, and decorative concerns intersect is in the construction of multiple altars in churches. As the dedication ceremonies and prayers for a church indicate, altars have a twofold purpose: for use in the confection of the presence of God in Christ's body, and for the commemoration of saints entombed within the altar.[10] And so from the late eighth century onward, as more religious became priests, as daily celebration for each priest became more common, as votive Masses multiplied, and as traffic in relics increased, provision had to be made for multiple altars and access to them. Here the studies for the early Middle Ages of the monastic churches of Saint-Riquier and Saint-Gall are important for their demonstration of the relationship between architectural and liturgical concerns in the multiplication of altars.[11] For the high and later Middle Ages, similar work begs to be done very much along the lines suggested by Klukas's study of Durham in this volume or the recent study of Edward Foley on the relationship of the first ordinary of the royal abbey of Saint-Denis to the spatial requirements of the multiple altars in Suger's basilica.[12] Such questions as the decline of lay communion, visual communion versus actual communicating, changes in Eucharistic theology, the practices in saying the Office – all have to be examined for their architectural and decorative implications, especially for continental churches.

One must remain aware of the constant phenomenon of pilgrimage and its relation to liturgy, architecture, and the decoration of churches. In pilgrimage there are elements of both procession and the veneration of saints, and hence the needs we have mentioned in regard to these are also present with respect to pilgrimage – processional space, accommodation of crowds, access to the relics both in altars and elsewhere, and appropriate decorative elements in the church.[13]

For the high and later Middle Ages, a further impingement of liturgical considerations on the design of churches came with preaching.

Although preaching and sermons did take place in the early Middle Ages, the somewhat low esteem in which they were held in the liturgical context is reflected in the complete omission of a sermon in the famous eighth-century *Ordo Romanus Primus*, or in the replacement of sermons by such things as the Creed in the tenth-century *Pontificale Romano-Germanicum*.[14] But as popular preaching increased in the twelfth century - to be institutionally epitomized in the formation of the preaching orders in the thirteenth century – so architectural accommodations had to be made, and one finds these reflected in the Gothic hall church type of Germany or at Santa Croce and Santa Maria Novella in Florence.

All of this brings us to the matter of where one might look for evidence beyond the monuments themselves to demonstrate the intersection of liturgy and ecclesiastical architecture and decoration. Here, as Klukas has emphasized, art historians must pay more attention to the written liturgical sources that specifically mention architectural and decorative features of churches in a liturgical context. Although certainly much liturgical knowledge was transmitted orally, the liturgical scholar still prefers to see textual evidence.

Most people, when thinking of these written liturgical sources, immediately seize on the sacramentaries, missals, and books of the Office. Sadly, these types of books rarely mention architectural and decorative features of churches, although they can be useful for their calendric references and occasional *ordo* for the performance of a liturgical ceremony. Of much greater help are several other types of liturgical sources. First, there are the *ordines*, ordinaries, ceremonials, and *consuetudines* or customaries with their extensive directions. Here, one thinks, for example, of the early medieval *ordo* of Angilbert of Saint-Riquier or the thirteenth-century Mazarine ordinary for Saint-Denis.[15] Pontificals and rituals offer descriptions of liturgical rites beyond the Mass and Office.[16] Finally, there are the *processionalia* describing the routes of processions, processional paraphernalia, the architectural setting, and processional "props."[17]

Art-historical scholars cannot afford to wait for the handful of living liturgiologists to publish these texts that might demonstrate how liturgy impinges on their studies of the designs and decorations of their monuments. Rather, as Sheila Bonde, Edward Boyden, and Clark Maines have recently done in their study of Saint-Jean-des-Vignes, Soissons,[18] they will have to enter the field for themselves, searching for and examining liturgical documents relating to their particular monuments.

To return to the theme of this collection of essays, "artistic integration," I may have given the impression that I believe the monuments we have studied were designed only with liturgical purposes in mind. This would mean that existing liturgical practice dictated the design and decoration of these buildings. In part, this is probably true, and the maintenance of older designs, Lady chapels, Anglo-Saxon fonts, and the like may reflect this attitude. But I also believe that liturgical practice often was made to conform to existing buildings. We see evidence for such conformity in the patristic era and in very early medieval churches where liturgy was accommodated to existing basilicas, civil buildings, and pagan temples. In the prayers of dedication for a church, the dominant theme is not so much liturgical practice in the building but its function as a house of God and a place where the saints repose.[19] Designers and artisans worked to glorify God and the saints in their creative artistic endeavours, letting the liturgists accommodate their own artistic liturgical practices to the architectural and decorative framework in which they found themselves. In short, the designers of Gothic cathedrals, whether the buildings were created in a long or short period of time, must have had to adapt to the liturgy; but liturgy, on the other hand, also had to be accommodated to the structural and ornamental features of the churches in which it was housed. We cannot study one issue without the other.

SELECTED BIBLIOGRAPHY

This selected bibliography has been provided by the editors on the issue of the relationship of liturgy to architecture.

Arens, Fritz, "Die Raumaufteilung des Mainzer Domes und seiner Stiftsgebäude bis zum 13ten Jahrhundert," In *Willigis und seiner Dom, Festschrift zur Jahrtausendfeier des Mainzer Domes 975–1975*, ed. Anton Brück, pp. 185–250, Mainz, 1975.
Blau, Sible de, "Architecture and Liturgy in Late Antiquity and the Middle Ages: Traditions and Trends in Modern Scholarship," *Archiv für Liturgiewissenschaft* 33/1 (1991), 1–31.

Borg, Alan, and Andrew Martindale, ed. *The Vanishing Past: Studies of Medieval Art, Liturgy and Metrology Presented to Christopher Hohler.* Oxford, 1981.

Harper, John, *The Forms and Orders of Western Liturgy from the Tenth to the Eighteenth Century: A Historical Introduction and Guide for Students and Musicians.* Oxford, 1991.

Chaillev, Jacques, "Du drame liturgique aux prophètes de Notre-Dame-la-Grande," In *Mélanges René Crozet*, vol. 2, pp. 835–41, Poitiers, 1966.

Fassler, Margot, *Gothic Song – Victorine Sequences and Augustinian Reform in Twelfth-Century Paris.* New York, 1993.

– "Liturgy and Sacred History in the Twelfth-Century Tympana at Chartres," *Art Bulletin* 75 (1993), 499–520.

Karp, Theodore, *The Polyphony of St. Martial and Santiago de Compostela.* Oxford, 1992.

Hiley, David, and Susan Rankin, eds. *Music in the Mediaeval English Liturgy.* Oxford 1993.

Lewine, Carol, *The Sistine Chapel Walls and the Roman Liturgy.* University Park, PA, 1993.

Mathews, Thomas F. *The Early Churches of Constantinople: Architecture and Liturgy.* University Park, PA, 1971.

Parsons, David, *Tenth-Century Studies: Essays in Commemoration of the Millennium of the Council of Winchester and "Regularis Concordia."* London, 1975.

Robertson, Anne Walters, *The Service Books of the Royal Abbey of Saint-Denis: Images of Ritual and Music in the Middle Ages* [chapter dedicated to Art, Architecture and Politics]. Oxford, 1991.

Rasmussen, Niels Krogh, O.P. "The Liturgy at Saint-Denis: A Preliminary Study," In *Abbot Suger and Saint Denis: A Symposium*, ed. Paula Lieber Gerson, pp. 41–7. New York, 1986.

Rasmussen, Niels Krogh, O.P., and Eric Palazzo, "Messes privés, livres liturgiques et architecture: À propos du Ms. Paris Arsenal 610 et de l'église abbatiale de Reichenau-Mittelzell," *Revue des sciences philosophiques et théologiques* 72 (1988), 77–87.

Sheingorn, Pamela, "The Easter Sepulchre: A Study in the Relationship between Art and Liturgy." Dissertation, University Microfilms, 1976.

– *The Easter Sepulchre in England.* Kalamazoo, MI, 1987.

Sinding-Larsen, Staale, *Iconography and Ritual: A Study of Analytical Perspectives.* Irvington-on-Hudson, NY, 1984.

Speer, Andreas, "Kunst als Liturgie: zur Enstehung und Bedeutung der Kathedrale," In *Kein Bildnis machen: Kunst und Theologie im Gespräch*, ed. Christoph Dohmen and Thomas Sternberg, pp. 97–117, Würzburg, 1987.

66   Roger E. Reynolds

Sturgis, Alexander, "The Liturgy and Its Relation to Gothic Cathedral Design and Ornamentation in Late Twelfth-Century and Early Thirteenth-Century France. Dissertation, University of London, 1991.

Van der Ploeg, Kees, *Art, Architecture and Liturgy: Siena Cathedral in the Middle Ages*. Groningen, 1993.

Walker, Christopher, *Art and Ritual of the Byzantine Church*. London, 1982.

Wright, Craig, *Music and Ceremony at Notre-Dame of Paris, 500–1550*. Cambridge, 1989.

Yates, Nigel, *Buildings, Faith, Worship: The Liturgical Arrangement of Anglican Churches 1600–1900*. Oxford, 1991.

NOTES

1 Joannis Pauli II Summi Pontificis, *Constitutio Apostolica*, "*Sapientia Christiana*" *de studiorum universitatibus et facultatibus ecclesiasticis* (Vatican City, 1979), pp. 29, 50.

2 Michel Andrieu, *Le pontifical romain au moyen-âge*, Vol. 1: *Le pontifical au XIIe siècle* [Studi e testi 86] (Vatican City, 1938), pp. 179, 184.

3 It is to be regretted that the question of acoustics has not been addressed by any of the essays in this collection.

4 On the dramatic aspect of postures, hand movements, and the like, see O.B. Hardison, Jr, *Christian Rite and Christian Drama in the Middle Ages: Essays in the Origin and Early History of Modern Drama* (Baltimore, 1965), pp. 48–79.

5 On the variety of processions, see Aimé-George Martimort, "Les diverses formes de procession dans la liturgie," *La Maison-Dieu* 43 (1955), 43–73; and on the Corpus Christi processions, see Miri Rubin, *Corpus Christi: The Eucharist in Late Medieval Culture* (Cambridge, 1991), pp. 243–71.

6 See Charles B. McClendon, *The Imperial Abbey of Farfa: Architectural Currents of the Early Middle Ages* (New Haven, 1987), pp. 100–2. On the use of bells in the Eucharist, see Rubin, *Corpus Christi*, pp. 58 f.

7 See Otto K. Werckmeister, "Cluny III and the Pilgrimage to Santiago de Compostela," *Gesta* 27 (1988), 103–12.

8 For the architectural needs of processions in the early Middle Ages, see Carol Heitz, *L'architecture religieuse carolingienne. Les formes et leurs fonctions* (Paris, 1980), pp. 51–62; and for the later Middle Ages, see Edward B. Foley, *The First Ordinary of the Royal Abbey of Saint Denis in France* (Paris, Bibliothèque Mazarine 526) [Spicilegium Friburgense 32] (Fribourg/Switzerland, 1990), pp. 183–260.

9 Certainly this processional need was operative in classical times from the evidence of triumphal arches and the like.

10 In the prayers of consecration of the altar in the dedication of a church, these themes are clear: "Lord we humbly implore your majesty, that you might deign to bless and sanctify with power this altar which has been anointed with a libation of sacred ointment for the purpose of offering the gifts of your people ... so that whatever is offered or consecrated on it might be in your eyes a worthy holocaust and the sacrifices of all people making offerings here (might be accepted) by you ... God, who from every gathering [joining] of the saint [holy things] establishes an eternal dwelling place for your majesty, grant heavenly increase to what you have built, so that we may be always aided by the merits of those whose relics we enclose [honor, embrace] with pious love." [Ed. note: The alternative reading of several words are enclosed in brackets in order to suggest the richness of the Latin poetic resonances.]

11 See Carol Heitz, *Recherches sur les rapports entre architecture et liturgie à l'époque carolingienne* (Paris, 1963); and Walter Horn and Ernest Born, *The Plan of Saint Gall: A Study of the Architecture and Economy of, and Life in a Paradigmatic Carolingian Monastery*, I (Berkeley, Los Angeles, and London, 1979), pp. 208–11; Lorna Price, *The Plan of St Gall: In Brief* (Berkeley, Los Angeles, and London, 1982), pp. 20–2.

12 Foley, *The First Ordinary*, pp. 183–260.

13 On the antiquity of pilgrimage processions, see Martimort, "Les diverses formes de procession," pp. 63 f.

14 Michel Andrieu, *Les Ordines Romani du haut moyen âge*, II, *Les Textes* [Spicilegium sacrum lovaniense, Etudes et documents 23] (Louvain, 1948), p. 90; and Cyrille Vogel and Reinhard Elze, *Le pontifical romano-germanique du dixième siècle*, vol. 1 [Studi e testi 226] (Vatican City, 1963), p. 325.

15 See *Institutio sancti Angilberti abbatis. De diversitate officiorum (800–811)*, ed. K. Hallinger, M. Wegener, and H. Frank [Corpus Consuetudinum Monasticarum I] (Siegburg, 1963), pp. 283–303; and Foley, *The First Ordinary*. Sadly, the publication of this type of text does not seem to be a special priority of liturgical or historical scholars.

16 Although great advances were made by Andrieu and others in the publication of the Roman pontifical, precious little has been done for other rites and local usages. Also little has been done in the field of rituals.

17 Only a few of these *processionalia* have been published. In fact, simply for a basic orientation to this vast field, scholars eagerly await the list of processional manuscripts promised by Michel Huglo. Undoubtedly even some of the early printed processionals now listed in the *RELICS*

project at the University of Michigan would reflect late medieval usage.

18　Sheila Bonde, Edward Boyden, and Clark Maines, "Centrality and Community: Liturgy and Gothic Chapter Room Design at the Augustinian Abbey of Saint-Jean-des-Vignes, Soissons," *Gesta* 29 (1990), 189–213.

19　See above, notes 2 and 10.

5

Durham Cathedral in the Gothic Era: Liturgy, Design, Ornament

Arnold Klukas

The author addresses the monument as a physical presence, a product of a complex set of circumstances, exerting its influence over time. Klukas sees the monument as central to our discourse. He sees the value – indeed, necessity – of interrogating it from many more perspectives than were available to previous generations of scholars. In Klukas's view, the fabric of the building is not separated from liturgy or decoration, nor are subsequent transformations (accretions) divorced from the monument's purported "meaning." He does not believe that our methodology is comprehensive enough, nor that our knowledge of a patron's conscious or unconscious agendas is infallible enough for any historian to promulgate the final word on a programmatic intention, but he accepts – at least as a postulation – that Gothic churches were constructed according to a schedule of "essentials" that included liturgical function and iconographic meaning.

He approaches Durham's Gothic past by a form of "reverse archaeology," admitting that the present reconstruction of Durham is highly flavoured by the Romantic ideals concerning a purported "Age of Faith" shared by nineteenth- and early twentieth-century antiquarians. This thin overlay was imposed on an interior stripped and functionalized by Sir Gilbert Scott (1811–1878). The cathedral can be glimpsed through restorations following the Puritan era, and eventually to the building as it stood on the eve of the Act of Dissolution of Henry VIII. In analysing the evidence of the building and decorative campaigns, Klukas distinguishes phases of construction that he terms structural or aesthetic. His argument approaches that of Draper, who comments on the construction of Wells and Glastonbury, where the canons shared a sense of "decorum," that is, a sense of decoration appropriate to the embellished structure. Klukas, like Reynolds, sees phases of construction and reconstruction predicated on shifts in liturgical practice that were themselves expressions of shifts in theology and devotion. Despite what Klukas sees as a remarkably unified iconography in glass, statuary, and furnishings, he does not believe that one must necessarily see a "master plan." He suggests, instead, that communities can often retain implicit, if not explicit, consensus of symbolic language over time. Such arguments also appear in Raguin's analysis of the architecture, sculpture, and glass of Poitiers.

The title of this volume, *Artistic Integration in Gothic Buildings*, presumes a search for unity, and therefore, a search for intentionality. From the various ways in which such a search can be pursued, we may begin with two seemingly opposed viewpoints represented by Christopher Brooke and Paul Crossley. In his homage to Edmund Bishop, Brooke writes: "[Bishop] showed in a profound and convincing way that major elements in liturgical practice and church design are not due to whims of taste and fashion, but also express widely felt sentiments and attitudes; or, as I should put it, in every substantial variety in church design one may find an attempt to solve a problem in a church's function ... to reflect in an appropriate way some of the religious sentiments of the age."[1] And in a recent article, Paul Crossley states: "The *Gesamtkunstwerk* of a cathedral represents an accumulation of ambiguous and contradictory meanings, not just the embodiment of a philosophical system."[2]

Are these two perspectives mutually exclusive? I do not think so. Certainly, my continuing interest in liturgy and spirituality predisposes me to what has been termed a "functionalist/intentionalist" approach, but I do not think that either my methodology is comprehensive enough or our knowledge of a patron's conscious or unconscious agendas is infallible enough for any historian to promulgate the final word on programmatic intention. I do accept – at least as a postulation – that Gothic churches were constructed according to a schedule of essentials which included liturgical function and iconographical meaning. Our own twentieth-century agendas and tacit assumptions – especially our fascination for art devoid of meaning – obstructs our ability to perceive the intentions of the patrons and artists within the Gothic era.

Reverse Archaeology

To place my own work in context, I wish to approach Durham's Gothic era by a form of reverse archaeology – that is, to indicate the various assumptions made about Durham as a work of art from our own time back into the past. For example, the interior view of the Galilee (fig. 1) as it is today is the result of the ardent fervour of St John Hope, Percy Dearmer, and other members of the Alcuin Club who wished to return the Church of England to the glorious days of the fourteenth century.[3] St John Hope's liturgical plan of Durham cathedral on the eve of the Reformation was published in 1903 (fig. 2), but it was not until after the First World War, when the clergy of Durham (and the rest of the clergy in the Church of England) had imbued enough of the Alcuin Club's agenda, that they began to restore the side altars and shrines indicated in St John Hope's plan.[4] I am also addicted to the fragrant opiate of the romantic vision of a perfectly medieval English Use, which the Alcuin Club so ardently advocated, but I am equally aware that much of the aesthetic viewpoint of the Dearmerites owes more to the Arts and Crafts movement of the last century than it does to the Middle Ages.[5]

What is visible within the interior of Durham cathedral today reveals more about the ideals and romantic reconstructions of early twentieth-century liturgical antiquarians than it does of the interior as it looked on the eve of the Reformation. In particular, the austere masonry devoid of paint, the open access to all parts of the building allowed to the visitor, and the tastefully coordinated liturgical furnishings appeal to our modern tastes but were not true of the interior in the Gothic era. Thus our most recent archaeological layer is actually a very thin stratum which rests upon the massive deposits of Sir Gilbert Scott (1811–1878) and his Victorian perspective of the 1870s. Scott had imbibed enough of Viollet-le-Duc's notion of Gothic structuralism that his efforts were oriented to revealing the architectonic qualities of the interior at the expense of antiquarian nostalgia or liturgical propriety.[6] Scott stripped the walls, restored missing fragments of masonry, and provided the ponderous choir screen and pulpit which dominate the interior today (fig. 3). Scott had found his predecessors' work, notably that of Sir James Wyatt (1746–1813), sufficiently wanting to eradicate it.

Scott's demolition of Wyatt's work was quickly accomplished, for the stratum attributable to Wyatt is more important for what he demolished or wished to demolish than for what he actually constructed. Wyatt had intended to demolish the Neville screen so as to allow an unobstructed vista from one end of the interior to the other. He also proposed the demolition of the Galilee to provide access to the west portal for horse-drawn vehicles. The protests of local antiquarians prevented the execution of his plans. That Wyatt's own work at Durham was later demolished was poetic justice, for he was given the epithet "Wyatt the Destroyer."[7]

One hundred years before Wyatt, in the 1670s, Bishop Cosin returned to a church that had been vandalized as much by Puritan fanatics as by Scottish soldiers.[8] Cosin was dismayed to find that nearly all the windows had been smashed, the woodwork burned, and the organs destroyed. Cosin's antiquarian tastes and his Laudian liturgical principles were combined in his program to restore the choir interior with "Gothic" stalls and a stone altar before the Neville screen. His fittings were not intended to restore the choir to its fourteenth-century appearance, but rather to accommodate his view of how the restored *Book of Common Prayer* should be suitably performed.[9] Cosin's quiet restoration was built upon 140 years of destruction and dissolution, a very nasty archaeological layer of *destrutis*. The shrine of Saint Cuthbert had been confiscated in 1538 and the monastery had been surrendered in 1540.[10] Durham remained a cathedral, however, and as a result canons and schoolmasters replaced the monks and filled the vacuum left in the cloister.[11]

The Interior in the Late Gothic Era

But now we come to the richest layers of our archaeological descent. The cathedral interior of 1538 was the result of a renovation and remodelling over a period of one hundred years that had transformed the east and west ends of the church into brightly lit, delicately detailed compartments. Although very little of the glass and other appointments remain from this era, a remarkable book does survive which documents the liturgical practices and the visual environment of the church as it was before the surrender of the monks. Although the author of *The Rites of Durham* is not known, it is assumed that he was a former monk of the priory who wrote his manuscript partly from memory, and partly from careful observation of the extant fabric.[12] We will follow closely his descriptions.

The Galilee had been refurbished by Bishop Langley, who made a chantry chapel before the Lady altar at the central west door.[13] The foundation included two chantry priests who were required to sing a Lady Mass there each day. The windows were filled with scenes from the life of the Virgin Mary, and records tell us they were in place by 1435. Remaining fragments show a close connection to the York Master workshops.[14]

The nave was basically untouched from the Norman era, with the exception of the renewal of the west window and aisle windows in the fourteenth century. At the eastern termination of the nave, a stone screen blocked access to the crossing and provided a Jesus altar for the use of laymen. The extant nave screen at Saint Albans is of a similar date and scale to that at Durham (fig. 4). On Fridays a sung mass and a vesper antiphon were performed here, accompanied by organs and singers who were placed on galleries set within the arcading.[15] The eastern termination of the nave south aisle was fitted with the delicate carved work of the Neville chantry chapel, probably of a similar effect to that extant in the Bishop Alcock chantry at the end of the south choir aisle of Ely cathedral (fig. 5).[16] Laymen were not admitted beyond these screens which prevented their access into the transepts or choir of the monks' church, except on the feast days of Saint Cuthbert, when they were allowed access to the shrine by the opening of gates to the transept and north choir aisle. Until the Dissolution, women were not admitted anywhere in the cathedral except for the Galilee and first bays of the nave. A line of blue marble was set into the pavement to indicate how far women were allowed into Saint Cuthbert's misogynist precincts.[17]

The transepts and choir were reserved solely for the Benedictine community. In the rebuilding of the eastern portions of the church in the Early Gothic era, the structure of the Norman church remained intact, but donations of large decorated-style windows for the transept terminations in the 1340s brightened the interior.[18] The *Rites of Durham* tells us that the transept north window honoured the Doctors of the Church, while the south window displayed the Te Deum. The windows above the six transept chapels held fourteenth-century images of the saints to whom each chapel was dedicated.[19] The choir was entered either under porches (with a chapel above on the north) in the choir aisles or through the stone *pulpitum*. This was contributed by Prior Wessington (d. 1446) and was said to be comparable with the one in York Minster (fig. 6).[20] The choir was a sumptuous and unified display of fourteenth-century craftsmanship. From the oak stalls of the monks, which were enriched with elaborate canopies, the eye was led eastwards to the decorated throne and chantry of Bishop Hatfield on the south and the chantry of Bishop Skirlaw on the north.[21] At Eastertide, a wooden platform was erected to support the seven-branched paschal candle of curious antique work in bronze and crystal, the central candle of which extended almost up to the height of the vault. After Ascension Day this was taken down and stored in pieces under the night stairs during the rest of the year. Its date is unknown, but parallels have been drawn with the Leau candlestick (ca. 1200) and the Milan lectern.[22] The eastern end of the choir terminated in the splendid Neville screen (fig. 7) made of Caen stone enriched with gilt alabaster figures.[23] Above the altar, the Reserved Sacrament hung in a canopied pyx and was flanked by the images of Saint Cuthbert and Saint Mary.[24] The screen was the gift of Lord Neville, who had also given a new base to the shrine of Saint Cuthbert.[25]

The Shrine of Saint Cuthbert

Saint Cuthbert still resides beyond the screen, for at the Dissolution his body was reburied on the site of the shrine. The *Rites of Durham* describes the shrine as follows (this description is paralleled by a Romantic drawing by William Burgess, fig. 8):

In the midst whereof his sacred shrine was exalted with most curious workmanship of fine and costly marble all limned (painted) and gilded (gilt) with gold, having four seats or places convenient under the shrine for the pilgrims or laymen sitting on their knees to lean and rest on ... At the west end of this shrine of Saint Cuthbert was a little altar adjoined to it for mass to be said on only upon the four great and holy feasts of Saint Cuthbert ... And at this feast and certain other festival days in the time of divine service they (the monks) were accustomed to draw up the cover of Saint Cuthbert's shrine.[26]

Access to the shrine was either by way of the two doors in the Neville screen or through doors set between the screen and the retrochoir crossing piers. Above the north door leading into the shrine area, an anchorage allowed a monk to watch the visitors to the shrine. A comparable watching chamber is still extant in a similar location at Saint Albans (fig. 9).[27]

All of this new work was nothing more than interior decoration, in that it was merely a refurbishing of an already established environment. The doors and screens merely replaced previous ones. Thus, the fourteenth-century layer of our archaeological dig is a purely aesthetic rather than a functional one.

The last layer before we hit the bedrock of the Norman church is the extensive alterations and extensions undertaken during the priorship of Thomas de Melsonby.[28] The documents tell us that the original Norman vault above Saint Cuthbert's shrine was in danger of collapse, or so the indulgences issued by Bishop Northwold of Ely would have us believe.[29] The new retrochoir, or the Chapel of the Nine Altars, as it was called, provided far more than a new vault over the shrine – other factors must be taken into consideration. Before discussing this wider context we should examine the evidence from this stratum. The vast new transept, 160 feet in length, added to the east end of the Norman church, necessitated the demolition of the original Norman apse as well as the breaking-through of the chapels in the choir aisles to allow processional access to the new area. The original sites of the Norman high altar and shrine were left undisturbed. The floor level of the Chapel of the Nine Altars was set four feet lower than the Norman level in order to give the chapel increased height while yet maintaining the same ceiling level as the Norman vaults of the older choir bays. The eastern wall of this new retrochoir was divided into nine bays, or three groups of three bays divided from each other by massive piers, so as to create a transept crossing over the shrine area. At the eastern side of this crossing, in the space created by the vaulting above the three middle bays of the retrochoir, a great rose window provided a termination to the axis of the entire length of the interior, visible above the transept and choir screens, and illumination for the shrine and high altar (fig. 10). Each eastern bay of the retrochoir was fitted up as a chapel, complete with an aumbry and piscina. Although the glass mentioned in the *Rites* dated from the fourteenth century, extent remains indicate that these windows replaced grisaille windows. The earlier glass appears to date to the mid-thirteenth century, or from approximately the same time as the Five Sisters windows of York Minster.[30] The altar dedications are known, and the later glass provided images appropriate to each dedication.[31]

The interior of the new work, begun ca. 1242 and in use by 1258, was elegant by early Gothic standards. It shares with its nearest formal relative, the Nine Altars retrochoir at Fountains Abbey, the same lavish use of marble, deep undercutting, and high textures.[32] The interior of the Durham retrochoir was originally articulated by the application of white, black, and red paint upon all its stone surfaces (this painting scheme is extant now only in one aisle bay of the nave) and this provided an added richness. Although no extant Durham document gives us a direct explanation for all this expense, the historical context of the 1220s does. The Fourth Lateran Council (1215–17) had required that bishops hold diocesan councils and that orders of monks hold triennial chapters to implement and enforce the statutes of the council. While many provinces were slack in their conformity, England was immediate in its compliance – especially among the Benedictines and in the Diocese of Durham.[33] Indeed, Richard Poore, bishop of Durham, was the English bishop who was most arduous in promulgating the statutes, first at Salisbury (1217–28) and then at Durham (1228–37).[34] The Northern Province of Black Monks first met in 1221 and every three years thereafter. The statutes they accepted were both proscriptive and prohibitive. Local peculiarities and other accretions to the classic monastic services were eliminated, while a daily office of Our Lady was required. Following the bishops' injunctions, secular clergy – and, of course, monks – were exhorted to live in total celibacy. As a means of assisting clergy in their vows of celibacy, screens were to be erected in churches to prevent communication with laity. Greater reverence should be shown to the Blessed Sacrament, especially in securing it under lock and key; and more care was to be given to the authenticating and displaying of relics.[35]

These canonical rules were the expression of shifts in theology and devotion that had begun a century before. Their practical consequences, however, were not manifest until the first decade of the thirteenth century. At Durham, they were not evident until the arrival of Bishop Poore in 1228, for it was he who began the campaign for a new eastern extension.[36] If Poore was to be true to his statutes, a new east end was inevitable. The Norman church did not adequately separate the clergy from the laity, especially in terms of access to the shrine; nor did it provide the proper situation for the celebration and reservation of the Sacrament. If the new construction eliminated two altars, it provided nine in their place – each with a footpace, an aumbry for the storage of vessels and vestments, and piscinas for the proper disposal of blessed water and wine.[37] The shrine was now more prominently displayed and accessible from the Chapel of the Nine Altars. Both the high altar and the shrine were nobly situated in a realm of light, the high altar secured from access by the laity and appropriately provided with aumbries and piscinas as well. Durham was now fully in conformity with the requirements of the reform movement, though it was exceptional in having the Lady chapel at the west end of the church. As a Durham legend goes, Bishop Hugh le Puiset (d. 1195) had intended to build a Lady chapel at the east end, but after several unsuccessful attempts at laying the foundations, he realized that Saint Cuthbert, who had a reputation as a misogynist, did not wish to risk the proximity of women to his shrine. Sometime before 1189, Le Puiset built the Galilee instead and placed a Lady altar within it.[38]

Bedrock

We are now at bedrock, and so we must begin to reconstruct our layers of sedimentary evidence so that we may clearly see the successive layers of activity in their proper perspective. It should now be clear to us that, within the Gothic era, Durham went through two major transformations, the first structural and the second aesthetic. The structural changes envisioned by Bishop Poore and completed by 1253 brought the monastic community of Durham into conformity with the new legislation of the Fourth Lateran Council in regard to the protection of relics, clerical separation, and Eucharistic celebration and reservation. The aesthetic environment created by this new work does not seem to have had any related elaborate iconographical program. The surviving evidence of paint and glass suggests patterns rather than pictures. Certainly the shrine and altar were now more nobly displayed, but this display was no more the City of God than many Romanesque or Early Christian liturgical environments.[39] The greater brightness and regularity of the retrochoir may be tied to the scholastic notions of beauty as *claritas*, but that is not visually or textually proven.[40]

If the first Gothic work at Durham indicates a functional *raison d'être*, the second layer of Gothic work suggests an aesthetic rather than a functional intention. Although the various additions of furniture throughout the fourteenth century are spread over one hundred years, they are all the result of in-house patronage. The glass, the throne, the partitions – everything but the Neville screen – were the gifts of the Durham cathedral household.[41] No extant documents indicate a master plan for this refurbishing, but the *Rites of*

Durham suggests a remarkably unified scheme of iconography in glass, statuary, and furnishings. Furthermore, the delicate pinnacle work of the throne, screens, and chantry do show a parallel in conception and in aesthetic forms. As Madeline Caviness has noted, communities often hold on to an implicit if not explicit consensus of symbolic language over generations in time.[42] Just as the fourteenth-century work surrounded an altar and shrine unmoved since 1104, and a paschal candle was kept in use, which was at least two hundred years out of style, so the community compartmentalized the choir according to the taste and orientation of the fourteenth century while maintaining a liturgical and iconographical continuity with its own past.

Conclusion

As we review our eight strata of superimposed sediment in the architectural history of Durham, three methodological observations may be made:

1. Every age or era has its own vision of the past, and brings its own unique questions to the material. If we choose an antiquarian, an archaeological, or a deconstructivist approach, the perspective says more about us than it does about our subject.
2. The two approaches represented by Brooke and Crossley are both valid. Brooke is right in suggesting that changes in church design are usually the result of an attempt to resolve liturgical problems, and Crossley is right in suggesting that, in looking back to the past, we are observing an accumulation of ambiguous and multivalent meanings. But to this *sic et non* of scholastic compromise, a third point may be added:
3. In spite of many a patron's *vanitas*, many a mason's *hubris*, and many a historian's prejudice, a Gothic church was and is, fundamentally, the servant of the liturgy and the vehicle of human aspiration towards the Divine.

NOTES

1   Christopher Brooke, "Religious Sentiment and Church Design in the Later Middle Ages," *Medieval Church and Society* (London, 1971), p. 163.

2 Paul Crossley, "Medieval Architecture and Meaning: The Limits of Iconography," *The Burlington Magazine* 130 (1988), p. 120.

3 The Alcuin Club was founded in 1897 in the midst of ritualist controver-
sies in the Church of England. For a brief history see Peter Jagger, *The
Alcuin Club and Its Publications: An Annotated Bibliography, 1897–1987* (London, 1988). Percy Dearmer was a key member of the club and was the
author of the most influential *Parson's Handbook*, first published in 1899
and in its twelfth edition by 1932. St John Hope added an archaeological
dimension to the club by providing detailed reconstructions of church
interiors as they might have been in the fourteenth century.

4 St John Hope provided a reconstruction of the liturgical arrangements at
Durham ca. 1500 for the Reverend Canon Fowler's edition of *The Rites of
Durham* [Volume CVII of the Surtees Society] (Durham, 1903) and his plan
was attached to the end page.

5 Percy Dearmer was the founder of the Warham Guild of crafts people and
encouraged the revival of handicrafts according to the ideals of William
Morris. See Nan Dearmer, *The Life of Percy Dearmer* (London, 1941), pp.
168ff.

6 For Gilbert Scott's work at Durham, see C.J. Strank, *This Sumptuous
Church* (Durham, 1973). For Scott's relation to Viollet-le-Duc and structur-
alism, see Nikolaus Pevsner, *Some Architectural Writers of the Nineteenth
Century* (Oxford, 1973), pp. 168ff.

7 For Wyatt's work at Durham, see Ian Curry, "Restorations and Repairs to
the Fabric of Durham Cathedral, 1777 to 1803," *The British Archaeological
Association Conference Transactions for the year 1977*, vol. 3: *Medieval Art and
Architecture at Durham Cathedral* (1980) (hereafter, *BAACT Durham*), pp.
130–9.

8 Strank, in *Sumptuous Church*, lays out the evidence.

9 For Bishop Cosin, see G.W.O. Addleshaw, *The High Church Tradition* (London, 1947), pp. 31ff. Cosin's opinions are recorded in his own words in
John Cosin, *The Religion, Discipline, and Rites of the Church of England* (London, 1870).

10 See R.B. Dobson, *"Mynistres of Saynt Cuthbert": The Monks of Durham in the
Fifteenth Century* (Durham, 1972), for pre-Dissolution circumstances. See
James Wall, *Durham Cathedral* (London, 1930) for the chronology.

11 For the transition from monastery to secular cathedral, see Wall, *Durham
Cathedral* and M.E.C. Walcott, *Traditions and Customs of Cathedrals* (London,
1872), pp. 24ff, which explains the post-Reformation system in detail.

12 The Rev. Canon Fowler, editor, provides an introductory text with notes
and suggests the probable author to be an ex-monk of Durham.

13 See M.G. Snape, "Documentary Evidence for the Building of Durham Cathedral and Its Monastic Buildings," *BAACT Durham*, pp. 20–36.

14 See Jeremy Haselock and David E. O'Connor, "The Medieval Stained Glass of Durham Cathedral," *BAACT Durham*, pp. 105–29.

15 *The Rites*, pp. 32ff. A discussion of the music and liturgy performed at the Jesus altar is found in F. Harrison's, *Music in Medieval Britain* (London, 1963), p. 41.

16 *The Rites*, pp. 58–9, describes the chantry; Fowler's notes, pp. 244–5, give the documentary and archaeological evidence. It was of a similar style to the Neville screen and followed the pattern of richly ornamented enclosed chapels. For a comparison with Bishop West's chantry at Ely, see T.D. Atkinson, *An Architectural History of the Benedictine Monastery of Saint Etheldreda at Ely* (Cambridge, 1933).

17 *The Rites*, pp. 35–7, narrates the legend that Saint Cuthbert prohibited all women from entering his churches and that a line of blue marble was inlaid across the paving of the nave at its west end to indicate how far women were allowed to go. Severe penalties were incurred by any woman who ignored the line.

18 *The Rites*, pp. 31–2, describes the transept windows. Haselock and O'Connor, in "Stained Glass," give a complete analysis of the evidence (pp. 105–29) and discuss the style and iconography of each window.

19 Haselock and O'Connor, in "Stained Glass," p. 114, give the documentation.

20 *The Rites*, pp. 30–2 describes the porches. The *Durham Annals* note that John Wessington (d. 1446) gave the screen. See Snape, "Documentary Evidence," pp. 30–1.

21 *The Rites*, p. 19, describes the chantry and throne.

22 *The Rites*, pp. 10–11, describes the paschal candlestick; Fowler gives a commentary on pp. 202–3. See Jane Geddes, "The Twelfth-Century Metalwork at Durham Cathedral," *BAACT Durham*, pp. 146–8 for the stylistic comparison with Leau and Milan.

23 *The Rites*, pp. 7–9, describes the screen and high altar in detail. See also Christopher Wilson, "The Neville Screen," *BAACT Durham*, pp. 90–104.

24 *The Rites*, pp. 12, 205, notes the suspended pyx and images. This was a common practice in England. See Archdale King, *Eucharistic Reservation in the Western Church* (New York, 1965), pp. 75ff. See also Daniel Cahill, *The Custody of the Holy Eucharist* (Washington, DC, 1950), and W.H. Freestone, *The Sacrament Reserved* [Alcuin Club Collections XXI] (London, 1917).

25 Snape, "Documentary Evidence," p. 27, and document no. 49.

26 *The Rites*, pp. 3–4.

27 See the feretory arrangement in St John Hope's plan, *The Rites*, pp. 17, 208–9, also C. Wilson, "The Neville Screen," p. 95. The "anchorage" of Saint Albans is still in place, see the *Royal Commission on Historical Monuments: A Guide to Saint Albans Cathedral* (London, 1952), pl. 3, and text on pp. 15–16.

28 For the documentation, see Snape, "Documentary Evidence," p. 24.

29 The indulgences are quoted and discussed in ibid., pp. 23–5 and note 23.

30 Haselock and O'Connor, "Stained Glass," pp. 109–11 and notes 48–50.

31 *The Rites*, pp. 2–3, 118–22. *The Rites* lists the dedications of the Chapel of the Nine Altars from north to south as: Saints Oswald and Lawrence, Saints Thomas Becket and Katherine, Saints John Baptist and Margaret, Saints Andrew and Mary Magdalen, Saints Cuthbert and Bede, Saint Martin, Saints Peter and Paul, Saints Aidan and Helen, Saint Michael. Haselock and O'Connor, in "Stained Glass," p. 110, discuss the windows.

32 For a discussion of the architecture of the Nine Altars' retrochoirs at both Durham and Fountains, see Peter Draper, "The Nine Altars at Durham and Fountains," *BAACT Durham*, pp. 74–86.

33 See M. Gibbs and B. Lang, *Bishops and Reform, 1215–1272* (Oxford, 1934), pp. 148ff. General chapters of monastic orders were to meet every three years to work on the reformation of their statutes so that they would be in accord with those of the Fourth Lateran Council. The first chapter of the Northern Province of Black Monks met in 1221 to draw up the statutes; they met at Durham in 1250 to enforce the statutes. David Knowles, in *The Monastic Orders in England*, vol. 1 (Cambridge, 1966), pp. 22ff, explains these changes in detail.

34 Bishop Poore was extraordinarily diligent in his implementation of the Fourth Lateran Council's statutes. He issued the most complete set of all thirteenth-century diocesan constitutions while he was at Salisbury (1217–28) and reused them for Durham while he was bishop (1228–37). See Gibbs and Lang, *Bishops and Reform*, pp. 106–9.

35 The above are my own "distillations" of those statutes which appear to influence most directly architectural arrangements in churches. For specific texts, see D. Whitelock, M. Brett, and C.N.L. Brooke, *Councils and Synods with Other Documents of the English Church* (Oxford, 1969). For the need for screens see item no. 12 (p. 1051) regarding the prohibition of all laymen from clerical association. Greater reverence for the Sacrament resulted in numerous rules about its consumption, ritual cleansing, and storage under lock and key (see p. 1061). The consecrated Host must be elevated for all to see (II, 298). Relics had to be authenticated

and properly venerated. See Gibbs and Lang, *Bishops and Reform*, pp. 180–2.

36 Documentation is found in Snape, "Documentary Evidence," p. 24 and notes 23 and 24. Poore intended to build the Nine Altars retrochoir but was prevented from doing so by his death in 1237. Prior Thomas de Melsonby began the new work in 1242.

37 Dom Gregory Dix has written a short but helpful explanation of the function of aumbries in *A Detection of Aumbries* (Westminster, 1948). For the origin and use of the piscina, see Ian Jessiman, "The Piscina in the English Medieval Church," *Journal of the British Archaeological Association* 20 (1958), 53–71, with plates.

38 For the legend of Saint Cuthbert thwarting the plans of Bishop le Puiset for an eastern Lady chapel, see J. Raine, ed., *Historia Dunelmensis Scriptores Tres* [Surtees Society 9 (1839)], pp. 11ff. For a detailed discussion of the construction and function of the Galilee, see R. Halsey, "The Galilee Chapel," *BAACT Durham*, pp. 59–73. For the Lady chapel, see Peter Draper, "Seeing That It Was Done in All the Noble Churches in England", *Medieval Architecture and Its Intellectual Context* (London, 1990), pp. 137–42.

39 Otto von Simson, in *The Gothic Cathedral* (New York, 1956), saw the Gothic cathedral as an "image" which was a direct reflection of ultimate reality. To prove his point he referred to traditional dedication liturgical texts – which is certainly a most appropriate source – but ignored the fact that most of these liturgical texts had their origins in Gallican and Carolingian rituals that predate the Gothic era by five hundred years. Thus, all the rich imagery to which Von Simson points is equally applicable to Carolingian or Romanesque monuments as well. For an early dedication text see Daniel Sheerin, "The Church Dedication 'Ordo' Used at Fulda, 1 November 819," in *Revue benedictine* 92 (1982), 304ff. For a comparison, see René Crozet, "Etude sur les consécrations pontificales," in *Bulletin monumental* 104 (1946), 5–46. Paul Crossley stresses the danger of identifying one iconographical meaning as appropriate to only one architectural feature; see Crossley, "Medieval Architecture and Meaning," pp. 120ff. A useful discussion of the iconography of heaven as defined in dedication rituals can be found in L. Stookey, "The Gothic Cathedral as the Heavenly Jerusalem," *Gesta* 8 (1969), 35–41.

40 John Gage, in "Gothic Glass," *Art History* 5 (1982), 36–45, distinguishes between two distinctly different concepts of light and their iconographical significance within the Early and Later Gothic eras. Thomas Aquinas and Albertus Magnus related beauty to *claritas*, and this became significant only to the Later Gothic era.

41 Snape, in "Documentary Evidence," pp. 20–36, lists all known documents that relate to patrons and projects at Durham. Item no. 49, the Neville benefactions, is the only secular benefaction.

42 Madeline Caviness, *Sumptuous Arts at the Royal Abbeys in Reims and Braine. Ornatus Elegantiae, Varietate Stupendes* (Princeton, 1990).

6

Suger's "Completion" of Saint-Denis

Eric C. Fernie

The abbey church of Saint-Denis has enjoyed a position of prominence in medieval studies. Since Emile Mâle's turn-of-the-century work, claiming the abbey as central to subsequent Gothic stylistic and iconographic development, it has been perceived as a seminal monument. The rare existence of a textual record by the building's patron, Abbot Suger (1122–1151), and the abbey's links to the concomitant rise of the Capetian monarchy increase its scholarly interest. It has been traditionally regarded as a "key" monument in assessing Gothic. In this volume, two essays are devoted to the building and its context.

Fernie demonstrates that important clues to the meanings this monument held for contemporary viewers are textualized by Abbot Suger, particularly in a thrice-voiced directive to the builders of Saint-Denis to harmonize the new work with the old. Fernie addresses the issue of text and monument, central in recent methodological approaches to the history of art. What did Suger actually say he was doing, as opposed to what we think he accomplished? He questions exactly how we may interpret the purported "new style" of Saint-Denis and hence the validity of calling Suger hypocritical when he expresses respect for the old building which he was demolishing.

If, on the contrary, we assume that his architect was responsible for the new style, then Suger's contribution can be read as a desire to renovate the old church by using significant elements from the preceding eight hundred years, to integrate the monument, as it were, with its own past. In this assessment Suger's words are entirely compatible with his actions.

The twelfth-century abbey church of Saint-Denis is one of the most innovative buildings in the history of architecture. It was also one of the prime interests of Abbot Suger, who had dreamt of rebuilding it from his youngest days as a monk, and who devoted a substantial amount of time to it throughout the second half of his demanding working life. It is therefore not surprising that many scholars have seen Suger as the inventor of Gothic, a man with an architectural vision who would not be thwarted in his desire to express it, whatever the opposition to his demolition of the revered old church. This in turn has led to the conclusion that his claims of respect for the old building were mere hypocrisy and manipulation.[1]

This, however, may be an anachronistically modern view of the matter. In the first place, there are good grounds for assuming that no building as technically revolutionary as Saint-Denis could have been designed by an amateur, and that what was really new about it in the longer perspective of the twelfth and thirteenth centuries was the work of a talented master mason and not of Suger himself. Suger's undoubted contribution would instead have consisted of the opinions and tastes of an educated churchman. This is not the place to set out the evidence in favour of this contention, but if it is accepted for the sake of the argument it enables one to propose a reading of Suger's attitudes which makes them neither hypocritical nor contradictory. On the contrary they provide an excellent illustration of a cast of mind common in the Middle Ages in which the past and present could be integrated in architectural forms in a way almost incomprehensible to the twentieth century.

Suger's protestations of unhappiness over the demolition can thus be seen as entirely consistent with what he was attempting to do – namely, to build, not a church in a ravishing new style, but one which encapsulated in perfect form the most important characteristics in the Christian architecture of the preceding eight hundred years, and in particular of the previous and, as he believed, Merovingian, church of Saint-Denis.

The references in his writings are as follows.

In the *De administratione*, Suger records how, after a successful program of fund-raising, he caused the walls of the old church "to be repaired and becomingly painted with gold and precious colors" (XXIV).[2] An expensive restoration of the old fabric does not sound like the act of someone about to embark on demolition and replacement, but we have to accept that that was precisely what Suger intended to do. To see this action as hypocritical involves accepting a quite astonishing degree of expense, and on the contrary it makes more sense to see it as a simple mark of respect.

This is consistent with the ways in which he discusses the new building itself. In a chapter entitled "the first addition to the church" (*de ecclesiae primo augmento*), Suger describes how he began "to enlarge and amplify the noble church consecrated by the Divine Hand" (*ad augmentandum et amplificandum nobile ... monasterium*), beginning "the enlargement of the body of the church" with the narthex (XXV), and then proceeding to the eastern arm, in a chapter entitled "on the addition of the upper part" (*de augmento superioris partis*) (XXVIII). Finally he turns to the nave, attempting to retain as much as possible of the old walls, and linking the old work to the new by extending the aisles (XXIX). Excavations have revealed that a completely new nave was begun, though it is not known if this was before or after Suger's death.[3] If it was before his death, then (as with the repairs) it is possible to see the retention of the old walls as hypocritical, but once again one is confronted with the problem of the disproportionate expense involved.

Similarly, in the *De consecratione* (especially chapters II and IV) Suger refers to enlarging, to making additions, and to establishing a concordance between the old and the new, so that, for example, the widths of the naves and aisles of the eastern arm should be equalized, in order to "respect the very stones, sacred as they are, as though they were relics."

All of these quotations, with their references to addition, enlargement, amplifying, and renewing, are commensurate with the idea that Suger saw himself as contributing not to a revolution but to a revival. The evidence of the building itself supports this contention, as it contains numerous architectural references to contemporary monuments in Italy (which one can assume would have appeared traditional to northern eyes) as well as revivals of things Antique and Early Christian (that is, Italian in the widest sense), and Merovingian and Carolingian (that is, Frankish in the widest sense).[4] These contentions can be illustrated from the various parts of the building in turn, beginning with the west end.

The narthex is an old-fashioned building type, having more in common with a Carolingian westwork than with the two-towered façades of eleventh-century Normandy and the formula of the later Gothic buildings. Thus, the rose in the façade does not communicate with the nave, as it does, for example, at Reims and Amiens. (Despite these associations with the westwork one must be cautious of claiming that the narthex contained any of the symbolism of the "city gate" other than of the most diffuse kind, since Suger describes the crenellations on the façade as being intended for beauty or practicality, without mentioning any meaning or reference they might contain [*De admin*. XXVII].)

The left-hand doorway of Saint-Denis had a mosaic in its tympanum, which Suger refers to as "contrary to modern custom" and which clearly calls to mind a Carolingian or Early Christian context.

The bronze doors which Suger describes have clear southern and *antiquisant* associations, the inscription in metal letters in particular being reminiscent of, for example, that of Carolingian date from the façade of San Vincenzo in Volturno, recently excavated.[5]

The portal sculpture has a number of Italian references, including, as George Zarnecki has shown, the atlases and the column figures.[6]

Lastly (as far as the west front is concerned), according to the *De administratione* (XXVI), the doorway from the old west end into the cemetery was conserved and re-erected in the new block.

Turning now to the eastern arm, in the crypt the axis of the new building lies between the axis of the old church and that of Hilduin's ninth-century extension. Indeed, it is possible that it was intended to bisect the existing angle, thus giving material form to one aspect of Suger's description of the "equalizing" of the old and new east ends by geometrical and arithmetic means.

Hilduin's ninth-century extension is retained, and Suger's crypt wrapped around it like a latter-day outer crypt, suitably vaulted with archaic groins rather than up-to-date ribs.

The raised eastern arm is also out of place in a twelfth-century French context, reminiscent of numerous older examples extending back to the Carolingian origins of the type.

In the upper church, the columns of the ambulatory and those which must have supported the main arcade can also be seen as backward-looking. It is true that columns are common in the apses of Romanesque churches, but the significance lies in Suger's church being entirely columnar, a characteristic of pre-Romanesque buildings. The importance of these elements to Suger is also indicated by the fact that the only architectural features of the old church which he singles out for special comment are its marble columns (*De consec*. II).

The elevation of the eastern arm is usually reconstructed with three or even four storeys, placing the design firmly in the architectural context of the eleventh or twelfth century. Yet it is likely that it had only two storeys – namely, a main arcade and a clerestory. This suggestion is based on two observations. First, the common type of elevation in the Paris basin at the time was not of three or four storeys, but two, as for example at Saint-Martin-des-Champs in Paris and in the churches at Morienval and Bury, both in the adjacent *département* of Oise. Second, and more important from the point of view of this essay, there is the near certainty that the old church had two storeys; so that at the very least Suger's new bays at the west end linking the old nave to the new narthex would have been similarly arranged.

Suger was equally solicitous of the integrative effect of the pieces of furniture of early dates, reusing the altar frontal of the time of Charles the Bald, renewing the "Holy Altar" in front of which Charles "III" had been buried, and restoring the ivory-covered pulpit and the "throne of Dagobert" (*De admin.* XXXIII, XXXIV).

Even Suger's attitude to the metaphysics of light provides evidence more for his wish to integrate the old than an awareness of the qualities of the new. Panofsky considers Suger's description of the new eastern arm as an application of such metaphysics to an aesthetic experience: "the new, transparent choir, which had replaced the opaque Carolingian apse, would be matched by an equally "bright" nave ..."[7] Against this, however, one can quote Suger's description, not of his own church but of the old one, as being so constructed and decorated that it "might shine with inestimable splendor" (*De consec.* II). There is also a good case for arguing that the existing apse need not have appeared opaque to contemporaries, especially if it had anything in common with Early Christian examples such as that of Santa Sabina in Rome, which introduces a blaze of light to the interior.

For a final comment on the question of how Suger describes his building, I would like to return to the quotation from Panofsky in the preceding paragraph: in order to illustrate that Suger was "fully aware of the new style's distinctive aesthetic qualities" Panofsky argues that Suger "felt, and makes us feel, its spaciousness when he speaks of his new chevet as being 'ennobled by the beauty of length and width'; its soaring verticalism when he describes the central nave of this chevet as being 'suddenly raised aloft' by the supporting columns; its luminous transparency when he depicts his church as 'pervaded by wonderful and uninterrupted light of most luminous windows.'"[8]

Compare, however, the following: "Although I am myself a useless little man, an inhabitant only of the earth, I greatly dislike little buildings, and although poor in goods, I design great things. And so, if given the means, I would not allow buildings although esteemed to stand, unless they were, according to my idea, glorious, magnificent, most lofty, most spacious, filled with light, and most beautiful."[9] The words are those of Goscelin of Saint Bertin in his *Liber confortatorius*, written in England around 1080, more than half a century before the advent of Gothic. If we ignore Panofsky's glosses and parallel Suger's terms directly with those of Goscelin, they will be found to coincide almost exactly: "ennobled by the beauty of length and width" / "most spacious ... and most beautiful"; "suddenly raised aloft" / "most lofty"; "pervaded by wonderful and uninterrupted light of most luminous windows" / "glorious, magnificent, ... filled with light." Suger is therefore at least in part adopting a traditional mode of speaking, as even Goscelin's reference to restricted stature may be another *topos*, the equivalent of Suger's praise to the Lord for having "reserved so great a work to so small a man" (*De consec.* IV).

To sum up, there is no need to assume that Suger's expressions of veneration for the old building cloaked a hidden agenda. When he succeeded, with the aid of his architect, in realizing his vision in stone, glass, and metal, he did not see himself as inventing a new style. On the contrary, whether out of respect for the venerable status of the standing church or because he saw the architectural possibilities of the old building, there seems to be little doubt that his work harks back to earlier architecture in a way which makes the twelfth-century church at Saint-Denis, at least in his own eyes, first and foremost a revivalist building, a columnar earlier Christian church with "Merovingian" narthex, mosaic, bronze doors, crypt, and furnishings. Thus Suger can be seen as in effect "completing" and "integrating" the church of Saint-Denis which his predecessors had bequeathed to him, which is no more and no less than he says he did in his comments on the building.

NOTES

1 See for example Erwin Panofsky, ed., *Abbot Suger on the Abbey Church of Saint-Denis and Its Art Treasures* (1946; 2d ed. by Gerda Panofsky-Soergel, Princeton, 1979), p. 37; Otto von Simson, *The Gothic Cathedral*, Bollingen

Series 48, 2d ed. (New York, 1965), pp. 66–7, 95–8; and Sumner McKnight Crosby, "Abbot Suger, the Abbey of Saint-Denis, and the New Gothic Style," in *The Royal Abbey of Saint-Denis in the Time of Abbot Suger (1122–1151)* [exh. cat., Metropolitan Museum of Art] (New York, 1981), p. 17.

2 The translations are from Panofsky, ed., *Abbot Suger*.

3 Sumner McKnight Crosby, *The Royal Abbey of Saint-Denis: From Its Beginnings to the Death of Suger, 475–1151*, ed. Pamela Blum (New Haven, 1987), p. 267.

4 Ernst Gall, *Gotische Baukunst in Frankreich und Deutschland* (Leipzig, 1925), p. 110, and Peter Kidson, *The Medieval World* (London, 1967), p. 97, present the building as Late Romanesque. Beat Brenk, "Sugers Spolien," *Arte medievale* 1 (1983), 101–7; Jean Bony, "What Possible Sources for the Chevet of Saint-Denis?" in *Abbot Suger and Saint-Denis*, ed. Paula Lieber Gerson (New York, 1986), pp. 131–43; and William Clark, "Suger's Church at Saint-Denis: The State of Research," in ibid., pp. 105–30, have discussed the wider range of Suger's interests in the first millennium. Clark's essay in this volume discusses in detail the relevance of the capitals in the crypt and the architectural landscape of contemporary Paris to the same question. Our conclusions appear to support one another.

5 John Mitchell, "Literacy Displayed: The Use of Inscriptions at the Monastery of San Vincenzo al Volturno in the Early Ninth Century," in *The Uses of Literacy in Early Medieval Europe*, ed. R. McKitterick, pp. 205–16, (Cambridge, 1990).

6 George Zarnecki, *Later English Romanesque Sculpture, 1140–1210* (London, 1953), pp. 21–5. For parallels to the column figures, see those in the Archiepiscopal Museum in Ravenna.

7 Panofsky, ed., *Abbot Suger*, p. 22. Peter Kidson, in "Panofsky, Suger and Saint-Denis," *Journal of the Warburg and Courtauld Institutes* 50, (1987), 1–17, supplies good grounds for rejecting this view; see also Michael T. Davis, review of Crosby (1987), *Speculum* 66 (1991), 139–43, for other references. Conrad Rudolph, in *Artistic Change at St-Denis: Abbot Suger's Program and the Early Twelfth-Century Controversy Over Art* (Princeton, 1990), discusses related matters, though not primarily concerning the architecture (see p. 66); Rudolph also rejects the relevance of light metaphysics to the new building (p. 74 and passim), and affirms that Suger "was inherently traditional in the area of art" (p. 33).

8 Panofsky, ed., *Abbot Suger*, p. 37.

9 Ego inutilis homuncio, qui tantum terram occupo, plerumque indignor pusillis edificiis, et inops rerum magna propono, ut data facultate non paterer stare templa quamuis spectata, nisi scilicet fuissent ad uotum

meum inclita, magnifica, precelsa, perampla, perlucida et perpulchra: C. Talbot, "The Liber confortatorium of Goscelin of Saint Bertin," *Analecta Monastica* series 3, 37 (1955), 93; the translation of the passage from Goscelin is taken from Frank Barlow, *The English Church 1000-1066* (London, 1963), p. 167.

7

"The Recollection of the Past Is the Promise of the Future." Continuity and Contextuality: Saint-Denis, Merovingians, Capetians, and Paris

William W. Clark

Clark's essay deals with the integration of the twelfth-century construction of Saint-Denis in the context of self-reflective political strategies by the Capetian monarchs and Suger, Saint-Denis's abbot. Like Fernie, he argues that many of the features modern scholarship has often regarded as "new" in Suger's commissions at Saint-Denis can be understood as deliberate appropriations and/or imitations of Merovingian forms found in the old abbey church. He suggests that twelfth-century audiences in Paris may have attached historical significance to the Merovingian capitals and columns deliberately reused or imitated in the abbey. Like Draper, he attempts to evaluate architecture in terms that would have been understood by those for whom it was built.

Clark concludes with an analysis of Capetian and Merovingian ties, for example, in royal seals. He notes that the seal of Louis VII, dating to 1141, not only shows the king seated on the throne of Dagobert, but also appropriates the Merovingian image of the long-haired king, to complete the process of Capetian association with the descendants of Clovis begun by Louis VI, the first king since Merovingian times to make Paris his principal residence. The Merovingian elements in Parisian Early Gothic architecture should be recognized as yet another aspect of this revival. The buildings become another manifestation of the national historical memory that was being created in the texts through the association of the abbey and patron saint with the monarchy in the first continuous histories linking Merovingians, Carolingians, and Capetians. He includes a selective bibliography of recent work on Saint-Denis and its historical context.

Near the end of his reign, ca. 1130, Louis VI (1108–1137) became the first Capetian king to make his principal royal residence in Paris, which had only just begun to expand beyond the physical limits of the old Roman and Frankish (Merovingian) city.[1] Residence was followed almost immediately by selective royal patronage of the old religious foundations in and around Paris. This patronage of the oldest houses by Louis VI and his son and successor, Louis VII (1137–1180), seems to be a deliberate attempt to associate themselves with Clovis (482–511), the first king to make Paris his capital, and his Merovingian successors.[2] Royal patronage was imitated by the old noble families and by ambitious ecclesiastics vying, as it were, for royal favour by openly proclaiming ties to royalty through their Merovingian antecedents.[3] As the largest and most prosperous city in northern Europe in the twelfth century, Paris may provide a unique instance in which sufficient evidence remains to establish the historical integration of twelfth-century buildings with their illustrious and then still surviving Merovingian predecessors. Above all, then, for Paris we need to examine historical contextuality. While the series of intentional appropriations and imitations of Merovingian architectural and sculptural forms [4] found in a number of twelfth-century Parisian and nearby churches raises the possibility of specific political and ideological associations with Capetian kingship and the selection of Paris as the capital city, the present discussion, for reasons of space, will be limited to the work commissioned by Abbot Suger at the abbey church of Saint-Denis.[5]

Both the importance of the continuity of site and the associations and correspondences between different construction periods at Saint-Denis have been all but ignored in favour of isolating each stylistic moment and championing its newness.[6] Yet we must remember Suger's own words: "my first thought was for the concordance and harmony of the ancient and the new work."[7] When the abbot died in 1151, the church consisted of the repaired eighth-century nave, framed by the added westwork and connecting nave bays, and the new chevet to the east (fig. 1). The nave incorporated marble bases, columns, and capitals from Dagobert's seventh-century Merovingian structure, although it is usually termed "Carolingian" by modern scholars because of its eighth-century date.[8] For Suger, the monks, and their contemporaries, that structure was the Merovingian church of the founder, Dagobert: "the glorious and famous King of the Franks, Dagobert, ... had constructed this [basilica] with a marvelous variety of marble columns ... [so that it] might shine with inestimable splendor."[9] In his texts the abbot, being fully aware of its miraculous consecration by Christ himself, went to considerable lengths to justify rebuilding parts of this venerable structure.[10] Thus it is not surprising that this early structure not only affected decisions made by the twelfth-century builders, as Crosby has shown, but also, I suggest, determined the choices of the patrons.[11]

Eric Fernie's essay in this volume is the most recent and one of the more thoughtful discussions of the Carolingian precedents for the westwork and the outer crypt and lists a number of "antiquisant" features in the work created for Suger.[12] However, I find at least three categories of associations with the earlier structures on the site. First, there are the dimensional and proportional transfers from the old church to the new additions, principally the western bays. Second, there are the inclusions of actual pieces from the old church in the new east end; and, third, there are the imitations of older forms by the two twelfth-century builders, most likely at the request of the patron, for the purposes of enhancing the meaning and emphasizing the historical integration of the new work.

The first category includes the obvious continuations of the dimensions of the nave and aisles in the added nave bays.[13] Crosby showed how the dimensions of the eighth-century transept were used to lay out the western bays and how the aisle widths determined the lateral portal widths. Other than making the new chevet equal the width of the old transept, the second builder did not rely on the dimensions of the earlier building, although we can find ample demonstrations of his more subtle geometric manipulations. Fernie has suggested, for example, that the second builder "corrected" the longitudinal axis of the new chevet by bisecting the angle between the two earlier axes, that of the chevet of Dagobert's church and that of Hilduin's chapel. In addition, Crosby demonstrated how this builder used both the actual dimensions and the proportional relationships of height to width from the Merovingian and Carolingian architectural elements in the old nave for the bases, columns, and capitals in the new chevet.[14] These decisions undoubtedly reflect Suger's directions, thrice-voiced, to harmonize the new work with the old.[15]

The second category of continuity consists of the reuse and repositioning of actual architectural elements, chiefly Merovingian marble columns and capitals, from the old church in the new. At least six Merovingian marble capitals and columns were prominently reused in the crypt and another six (or more) were installed in the new upper chevet.[16] Downstairs, pairs of marble columns were displayed at the bottom of the steps on both sides as one entered the crypt; and the other two were disposed singly against the outer wall as one passed from the side corridors of Hilduin's chapel into the new ambulatory and chapels (figs. 2–4). Upstairs, six more marble columns, no longer extant, were apparently installed against the outer wall, one between each radiating chapel (fig. 5).[17] Like the reinstallation of the old cemetery door in the new west bays and the utilization of "old" bronze doors in the northwest portal,[18] these Merovingian columns are not accidental reuses, but intentional, even prominent displays. They should be understood as the architectural equivalents of such restored liturgical furnishings as the altar frontal of Charles the Bald, the altar cross of Saint Eloi, and the refurbished throne of Dagobert.[19] At the same time, a number of ancient objects in the abbey treasury were fashioned into new liturgical pieces, among the best known are the chalice, now in Washington, and the eagle-vase, now in the Louvre.[20] Indeed, the repair and refurbishing of the coronation regalia housed at Saint-Denis for the crowning of Louis VII at Reims in 1132, after the accidental death of his older brother, Philip, also falls in this category.[21] Like the restoration of the regalia, the reuse of the Merovingian marbles, however, has a significance greater than merely harmonizing the old with the new, a point to which I shall return.

Finally, there is the third category of continuity, the conscious imitation of older forms, variously identified in later scholarship as Early Christian, Merovingian, and Carolingian. This category includes the twelfth-century bronze doors, tympanum mosaic, floor mosaics, and free-standing columns that have associations with Early Christian Italy, a reminder that Suger was several times in Rome.[22] Fernie discusses the continuity of such Carolingian features as the westwork, the outer crypt, the two-level sanctuary, and the *confessio*. Most important, all of these features, with the exception of the tympanum mosaic and, possibly, the raised sanctuary, existed in the abbey church prior to Suger's constructions.[23] The free-standing columns might have evoked precedents in Rome, but they would more likely have been associated with the church of Dagobert, which, according to Suger, had "a marvelous variety of marble columns."[24]

Crosby's excavations have enabled us to recognize other continuities between the old and new work in this third category. At the west end of the eighth-century church, he uncovered two successive layers

of façade foundations. The lower level is continuous with the fragments of the outer walls of Dagobert's church, while the upper level
should most likely be identified with the façade structure, a sort of
westwork, built on Charlemagne's orders over the burial site of
Pepin, his father, just as Suger described it.[25]

We might further speculate that the eighth-century arrangement of
the sanctuary, which allowed direct access to the *confessio*, was at least
partly two-level.[26] This would provide another, more immediate local
source for the two-level chevet consecrated in 1144. In fact, should we
not consider the twelfth-century chevet a synthesis of two features
from the old church, the two-level sanctuary and the outer crypt?
Suger wrote of "respect[ing] the very stones, sacred as they are, as
though they were relics" as well as using "the upper surface of the
crypt ... as a pavement."[27] Certainly the addition of the ambulatory
and radiating chapels around Hilduin's chapel, that is, the outer
crypt, not only creates a level platform for the upper storeys, but also
unifies the previously separated crypt elements into a more ordered
spatial progression.

The list of features from the old work imitated in the new also
includes, in addition to the free-standing, monolithic columns
already mentioned,[28] the many, small detached shafts used against
the outer wall in the upper level of the chevet [29] (fig. 6) and the new
types of acanthus ornament on the capitals. While detached shafts
were common in all periods of medieval architecture, Merovingian
through Romanesque, these at Saint-Denis are unusual in that they
frequently have the little ring moulding at the top carved with the
shaft, in imitation of Merovingian practices, as can be seen in the
larger shafts reinstalled in the crypt.[30]

The new types of acanthus ornament are found in one series in the
centre west bay of the façade block, and in another in the crypt.[31]
Acanthus capitals, as is well known, have a continuous history in the
Middle Ages, but in these two areas the same group of sculptors who
executed capitals everywhere at Saint-Denis abruptly shifted capital
design, style, and technique.[32] Neither casual nor accidental, the
changes in foliage design must result from sculptors being specifically directed to copy Merovingian marble capitals. This happened
first during the construction of the western bays, where we can see
changes in the design and organization of the foliage on the four most
prominent capitals in the centre west bay (figs. 7 and 8). Unprecedented at Saint-Denis, these new designs, which are directly behind

the central portal of the façade, were introduced only after the construction and decoration of the lateral bays and the carving of the capitals in all three portals. The four angled capitals in the centre bay have simpler overall designs, organized in two or three layers of leaves in alternating patterns (fig. 8). These are not the work of different sculptors but result from different conceptions of arranging foliage around the core of a capital. Comparison with one of the two nearly identical Merovingian marble capitals from Saint-Denis, today in the Musée National du Moyen Age, formerly the Cluny Museum, in Paris (fig. 9), confirms that one of the twelfth-century capitals is a direct copy of the Merovingian marble,[33] itself simplified from the classical acanthus capital. The twelfth-century sculptor isolated and emphasized precisely the same element of design, the acanthus bud, as had the Merovingian carver before him. Since the other three west capitals are equally different from adjacent twelfth-century examples, they were probably copied from Merovingian marbles that are no longer extant.

The second significant change in capital decoration occurred in the twelfth-century work in the crypt, amidst an even more complex series of incorporations and imitations. The Merovingian marble capitals newly installed in the crypt, in fact, presented new models for the sculptors, the same sculptors who had copied other marble capitals for the centre bay in the western block. The results of their copying in the crypt appear on the polygonal piers that separate the radiating chapels. Although heavily restored and recut, these capitals retain enough of the original foliate patterns and motifs to be recognized as a series of imitations and variations on the marbles still found in the crypt (fig. 3).[34] Thus, walking around the new crypt ambulatory at Saint-Denis, the twelfth-century viewer would have been able to see both the authentic Merovingian pieces as well as constant variations on them along the polygonal piers separating the crypt chapels.[35] This combination achieved what Suger requested of his builder, the integration of the new with the old.

In the centre west bay the capitals should be read within the context of the special historicizing character of that bay. The unusual octagonal shape of the bay, resulting from the size and plan of the massive piers alternating with arched openings, was recognized by Crosby, but he did not relate it to its obvious predecessor, the polygonal bay in the westwork, thought in the twelfth century to have been constructed by Charlemagne around the burial site of Pepin.[36] That the capitals were copied after Merovingian originals in the eighth-century nave would have confirmed for the viewer the association of the new work with its historical predecessor. In fact, this bay was part of an iconographic sequence that began with the new façade and its twin towers and crenellations, at once triumphal arch, city gate, and fortress church: the visitor passed through the portals, with their oft-cited royal associations, into the westwork evoking Pepin and Charlemagne and hence into the nave of Dagobert. The experience became a royal journey back in time to the high altar above the original burial place of Denis. This symbolic journey in space complemented the newly compiled histories begun under Abbot Adam and completed under Suger.[37]

The Merovingian pieces in the crypt, together with the capitals on the piers at the chapel entrances, would have been visible reminders of the antiquity of the abbey, and, I suggest, signified historical continuity, direct links to Dagobert and Denis himself.[38] They are intended to evoke religious historical memory.[39] Descending from their place in the choir into the crypt around the original burial spot of Denis, the monks made a religious pilgrimage through the history of the abbey: from the altar of the Holy Trinity to the original burial spot of the patron saint, with its remembered associations with Saint Geneviève; beside the apse of Dagobert, with the tombs of the founder, Charles the Bald, and, after 1137, Louis VI; through Hilduin's chapel; and into the ambulatory and chapels of Suger, the new founder.[40]

Likewise we must endeavour to understand the multivalent meanings inherent in the upper level of the chevet, the new resting-place for the bodies of the saints, Denis, Eleutherius, and Rusticus – "that noble edifice," "that magnificent building," "that chamber of divine atonement," – in Suger's own words. The setting created by the upper level of the chevet was conceived as the site for the apotheosis of the three saints. What is embodied in the physical structure of the building, the ultimate synthesis of past and present, culminated in the translation of the holy bodies, in "the venerable shrines executed under King Dagobert," from their original burial place in the crypt up to the new chevet. Religious past and secular present were conjoined as Louis VII, the "Most Serene King of the Franks," carried (devoutly and nobly, according to Suger) the *châsse* of Saint-Denis to its new place in the chevet. When Suger discussed that culminating event, interspersed in his text were the words "King Dagobert," and "our Lord the King [Louis VII] himself." Like "the glorious and famous

King of the Franks, Dagobert," Louis VII showed his special devotion to the patron saint of the church and the realm. Just as the pageant itself evoked the history of the abbey from Denis and Dagobert to the present, so the physical setting – architecture, decoration, and furnishings – evoked a continuous line of royal history, from Merovingians to Capetians. The newly enlarged church became the fulfilment of Abbot Suger's "first thought ... the concordance and harmony of the ancient and the new work": the physical embodiment of the historical memory of the French nation, the living bond between patron saint, monastery, monarch, and nation.[41]

Capetians and Merovingians

Although the texts of Abbot Suger make Saint-Denis the best documented example, in the broader context of Parisian and regional monuments it is hardly unique. The Musée Carnavalet survey now documents some thirty-five to thirty-eight Merovingian ecclesiastical foundations within the modern limits of the city, many of which were still standing in the second quarter of the twelfth century.[42] The ninth-century Norman sieges and other damage notwithstanding, both the textual and archeological evidence indicate there was little important building activity in Paris between the end of the Merovingian dynasty and the decision of Louis VI to settle there.[43] Thus, the twelfth-century builders had before them a number of surviving Merovingian structures, as well as a number, like Sainte-Geneviève and the nave at Saint-Germain-des-Prés, that were identified as ancient by virtue of having been erected directly on Merovingian foundations. It is important to remember that in the eyes of the twelfth-century viewer, whether learned or not, all of the old churches would have been considered ancient, if not actually called "Merovingian" or "Carolingian," because their classification would have been by foundation dates.

Most of these repaired Merovingian structures were rebuilt or significantly altered during the reigns of Louis VI and Louis VII (1137–1180). In the architecture, there were both intentional appropriations and conscious imitations of Merovingian forms, such as we have seen at Saint-Denis, which were intended to symbolize continuous royal presence in Paris, visible links from Merovingians and Carolingians to Capetians.[44] Thus, many of the more distinctive features that appear "new" to us and that we associate with the beginnings of the

Gothic style in Paris would just as surely have had other, quite different references to the twelfth-century audience.[45] Free-standing columns, acanthus capitals, and detached shafts might just as easily have meant "ancient" to this audience. They would have been seen as references to the past, but also understood as symbolic of the continuous, living history of the community. In addition, we must recognize that these Merovingian revival elements are related to the creation of the Gothic style in Paris.[46] In our quest for newness and our study of buildings, parts of buildings, and architectural elements in isolation, we have failed to see them in their historical context and to recognize that even architectural elements can embody historical integration.

That the deliberate references to the Merovingian past found in twelfth-century Parisian buildings are not accidental can be quickly confirmed by examining twelfth-century Capetian royal seals, as Bedos-Rezak has shown.[47] If we compare the seal of Louis VI (dated 1108) with that of Louis VII (dated 1141), at first glance they appear to be typical Capetian royal seals carrying the frontal image of the king seated on a throne. But the 1141 image of Louis VII differs in two dramatic details: Louis VII is seated on the throne of Dagobert and he has shoulder-length hair. The image intentionally associates him with the "long-haired kings," the descendents of Clovis.[48] The seal provides a visual corollary to the histories and chronicles compiled at Saint-Germain-des-Prés and then being collected at Saint-Denis,[49] and indicates a conscious political revival – a *renovatio* – of the Merovingian past. It has its parallels with Suger's text that, in the same passage, simultaneously lauded "the glorious King Dagobert" as well as "the Most Serene King," namely, Louis VII.[50] The association of the image of Louis VII with Clovis and his successors – I remind you that Clovis and Louis are the same name – created a continuous history of French kingship linking the Capetians to their Carolingian and Merovingian predecessors and provided new meanings in terms of legitimacy and of historical genealogy.

NOTES

The present study, like the paper at the 1989 conference, is an excerpt from a much larger project analysing historical integration in Parisian and regional churches from ca. 1130 to ca. 1160. The book is provisionally titled *Capetian Kings in Merovingian Paris: Continuity and Contextual-*

ity in Early Gothic Architecture. The original conference paper was titled, "Capetians in Merovingian Paris: Architecture and Its Audience at the Beginning of the Gothic Period," and considered problems at Saint-Germain-des-Prés, Saint-Pierre de Montmartre, Sainte-Geneviève, and Notre-Dame, as well as Saint-Denis. Thanks are due to Richard Schneider, organizer of the conference from which this volume developed, who offered valuable support at the onset of the project. Thanks are also due to the participants and audience at the conference for their friendly advice and sage criticism, and to the editorial committee for their help. Special thanks are reserved for V.P.C. for her probing questions and repeated refusals to accept pat answers. To lessen the scholarly apparatus a lengthy bibliography of the most recent and relevant sources has been added. References in the notes to works in the bibliography are limited to the author's name, followed by pages. This study has been aided by a PSC-BHE Research Award for 1994–5 from the Research Foundation of CUNY.

1   All investigations of Merovingian Paris must begin with the Musée Carnavalet publications listed in the bibliography. The most important studies of twelfth-century Paris are also listed there and include: Friedmann; Boussard; Bautier and Willesme.

2   Patronage is discussed by Gardner, Dufour, and Sassier, etc.

3   On the old families in royal service, see Bournazel; on the ecclesiatic climate, see Fassler.

4   "Merovingian," as it is used here, refers to the time of Clovis and his successors, 500–768, as well as to works the twelfth-century viewer might have believed to be Merovingian. The evidence suggests that Frankish builders continued the Late Antique practice of reusing architectural elements. Thus, some of the *spolia* here are older but are considered Merovingian from their context. Given the evidence, a thorough investigation of the Merovingian use of *spolia* is impossible, but the imitation and continuation of Roman practice, as in the case of the forum of Paris, seems likely. See *Lutèce,* and P.-M. Duval.

5   From the enormous bibliography on Saint-Denis a few relevant items, in addition to Crosby, must be mentioned. Panofsky; Bony; Brenk; Gardner; Winterfeld; Losowska; Nebbiai-Dalla Guarda; Gerson; Bony, "What Possible Sources for the Chevet of Saint-Denis?" in *Abbot Suger,* pp. 131–42; Clark, "Suger's Church at Saint-Denis: The State of Research," in *Abbot Suger,* pp. 105–30; Kidson; Adams; Foley; Rudolph; Périn, 1991; Robertson; Suckale; Bur; Blum; Suger; Clark, 1993 and 1994; Dubois; and Wyss.

6   This unfortunate habit of scholarship can be traced to the beginning of the

nineteenth century and the first attempts to identify Saint-Denis as the first Gothic building.

7 Panofsky, pp. 90–1. Pending the publication of a new, complete English translation and critical edition by Thomas Waldman, quotations are taken from the Panofsky edition. The texts of Abbot Suger, including those translated by Panofsky, and the life of Louis VI (bibliography, Suger), are primary sources, but they have led scholars to attribute to Suger attitudes that he might have inherited from Abbot Adam (1094–1122), the man Suger calls his "spiritual father and foster parent," as well as projects initiated by Adam and completed under Suger. See Benton, in *Abbot Suger*, pp. 3–15. It was Adam, for example, who established the anniversary of Dagobert, although it was the income from Berneval, a priory under Suger's control, that provided the resources: R. Barroux, "L'anniversaire de la mort de Dagobert à Saint-Denis au XIIe siècle: Charte inédite de l'abbé Adam," *Bulletin philologique et historique*, 1942–3, 131–51. It was Adam who began the collection of texts that led to the establishment of a continuous royal history under Suger. See Spiegel and Guenée, in Nora, *La Nation*, 1, pp. 5–30. Guenée, p. 22, also points out that Suger certainly recognized the significance of the gift of the crown of Philip I by Louis VI in 1120, because he moved the event forward into his own abbacy, 1124, in the life of Louis VI (Suger, p. 131).

8 On Fulrad's eighth-century church, in addition to Crosby, pp. 51–83, see Heitz; Jacobsen; Semmler; Périn, 1991; and Stoclet.

9 Panofsky, pp. 86–7.

10 Ibid., pp. 44–5, 50–3.

11 Crosby, Part Two, discusses the influence of the earlier nave on the new work. Bony, 1983, p. 94, and notes 16–17 (pp. 479–80), speaks of the columns from the old nave and the new chevet as the source for those of Suger's projected nave. See also, Bony, 1980, and in *Abbot Suger*, pp. 131–42, as well as Clark, in *Abbot Suger*, pp. 105–30.

12 I cannot agree with Fernie's proposal that the upper level of Suger's chevet had a two-storey elevation. My three-storey reconstruction differs slightly from those published in Crosby, p. 264, and Gardner, 1989, fig. 10. The latter based his reconstruction, with only minor modifications, on that of Kenneth John Conant, *Carolingian and Romanesque Architecture 800 to 1200*, 2d ed. (New York, 1979), pp. 462–5. The reconstruction by Christopher Wilson, in *The Gothic Cathedral* (London, 1990), p. 39, is without foundation.

13 Crosby consistently spoke of five added nave bays because there were four added nave columns on each side. That presupposes the reconstruc-

tion of the final nave bay of the old church, although I believe the builders would have made every effort to preserve it.

14 Crosby, Appendix J, pp. 370–1. Clark, with Crosby's permission, published Crosby's earlier analysis of the chart (deleted from Crosby's final text), in *Abbot Suger*, p. 111.

15 Panofsky, pp. 50–3, 90–1, and 100–1.

16 Presently in the crypt there are only three marble capitals and three marble columns, as well as several marble colonnettes installed in the wall arcading, of Hilduin's chapel. This arcading. like the strengthening of the wall of the apse of Dagobert's church, is the work of Suger's builders in the twelfth century.

17 Removed by Lenoir for his museum, they were initially replaced by black marble columns from the church of the Grands Augustins, given to Saint-Denis by Napoleon and installed with new, Corinthian-style capitals by Legrand in 1806. These in turn were taken out by Viollet-le-Duc and replaced by the six thin shafts that stand between the chapels today. Clark, 1994, and Wyss present the documents and preliminary analyses. A more complete analysis will appear in my book.

18 Panofsky, pp. 46–7, 161. Both Panofsky and Crosby, pp. 99 and 188, agreed that these now lost doors dated to the eleventh century.

19 *Le trésor de Saint-Denis*, pp. 119–87.

20 Gaborit-Chopin, in *Abbot Suger*, pp. 283–93; Wixom, in *Abbot Suger*, pp. 295–304; *Le trésor*, pp. 119–87; and Gaborit-Chopin, "Le trésor au temps de Suger," *Dossiers d'archéologie* 158 (March 1991), 2–19.

21 D. Gaborit-Chopin, *Regalia: Les instruments du sacre des rois de France; les "honneurs de Charlemagne"* (Paris, 1987), with bibliography. Louis VI had been crowned at Orléans by the Archbishop of Sens, rather than at Reims. See Le Roy.

22 Panofsky, pp. 90–3; J. Benton, in *Abbot Suger*, pp. 3–15; and Crosby, p. 116. It is likely that the columns Suger considered importing from Rome were for the nave extension. Thus, to contemporary eyes, the twelfth-century bays would have looked like, and thus would have been, the nave of Dagobert. On the mosaic floors, see C. Norton, "Les carreaux de pavage du moyen âge de l'abbaye de Saint-Denis," *Bulletin monumental* 139 (1981), 69–100; and X. Barral i Altet, in *Abbot Suger*, pp. 245–55.

23 M. Vieillard-Troïkouroff, "L'église de Sainte-Geneviève de Paris au temps d'Etienne de Tournai," *Bulletin de la Société nationale des Antiquaires de France* (1961), 131–48, gives the reference to mosaics at Sainte-Geneviève, which might have been a local source for Suger.

24 Panofsky, pp. 85–6. The association of columns and the number twelve is

an obvious reference to the Apostles, but Suger's mention of *marble* columns is not a literary convention. See B. Reudenbach, "Säule und Apostel. Uberlegungen zum Verhältnis von Architekturexegetischer Literatur im Mittelalter," *Frühmittelalterliche Studien* 14 (1980), 310–51; and J. Onians, *Bearers of Meaning: The Classical Orders in Antiquity, the Middle Ages, and the Renaissance* (Princeton, 1988), esp. pp. 86–7. In fact, there were twelve columns in the inner rank of the upper chevet, which obviates the possibility of double columns, recently raised by P. Kidson, in "Gervase, Becket, and William of Sens," *Speculum* 68 (1993), 969–91, esp. p. 988.

25 Crosby, pp. 53, 68–9, and Panofsky, pp. 44–5.

26 Crosby, pp. 59–61, discusses the annular crypt. See also C. Heitz in *Une village au temps de Charlemagne: Moines et paysans de l'abbaye de Saint-Denis du VIIe siècle à l'an mil* [exh. cat., Musée National des Arts et Traditions Populaires] J. Cuisenier et al. (Paris, 1988), pp. 50–9; and Heitz.

27 Panofsky, pp. 100–1.

28 Clark, in *Abbot Suger*, discusses these features in the context of the creation of the new style. Bony, 1983, p. 95, derived the free-standing, monolithic columns for Suger's projected nave from those in the chevet, which in turn were based on the old nave columns. I believe Suger intended to reuse the marble columns from the old nave in the new nave, another example to be added to the list given above.

29 Detached shafts may have been used in the remodelled crypt at Sainte-Geneviève in the 1130s. They also appear in Saint-Aignan, but not in the work associated with the 1119 charter. Yvan Christ, "La chapelle Saint-Aignan," *Paris foyer d'art au moyen âge*, [Document archéologia No. 3], 1973, 28–33; and Anne Prache, *Ile-de-France roman* (La Pierre-qui-Vire, 1983), pp. 45–6.

30 Merovingian examples can also be seen in the crypt at Jouarre and the baptistry at Poitiers.

31 Earlier studies of the capitals did not note this change. Wulf chiefly investigated twelfth-century precedents. The Merovingian revival capitals are discussed at greater length in Clark, 1993. The twelfth-century capitals added to the reinforcements of the apse and to the walls of Hilduin's chapel include one deliberate copy of an eighth-century capital, but none that copy known Merovingian designs.

32 See *L'acanthe dans la sculpture monumentale de l'antiquité à la renaissance* (Paris, 1993); and Eliane Vergnolle, "Fortune et infortunes du chapiteau corinthien dans le monde roman," *Revue de l'art* 90 (1990), 21-34.

33 Caillet, *L'Antiquité*, pp. 73–4. Fossard; Fossard, Vieillard-Troïekouroff,

and Chatel; and Vieillard-Troïekouroff, 1976, 1982, and 1983.

34 Pamela Blum, as in note 35, suggests that the marble capital now installed at the north entrance to the crypt is a twelfth-century copy because it lacks the bottom ring carved with the capital. If true, this would provide a convincing demonstration of the ability of the sculptors to copy precisely. Recutting a Merovingian marble capital presents formidable physical and technical problems. It would invariably result in either a smaller capital (the Sainte-Geneviève capital of Daniel, now in the Louvre) or in one with only minimal surface changes, or in one with little detail (as in the Musée de Cluny capital discussed below, note 35. See Vieillard-Troïkouroff, 1976).

35 The reinforcements Suger's workmen applied to the older parts of the crypt would effectively have brought them into the new work. The extensive restorations and shifting of capitals in the crypt are discussed by Crosby, pp. 222–32, and, for the figural capitals, more thoroughly by P. Blum, "The Saint Benedict Cycle on the Capitals of the Crypt at Saint-Denis," *Gesta* 20 (1981), 73–87. Several of the twelfth-century capitals are given doubtful early dates by J. Formigé, in *L'abbaye royal de Saint-Denis* (Paris, 1960), figs. 47, 157, 158, and 166, when they are plainly copies of eighth-century originals. Another marble capital in the collection of the Musée National du Moyen Age proves instructive. Vieillard-Troïekouroff, 1976, argued persuasively that it is a Merovingian original which someone at Saint-Denis in the twelfth century attempted to recarve. For reasons we do not know, the sculptor did not complete the recarving, but he carved enough for us to be certain that he was one of Suger's workmen because the capital most closely resembles twelfth-century capitals in the east end at Saint-Denis. We can also recognize that the original capital and the model for the recarved design (which may not have been one and the same) were Merovingian.

36 Crosby, pp. 121–58, places less emphasis on the special character of the centre space than he did in "The Plan of the Western Bays of Suger's New Church at St. Denis," *Journal of the Society of Architectural Historians* 27 (1968), 39–43. Suger's text describing the construction of Charlemagne is translated by Panofsky, pp. 44–5.

37 Spiegel; Guenée, "Chancelleries et monastères," in *Les lieux de mémoire*, II, *La Nation*, vol. 1, ed. P. Nora (Paris, 1986), pp. 5–30, esp. 21–7; and Beaune, "Les sanctuaires royaux," in *La Nation*, vol. 1, pp. 57–87, esp. 58–70.

38 See Clark, 1993, 1994, and my forthcoming book, cited in note 1.

39 This is analysed at greater length in Clark, 1993, and my forthcoming book.

40 In "The Recollection of the Past Is the Promise of the Future: Abbot Suger and Dagobert's Church," a paper presented at the 25th International Congress on Medieval Studies, Kalamazoo, MI, May 1990, I suggested that Suger identified with Dagobert and saw himself as the new "founder." On the other hand, he may be intentionally linking Louis VII with Dagobert, just as he so often mentions the gifts of Louis VI and Charles the Bald at the same moment. It should also be recalled that Suger's texts never mention other building abbots, such as Hilduin and Fulrad.

41 The vertical axis of burial site and altar became the goal of the royal visitor, a physical demonstration of the continuous links between the abbey and kings forged by the historical procession from façade to altar. Suger was all too aware that Philip I had favoured Saint-Remi in Reims over Saint-Denis and had chosen to be buried at Saint-Benoît-sur-Loire in 1108, a slight he takes pains to justify in terms of the king's actions (see Bur, 1986 and 1991). The cadet Philip, who died as a result of a freak accident in 1131, was buried at the abbey, which may indicate Suger's success. And, of course, Louis VI himself chose to be buried at Saint-Denis in 1137. The bond Suger forged between saint, abbey, and monarchy was not irrevocable. In 1180, Louis VII chose burial at the Cistercian abbey of Barbeaux. Two final points must be kept in mind: first, Suger intended to tear down the eighth-century nave and replace it with a five-aisled structure, an Apostle's church scheme (Crosby, pp. 267–77; and Bony, 1983, p. 95); and second, the Dionysian aesthetic of extraordinary variety in details (Clark, in *Abbot Suger*, p. 116) originated in the old nave.

42 See the map and the list in *Collections mérovingiennes*, pp. 603–4 and passim. The map does not include Saint-Denis or any of the other nearby abbeys of Merovingian foundation, such as Chelles, Jouarre, or Saint-Maur-des-Fossés. The new list, see N. Duval et al., gives only thirty-five Merovingian foundations.

43 The exceptions are Sainte-Geneviève and Saint-Germain-des-Prés, where extensive eleventh- and early twelfth-century construction is evident. No known Merovingian elements were incorporated in the two Parisian twelfth-century churches, Saint-Martin-des-Champs and Saint-Julien-le-Pauvre, for which there are donations made by Henri I (1031–60). On the other hand, the twelfth-century crypt of Saint-Marcel had at least one Merovingian marble capital, which was, along with two limestone capitals and a marble shaft, removed by Lenoir in 1806. Unfortunately, none of these pieces has been identified in Parisian collections. See Vieillard-Troïekouroff, Fossard, Chatel and Lamy-Lasalle, 127; and *Collections mérovingiennes*, passim. See Bautier, 1993.

44 My forthcoming book discusses the individual twelfth-century churches and their distinctive Merovingian revival elements in detail. This varies in each example and may also extend to church planning. The distinctive triapsidal plan now best exemplified by Saint-Julien-le-Pauvre should also be regarded as a deliberate revival.

45 The distinctive character of the Gothic style in Paris is stressed by Bony, "Essai sur la spiritualité de deux cathédrales: Notre-Dame de Paris et Saint-Etienne de Bourges," in *Chercher dieu* (Paris, 1943), pp. 105–67. The style should not be defined simply by stylistic features, such as pointed arches or rib-vaults, but by the changes in thinking that distinguish the work of the second builder at Saint-Denis from his predecessors; see Radding and Clark, 1988, and 1992, pp. 57–76.

46 These questions have not been taken up in the standard histories of Gothic architecture. See, most recently, Bony, 1983; Dieter Kimpel and Robert Suckale, *Die gotische Architektur in Frankreich 1130–1270* (Munich, 1985) and *L'architecture gothique en France 1130–1270*, trans. by Françoise Neu (Paris, 1990).

47 L. Douët d'Arcq, *Collection de sceaux, Archives de l'Empire, Inventaire et documents*, 3 vols. (Paris, 1863–8), vol. 1, 271; B. Bedos-Rezak, in *Abbot Suger*, pp. 95–103, citing Marjorie Caucheteux-Chavannes, "Les sceaux des rois de France, d'Hugues Capet à François Ier (987–1547)," Dissertation, Ecole des Chartes (Paris, 1962); Bedos-Rezak; and Dalas.

48 The phrase is found in Gregory of Tours; the image on the seal ring of Childeric.

49 See the works cited above in note 37.

50 The parallels are most obvious in the description of the consecration ceremonies for the chevet. Panofsky, pp. 110–21.

SELECTED RECENT BIBLIOGRAPHY

Adams, J. duQ. "The Patriotism of Abbot Suger," *Proceedings of the Annual Meeting of the Western Society for French History* 15 (1988), 19–29.
- "The *Regnum Francie* of Suger of Saint-Denis: An Expansive Ile-de-France," *Historical Reflections* 19 (1993), 167–88.
Bautier, R.-H. "Le rôle de Paris au Haut Moyen Age," In *l'Ile-de-France de Clovis à Hugues Capet*, pp. 125–34, Guiry-en-Vexin, 1993.
- "Paris au temps d'Abélard," In *Abélard en son temps. Actes du colloque international organisé a l'occasion du 8 centenaire de la naissance de Pierre Abélard (14–19 Mai 1979)*, ed. J. Jolivet, pp. 21–7, Paris, 1981.

- "Quand et comment Paris devint capitale," *Bulletin de la Société de l'Histoire de Paris et de l'Ile-de-France* 105 (1976), 17–46.

Beaune, C. *Naissance de la nation France.* Paris, 1985.

- "L'ancêtre de tous les rois de France," *Les temps des mérovingiens* [Historia Speciale 30] (July-August 1994), 108–13.

Bedos-Rezak, B. "Mythes monarchiques et thèmes sigillaires du sceau de Louis VII aux sceaux de Charles VII," In *XV Congreso internacional de la ciencias genealógica y heráldica, Madrid, 1982,* pp. 199–213, Madrid, 1982.

Beech, G.T. "The Eleanor of Aquitaine Vase: Its Origins and History to the Early Twelfth Century." *Ars Orientalis* 22 (1992), 69–79.

- "The Eleanor of Aquitaine Vase, William IX of Aquitaine and Muslim Spain." *Gesta* 32 (1993), 3–10.

Belaubre, J. *L'ère du dernier.* Monnaies médiévales 1, Les collectiones monétaires 2. Paris, 1987.

Blum, P. *Early Gothic Saint-Denis: Restorations and Survivals.* Berkeley, 1992.

- "Fingerprinting the Stone at Saint-Denis: A Pilot Study," *Gesta* 33 (1994), 19–28.

Bony, J. *French Gothic Architecture of the 12th and 13th Centuries.* Berkeley, 1983.

- "The Genesis of Gothic: Accident or Necessity?" *Australian Journal of Art* 2 (1980), 17–31.

Bourderon R., and P. de Peretti, dir. *Histoire de Saint-Denis.* Toulouse, 1988.

Bournazel, E. *Le gouvernement capétien au XIIe siècle, 1108–1180.* Paris, 1975.

Boussard, J. *Nouvelle histoire de Paris: De la fin du siège de 885–886 à la mort de Philippe Auguste.* Paris, 1976.

Brenk, B. "Sugers Spolien," *Arte medievale* 1 (1983), 101–7.

Brown, E.A.R. "La généalogie capétienne dans l'historiographie du Moyen Age," In *Religion et culture autour de l'an mil,* ed. D. Igona-Prat and J.-C. Picard, pp. 199–214. Paris, 1990.

Bur, M. "Saint-Denis et Saint-Remi, à propos d'un livre récent," *Francia* 14 (1986), 578–81.

- *Suger: Abbé de Saint-Denis, Régent de France.* Paris, 1991.

Clark, W. "Merovingian Revival Acanthus Capitals at Saint-Denis," In *L'acanthe dans la sculpture monumentale de l'antiquité à la renaissance,* pp. 345–56. Paris, 1993.

- "New Light on Old Stones: Quarries, Monuments, and Sculpture in Medieval France. An Introduction," *Gesta* 33 (1994), 3–9.

- "Spatial Innovations in the Chevet of Saint-Germain-des-Prés," *Journal of the Society of Architectural Historians* 38 (1979), 348–65.

Crosby, S. *The Royal Abbey of Saint-Denis from Its Beginnings to the Death of Suger, 475–1151*, ed. P. Blum. New Haven, 1987.

Dalas, M. *Les sceaux des rois et de régence* [Corpus des sceaux français du moyen âge, vol. 2]. Paris, 1991.

Dubois, C. "Genése de la legende de Saint Denis de Paris," Master's thesis, University of Paris X - Nanterre, 1993.

Dufour, J. "Louis VI, roi de France (1108–1137), à la lumière des actes royaux et des sources narratives." *Comptes-rendus de l'Académie des Inscriptions et Belles-Lettres* (1990), pp. 456–82.

Dufour, J. ed. *Recueil des actes de Louis VI, roi de France (1108–1137).* 4 v. Paris, 1992–4.

Dumolin M., and G. Outardel, *Les églises de France. Paris et la Seine.* Paris, 1936.

Dunbabin, J. "What's in a Name? Philip, King of France." *Speculum* 68 (1993), 949–68.

Duval, N., ed.,*Naissance des arts chrétiens: Atlas des monuments paleochrétiens de la France.* Paris, 1991.

Duval, N., P. Périn, and J.-C. Picard, "Paris," In *Topographie chrétienne des cités de la Gaule des origines au milieu de VIIIe siècle*, ed. N. Gauthier and J.-C. Picard, Vol. 8, *Province Ecclesiastique de Sens*, 97–129. Paris, 1992.

Duval, P.-M. *Nouvelle histoire de Paris: De Lutèce oppidum à Paris capitale de la France (vers -225?/500)*, Paris, 1993.

Fassler, M. *Gothic Song: Victorine Sequences and Augustinian Reform in Twelfth-Century Paris.* Cambridge, 1993.

Foley, E.B. *The First Ordinary of the Royal Abbey of St.-Denis in France* [Spicilegium friburgense 32]. Fribourg, 1990.

Fossard, D. "Les chapiteaux de marbre du VIIe siècle en Gaule, style et évolution," *Cahiers archéologiques* 2 (1947), 69–85.

Fossard, D., M. Vieillard-Troïekouroff, and E. Châtel, *Recueil général des monuments sculptés en France pendant le haut moyen âge (IVe–Xe siècles)*, vol. 1: *Paris et son département.* Paris, 1978.

Friedmann, A. *Paris, ses rues, ses paroisses, du moyen âge à la révolution française.* Paris, 1959.

Gardner, S. "The Theory of Centripetal Implosion and the Birth of Gothic Architecture," In *World Art*, ed. I. Lavin vol. 1, pp. 111–16. University Park, PA, 1989.

– "Two Campaigns in Suger's Western Block at St.-Denis," *Art Bulletin* 66 (1984), 574–87.

Gerson, P., ed., *Abbot Suger and Saint-Denis: A Symposium.* New York, 1986.

Guenée, B. "Etat et nation en France au moyen âge," *Revue historique* 237 (1967), 17–30.

– *Histoire et culture historique dans l'occident médiéval*. Paris, 1980.

– "Les Généalogies entre l'histoire et la politique: La fierté d'être capétien, en France, au moyen âge," *Annales ESC* 33 (1978), 450–77.

Guiry-en-Vexin, Musée archéologique Départemental du Val d'Oise, [Exh. cat.] *l'Ile-de-France de Clovis à Hugues Capet*. Guiry-en-Vexin, 1993.

Heitz, C. "Architecture et monuments de Neustrie," In *La Neustrie: Les pays au nord de la Loire de 650 à 850; colloque historique international*, ed. H. Atsma, pp. 187–208. [Beihefte der Francia 16/2]. Sigmaringen, 1989.

Jacobsen, W. "Die Abteikirche von Saint-Denis als kunstgeschichtliches Problem," In *La Neustrie*, pp. 151–85.

Kidson, P. "Panofsky, Suger and St. -Denis," *Journal of the Warburg and Courtauld Institutes* 50 (1987), 1–17.

Krüger, K.H. *Königsgrabkirchen des Franken, Angelsachsen und Langobarden bis zur Mitte des 8. Jahrhunderts. Ein historischer Katalog* [Münstersche Mittelalterschriften 4]. Munich, 1971.

Labande, E.R. "Memoria Sugerii abbatis," *Cahiers de civilisation médiévale* 25 (1982), 121–7.

Lafaurie, J. *Les monnaies des rois de France de Hugues Capet à Louis XII*. Paris, 1951.

Le Roy, Y. "La *Chronique de Morigny* et le sacre de Louis VII. Le pouvoir royal vers 1131," *Revue historique de droit français et étranger* 65 (1987), 527–44.

Lewis, A.W. *Royal Succession in Capetian France: Studies on Familial Order and the State*. Cambridge, 1981.

Lombard-Jourdan, A. *Fleur de lis et oriflamme*. Paris, 1991.

– "Leucothéa et sainte Geneviéve, protectrices de Paris. Mythe et hagiographie." *Paris et l'Ile-de France* 42 (1991), 7–59.

– "*Montjoie et saint Denis!*." Paris, 1989.

Losowska, H. *Recherches sur l'état des fonds concernant la basilique Saint-Denis au XIXe siècle*, 3 vols. Paris, 1985?

Nebbiai-Dalla Guarda, D. *La bibliothèque de l'abbaye de Saint-Denis en France*. Paris, 1985.

Nora, P., ed., *Les lieux de mémoire*, I, *La République*. Paris, 1984; II, *La Nation*, 3 v. Paris, 1986; III, *Les France*, 3 v. Paris, 1992.

Panofsky, E., ed., *Abbot Suger on the Abbey Church of St.-Denis and Its Art Treasures*, 2d ed. by G. Panofsky-Soergel. Princeton, 1979.

Paris, Musée Carnavalet. *Collections mérovingiennes*, Catalogues du musée Carnavalet 2, P. Périn et al. Paris, 1985.

– [Exh. cat.] *La Montagne Sainte-Geneviève*, B. de Mongolfier et al. Paris, 1981.

– [Exh. cat.] *Lutèce. Paris de César à Clovis*, B. de Montgolfier, P. Périn et al. Paris, 1984.

- *Paris de la préhistoire au moyen âge*, P. Velay, Bulletin du musée Carnavalet 43. 1990.
- [Exh. cat.] *Paris mérovingienne*, P. Périn and P. Velay, Bulletin du musée Carnavalet 33. 1980.
- *Sculptures médiévales (XIIe siècle – début du XVIe siècle)*, Catalogues du Musée Carnavalet 1, J.-P. Willesme. Paris, 1979.

Paris, Musée du Louvre, [exh. cat.], *Le trésor de Saint-Denis*, D. Gaborit-Chopin et al. Paris, 1991.

Paris, Musée National des Arts et Traditions Populaires, [Exh. cat.] *Un village au temps de Charlemagne*. Paris, 1988.

Paris, Musée National du Moyen Age (formerly, Musée de Cluny). *L'Antiquité classique, Le haut moyen âge et Byzance au Musée de Cluny*, J.-P. Caillet. Paris, 1985.

Périn, P. *Clovis et la naissance de la France*. Paris, 1989.
- "Paris mérovingien, *sedes regia*," *Klio* 71/2 (1989), 487–506.
- "Quelques considérations sur la basilique de Saint-Denis et sa nécropole à l'époque mérovingienne," In *Villes et campagnes au moyen âge: Mélanges Georges Despy*, ed. J.-M. Duvosquel and A. Dierkens pp. 599–624. Liège, 1991.

Plagnieux, P. "Le chevet de Saint-Germain-des-Prés et la définition de l'espace gothique au milieu du XIIe siècle," PhD, University of Paris VI – Sorbonne, 1991.

Plongeron, B. ed. *Histoire de diocèse de Paris*, I, *Une histoire religieuse des origines à la Revolution* [Histoire des diocèses de France 20]. Paris, 1987.

Poisson, G. "Paris, capitale depuis quinze siècles." *Les temps des mérovingiens* [Historia Speciale 30] (July–August 1994), 62–7.

Radding C., and W. Clark, "Abélard et le bâtisseur de Saint-Denis: Études parallèles dans l'histoire des disciplines," *Annales ESC* 43 (1988), 1263–90.
- *Medieval Architecture, Medieval Learning, Builders and Masters in the Age of Romanesque and Gothic*. New Haven, 1992.

Robertson, A.W. *The Service Books of the Royal Abbey of Saint-Denis: Images of Ritual and Music in the Middle Ages*. Oxford, 1991.

Romero, A.-M. *Saint-Denis*. Paris, 1992.

Rudolph, C. *Artistic Change at Saint-Denis*. Princeton, 1990.

Sassier, Y. *Louis VII*. Paris, 1991.

Schneidmüller, B. *Nomen Patriae. Die Entstehung Frankreichs in der politisch-geographischen Terminologie (10.–13. Jahrhundert)* [Nationes, 7]. Sigmaringen, 1987.

Semmler, J. "Saint-Denis: Von der bischöflichen Coemeterialbasilika zur königlichen Benediktiner-abtei," In *La Neustrie: Les pays au nord de la Loire de 650 à 850; colloque historique international*, ed. H. Atsma, pp. 75–123. [Beihefte der Francia 16/2]. Sigmaringen, 1989.

Spiegel, G. *The Chronicle Tradition of Saint-Denis: A Survey*. Brookline, MA, and Leyden, 1978.

Suckale, R. "Neue Literatur über dei Abteikirche von Saint-Denis," *Kunstchronik* 43 (1990), 62–80.

Suger, *La geste de Louis VI et autres oeuvres*, ed. M. Bur. Paris, 1994.

– *The Deeds of Louis the Fat*, trans. R. Cusimano and J. Moorhead. Washington, DC, 1992.

Stoclet, A. *Autour de Fulrad de Saint-Denis* [Hautes études médiévales et modernes, 72]. Geneva, 1993.

Theis, L. "Dagobert, Saint-Denis et la royauté française au Moyen Age," In *Le métier d'historien au Moyen Age* [Publications de la Sorbonne, Etudes 13], ed. B. Guenée, pp. 19–30. Paris, 1977.

Velay, P. *From Lutetia to Paris*. Paris, 1992.

Verdier, P. "La politique financière de Suger dans la reconstruction de Saint-Denis et l'enrichissement du trésor," In *Artistes, artisans et production artistique du Moyen Age*, II: *Commande et travail*, ed. X. Barral i Altet, pp. 167–82. Paris, 1987.

Vieillard-Troïekouroff, M. "Les chapiteaux de marbre du haut moyen âge à Saint-Denis," *Gesta* 15 (1976), 105–12.

– "Récentes découvertes du Paris mérovingienne, extra muros," *Bulletin archéologique* n.s. 19 (1983), 97–105.

– "Supplément au Recueil général des monuments sculptés en France pendant le Haut Moyen Age (IVe–Xe siècles), I: Paris et son département," *Bulletin archéologique* n.s. 15 (1982), 181–227.

Vieillard-Troïekouroff, M., D. Fossard, E. Chatel, and C. Lamy-Lasalle, "Les églises suburbaines de Paris du IVe au Xe siècle," *Paris et Ile-de-France* 11 (1960), 17–282.

Waldman, T. "Saint-Denis et les premiers capétiens," In *Religion et culture autour de l'an mil*, ed. D. Igona-Prat and J.-C. Picard pp. 191–7. Paris, 1990.

Werner, K.F. "Kingdom and Principality in Twelfth-Century France," In *The Medieval Nobility*, ed. T. Reuter pp. 243–90. Amsterdam, 1979.

– "Les nations et le sentiment national dans l'Europe médiévale," *Revue historique* 244 (1969), 285–304.

– *Les origines, histoire de France*, vol. 1, ed. J. Favier. Paris, 1988.

– "Les sources de la légitimité royale a l'avènement des capétiens (Xe–XIe siècles). In *Le sacre des rois*, Actes du colloque international d'histoire sur les sacres et couronnements royaux (Reims, 1975), pp. 49–60. Paris, 1985.

– *Vom Frankreich zur Entfaltung Deutschlands und Frankreichs* [collected papers with bibliography]. Sigmaringen, 1984.

Willesme, J.-P. "Paris de la fin du Xe siècle à l'aube de la Renaissance," In *Paris de la préhistoire à nos jours*, ed. M. Le Clère pp. 109–221. Saint-Jean-d'Angély, 1985.

Winterfeld, D. Von. "Gedenken zu Sugers Bau in St.-Denis," In *Martin Gosebruch zu Ehren*, ed. F. Steigerwald pp. 92–107. Munich, 1984.

Wulf, W. *Die Kapitellplastik des Sugerbaus von Saint-Denis* [Europäische Hochsculschriften, 28, Kunstgeschichte, 10]. Frankfurt, 1979.

Wyss, M., dir. *Atlas historique et archéologique de la ville de Saint-Denis (Un recueil des sources)*. Saint-Denis, 1995.

– "Saint-Denis, I, Sculptures romanes découvertes lors des fouilles urbaines." *Bulletin monumental* 150 (1992), 309–54.

8

Interpreting the Architecture of Wells Cathedral

Peter Draper

Draper's essay on the late twelfth-century architecture of Wells cathedral, like Fernie's, stresses the need to seek ways of evaluating architecture in terms that would have been understood by those for whom it was built. Integration is considered here as the deliberate use of architectural features to create a distinctive overall effect with a purposeful sense of decorum. Wells forms a highly important case-study since much of the original fabric survives intact and with little alteration, save the loss of all the early glass. Draper deals, as do Brenk and Klukas, with the roles played by the specific patrons of the building, and here posits a self-conscious awareness by the secular canons at Wells concerning the appearance of the design. To contextualize his analyses, Draper draws upon an understanding of specific legislation by the Cistercians and contemporaneous descriptions of sumptuous settings and shrines. He argues that the artistic qualities peculiar to Wells appear to have been a deliberate choice of the builders.

Draper confronts the issue of "stylistic continuum" that has so frequently been a part of art-historical studies since the turn of the century. He analyses the historiography of the scholarship on Wells that projected different assessments of its formal character. Wells has been interpreted variously as a building exhibiting progressive or traditional, Gothic or Romanesque, characteristics. Draper suggests that such arguing over stylistic criteria and placement in a continuum may reveal more about the motivations of the modern authors than it does about the buildings themselves, issues also addressed by Brush in her study of the historiography of Gothic sculpture. He suggests that we can replace taxonomic formalist approaches to stylistic unity with the attitudinal term "coherence." We can also avoid the modern notion of "artistic style" and replace it with the arguably more medieval notion of "decorum," admitting that the medieval viewer could see a building as coherent that we today see as jarringly uncoordinated.

In a manner similar to that of the social approach of Bedos-Rezak and Abou-El-Haj, Draper addresses the political rivalries between the canons at Wells and the monks of Bath and Glastonbury. The decision by the canons at Wells may have been affected not only by their attitudes towards issues of size and importance, but by conscious awareness of architectural forms that conveyed contemporaneous impressions of sobriety or luxury.

Historians concerned with style and formal analysis have long been open to the fundamental criticism that their methodology involves models of classification which belong to their own time and would have had little or no meaning for those responsible for the design of medieval buildings. Medieval historians concerned with iconography, on the other hand, have had to base their interpretations much more securely on evidence drawn from the Middle Ages. The concern of this essay is to suggest ways in which the conventional terminology of stylistic analysis might be replaced by an approach which is more closely related to medieval modes of thought. The basis of this approach is that as the design of all these Early Gothic monuments was based on a series of choices, our enquiries should be focused on trying to establish why one form (or a particular combination of forms) was preferred over another.

The reference to choice begs obvious questions as to who was responsible for making that choice and what evidence can be used to elucidate the roles of those most concerned: the patrons and the craftsmen. Documentary sources by their very nature are not concerned with the intentions of craftsmen, and while they may give some indication of the general aspirations of patrons they are rarely informative about more specific intentions. With the traditional reliance on the evidence of documentary and textual sources being increasingly questioned, particularly in the interpretation of pictorial images, greater emphasis has to be placed on the evidence to be derived from the works themselves. Such emphasis in turn concentrates attention more forcefully on the methodology of interpretation and on the ways in which we focus our enquiry. In relation to Gothic architecture, it has become increasingly evident that our historical understanding is hampered by the conventional specialization of historians on one particular aspect of complex monuments such as cathedrals, as Willibald Sauerländer and Kathryn Brush demonstrate so lucidly in this volume. The challenge facing the architectural historian is to try to avoid the distorting effects of this specialization and to understand the monument as a whole in its historical context, seeking an interpretation which is related closely to concepts and modes of thought current at the time of its conception.

This study focuses on the late twelfth-century cathedral of Wells (fig. 1) and attempts to suggest possible ways in which the design and the image of this building were defined. Following an analysis of the main features of the design, the circumstances in which the building was undertaken are examined, particularly in relation to the contemporaneous rebuilding of the nearby Benedictine abbey of Glastonbury. An important advantage in studying Wells is that the twelfth-century church has survived largely intact with remarkably few alterations. Even the extension and remodelling of the east end in the fourteenth century preserved much of the twelfth-century structure, although the layout of the original east end remains conjectural.[1] The only appreciable change to the architecture of the nave and transepts has been the insertion of tracery in all the windows in the early fifteenth century. This has had little effect on the architecture, but it has resulted in the destruction of all evidence concerning the original glazing of the church. The two western towers were laid out as part of the original design, but, when the west front was built in the second quarter of the thirteenth century, a different architectural vocabulary was employed. The possible significance of this will be addressed later.

In the literature on medieval architecture the late twelfth-century work at Wells has long been classified as a significant monument in the transition from Romanesque to Gothic, and although there has been widespread agreement among historians in their estimation of the clarity and consistency of the design, there has been considerable controversy about the stylistic category in which Wells should be placed. Arguably Gothic, in the traditional sense, is the consistent use of the pointed arch and quadripartite rib-vault throughout and the complex linearity of the piers and arcades, but the thick-wall construction, with its clerestory passage and pilaster buttresses, has been seen as firmly rooted in the Anglo-Norman tradition. These problems of interpretation are highlighted when placed alongside the comparable difficulties experienced in the critical evaluation of the architectural quality of the Vetusta Ecclesia or Lady chapel at Glastonbury (figs. 2 and 3). There are good grounds for considering these two buildings together: they are only ten kilometres apart; they were under construction at the same time; they share the same regional tradition, even to the extent of being built of limestone from the same quarries; and almost certainly some of the masons worked on both sites.[2] The rebuilding of Glastonbury is reasonably securely dated to the years immediately following the devastating fire of 1184, but at Wells the surviving evidence does not allow the starting date to be established with such certainty, so the precise chronological relationship between the two buildings has been open to question.

Given that the two buildings are so closely associated in some respects and yet so obviously different in others, the critical assessments that have been made of them are particularly revealing of the tacit assumptions which underlie these evaluations and of the serious limitations of traditional stylistic categories for an understanding of these buildings within their historical context. For Francis Bond, writing in 1906, Glastonbury was clearly a Transitional building, but he saw Wells, which he dated ca. 1170, as "the first important English church ever built in the Gothic style."[3] John Bilson rejected this early dating and despite the strong indications of a starting date before 1186, argued from the documents by Armitage Robinson, he preferred a date of ca. 1190 because he considered Wells to be stylistically more advanced than Glastonbury, which to him still showed clear signs of Romanesque, especially in the ornament.[4] Bilson's conclusions were based on a very detailed comparison of the two buildings which revealed a number of close correspondences. He saw both buildings as the culminating achievement of the local western manner which had been "continuously influenced by the much more advanced schools of the Ile-de-France." Tom Boase, too, detected "traces of the Romanesque idiom" at Glastonbury, but of Wells, for which he dated the start of work between 1184 and 1191, he said that "from the first its builders used the Gothic style with an ease and fluency not yet seen in England."[5] More recently, Jean Bony placed Wells, for which he asserted a starting date of 1189, alongside Lincoln as one of the key monuments in the formation of the "English styles of Gothic." At the same time he revised radically the traditional assessment of Glastonbury by emphasizing the progressive elements in its design. He suggested that the crocket capitals showed the influence of Canterbury and he noted the strong French influence in the mouldings, especially in the use of stilted wall ribs of a more up-to-date form than is to be found at Canterbury.[6] To these fashionable features one could also add the lavish use of dark shafts *en délit* (now lost) for the internal and external arcading.

The later date for Wells, which was based primarily on stylistic comparison with Glastonbury, could no longer be maintained following Linzee Colchester's identification of one of the witnesses to a crucial charter at Wells, which enabled him to establish that work on the cathedral was under way by 1186. Further archaeological evidence, in the form of a change in the stone employed in the transepts, strongly suggested that work had begun at the east end by ca. 1180, if not earlier. The chronological relationship between the two monuments was now reversed, but this only served to provoke a tenacious and determined effort to maintain the traditional stylistic assessment by arguing that the revolutionary design of Wells should be attributed to a brilliant young man, while the transitional character of Glastonbury must be the work of a conservative older man.[7] This position is taken to even greater extremes in a recent monograph on Wells in which John Harvey asserts that Wells was not only the culmination of the West Country school, showing no sign of influence from contemporary France or from Canterbury, but that it was "the first building in the world, not merely in Britain, to proclaim the emancipation of the new Gothic style. The runners-up, the cathedrals at Bourges and Lincoln, were both begun in 1192, more than five years after Wells at the most modest computation."[8] This markedly nationalistic outlook, together with the somewhat idiosyncratic definition of Gothic, serve to emphasize the point that all these assessments tell us much more about the interests of the authors than about the buildings themselves.

Interesting though these assessments may be from an historiographical point of view, they all resolutely avoid questions which are crucial to our understanding of these buildings. By what standards would they have been judged in the twelfth and early thirteenth centuries? Which aspects of the design or which architectural features would contemporaries have considered to be the most significant in establishing the essential character of the building? I use the term "character" rather than "style" because, instead of seeking to place buildings within arbitrary stylistic categories such as Romanesque or Gothic, which would have had no meaning for the twelfth century, I would prefer to see attention focused on determining the character or manner of building. An approach on these lines seems to me to accord better with such evidence as there is of the medieval perception of architecture.

For the most part the kind of adjectives that are employed in the Middle Ages to describe buildings – *ornatus, nitidus, splendens, sumptuosus* – though unspecific are suggestive of the qualities that were identified for admiration,[9] or, on occasions, for condemnation. Relevant in this connection are the attempts by the Cistercians to establish a recognizably austere or chaste manner of building even though the architectural vocabulary of their churches varied considerably in different parts of Europe. The evidence of the intentions of the order rests mainly in the architecture itself because the legislation was not prescriptive but retrospective, aimed at rectifying abuses after they had occurred, and the degree of decoration or the use of certain features, such as towers, could be seen to be incompatible with the spirit of the order.[10] The Cistercian acceptance of the diversity of local building traditions, while aiming for a common manner of building, is a helpful model to bear in mind when analysing the respective roles of patron and mason in the process of design of other buildings. Regional architectural forms, provided by the mason, could be selected or modified to accord with the expressed taste of the patron. That it was possible for an interested non-professional observer to be aware of the role of individual architectural features in the creation of the overall character of the building is evidenced by the well-known attempt by Gervase, a monk at Canterbury, to explain the novelties of the new work in comparison with Conrad's Glorious Choir.[11] Unfortunately, no other such document has survived, so for Wells and Glastonbury, as for most other buildings, we have to rely on the evidence of the buildings themselves.

It is the approach to the interpretation of this evidence which is at the heart of this enquiry. Reference has already been made to the dangers of foisting onto the builders of these monuments the preoccupations and constructs of the twentieth century. Here I would like to stress the importance of placing due emphasis on the interests of the patrons by looking carefully into the historical context in which the building was produced and in which the design was defined in relation to other buildings. These exemplars may be contemporary buildings in the same region or famous monuments at some geographical distance, or even from a historic past. The nature of such emulation or rivalry will vary, and recognition of such resonances is not always easy. The mason will usually work with the local or regional architectural vocabulary, but too often regional schools or styles are defined almost exclusively in terms of the identification of common features, and too little attention is given to the overall effect of the use of those features in each building.[12] Very different effects can be obtained by employing similar features in different ways and in varying combinations. The late twelfth-century works at Wells and Glastonbury provide good examples of this in that they have a number of features in common, even though the overall effect of the two buildings is completely different. This difference is most plausibly explained as the result of conscious rivalry. To understand this rivalry we need to consider the specific historical circumstances in which the building of the church at Wells was undertaken and of its competition during the twelfth century with the Benedictine abbeys of Bath and Glastonbury for the seat of the bishopric.[13]

The initial foundation of an ordered religious life at Wells, as a community of canons, had been made under Bishop Giso (1061–1088) in the 1060s and 1070s. His successor, John of Tours, transferred the see to Bath, and the community at Wells suffered severely. The fortunes of the canons revived following the election in 1136 of Bishop Robert of Lewes, a Cluniac monk and former Prior of Winchester (an appointment he owed to Henry of Blois, who held the abbacy of Glastonbury in plurality from 1123 to 1171). Robert retained the see at Bath but refounded the community of canons at Wells under a dean, following the model of the Institution of St Osmund at Sarum Cathedral. There is no evidence, however, that Robert intended to move his see from Bath. On the other hand, in a bull of Pope Hadrian IV (1154–9) there is express mention of Bath as the only see in the diocese of Somerset, which may indicate a defensive stance being taken by the chapter there against a putative rival at Wells. The present church was started during the episcopate of Reginald (1174–91), who was, according to a thirteenth–century source, elected jointly by the two chapters of Bath and of Wells in accordance with a charter of Pope Alexander III (confirmed in 1176). The papal charter ordained that the two churches of Bath and Wells were to be equally the seat of the bishop, and that the bishop should be elected by representatives of the two chapters. It must be acknowledged, however, that serious doubt has been cast on the authenticity of these charters:[14] formal recognition of the title of the see as Bath and Wells came only in the thirteenth century under Bishop Jocelin. Yet, however equivocal the textual sources may be, it is hard to escape the conclusion that such a monumental building campaign was undertaken in anticipation of the restoration of cathedral status to the church at Wells.

In support of this interpretation may be cited the evidence of the promotion at this same period of the Saxon history of the see of Wells. This effort to preserve and promote a past tradition involved, as Fernie and Clark demonstrate for Saint-Denis, the incorporation of extant elements of previous buildings on the site and the revival of earlier design motifs.[15] At Wells the new church was being built on a new site just to the north of the Anglo-Saxon church, but in 1196 it was decided to preserve the eastern chapel of the earlier church, even though it was way out of alignment with the new building. This became the Lady chapel *iuxta claustrum* to differentiate it from the Lady chapel at the east end of the new church. It is also possible that the original font was preserved and moved into the new church, for the present font may well be the Anglo-Saxon font remodelled. The clearest manifestation of this interest was the commissioning of a series of effigies of the Saxon bishops to surround the choir of the new church. On stylistic grounds the effigies would seem to date from the 1190s or ca. 1200 and it must have been in this decade that the remains of the Saxon bishops were being exhumed as the old church was being demolished.[16] It was, surely, more than coincidence that Wells should have shown such obvious interest in its Anglo-Saxon past in the years so closely following the discovery at Glastonbury of Saint Dunstan's relics in 1184 and the tomb of King Arthur and his queen in 1192. This circumstantial evidence becomes more convincing when it is remembered that it was at about this time, too, that the Historiola was compiled in which was recounted the earlier history of the see of Wells, including its legendary foundation by King Ine. This again suggests a conscious attempt to emulate the history of Glastonbury since that religious community was also reputedly founded by King Ine.[17]

The decision by Bishop Robert to take Osmund's constitution for the cathedral of Old Sarum as the model for the canons at Wells, however auspicious for the later history, cannot be taken as a certain indication of the aspirations of the Wells chapter. The Sarum constitution and customs may have been chosen as the most orderly and systematic available and not necessarily because Sarum was a cathedral.[18] Liturgical usage, as discussed by Klukas and Reynolds, was an important factor in the conception of church architecture and it is clear that significant aspects of the plan of Wells, for example, the rectilinear east end, the unusual double-aisled transepts, and the two-towered west front, were modelled on Bishop Roger's enlargement of Old Sarum. Certainly, the plan of Wells was admirably suited to accommodate the Sarum customs;[19] all the chapels were correctly oriented and easily accessible and the religious observance of the canons was carefully protected from disturbance by screening off the eastern part of the church on the west side of the transept. This was necessary because, up to the late thirteenth century, the north transept served as the chapter house; its western aisle housed a library, while the western aisle of the south transept allowed access to the cloister for processions, which re-entered the church either through the richly decorated door in the southwest tower or, by way of the lay cemetery, through the west front. The church at Wells is undoubtedly on the requisite scale for a cathedral, and the recognizably impressive features in the plan would be entirely appropriate to pretensions to cathedral status.

In this respect the architecture of Wells provides valid evidence of the aspirations of the chapter and these should be seen in the context of other rivalries for the seat of the bishop between secular and monastic chapters.[20] Bishop Reginald had tried to establish his jurisdiction over Glastonbury and the active support by the canons of Wells for Bishop Savaric in his forcible attempt to establish his seat at Glastonbury in the 1190s might be explained as being seen as the most effective way to curb the independence of this powerful Benedictine neighbour.[21] It is a reasonable assumption that this political rivalry between the chapters of Glastonbury and Wells would be reflected in the architecture. Could it not be that, in pursuance of their historical claim to have the seat of the bishop in Wells, the chapter there sought a design for their new building that would be appropriate to a cathedral church as well as being distinctive and obviously different from the rival Benedictine houses of Bath and Glastonbury? At the time work began at Wells, ca. 1180, the architectural design would have been responding to the abbey at Glastonbury as it existed before the fire, especially the buildings that had been completed by Henry of Blois. Following this same idea, the exceptionally lavish and highly fashionable architectural vocabulary of the Lady chapel of Glastonbury, as it was rebuilt after 1184, could be seen as a conscious restoration of the splendor of the destroyed buildings and as a reflection of the desire of the Glastonbury monks to re-establish their position vis-à-vis the new building under construction for the assertive chapter at Wells. The undoubted similarities between the two buildings noted by Bilson are confined mainly to details: the visual effect of the two buildings is quite distinct. It is not unreasonable, it seems to me, to assume a critical awareness of such visual effects on the part of masons and leading ecclesiastics, without having to postulate that they had a concept of style as we understand it.

The question that needs to be addressed here is which aspects of the two buildings would have seemed of particular significance in the late twelfth century. In order to attempt to answer this, it is essential to keep in mind the architectural qualities in relation to the particular requirements that each building was designed to fulfil. Glastonbury was among the largest and wealthiest Benedictine abbeys, and in the rebuilding after the fire there would be a need to reflect the illustrious history of the monastery, especially to restore the richly decorative character of the buildings constructed under Henry of Blois. The church at Wells, on the other hand, was built in conscious rivalry with Glastonbury by an aspiring community of secular canons. A comparison of the architectural and decorative vocabulary employed in these two buildings will help us to identify those elements that were of particular importance in determining the overall character of each building.

The lavish decoration of the Vetusta Ecclesia at Glastonbury – the show-piece of the monastery – reflected the importance of this venerable site. The main impression would have been created by the extensive arcading which dominates the exterior as well as the interior walls (fig. 4). The use of intersecting arcading increases the richness of effect, with the soffits ornamented with bold chevron and the sumptuous effect enhanced with shafts of polished blue lias to simulate marble. Externally, even tighter intersecting arcading completes the upper part of the four corner turrets. Complex and deeply cut chevron ornament decorates both sides of the window heads, and the vault ribs. In this connection it is significant that chevron is a notable part of the ornament of the exquisite blue lias capitals from the cloister built during the abbacy of Henry of Blois.[22] The concentration on surface enrichment in the interior is very striking and was originally emphasized by painted decoration as well, clear traces of which survive. It may be assumed too that the ensemble was completed by historiated glass windows. The north and south doors of the Lady chapel would have been among the most elaborately sculptured doorways in England, with four orders of enriched carving embracing the jambs as well as the arch.[23] In the main church, although there are many architectural and sculptural details which are almost identical to comparable features at Wells, the use of the monumental giant order (fig. 5) would have provided a very different overall impression to the compact sturdiness of the Wells elevation. The main arches are pointed and are often enriched, unlike those at Wells, with at least one order of chevron, but the *triforium* retains round-headed arches with trefoil cusping, foliate sculpture in the spandrels, and fashionable crocket capitals on detached shafts.

In marked contrast, in the new building for the community of canons at Wells, detached shafting in freestone or marble is conspicuously absent, as is any form of chevron or surface embellishment of mouldings. The elaboration of architectural features has been confined to the lower parts of the building, to the arcade piers and mouldings and to the capitals, but even at this level there is a conspicuous absence of arcading in the aisles. The multiplicity of the arcade mouldings is retained in the middle storey, although the mouldings are now continuous and without capitals. There is an obvious contrast here between the intersecting arcading of Glastonbury, which in a sense denies its architectural quality in favour of textural richness, and the continuous rows of arches in the Wells *triforium*, where each arch retains its separate architectural identity and sculpture is tightly contained within this architectural framework. In the eastern parts of the church, sculpture is confined to capitals and to the corbels of the vaulting shafts, whereas in the nave the *triforium* has head stops for the hood moulds, foliated *tympana* for the subarches, and foliate *paterae* in the spandrels. Figure sculpture in the capitals of the main arcade begins on the west side of the south transept and continues through the nave. The possible significance of the occurrence of the figure sculpture is difficult to assess as it does not coincide with the liturgical division of the church: the screens dividing nave and choir were aligned with the west wall of the transepts. In this case it may be explained as the result of the tendency towards greater elaboration as the building progressed, which is also evident here in the addition of fillets to the mouldings in the western part of the nave. This common tendency towards greater elaboration may complicate the kind of analysis that we are attempting in that we have to assess whether the changes were envisaged as part of the original design or whether they represent a significant modification of that design. Given that the main elements of the architectural design at Wells remain remarkably consistent throughout the building, I do not see any reason to attach particular importance to these changes in details.

In the upper parts of the elevation, the clerestory and the vault, a markedly less enriched, almost chaste, character is evident: the clerestory windows have plain chamfers, and the vault ribs have simple mouldings with bosses only at the intersection of the diagonal ribs. No trace of the original twelfth-century glass has been found, but it is perhaps reasonable to assume that, like at Salisbury in the thirteenth century, much of the glass was grisaille, with any historiated glass confined to the east end and to windows above altars. Externally, Wells has very simple articulation with horizontal string courses, simple hood moulds, and plain chamfered surrounds to the windows (fig. 6), whereas at Glastonbury the heads of the very similar form of windows are enriched with chevron ornament (fig. 2). Apart from the west front, the only enrichment with arcading on the exterior of Wells occurs on the north transept façade. Even here all the arches have continuous mouldings and no capitals, but the contrast with the simplicity of the south transept suggests that a slightly enriched vocabulary was employed on the more visible, "public" north facade.

The clarity and consistency of the late twelfth-century and early thirteenth-century work is highlighted by what seems to us the very abrupt change in the manner of building introduced with the west front (fig. 7). In fact, it is in the north porch and on the processional doors from the cloister into the church that we find the first indications of this new vocabulary: the use of shafts *en délit*, foliate ornament, and a marked spatial emphasis in the enriched intersecting arcading (fig. 8). Although underlying these new features there is much that shows continuity with the earlier work, especially in the use of continuous mouldings and the very simple quadripartite vault of the north porch, it is important to recognize the distinctive vocabulary which has been applied to the entrances to the church. Some of the simpler, original mouldings are found on the west front alongside the new vocabulary, but there the spatial, skeletal effect was pursued much further, most obviously in the prominent "marble" shafting, in the canopied niches, and in the towers which were originally open prior to the fifteenth-century infilling.

To us the present west front may seem an uneasy conjunction of elements with massive projecting towers overlaid by a gigantic screen whose architectural vocabulary would seem to represent the supplanting of the earlier local manner by a new mason bringing a fashionable and up-to-date vocabulary stemming ultimately from Canterbury. There is every indication that this is a new vocabulary and that it must therefore represent a change to the original design. But does it follow that this change would necessarily have disrupted the coherence of the monument as perceived in the thirteenth century? Could it be that by their very nature the entrances to the church and the screen-like west front were felt to require a different vocabulary: one appropriate to their function? Might not the obvious contrast with the previous simplicity be intentional?

Such questions need to be posed in order to challenge traditional assumptions that a change in "style" necessarily implies chronological sequence. It may do so, of course, and the addition of the Nine Altars at Fountains Abbey would seem to be an obvious instance of the importation of the grand new cathedral vocabulary which marks the end of any attempt to maintain a sense of restraint and austerity. But how are we to judge the juxtaposition of the elaborately moulded and sculptured doorway of the Temple Church in London with the seemingly quite different qualities of the nave (figs. 9 and 10)? Here there is no reason to suppose any difference in date, so it is reasonable to assume that they were planned together as part of the same design, employing what seemed to be the most appropriate vocabulary for each part of the building. It is in these terms that we should be trying to assess medieval buildings, to step back from the traditional stylistic constructs, to be less rigid in specifying what constitutes unity of style, and to be prepared to accept that recognizable diversity of forms might be intentional. We should be prepared to allow that certain architectural features – pointed as opposed to round arches, or a certain repertoire of moulding profiles and ornament – could have had connotations and typological associations in the same way as is accepted for the overall form of a building.

In context, the particular qualities of the design of Wells can be interpreted in a very positive light as being consciously defined against the contemporary work of the great rival Benedictine abbey of Glastonbury. Compared with the customary ostentation of the Benedictines, the clarity and regularity of Wells might well have been seen as more appropriate to the ordered religious life and liturgical customs of a regulated community of canons, while at the same time including the features requisite for a church of cathedral status.[24] This interpretation of the nature and character of the twelfth-century work at Wells is that it provided the canons with a distinctive building, within the traditions prevailing in the West Country, admirably suited to its liturgical functions, and of striking visual effect: an effect which in many ways seems to have been consciously preserved though the later Middle Ages.[25]

A further question remains within the context of the present discussion: to what extent should the character of the building – resulting from the particular combination of features in the architecture, the sculpture, and the presumed grisaille glass – be described as "artistic integration"? The doubt arises from the dangers that the use of such a term may give too much emphasis to the connotations of the creative act of an artist or artists and that it may imply "a belief that an image or a building must possess a unity of style and that it is the art historian's condemned duty to recognize this unity."[26] Integration should not be interpreted as a synonym for unity of style.

The overall effect of a building is made up of the particular combination of architectural features, but we need to do more than to chart the derivations and affiliations of the individual elements of the architectural vocabulary. We must also seek to elucidate their connotations and associations and to explore the ways in which they might have been employed with a conscious sense of decorum to serve the ambitions and expectations of the patrons. We can never reconstruct the process by which any particular design was arrived at, nor the relative contribution to it of the patron and mason, but we can seek within the historical context of a commission to identify the factors that might have influenced the choice of specific features in order to create a particular kind of overall effect. Such a sense of decorum is well attested in many different aspects of medieval culture, and it does provide a flexible model within which the interactive roles of patron and mason can be understood. A study of the detailed elements of the building will tell us much about the training and experience of the mason but such details are unlikely to have been of interest to the patron except in so far as they contributed to the overall character of the building.[27] The primary concern of the patrons would have been that the selection of the architectural vocabulary should be appropriate to the building and that it should be employed in a manner which matched their aspirations.

NOTES

1 From archaeological evidence it can be shown that there was an eastern aisle, and it is known from documentary evidence that there was an eastern Lady chapel, at least from the thirteenth century and so, in all probability, from the beginning. The precise form of the chapel cannot be established without further archaeological excavation, but it is usually and plausibly shown as a two-bay rectangular extension. See C.M. Church, *Early History of the Church of Wells* (London, 1894); John Bilson, "Notes on the Earlier Architectural History of Wells Cathedral," *Archaeological Journal* 85 (1928), 23–68, plan on p. 27; Peter Draper, "The Sequence and Dating of the Decorated Work at Wells," *Art and Architecture at Wells and Glastonbury*, British Archaeological Association Conference Transactions (1981), p. 20; John Harvey, "The Building of Wells Cathedral, I: 1175–1307," in *Wells Cathedral: A History*, ed. L.S. Colchester (Wells, 1982), pp. 59–60.

2 Bilson, "Notes on the Earlier Architectural History," note 2.

3 Francis Bond, *Gothic Architecture in England* (London, 1906), p. 105.

4 J. Armitage-Robinson, "Documentary Evidence Relating to the Building of the Cathedral Church of Wells," *Archaeological Journal* 85 (1928), 1–22; Bilson, "Notes on the Earlier Architectural History," pp. 25 and 36–7.

5 T.S.R. Boase, *English Art 1100–1216* (Oxford, 1953), p. 62.

6 Jean Bony, "French Influences on the Origins of Gothic Architecture in England," *Journal of the Warburg and Courtauld Institutes* 12 (1949), 12–13.

7 L. S. Colchester and John Harvey, "Wells Cathedral," *Archaeological Journal* 131 (1974), 200–3.

8 John Harvey, "The Building of Wells Cathedral, I," pp. 53–5.

9 As for example in the *Metrical Life of St. Hugh*, lines 890–6, "Mille collumnellas ibi; quae rigidae, pretiosae / Fulgentes, opus ecclesiae totale rigore / Perpetuant, pretio ditant, fulgore serenant. / Ipsarum siquidem status est procerus et altus / Cultus sincerus et splendius, ordo venustus / Et geometricus, decor aptus et utilis, usus / Gratus et eximius, rigor inconsumptus et acer": J.F. Dimock, *The Metrical Life of St Hugh of Lincoln* (Lincoln, 1860).

10 All the Cistercian statutes concerned with artistic matters are now conveniently collected in Christopher Norton and David Park, ed., *Cistercian Art and Architecture in the British Isles* (Cambridge, 1986), pp. 315–93.

11 For an evaluation of the architectural writings of Gervase, see Paul Frankl, *The Gothic: Literary Sources and Interpretations through Eight Centuries* (Princeton, 1960), pp. 24–35.

12 For relevant examples of this approach, see Harold Brakspear, "A West Country School of Masons," *Archaeologia* 81 (1931), 1–18; Christopher Wilson, "The Sources of the Late Twelfth-Century Work at Worcester Cathedral," in *Medieval Art and Architecture at Worcester Cathedral*, British Archaeological Association Conference Transactions (1978), pp. 80–90.

13 C.M. Church, *Chapters in the Early History of the Church of Wells* (London, 1894). The most recent account is by Antonia Gransden, "The History of Wells Cathedral c. 1090–1547," in *Wells Cathedral: A History*, ed. L.S. Colchester, pp. 24–35.

14 Gransden, "History," pp. 33–5. If fabricated at a later date, the fabrication would indicate an attempt to antedate the aspirations of the Wells chapter.

15 Recently, Peter Kidson has argued persuasively for a comparable influence of many aspects of Old Sarum on the design of the new cathedral of Salisbury. Thomas Cocke and Peter Kidson, *Salisbury Cathedral: Perspectives on the Architectural History* (London, 1993), esp. pp. 52–6.

16 Warwick Rodwell, "The Anglo-Saxon and Norman Churches at Wells," in *Wells Cathedral: A History*, ed. L.S. Colchester, pp. 17–21; Pamela Tudor-Craig, "Wells Sculpture," in ibid., pp. 102–5, suggests a date of ca. 1200 for all but two of the effigies. I would favour this date in preference to the slightly later date suggested by Gransden, in "History," p. 33.

17 Gransden, in "History," pp. 33–4, argues that the promotion of cathedral status for Wells did not take place until the early thirteenth century under Bishop Jocelin. This view does not take sufficient account of the evidence of the building itself. For a fuller discussion of the evaluation of the building itself as primary evidence, see Madeline Caviness, "Saint-Yved of Braine: The Primary Sources for Dating the Gothic Church," *Speculum* 59 (1984), 524–58.

18 Unfortunately, so little survives of the twelfth-century abbey of Bath that it cannot be included in this discussion.

19 Arnold Klukas, "The *Liber Ruber* and the Rebuilding of the East End of Wells," *Medieval Art and Architecture at Wells and Glastonbury*, British Archaeological Association Conference Transactions (1981), pp. 30–1.

20 For the background to the pressure to have bishops associated with chapters of canons rather than monks, see Dom David Knowles, *The Monastic Orders in England 940–1216*, 2d ed. (Cambridge, 1963), pp. 619–31. The contemporary litigious rivalry between the canons of Lichfield and the Benedictine chapter of Coventry provides an instructive parallel to the case argued here for Wells.

21 Gransden, "History," pp. 25–31.

22 Fragments are preserved in the Glastonbury museum. See George Zar-

necki in *English Romanesque Art 1066–1200*, [exh. cat., Hayward Gallery] (London, 1984), nos. 149a–g.

23 I see no reason to doubt that the carving of these doors is contemporaneous with the construction of the chapel, and I agree with the dating proposed by Deborah Kahn, in *Bulletin monumental* 146 (1988), 330. Previous attempts to date them on stylistic grounds have resulted in dates of ca. 1210 by George Zarnecki, *Later English Romanesque Sculpture 1140–1210* (London, 1953), pp. 50 and 63, and even of ca. 1220–30 by Paul Williamson, in *The Age of Chivalry: Art in Plantagenet England 1200–1400* [exh. cat., Royal Academy], ed. Jonathan Alexander and Paul Binski (London, 1987), p. 99.

24 I have argued elsewhere for a comparable interpretation of the thirteenth-century cathedral of Salisbury. See "Architecture and Liturgy" in *The Age of Chivalry*, ed. J. Alexander and P. Binski, pp. 83–91.

25 It is remarkable how sympathetically the fourteenth-century additions seem to be designed in relation to the twelfth-century work (e.g., the strainer arches in the crossing, the remodelling of the choir, and the heightening of the towers), and although an interpretation on these lines is admittedly more subjective in approach, this is not an isolated example of such conformity, and further study might give some indication of later medieval perceptions of the qualities of the work of earlier periods.

26 Willibald Sauerländer, "Style or Transition? The Fallacies of Classification in the Light of German Architecture 1190–1260," *Architectural History* 30 (1987), 12.

27 See for example the quotation from the *Metrical Life of St Hugh* in note 9 above.

9

Chartres Cathedral as a Work of Artistic Integration: Methodological Reflections

Peter Kurmann and Brigitte Kurmann-Schwarz

This essay explores the issue of "artistic integration" at Chartres, a cathedral traditionally praised for its visual coherence, by attempting to integrate both art-historical and historical methods and evidence. Pointing first to the paucity of documents chronicling the construction of the cathedral, the authors, like Draper, Raguin, and Brenk, emphasize the importance of consulting the fabric itself in order to determine whether or not the architecture, stained glass, and sculpture cohered to one unified plan from the outset. Like Reynolds and Klukas, they evaluate particular formal and iconographic features of the building and its decoration in relation to liturgical usage and conditions of the patronage. The authors note that, although there were definite points of formal and iconographic contact between the architecture, stained glass, and sculpture, it appears that these three media developed largely independently as the campaign progressed. It seems, for instance, that although a rough programmatic scheme for the stained glass existed from the beginning, the specifics of the iconography and placement of the windows responded in somewhat haphazard fashion to the exigencies of the moment. Sauerländer addresses this same issue in his discussion of the introduction of the cult of Saint Anne at Chartres. Kurmann and Kurmann-Schwarz emphasize that the iconography of glass reflected the wishes of the individual patrons, which included royalty, the canons, and a variety of nobles, as well as guilds, rather than to a preconceived integration with the architecture and sculpture.

In the second part of the essay, like Bedos-Rezak and Abou-El-Haj, the authors place their assessment of the fabric in relation to the local economic and historical context of Chartres. With fresh insights, Kurmann and Kur-

mann-Schwarz draw on recently published historical studies of Chartres to show that the local historical constellation was less politically, socially, and economically unified than earlier art-historical studies have projected. First, rather than viewing the cathedral as a microcosm of the entire community, the authors stress that the principal financier of the cathedral was the chapter which was in frequent conflict with local secular authorities. Indeed, historical documents indicate that the donations of other groups (such as the nobility or guilds) were relatively insignificant in comparison. Furthermore, while the chapter's finances were in relatively good shape during the late twelfth and early thirteenth centuries, the economy of the town was underdeveloped and the pilgrimage to Chartres was not attracting large crowds. In addition to serving its primary religious function, then, the cathedral might be regarded as a self-conscious expression of capitular concerns. Following their assessment of the artistic and historical aspects of the building campaign at Chartres, Kurmann and Kurmann-Schwarz conclude that an "integrated" view of the broader context points to a number of disjunctures in the general perception of Chartres cathedral as an integrated structure.

Note: Numbers for the windows are given first in the Corpus Vitrearum system and second in the system used by Delaporte.

Perhaps more than any other medieval monument, Chartres cathedral (fig. 1) invites investigation as an integrated undertaking. Good fortune has preserved in large part the sculptural decoration, stained glass, and architectural polychromy of the interior.[1] Despite the monumental scale of the episcopal church, the period of construction was remarkably short and the few documents that have survived from this period allow us to establish both beginning and completion dates for this *Gesamtkunstwerk*.[2] We know that in 1194 a fire destroyed the earlier church.[3] A document contained in the cartulary of the chapter indicates that the canons occupied the choir-stalls in 1221 in a specific hierarchical seating arrangement.[4] The entire building must have been essentially complete for the dedication ceremony of 1260.[5]

Before beginning an integrative analysis of this monument we believe to have been planned and constructed through interactive building strategies, we need to define our methodology concerning "artistic integration." The first phase of inquiry must involve an examination of the physical evidence of the monument itself – that is, the architecture, stained glass, and sculpture – first as separate entities and then as a collective whole. A more interdisciplinary inquiry comes on a second level. Here we investigate the historical period in which the monument was produced as well as its relationship to other artistic developments of its era. The tools we use include the study of written sources, evidence drawn from archaeology, and stylistic analysis of the character of the building. Once these substrata are established, we turn to a third level of broader and more theoretical historical inquiry. This third stage is predicated on the belief that the issue of historical context has two sides. On one hand, the work of art was produced in response to specific historical circumstances. Yet, on the other hand – and this is particularly operative for so massive and complex a work as Chartres – the monument itself "provoked" history in that it compelled the viewer to adopt a specific interpretative stance vis-à-vis these historical circumstances.

The visual unity of the physical structure of Chartres argues that the builders adhered to a single basic plan that was probably developed just after the fire of 1194. It is hardly thinkable for practical reasons that the cathedral chapter would embark on such an enormous undertaking without a precise proposal for the form and dimensions of the building. In contrast to some scholars, who posit an initial, but later discarded, plan for a totally new building,[6] we would argue that the twelfth-century west façade and the crypt, with its Romanesque and pre-Romanesque fabric, were intended to be incorporated into the new building from the very outset. Probably, too, the designer or designers planned a transept having façades with three portals and porches as early as 1194. Unlike the pre-existent supports for nave and choir, entirely new foundations had to be laid for the projections of the transept arms. Changes in design do appear, but only later, during the construction of the southern transept in the 1230s (fig. 3) and with increasing frequency during the erection of the north transept façade and the buttressing of the choir (fig. 4).[7] These progressive tendencies are confined to the decorative, not structural elements of the architecture. They reflect the architectural changes in the region of the Ile-de-France where a shift to a style we have come to define as *rayonnant*, as opposed to High Gothic, occurred in the early 1230s. The impact of these new developments soon appeared at other major building sites across Europe.

We now turn our attention to the painted and sculpted decoration of the cathedral, beginning with the justly renowned stained glass.[8] The large size of the windows, particularly in the clerestory, made swift glazing necessary, for otherwise the building was open to the vagaries of wind and weather.[9] Clearly, the task of glazing 173 windows at Chartres far exceeded the capabilities of a single local workshop.[10] The procurement of such large quantities of coloured glass and lead, as well as the complexity of the cutting, painting, firing, and assembling of windows, demanded considerable advance planning.[11] It is reasonable to assume, then, that production of stained-glass windows was under way and that the sequence of glazing had been determined as soon as construction began. At the same time, efforts would have been made to solicit donations which would ensure the financing of the panels.[12] It is most reasonable to conclude from such observations that masons and glass painters worked quite literally hand in hand.[13]

As a rule, multiscened legendary windows (fig. 6) were mounted in the openings of the ground floor, while monumental figural compositions were placed in the lights of the clerestory (figs. 7 and 10). This suggests that the planners had a relatively precise mental image of the glazing of the cathedral, at least in terms of its formal character, when work on the project commenced. A general idea of the iconographic program must also have been projected in 1194. Programs that complement and amplify each other appear in the clerestory windows of the choir and in the north, west, and south façade openings.[14] At first glance, the legendary windows of the ground floor present less coherently organized themes. In the three major chapels of the ambulatory, the subjects of the windows follow the altar dedications, to the martyrs (north), the apostles (east), and the confessors (south).[15] The Confessors chapel, however, not only contains windows of the confessors Remigius [12/28] and Nicholas [10 & 14/29 & 27], but also the martyrs Thomas Becket [18/25] and Catherine and Margaret [16/36] (fig. 2).[16] We may conclude in this case that the iconography of the stained glass responded to both the requirements of the liturgy and the wishes of the patrons. Marguerite de Lèves donated the window depicting Margaret and Catherine with the common desire to see the scenes of her patron saint included in the program.[17]

Other windows were also determined by altar dedications. Evidence for this practice is not always available from the windows now in situ, but the practice is documentable through written texts that may be compared with what now remains of the original program. We find still extant, however, the window of Saint Julian the Hospitator [21/45] in the central bay of the northern ambulatory chapel dedicated to this saint (fig. 2).[18] The adjacent chapel to the west, now provided with predominantly non-figural grisaille glass produced in the years around 1260,[19] contains an image of the martyrdom of Saint Lawrence in the right lancet [25/47] (fig. 5). The image is a reminder of the former dedication of the chapel's altar to Saint Lawrence.[20] An early eighteenth-century text records the existence of now lost windows depicting the legend of Saint Lawrence in the west wall of the north transept [33/57]. In 1791 the figural panels were removed. Remaining in the window are two ranges of border designs, the outer border of figures of angels in half-circles of later date than the inner border of small palmettes typical of Early Gothic ornament. Scholars have long recognized that this window, dismantled in 1791, had already come from another site in the cathedral. This, we posit, was the opening now filled by the grisaille window with the medallion of Lawrence's martyrdom.

Further clues in this reconstruction are provided by textual sources that record the 1259 dedication of an altar honouring the Holy Angels in the north transept.[21] In that year Louis IX released the bishop of Chartres from the "droit de gîte," the often onerous obligation of providing lodging and appropriate hospitality for the king and his retinue in the episcopal palace. In return for this exemption, the bishop was to assume the costs of new altars in the north transept honouring the Virgin Mary and the Holy Angels.[22] Stylistic analysis of the figures of the angels and the Saint Lawrence medallion argue that both were designed at the same time in a coarse, rather modernized deepfold style. This style was employed at Chartres well into the late 1250s, although elsewhere the High Gothic large-fold style was generally adopted.[23] We conclude that the original window of Saint Lawrence was transferred to the south transept and provided with a border of angels in half-circles at this time. It is very possible that the reasoning for the shift of fully saturated coloured glass to the transept arm was to allow grisaille glazing that would provide more light to the north ambulatory.

Additional windows formerly in the Laurentian chapel can be identified. The Ordinary containing the ritual obligations of the canons of Chartres prescribed a procession to the altar of Saint Lawrence on the feast day of Saint Apollinaris. Delaporte admitted that the logic for seeking out this altar on the feast day of the Ravennate saint seemed elusive.[24] A legendary window depicting the life of Saint

Apollinaris is now located in the south transept [36/10] (fig. 6). Like the fragments from the Saint Lawrence window discussed above, these panels give every evidence of reuse.[25] We would argue that it is most likely that the window of Saint Apollinaris was originally located in the left lancet of the chapel of Saint Lawrence, thus giving perfect sense to the thirteenth-century rubric instructing the procession to visit the altar of Saint Lawrence on Saint Apollinaris's feast. Relics, like major altar dedications very probably influenced the program of the stained glass. Often iconographic traditions will appear arbitrary until compared with specific Chartrain traditions. The window of Saint Thomas the Apostle [23/46] presents narrative irregularities that defy any known written or figurative account of the saint. The scenes showing the Incredulity of Thomas (John 20: 24–9) are emphasized in a such way that the window loses its compositional and chronological coherence. The depiction of the saint touching Christ's side is completely isolated in the lowest portion of the window.[26] The reason for such emphasis becomes apparent if we consider that the finger with which Saint Thomas touched Christ's flesh was one of the most important relics possessed by the cathedral.[27] Manhes-Deremble recently suggested a new concept of iconographic program based essentially on the principles of opposition and contiguity. In addition to the influence of important donors and the liturgy, members of the ecclesiastical herarchy determined themes that reflected current theological concerns about sin and penance, the position of the Virgin (in particular her Immaculate Conception), and eucharistic suspension.[28]

Since the constructed shell and glass sheathing of the Gothic cathedral were mutually interdependent,[29] issues of style and dating for stone and glass are equally closely connected for both media. The structure of the cathedral could be considered complete only when the stained glass was mounted, so that we can follow the chronology of the glazing by examining the sequence of the building campaigns.[30] Thus it is significant that stylistic arguments for a chronology of the panels, the majority of which occupy the original positions, accord with our reading of the building campaign. Most scholars have dated the earliest stained glass in the side aisles and clerestory of the nave to about 1200–10. Because the construction of the nave was begun shortly after 1194, at least the windows of the aisles could have been mounted about 1200. This was followed by an early phase of glazing in the ambulatory and the production of all of the panels of the clerestory of the choir (1210–20, around 1210 the glazing of the ambulatory and 1210–20 the windows of the clerestory).[31] Then a break in operations ensued.[32] After 1230, work continued, but with a marked stylistic shift, as exemplified by the work associated with the Master of Saint Chéron.[33] The ambulatory openings, which until this date must have been walled with temporary materials, were glazed during this campaign. The clerestory openings of the transept, with the exception of the two windows that were glazed earlier [128/86, 87, & 88; 115/136, 137, & 138], also received windows at this time.[34]

As in the architecture, progressive tendencies are observable in the stained glass in the years approaching 1230.[35] A particularly striking illustration of these developments can be found in the four lancets of the south transept façade (fig. 8) which contain prophets carrying the evangelists on their shoulders [122/95 A–E]. In contrast to the earlier glazing of the choir (fig. 7) that was characterized by delicate, slender proportions in the figures, the prophets show far bulkier proportions and a distinctly three-dimensional rendering of the garments. The edges of their cloaks run up and down in a zigzag pattern above the strict horizontal formed by the hem of their tunics. They retain, however, many earlier conventions of draughtsmanship. The long, triangular forms that structure the gathered cloaks are formed according to conventionalized drop-like impressions. A fine web of thin parallel lines, a characteristic of the earlier workshop habits, appear within the folds. In other words, the stained glass displays a more progressive concept of the figure but a more *retardataire* decorative format. The architecture, as observed earlier, displays the diametric opposite. Here the structural conception of 1194 was followed, while a more progressive decorative overlay of *rayonnant* features was added to the transept façades and to the buttressing of the choir.

When we examine the portal sculpture, we are prepared to ask the same questions concerning its development: was there an initial over-riding plan, and did the construction issues determine the progress of the work? As we argued for the glazing, we are convinced that the canons must have been concerned with the decorative sculpture at the outset of the campaign and, at the very latest, the sculptural program had to be ready for mounting by the time work commenced on the transept façades. The acquisition of suitable material presented special problems in Chartres. The Berchères quarry, a site not far from Chartres,[36] used for the earlier church and for the Gothic building, provided an excellent hard building material but one wholly unsuitable for the carving of fine details.[37] Unlike the cathedral sites of the Ile-de-France, Champagne, and Picardy, no fine-grained stone was available in the near vicinity, and the twelfth-century sculpture of the Royal Portal had been carved using a fine-grained limestone from the valley of the Oise. The canons must have been aware of this situation and had already begun to organize the delivery of high-grade limestone from the Ile-de-France for the sculptural program at the time when the rebuilding of the church was agreed upon. They undoubtedly encountered problems of transport since the rivers in the region of Chartres, the Eure and the Loir, were unnavigable in the Middle Ages.[38] Stone destined for the sculpture could be transported by water only part way. Interruptions in the delivery of the material may have been one of the chief reasons for the prolongation of the carving for a period of approximately forty years.[39]

. Stylistic shifts, or as Peter Draper has phrased this issue, the elements of visual character of the building, are quite visible in these decisions. Shortly before work began on the south transept, sculptors with knowledge of the new "High Gothic" stylistic vocabulary arrived in Chartres (fig. 9).[40] It is likely that, like the stone itself, they were imports from the Ile-de-France.[41] Did the idea to incorporate newer forms of expression into the architecture depend on the building's supervisor, who summoned the young sculptors to the episcopal seat, or did the new ideas simply arrive with the sculptors? No written sources are available to answer such speculations. We would argue that the fresh outlook of the newly arrived sculptors impacted on the stained glass designers working on the windows of the ambulatory and south transept (fig. 10) shortly after 1230.[42]

Like the architecture, the portal sculptures were commissioned and planned by the chapter, and uninfluenced by the agendas of individual donors. The iconographic program, evidently drawn up by the clerics, has been treated in an exhaustive manner by Adolf Katzenellenbogen, so that we will leave this issue aside.[43] We wish, however, to emphasize an interpenetration among the media. The iconographic program of the sculpture of the three south portals repeats the subjects and placement of stained glass in the three eastern chapels of the ambulatory (fig. 2). The three portals show, from left to right, the martyrs, the apostles, and the confessors. When the visitor moves inside the cathedral and looks to the east, he or she encounters the altar of the martyrs surrounded by the legends of the martyr saints in the northern chapel of the ambulatory (left). In the axial chapel the altar and the stained glass are dedicated to the apostles. Finally, the confessors are venerated in the chapel on the south side of the choir (on the visitor's right) and some are represented in the windows. We may identify a further analogy between the portal sculpture of the south transept façade and the liturgically determined disposition of the interior furnishings and decoration. According to Roulliard, the altar of Saint Aegidius stood on the south side of the choir beside the chapel of the confessors. It is certainly not by chance that Saint Aegidius appears next to the confessors Nicholas and Martin in the upper zone of the portal of the confessors.[44]

We would like to suggest several general conclusions that may be based on this overview of the material evidence. The uniformity which distinguishes the entire monument and the speed of its construction would argue that a well-organized supervisory body must also have exercised control over the production of sculpture and stained glass. Links to the Ile-de-France must have resulted from the need to import all stone for the decorative and figure sculpture from this region. The communication among the workers in each medium permitted the sculptors' work to influence the glass painters and stone masons, who gradually incorporated more progressive stylistic concepts in their architectural work. This was done gradually, without losing the links to former stylistic expressions. Generally speaking, then, the development of style and content among the three media forming the *Gesamtkunstwerk* of the cathedral followed different routes. However, a supervisory body embracing all three media brought about contacts and mutual exchanges.

This brief overview of the iconography of the sculpture and stained glass makes evident the necessity for art history to collaborate with other disciplines, in particular liturgical studies and theology, an approach argued for with eloquence in this volume by both Bernard McGinn and Roger Reynolds. We wish, however, to examine the opportunities afforded by interdisciplinary or "integrated" study by examining the intersection of the disciplines of history and art history, a subject also undertaken by Brigitte Bedos-Rezak. Art-historical studies so frequently posit links between the monument and its historical circumstances that the ranks of documentary historians often become uneasy. The situation has been summarized by Arnold Esch in the following manner: "To suggest that art historians overlook these [historical and economic] questions is certainly untenable; the field often engages in self-reproach on just this issue. However, to look at current trends in art historical literature, one has the impression that too much has been done in this direction, at least there has been far greater integration of these disciplines into art history than art historical approaches being incorporated into other disciplines. Interdisciplinary work should not be discouraged; actually quite the opposite. There remain scholarly risks, however, for both sides of the collaboration."[45] Precision is all important. Often the art historian will strive for a synthetic overview, laudable but difficult. It is methodologically far more acceptable in current studies for historians to confine themselves to far narrower questions. A prime example is the work of the historian Chédeville, who published a chapter dealing with the relationship between the construction and decoration of Chartres cathedral and its larger historical context in his 1973 book on the history of Chartres.[46] His study was based on a very detailed investigation of local conditions and events. Chédeville's conclusions project a far less spectacular position for Chartres than, for instance, the most recent survey of Gothic architecture in France by the art historians Dieter Kimpel and Robert Suckale. These authors continue to depict the cathedral, quite inaccurately, as a collective effort of all of France under the direction of the royal house.[47] Esch's historical critique also suggests to art historians that local circumstances are usually far more significant for monumental building than far-flung general speculation.[48] According to Esch, the issue of patronage provides the most dynamic point of contact between the disciplines of history and art history.[49] Patronage, therefore, will serve as our point of departure to place the cathedral within its larger historical context.

As at most other episcopal seats, it was the cathedral chapter at Chartres which bore the financial burden of the building campaign.[50] Costs were met by the income and holdings of the fabric, which was administered by the chapter and its functionaries.[51] Unfortunately we are not informed about the size of the fabric's endowment, nor about the measures undertaken to secure the additional income needed in the course of the building campaign. Considerably more is known about the general state of the chapter's finances in the late twelfth century.[52] Secular and ecclesiastical lords began to make efforts to cultivate their lands for agricultural use in the late tenth century. This process reached its peak around the middle of the twelfth century. By 1200 it had slackened considerably; it came to a standstill around 1250.[53] With the support of the bishops, the chapter at Chartres had carried out substantial reforms in the administration of its holdings in the years between 1171 and 1193. At that time, the canons took over the administrative responsibilities from the stewards, and in so doing doubled their income.[54] Even before the fire of 1194, then, the canons were well prepared, financially speaking, for a new church.[55]

The *Miracula Beate Marie Virginis in Carnotensi ecclesia facta* claims that the canons and the bishop placed a portion of their income at the disposal of the building campaign for only three years. This three-year period cannot be considered accurate, at least not in relation to the chapter. The *Miracula* is a literary text written around 1210 to promote the pilgrimage to the Virgin at Chartres. Yet, art historians have cited this story all too frequently and uncritically as evidence for the progress of work following the destruction of the earlier church.[56] Certainly the great speed with which the church was built contradicts the notion that it was financed by voluntary donations. For at least fifty years the canons needed to transfer income to the fabric of the cathedral.[57] The contribution of the bishop to the campaign is uncertain because no written source deals with this topic, except for the *Miracula*. However, the source of the stone for the cathedral, the village of Berchères-les-Pierres, belonged to the bishop.[58] It is not known whether or not the bishop supplied the building materials without charge.

What about the generosity of the king, nobles, pilgrims, and citizens of Chartres, which has been stressed in art-historical studies of the building campaign? We know only that Philip Augustus expressly donated money to the episcopal church. In 1210 he negotiated peace between the church at Chartres and the count's vassals, who had become engaged in a bloody dispute. A stiff fine was imposed on the count's vassals. Half of this fine was to be paid to the chapter (for the construction of the cathedral?), while the other half was to go to the king and bishop. This donation of the king was a unique one and was not repeated on an annual basis, as Bulteau once claimed.[59] The king displayed his generosity more through the furnishings of the cathedral, especially the stained glass, than in the structure itself. The nobles in the vicinity of Chartres behaved in a similar fashion.[60] As for the pilgrims, their offerings have been portrayed, even recently, as one of the primary sources of income financing the new church. However, Chédeville's study shows clearly that the renown of Notre-Dame of Chartres was restrained, having far less status as a pilgrimage attraction than a site such as Mont-Saint-Michel. The Virgin of Chartres was venerated chiefly by members of the ecclesiastical and secular élite of France and by those dwelling in the region of Chartres.[61]

The role played by the citizens of Chartres is very difficult to assess. Taking the *Miracula* as their point of departure, Bulteau, von Simson, and others conveyed a harmonious picture of Chartrain society, united in its effort to reconstruct the cathedral.[62] This view is challenged in this volume by Barbara Abou-El-Haj. We know that the population was divided into two groups – namely, the vassals of the count and those of the church. Most of the city's inhabitants, except for those in the district of the cathedral, were subject to tax by the count. By promising to grant privileges to the citizens, and to craftsmen in particular, the chapter attempted repeatedly to lure these groups into the tax jurisdiction of the church. This resulted in continual struggle between ecclesiastical and secular powers, often involving bloodshed, as, for instance, during an uprising of 1210.[63] The economic status of goods produced at Chartres was far less important than believed by art historians such as Otto von Simson. Most of the wares were destined for local use. Only the cloth from Chartres was sold in foreign markets, and then only among wares of moderate quality. A money economy had hardly begun to develop for local citizens of Chartres at the beginning of the thirteenth century. Only the ecclesiastical institutions possessed considerable amounts of cash income. In view of these circumstances, it seems highly unlikely that the inhabitants of Chartres could have borne the costs of the building after the first three years largely by themselves.[64]

What, then, compelled the canons to assume the costs of a monumental building (figs. 1 and 3) and to provide it with luxurious furnishings such as the sculpture and stained glass? It seems to us that the building was intended to impress onlookers in two ways. On the one hand, the building campaign allowed the chapter to demonstrate its venerability and power. This was intended to deter anyone from attempting to trespass on the chapter's rights. On the other, the enormous and highly visible structure served as a beacon to attract people: to draw pilgrims to venerate the Virgin of Chartres, or to encourage craftsmen to place themselves under the jurisdiction of the chapter. The new cathedral must have also been intended to inject life into what had been until then a rather modest pilgrimage site.

The portal sculpture alludes indirectly to the frequent tensions between clerical and secular authorities of the region. It was not by chance that the canons emphasized the representation of *regnum* (kingship) and *sacerdotium* (priesthood) on the thirteenth-century façades. The Royal Portal had already incorporated a vision of uto-pian harmony between the two powers on the west façade.[65] On the south side of the cathedral, which originally faced towards the castle of the count,[66] the bishops stand in the tabernacles of the nave buttresses as representatives of the priesthood. The kings occupy the tabernacles between the pediments of the south porch as representatives of secular power. On the north porch, which was located across from the residence of the bishop, kings, prophets, and prefigurations of the church stand in harmony on the piers, while bishops and kings occupy the upper zone. The bishops are located in the pediments of the side portals, while the kings occupy the niches above the piers.[67] From the document, which mentions the 1259 dispensation, we know that the king and his retinue were lodged in the palace of the bishop when they visited Chartres. Thus, the sculptural program of both façades stresses that the prosperity of the church is guaranteed only by unity and balance between the two powers.

Our understanding of the cathedral of Chartres and its decoration can be extended in several directions by taking the historical context into account. Chédeville's study gives us clearer notions about the material conditions underlying the campaign, as well as about who financed it. As the theme of *regnum* and *sacerdotium* demonstrates, often the meaning and function of specific decorative programs can be comprehended only in relation to the local historical background. The circumstances at Chartres prove that the harmony expressed here was a utopian vision, and not a reflection of historical realities. The liturgy clearly impacted upon the form and subject-matter of the architecture, sculpture, and stained glass, but, as has been demonstrated by Manhes-Deremble, stained glass also influenced *post factum*, the development of new liturgical forms. The economic realities of the purchase of materials and the mechanics of the erection of the building also determined in many ways the spinning-out of the construction over time and the successive availability of newer stylistic vocabularies.

Investigation of the historical context, however, cannot shed light on the central and most complex issue of art history, the development and selection of visually different artistic forms. Despite the lure of interdisciplinary studies to give us a broader view of the monument, these approaches help explain only specific parts of the monument. Exchanges between art history and history enable us to gain concrete information about the material conditions and the individuals responsible for the monument. Liturgical studies can help to account, at least in part, for the iconographic choices. But for an understanding of the essential core of the monument, its particular physical presence – in a word, the "artistic" in this volume's title – we turn to the traditional aspects of the discipline of art history. The description and analysis of issues such as the choice of forms and stylistic changes, as we see developed in this volume by Peter Draper for Glastonbury and Wells, and Virginia Raguin for Poitiers, has been the particular province of the art historian. To "integrate" the information derived from several disciplines, we appear to return full circle to the first methodological step described in this essay, respect for the physical evidence of the building. We suggest that an integrated reading of these issues of history, liturgy, and theology in many cases depends on the ability of the art historian to relate all of this information to the compelling issue of the particular visual circumstance of the monument itself.

NOTES

German text translated by Kathryn Brush and revised and edited by Virginia Raguin. The authors wish to express their gratitude to both colleagues.

1 Jürgen Michler, "La cathédrale Notre-Dame de Chartres: Reconstitution de la polychromie originale de l'intérieur," *Bulletin monumental* 147 (1989), 117–31.
2 Literally translated, "totally unified work of art." The word became popular during the nineteenth century to describe the efforts of Wagner to produce spectacles that would unite the arts of drama, music, poetry, history, and the visual arts through his monumentally staged operas, such as the *Ring of the Nibelungs*. The term is frequently used by art historians to describe similar confluence of media in a single monument.
3 Jan van der Meulen, "Recent Literature on the Chronology of Chartres Cathedral," *Art Bulletin* 49 (1967), 153, and 165 note 11, where the original text of the *Miracula Beate Marie Virginis in Carnotensi ecclesia facta* is cited.

4 E. de Lépinois and L. Merlet, *Cartulaire de Notre-Dame de Chartres*, vol. 2 (Chartres, 1863), pp. 95–6. See also Van der Meulen, "Recent Literature," pp. 153 and 165, for the original text.

5 Van der Meulen, "Recent Literature," pp. 153–4.

6 Jan van der Meulen and J. Hohmeyer, *Chartres. Biographie einer Kathedrale* (Cologne, 1984), pp. 97–125.

7 Peter Kurmann and Brigitte Kurmann-Schwarz, "Die Architektur und Glasmalerei der hochgotischen Ostanlage der Kathedrale zu Chartres im Zeichen von Innovation und Tradition," *Die Kunst des 13. Jahrhunderts*, ed. W. Götz, J. Krause, and E. Lehmann (Weimar: forthcoming, 1996).

8 The study of Yves Delaporte, *Les vitraux de la cathédrale de Chartres* (Chartres, 1926), is still of fundamental importance. For recent summaries of the state of research, see *Les vitraux du centre et des pays de la Loire. Corpus Vitrearum France, Recensement* II (Paris, 1981), pp. 25–45; Claudine Lautier, "Les peintres-verriers des bas-côtés de la nef de Chartres au début du XIIIe siècle," *Bulletin monumental* 148 (1990), 7–45; and Colette Manhes-Deremble, *Les vitraux narratifs de la cathédrale de Chartres: Etude iconographique. Corpus Vitrearum France, Etudes* II (Paris, 1993).

9 The lancets of the windows in the upper portions of the nave, transepts, and choir measure ca. 6.8 metres in height and between 1.7 and 2.2 metres in width, and their roses about 5 metres in diameter. The windows in the lower parts of the church are taller, ca. 8.2 by 2.2 metres, and those of the hemicycle of the upper choir taller still, ca. 12.3 by 2.2 metres. The lancets of the transept façades measure about 7.5 by 1.6 metres, and the great roses 10.5 metres in diameter. The west rose is about 12 metres across.

10 Not counting the three twelfth-century windows of the west façade, there were 173 openings which required glazing. More than 150 of these still possess their medieval glass, either totally or in part. A. Chédeville, *Chartres et ses campagnes (XIe-XIIIe siècles)* (Paris, 1973), pp. 420–1, compares the great size of the cathedral to his estimates of a population of ca. 8,000 to 10,000 for the town. The population was at its peak in the thirteenth century and declined in the course of the fourteenth and fifteenth centuries. See C. Billot, *Chartres à la fin du moyen âge* (Paris, 1987), p. 90 (without exact numbers).

11 See Eva Frodl-Kraft, *Die Glasmalerei. Entwicklung, Technik, Eigenart* (Vienna and Munich, 1970), and Jean Lafond, *Le vitrail. Origines, techniques, destinées* (Lyon, 1988). For the organization of stained glass workshops, see Eva Frodl-Kraft, "Zur Frage der Werkstattpraxis in der mittelalterlichen Glasmalerei," *Glaskonservierung. Historische Glasfenster und ihre Erhaltung*

[Arbeitshefte des Bayerischen Landesamtes für Denkmalpflege 32]
(Munich, 1985), pp. 10–22.

12 The stained-glass windows were donated by members of the royal family, the local nobility, clerics, and the guilds. The nobles possessed fiefs or
land holdings in the immediate vicinity of the city, and a number of
donors of windows were related to members of the cathedral chapter. A
brother of Guillaume de la Ferté, a son of Jean Clément de Metz, and a
son of Robert de Courtenay were cathedral canons; a member of the
Beaumont family was subdeacon of the chapter in 1258. See Delaporte,
Les vitraux, pp. 441, 451, and 462; L. Merlet and R. Merlet, *Dignitaires de
l'église Notre-Dame de Chartres. Listes chronologiques.* (Chartres, 1900), p. 15
(Robertus de Curteneto); and Chédeville, *Chartres*, pp. 517–19. The position of the guilds as donors of windows has been debated in recent scholarship. Scholars still maintain the ability and willingness of the guilds to
finance such donations. See Delaporte, *Les vitraux*, and most recently
Wolfgang Kemp, *Sermo Corporeus. Die Erzählung der mittelalterlichen Glasfenster* (Munich, 1987) and "Les cris de Chartres. Rezeptionsästhetische
und andere Überlegungen zu zwei Fenstern der Kathedrale von Chartres," *Kunstgeschichte – aber wie?* (Berlin, 1989), pp. 189–220. Others have
challenged this view and interpret the representation of the guilds as the
canons' means of asserting hegemony over local means of production.
See Jane Welch Williams, *Bread, Wine, & Money: The Windows of the Trades
at Chartres Cathedral* (Chicago, 1993). For our opinion of these issues, see
Brigitte Kurmann-Schwarz, "Publications récentes sur les vitraux de la
cathédrale de Chartres," in *Bulletin monumental* (1995, forthcoming). This
review will include Manhes-Deremble, *Les vitraux narratifs*; Françoise
Perrot, "Le vitrail, la croisade et la Champagne: Réflection sur les fénêtres
hautes du choeur de la cathédrale de Chartres," in *Les Champenois et la
Croisade* [*Actes des quatrièmes journées rémoises, 27–8 Nov. 1987*], ed. Y. Bellenger and D. Quéruel (Paris, 1989), pp. 109–28; Jean-Paul Deremble and
Colette Manhes, *Les vitraux légendaires de Chartres. Des récits en images*,
(Paris, 1988); and Beat Brenk, "Bildprogrammatik und Geschichtsverständnis der Kapetinger im Querhaus der Kathedrale von Chartres," *Arte
medievale*, 2d series 5/2 (1991), 71–96. About the guilds, see also Manhes-
Deremble, *Les vitraux narratifs*, pp. 26–8. The author thinks that the guilds
gave the money, but they had neither the right to choose the subject of
the windows nor were they able to influence their forms, as Kemp pre-
tended.

13 This opinion has also been expressed by Alain Erlande-Brandenburg in
Chartres. Dans la lumière de la foi (Paris, 1986), p. 125. The speed of execut-

ing the building and the stained glass is also emphasized by Lautier, in "Les peintres-verriers," pp. 40–2.

14 The iconography of these windows will be treated in greater detail in Peter Kurmann and Brigitte Kurmann-Schwarz, *Die Kathedrale von Chartres* (Darmstadt, Wissenschaftliche Buchgesellschaft, forthcoming, 1996).

15 Yves Delaporte, "L'ordinaire chartrain du XIIIe siècle, publié d'après le manuscrit original," *Mémoires de la Société archéologique d'Eure et Loir* 19 (Chartres, 1953), 25.

16 Delaporte, *Les vitraux*, pp. 247–60.

17 The Catherine/Margaret window was presumably installed between 1231 and 1240. See also Delaporte, *Les vitraux*, pp. 247–60; R. Merlet, "Les vidames de Chartres au XIIIe siècle et le vitrail de sainte Marguerite," *Mémoires de la Société archéologique d'Eure et Loir* 10 (1896), 81–91; Jan van der Meulen, "Angrenzende Bauwerke der Kathedrale von Chartres," *Jahrbuch der Berliner Museen* 16 (1974), 30; idem, "Recent Literature," pp. 155–6. The choice of Catherine as the second saint may perhaps be explained by the fact that Hugues de Meslay, the brother-in-law of Marguerite de Lèves, had entered into a second marriage with a woman named Catherine. Manhes-Deremble, in *Les vitraux narratifs*, pp. 15–17, dates this window before 1215, the date of the marriage of Marguerite's sister Mabile to Hugues de Meslay. The author further assumes that Marguerite gave the window in conjunction with her husband and her brother-in-law. We do not agree with this suggestion primarily because Marguerite de Lèves is represented as a single donor kneeling before the Virgin. The window is more easily understandable as a memorial commemorating both Guérin de Friaize (d. before 1231) and Hugues de Meslay (d. 1227), made sometime between 1231 and 1240, the year of Marguerite's death.

18 S. Roulliard de Melun, *Parthénie ou histoire des la très-auguste et très-dévote église de Chartres* (Paris, 1609), fol. 142r. For the altar dedication, see Delaporte, *Les vitraux*, pp. 350–1.

19 Meredith P. Lillich, "Redating of the Thirteenth Century Grisaille Windows of Chartres Cathedral," *Gesta* 11 (1972), 13–14.

20 Roulliard, *Parthénie*, fol. 141v.

21 Delaporte, *Les vitraux*, pp. 363–5; for the Lawrence altar, p. 264; window no. 33/57, pp. 377–80. See also Lillich, "Redating," p. 14. Lautier, in "Les peintres-verriers," pp. 27–8 and note 99, dates the angel's border to the beginning of the thirteenth century and suggests that the artist who executed the border also worked on the window of Saint Mary Magdalene [46/5]. Manhes-Deremble, in *Les vitraux narratifs*, p. 72, suggests also an early date for the border.

22 Roulliard, *Parthénie*, fol. 139v.

23 Delaporte, in *Les vitraux*, p. 380, note 2, suggested that the angel from window 33/57 and the Lawrence medallion in the grisaille of the right lancet of window 25/47 were made by the same hand ca. 1259. The north rose also belongs to this stylistic group, although it is probably older (from the 1240s).

24 Delaporte, "L'ordinaire chartrain," p. 54. Manhes-Deremble, in *Les vitraux narratifs*, pp. 32–3, 75–8, suggests that the canons intended to give an impetus to a new liturgy through the iconographic program of the windows, above all by chosing lives of many saints who were not popular at Chartres at the time.

25 Delaporte, in *Les vitraux*, pp. 205 and 380, expressed this view.

26 Ibid., pp. 357–63.

27 L. Merlet, *Catalogue des reliques et joyaux de Notre-Dame de Chartres* (Chartres, 1885), pp. 96–8, and in an inventory of 1322 (discussed pp. 90–3, note 1). See also Jan van der Meulen, *Notre-Dame de Chartres. Die vorromanische Ostanlage* (Berlin, 1975), p. 78.

28 Manhes-Deremble, *Les vitraux narratifs*, pp. 37–50.

29 Van der Meulen, in "Recent Literature," refutes this notion, as on p. 154, note 2: "The windows ... do not form an integral part of the construction."

30 The authors address in detail the chronology of the architecture and stained glass of Chartres cathedral in the forthcoming study cited in note 7 above.

31 Different formal languages are still legible in the windows of the nave, indicating different origins for the glass painters. The workshop became more tightly organized in the course of time, as evidenced by the much more unified style of the glass of the ambulatory, chapels, and clerestory of the choir. Lautier, in "Les peintres-verriers," has examined the workshop organization at Chartres and suggests that master glass painters occasionally worked with others whose different style can be distinguished from the dominant style of the window. She sees a continuity of artists working from the nave aisles into the ambulatory.

32 The reasons for this pause in the campaign are examined in detail by the authors in the forthcoming study cited in note 7 above.

33 In contrast to earlier opinions, we do not believe that the group associated with the so-called Master of Saint Chéron was active at the same time as the glass painters who created the Charlemagne window [7/38] and others. For a review of the earlier argument, see *Recensement* II, pp. 27–32. This argument is countered by the orderly distribution of the work of the so-called Master of Saint Chéron in the windows located in the ground

floor of the choir. In each case they occupy either one or both of the openings which flank the axial windows of the large chapels in the ambulatory. The only exception to this rule are the panels of the legend of Saint Germanus in the left lancet of window no. 29ab, a pendant to window no. 30, which contains the twelfth-century image of Notre-Dame de la Belle-Verrière. In our view, the Gothic additions to the Belle-Verrière also appear to be of a later date. We believe that the windows containing glass by the Master of Saint Chéron were deliberately postponed during an initial phase of glazing (taking place between 1200 and 1210) in order to give priority to the more pressing need to glaze the clerestory openings of the choir. The clerestory windows were certainly finished by 1221 when the canons occupied the choir-stalls and recorded their seating arrangements. We suggest that the so-called Master of Saint Chéron was not at work in Chartres before the mid-1230s. This view is given further credence by the dates of Geoffroy Chardonnel, the patron of the Germanus window, as well as by those of Marguerite de Lèves, who donated the Margaret window [6/36]. See the authors' forthcoming study cited in note 7 above for a detailed explanation. For the Master of Saint Chéron, see L. Grodecki, "Les problèmes de l'origine de la peinture gothique et le 'Maitre de saint Chéron,'" *Revue de l'art* 40/41 (1978), 43–67. Lautier, in "Les peintres-verriers," however, believes that the glaziers of the Saint-Chéron group arrived at Chartres around 1200. The modern-looking heads in the nave windows may not be an indication of early work of this group, however, and bear further investigation. We feel that it is unwise to reject the possibility of early restorations, as Lautier does. Manhes-Deremble, in *Les vitraux narratifs*, pp. 15–17, follows the date of Lautier.

34 The lancets showing Saints Peter and Paul [128/86 and 87] and the lancets showing scenes from the life of Saint Eustache and scenes of Christ's Infancy [115/136, 137, 138] are from another campaign. These windows were glazed with the clerestory of the nave in the years around 1210 because they were built together with the easternmost bay of the nave. For this reason, the dates given in *Recensement* II (1230–35) are too late.

35 For a discussion of the relationships between architecture and stained glass, see L. Grodecki, "Le vitrail et l'architecture au XIIe et XIIIe siècles," *Gazette des Beaux-Arts* 6th ser., 36 (1949), 5–24.

36 For the quarry at Berchères, see Billot, *Chartres à la fin du moyen âge*, pp. 106–7.

37 "Chartres, Cathédrale, étude de statues, études des prélèvements et étude des échantillons provenant de carrières de l'Oise," typescript by Anne Blanche, 1969, deposited at the Centre des Recherches sur les Monuments

historiques, Paris, Palais de Chaillot. The authors wish to thank Alain Erlande-Brandenburg for informing them of this typescript.

38 Chédeville, *Chartres*, pp. 439–40. Billot, in *Chartres à la fin du moyen âge*, p. 106, claims that the Eure was navigable at least during the eleventh century because the materials for the tower of Saint-Père were transported by water from the region of Mantes.

39 For the dating of the sculpture, see Willibald Sauerländer, *Gotische Skulptur in Frankreich 1140–1270* (Munich, 1970), pp. 113–21 and P.C. Claussen, *Chartres-Studien. Zu Vorgeschichte, Funktion und Skulptur der Vorhallen* (Wiesbaden, 1975), pp. 103–25, esp. pp. 123–5.

40 Sauerländer, in *Gotische Skulptur*, pp. 113–14, 116, 118–19, argues that the first sculptors came from Laon and Sens. Since the architectural vocabulary of Chartres is derived from buildings of the Laon-Soissons region, it is reasonable to assume that sculptors also came from this area. For the sources of the architecture, see Bruno Klein, "Chartres und Soissons. Überlegungen zur gotischen Architektur um 1200," *Zeitschrift für Kunstgeschichte* 49 (1986), 437–66. Connections with Sens were probably encouraged by transportation links. The route connecting Orléans, Chartres, and Rouen, and the road leading from Chartres to Sens, were the oldest thoroughfares linking the city to other sites. During the Middle Ages the road to Sens was called the "Chemin de Saint-Mathurin" because it was used by pilgrims who travelled from Chartres to Saint-Mathurin in Larchant. See Chédeville, *Chartres*, pp. 440–1 and Billot, *Chartres à la fin du moyen âge*, p. 64.

41 Sauerländer, in *Gotische Skulptur*, p. 117, discusses Notre-Dame in Paris as source for the sculpture of the southern porch; Claussen, *Chartres-Studien*, pp. 123–5.

42 Delaporte, *Les vitraux*, pp. 440–1; Grodecki, "Les problèmes," pp. 57–8.

43 Adolf Katzenellenbogen, *The Sculptural Programs of Chartres Cathedral* (1959; repr. New York, 1964).

44 Roulliard, *Parthénie*, fol. 143v.

45 Arnold Esch, "Über den Zusammenhang von Kunst und Wirtschaft in der italienischen Renaissance," *Zeitschrift für historische Forschung* 8 (1981), 180.

46 Chédeville, *Chartres*, pp. 505–25 ("Le préstige de Chartres").

47 Dieter Kimpel and Robert Suckale, *Die gotische Architektur in Frankreich 1130–1270* (Munich, 1985), pp. 236–44 ("Geschichte") [trans. by Françoise Neu, *L'architecture gothique en France 1130–1270* (Paris, 1990)]. The authors" presentation relies chiefly on Otto von Simson, *Die gotische Kathedrale. Beiträge zu ihrer Entstehung und Bedeutung* [Darmstadt, 1972;

original English text, *The Gothic Cathedral: Origins of Gothic Architecture and the Medieval Concept of Order* (New York, 1956)], and Abbé Bulteau, *Monographie de la cathédrale de Chartres* 1 (1887). Often Bulteau's work does not distinguish between written sources and legends. For a critical assessment of von Simson's study, see Chédeville, *Chartres*, pp. 507–08, 523. Manhes-Deremble, in *Les vitraux narratifs*, p. 248, sees royalty encroaching on ecclesiastical power only in the latest phase of construction.

48 Esch, "Über den Zusammenhang von Kunst und Wirtschaft," p. 187.

49 Ibid., p. 196.

50 Chédeville, *Chartres*, p. 514: "[the chapter] which was, in reality, responsible for the project."

51 M. Jusselin, "La Maîtrise de l'Oeuvre à Notre-Dame de Chartres. La fabrique, les ouvriers et les travaux du XIVe siècle," *Mémoires de la Société archéologique d'Eure et Loir* 15 (1921), 233–343 (the fabric, pp. 256–63); Chédeville, *Chartres*, pp. 512–13. The latter contends that, while the endowment of the fabric was sufficient for the routine maintenance of the structure and its furnishings, it certainly could not have met the expenses of a large building campaign.

52 Chédeville, *Chartres*, pp. 183–5, 514–15.

53 Ibid., pp. 109–60, esp. p. 148 regarding dates.

54 Ibid., pp. 514–15.

55 Esch, in "Über den Zusammenhang von Kunst und Wirtschaft," p. 219, demonstrates that most patrons invested in art works and buildings only after a certain degree of wealth had been obtained and a slowdown in its growth occurred. The changes in the income structure of the chapter at Chartres and its role as patron correspond very closely to the notions put forward by Esch.

56 Von Simson, *Die gotische Kathedrale*, pp. 227–32; Kimpel and Suckale, *Die gotische Architektur*, pp. 236–37. Lautier, in "Les peintres-verriers," p. 41, suggests the same interpretation of these texts that we do.

57 Chédeville, *Chartres*, p. 519. Concerning the interpretation of written sources for the dating of a building, see also Madeline Caviness, "Saint-Yved of Braine: The Primary Sources for Dating the Gothic Church," *Speculum* 59 (1984), 524–48.

58 The village was also called Berchères-l'Evêque.

59 Bulteau, in *Monographie de la cathédrale*, I, p. 119, claimed that the king travelled to Chartres on a pilgrimage and from that time onwards gave an annual donation towards the north transept. He does not provide any source for this statement. The king's trip to Chartres was in fact connected with an uprising in 1210. See Chédeville, *Chartres*, pp. 499, 524 (uprising

of 1210), and pp. 518-19 (royal donations). Bulteau's statements were adopted uncritically by Kimpel and Suckale, in *Die gotische Architektur*, p. 244.

60 Chédeville, *Chartres*, pp. 517–18.

61 Ibid., pp. 509–12. By contrast, Kimpel and Suckale, in *Die gotische Architektur*, p. 240, claim that the bishop and chapter became wealthy because of the pilgrimage.

62 Most recently, Kimpel and Suckale, ibid., p. 240: "The inhabitants of the town, the king, and indeed all of France, supported the erection of the new church."

63 Chédeville, *Chartres*, pp. 493–504. See also the essay by Barbara Abou-El-Haj in this volume.

64 Chédeville, *Chartres*, pp. 446–9 (textile production), pp. 454–6 (production for the local market), pp. 457–9 (the lack of participation of Chartres in foreign trade, city markets visited by local populace only). Kimpel and Suckale,in *Die gotische Architektur*, p. 240, claim that the Beauce had already become the grain basket of France by the thirteenth century. By contrast, Chédeville, in *Chartres*, p. 456, shows that the Chartres region barely exported any grain. There is no proof of the "Halle de Beausse" in Paris prior to 1552. For the role of money in the Chartrain economy, see ibid., pp. 460–80 (money was probably concentrated in the city, mostly in the possession of ecclesiastical institutions). The money economy of Chartres was underdeveloped in relation to that of northern French and Flemish cities. Williams, in *Windows of the Trades*, pp. 103–38, however, attempts to assign a considerably more important role to a cash economy at Chartres. Although her argument is based on Chédeville, she arrives at an opposite result.

65 Katzenellenbogen, *The Sculptural Programs*, pp. 27–36, 101. Manhes-Deremble, in *Les vitraux narratifs*, pp. 239–48, emphasizes the desire of the canons of Chartres to show harmony and balance between the two powers.

66 Chédeville, *Chartres*, plan on p. 421.

67 For the north porch program, see Claussen, *Chartres-Studien*, pp. 126–52.

10

Integrated Fragments and the Unintegrated Whole: Scattered Examples from Reims, Strasbourg, Chartres, and Naumburg

Willibald Sauerländer

Sauerländer selects four major Gothic ensembles, addressing the unity of sculpture, architecture, furniture, and stained glass in each, and the issues of audience, use, and moment. The cathedral of Reims, the site of coronation rites of the French monarchy, is a telling case of simultaneous orchestration of architecture, stained glass, and sculpture. The exterior and interior of the building carry images of kings, angels, and the bishops of the ecclesiastical province of Reims, a program emphasizing the intersection of ritual function, articulation of power, and visual design.

The old south transept at Strasbourg was reconstructed by a Gothic workshop between 1220 and 1230. Fifteen statues and two sculpted tympana centred around Solomon as the prototype of Christ as compassionate but discerning judge were added to the exterior of the Romanesque façade. On the interior, an image of Christ as Judge appears in an extraordinary ensemble of angels and apostles clustered around a massive central pillar. The structural necessities of vaulting so large an interior space became the impetus for an unprecedented formal and iconographic whole.

At Chartres, Sauerländer analyses a specific cause of unified function and design. A relic of the head of Saint Anne, the mother of the Virgin Mary, had been acquired by the cathedral sometime between October 1204 and April 1205. This event transformed the iconographic program which had originally been centred on the genealogy of Christ and the lineage and glorification of his mother, Mary. A large statue of Saint Anne was added to the central portal of the north façade, and an identical image in stained glass was set in the central lancet below the rose of the transept, donations that reflected royal interest.

Naumburg shows an unusual harmony among sculpture, furniture, architecture, and stained glass in the western choir, constructed shortly after 1250. The choir-stalls for the canons are surmounted by life-size statues of donors to the chapter. Stained glass in the apse shows the heavenly choir of saints and apostles illuminating the terrestrial choir. It is a case of total integration of function for the donors are present in effigy, while the canons pray for their salvation and their entrance into celestial light.

Although noting such instances of integration, Sauerländer warns that they are found only in small and chronologically short-lived parts of the vast ensemble of the huge cathedrals. Holistic unity in the entire ensemble of a Gothic building, a point echoed by Klukas for Durham and by Raguin for Poitiers, is either a retrospective illusion or an impossibility.

I feel compelled to begin this essay with some methodological reminders and reminiscences. In December 1961, I had my last conversation with the late Paul Frankl. The topic was the statue columns of the Royal Portal of the cathedral of Chartres. Frankl, deeply concerned with the problem of stylistic classification, debated the definition of the Chartrain statues as "Late Romanesque" or as "Early Gothic." I can hear him still, concluding our conversation on a slightly ironic note: "So, I see that Dr Sauerländer thinks the heads of these statues are Gothic while their bodies still seem Romanesque." This anecdote shows how deeply imbued Frankl was with the belief in a system of stylistic principles which would be valid for the form of the rib-vaults in the interior of the western towers at Chartres as well as for the shape of the statues of the west façade. Frankl, a scholar brought up around 1900, and strongly influenced by Wölfflin, developed his dream of a great unity of design embracing architecture, furniture, decoration, and even dress, in the context of the turn-of-the-century designs of Henry van der Velde, Behrens, Berlage, Hoffmann, and others. It was this modernist commitment to a new, unified style created to overcome nineteenth-century eclecticism that Frankl and other art historians projected into the past. An early Gothic monument such as the west façade of Chartres must, of necessity, appear as a radiant example of unity of design embracing all of the branches of art and the crafts.

This dream of stylistic unity belongs to the past. The issue at the heart of this volume, the question of whether the design of the Gothic church was holistic, reflects an intellectual and social unease peculiar to our own historical context. We all suffer from a sense of isolation and alienation, exacerbated by the ever-growing specialization of fields in academe. We bemoan our situation of always studying the details and never the whole. We distinguish the building campaigns, we date and redate sculptures, we study technical details in stained-glass windows, but we never grasp the whole of a cathedral. Why should we not escape from our specialized marginalizion and seek more holistic approaches? Why should not the specialist in Gothic art and architecture, as have others, drink at the fountain of wholeness? I would say yes, granted that we avoid inebriation and retain our powers of reason and analysis.

Reason demands that we examine carefully our choice of words. What does "unity of design" mean in a Gothic monument – unity of planning, unity of program, or unity of style? Even with great effort, I feel unable to suggest a unity of style between, for example, the architecture of Senlis, with its simple and severe structure, and the lively figures on the west portal of the same cathedral. I would be equally reluctant to identify a stylistic unity between the heavy, even massive, nave architecture at Chartres and the narrative loquaciousness of the images in the stained glass of the nave windows, such as the miracles of Saint Lubinus. The different media of a great cathedral are the result of specialized craftsmanship, articulating various languages and rhetoric. The cooperation of different crafts may result in a coherent spectacle achieved with many different actors. An *a priori* stylistic unity in a Gothic cathedral embracing architecture, sculpture, stained glass, furniture, and the decorative arts, however, is a retrospective invention of modern art history.

So the unity, if unity can be assumed, must be looked for in a dimension of the Gothic cathedral which transcends the visual evidence of style and form. I suggest that even the grand unity of the iconographic program, which we often take for granted, is to a large degree a modern illusion. Emile Mâle read the program of the great cathedrals as an encyclopedia of sacred images.[1] He followed the model of the *Speculum Majus* of Vincent of Beauvais, but in many ways his classification seems closer to that of Linnaeus or Comte than to the Middle Ages. Unity of program is more complex and elusive than we generally admit. The meaning of images in their designated places within the cathedral can be understood fully only if we reconstruct their original function and topography. The cathedral emerges as more than an aesthetic or technical object of study for specialists in architectural history only when we read it as a "place of memory" housing cults, celebrations, shrines, and tombs in a meaningful, if not systematic, arrangement. To attempt such a reconstruction, however, precipitates practical difficulties.

We want to read and understand a text or a context – and a Gothic cathedral with its images and its furniture is a very complex text and context – but we have only fragmentary remnants of the original text. If we stand in the interior of the cathedral at Laon or at Noyon we are overwhelmed by the vast space. We feel as if we are standing in an interior by Nervi or Niemeyer. But we know nothing about the shrine of Saint Eligius, the ancient liturgical focal point of the choir at Noyon. The 1157 date of the solemn translation of the shrine means little more than a convenient means of dating the construction of the new cathedral. Noyon retains only a few remants of its stained-glass windows.[2] The choir screen has disappeared, and not even the most detailed monographs on this building inform us of the dedications of the former altars in the ambulatory and transepts. A holistic approach to such a building is doomed as long as we lack the most basic information on the original function of the building.

The case of Laon is no less dramatic. We know that the chapter of Laon was one of the richest in France and that the cathedral was lavishly furnished. Nothing of this former splendour remains with the exception of the stone shell of a building dating half from the Middle Ages and half from Boeswillwald's nineteenth-century restoration.[3] It is ironic that modern scholarship has interpreted the eastern piers of the nave, with their curious combination of central column surrounded by four free-standing responds, as a purely architectural experiment – a "pilier cantonné" *in statu nascendi* – until Eric Fernie observed that these odd pillars might be remnants of the original topography of the cathedral marking the western end of the chapter's choir.[4] Fernie has made "readable" again a small detail of a destroyed "text" establishing Notre-Dame at Laon as an accumulation of usages and rites which were staged in the huge building and connected with objects and images visible in the stained-glass windows, on the destroyed screen and altars, and on the portals.

Two of the western entrances of the cathedral at Laon show an iconographic program dedicated to the Virgin. Although awkwardly restored, the Marian program is quite discernible and was analysed in detail by Emile Mâle.[5] Until the eighteenth century, however, these representations of the Virgin were linked to the most famous image in the interior of the cathedral, the statue of "Notre-Dame-des-Miracles," which stood on an altar connected to the choir screen.[6] All of these images and objects in the cathedral of Laon formed a unity, but a unity that had never been systematically planned. It was the result of an accumulation over a very long history, beginning even before the erection of the present cathedral and continuing until the dissolution of the chapter in 1793. Old and new images and objects gave visual expression to the traditions of the church of Laon. A holistic approach to such a storehouse of religious treasures and images asks for a reconstruction of this destroyed ensemble. Architecture, stained glass, sculpture, and furniture were not necessarily planned together and they may not display a unity of style, but they formed together the stage where the living theatre of the liturgy and local customs were played. Only in a few instances, have we been able to reconstruct such holistic ensembles.

I begin with the choir of Notre-Dame at Reims (fig. 1). In order to understand the topography of the choir, we must turn to an eighteenth-century plan. The choir-stalls of the chapter at Reims stood in the three eastern bays of the nave, an arrangement visible today in the interior of the cathedral. The main altar of the cathedral stood in the crossing beneath the pseudo-tower visible on the exterior. East of the crossing was the sanctuary with the altar of the archbishop. The most prestigious rite celebrated in the cathedral at Reims, the "sacre," or anointing, and the coronation of the kings of France, did not take place in the sanctuary but was staged at the main altar in the crossing (fig. 2). After receiving the crown, the king mounted the choir screen at the western end of the choir and was installed on his throne.[7] This liturgical arrangement is reflected in a most impressive and majestic way in the iconographic and architectural program of the eastern parts of the cathedral. The windows of the clerestory of the sanctuary display a unique iconographic program. The central window depicts the Virgin and Christ, and beneath them an image of the cathedral of Reims with an angel holding a cross on its roof. Within the schematic representation of the cathedral appears Henry of Braine, archbishop from 1227 to 1240. The other ten windows of the sanctuary show apostles, and beneath them the ten suffragan bishops of the archdiocese of Reims with the images of their cathedrals. On the roofs stand angels sounding trumpets. The clerestory of the sanctuary is thus dominated by an image of ecclesiastic power, the bishops of Amiens, Arras, Beauvais, Cambrai, Chalons, Laon, Noyon, Senlis, Thérouanne, and Tournai assembled around the archbishop of Reims as if participating in a synod. It is possible that the sequence of the suffragan bishops corresponds to an order which had been established at a council held at Saint-Quentin in 1231.[8]

This unique program shaped the architectural design on the exterior of the sanctuary (fig. 3). The buttresses are crowned by huge, open tabernacles framing eight gigantic statues of angels. We find, therefore, a telling case of the simultaneous orchestration of architecture and sculpture. The tabernacles crowning the buttresses represent the gates of the Heavenly Jerusalem as they were depicted elsewhere on chandeliers and in manuscripts.[9] The architecture functions simultaneously as form and image. The angels enshrined by the tabernacles stand guard over the ecclesiastical province of Reims on the interior like angelic sentinels in the towers of the Heavenly Jerusalem. I would argue that in this instance we can assume that this integration of architecture, sculpture, and stained glass must be the result of unified planning.

If we move from the sanctuary to the transept of the cathedral, the place of the "sacre," the program changes. The tabernacles crowning the buttresses continue and increase in size. The angels, however, have been replaced by fourteen statues of kings. These images encircle the transept and frame, as it were, the altar where the kings of France were anointed and crowned. Since the kings of France are represented on the fourteenth-century gallery on the west façade, the fourteen statues on the transept may have been intended to function as Old Testament models for the Christian ruler.[10] Whatever their precise identity, the royal statues in the tabernacles around the transept visualize the sacred and political function of this part of the cathedral. Sculpture and architecture are again meaningfully integrated and must have been planned together. The message of this unified ensemble, however, becomes understandable only in light of the rituals and ceremonies which took place in this part of the building. There is no integration without liturgical or ceremonial function in a Gothic cathedral.

The coronation program in the cathedral of Reims continued into the eastern bays of the nave. This was the part of the cathedral in which the king was enthroned after his coronation, and the clerestory windows contain images of historical French kings and the archbishops who had crowned them.[11] Again we observe the simultaneous orchestration of the architecture and stained glass in a coherent program enhancing the sacred topography of the cathedral. As impressive as this example may be, even here the text – or context – that we wish to read remains fragmentary. The choir screen has been dismantled, the furniture of the sanctuary is missing, and the once venerated shrines have been melted down. We see today only one aspect or layer of the original integration of the structure, decoration, and ritual.

Let me approach the next great example. There is no other cathedral in Europe which contradicts more forcefully the idea of unified planning than the cathedral of Strasbourg. The eastern part of the building – the apse, the crossing, the giant cupola, and large transepts – was evidently begun with the intention of imitating the great imperial cathedrals of the eleventh and twelfth centuries at Speyer and Mainz. There were several radical changes in plan.[12] But when the first Gothic workshop assumed control somewhere between 1210 and 1220, a coherent program for architecture, sculpture, and stained glass was developed. The Romanesque double portal of the façade of the south transept facing the bishop's palace, was modernized by the addition of fifteen statues and two sculpted tympana. The iconographic program of these additions is complex, but was focused on the idea of the election of "Ecclesia" (the church) and the repudiation of "Synagoga" (the synagogue). "Ecclesia" is represented with the attributes of her victory, the chalice and gonfalon, faithfully looking up to Christ, whose bust appears in the centre of the double portal. "Synagoga" is shown as defeated and repulsed, blindfolded, with a broken lance and the tablets of the Old Law falling from her hands. Solomon appears between the figures of church and synagogue. Solomon, who had recognized the true mother and repulsed the false one was regarded as prototype of Christ who accepted the church and repudiated the synagogue.[13] But Solomon was also seen as the prefiguration of Christ the Judge who returns at the end of time to redeem the blessed and condemn sinners.[14] It is the fusion of these two roles that allows Solomon's presence to connect the exterior and interior decorative schemas of the south transept.

The interior decoration is an astonishing example of the integration of architecture and sculpture. The enormous transept was built on an early medieval foundation, and its vaulting necessitated a central pillar. The structure of the pillar, an octagonal nucleus with eight detached responds, was dictated by the design of the ribbed vaults that subdivide the transept into four bays. Clearly, the erection of this pillar was a technical necessity. It was the ingenious idea of the planners of the south transept, whether architect or canon, and more probably both parties together, to use the central pillar for a dramatic extension of the iconographic program. Entering the transept, the beholder stood beneath an emphatic representation of the Last Day. The central pillar was surrounded by twelve figures distributed in three tiers. In the lowest tier, the four Evangelists in dramatic posture announce the return of Christ at the end of time. In the next tier, four great angels bend down to sound the trumpets that call the living and the dead from all four corners of the world to appear before the Judge. Above, beneath the vaults of heaven, appears the Judge accompanied by three angels bearing his cross, nails, and the crown of thorns. *Crux micat in caelis* (the cross shines in the heavens) one reads in the ninth-century description of the Last Judgment in the *Carmina Sangallensia*.[15] No more telling illustration of this sentence could be conceived than the illusionistic arrangement of the twelve statues of Strasbourg's great pillar. It is, to me, the most spectacular case of integration of architecture and sculpture of the early thirteenth century. Clearly coherent planning for the vaulting of the transept and the placement of the sculpture must be assumed. Even the glazing of the south transept may have been a part of the same program. The huge figure of Saint Christopher in a window of the eastern wall of the transept, quite close to the central pillar, is in this sense very suggestive.[16] The figure of Saint Christopher was believed to be a protection against unexpected, and therefore unprepared-for, death.[17] Close to an image of the Judge and the resurrection of the dead, the presence of Saint Christopher promised protection.

The transept of Strasbourg presents us with a second case of simultaneous orchestration of architecture, sculpture, and stained glass. Yet certain reservations must be voiced. The erection of the central pillar was part of a dramatic change in the building campaign, so that the unity of design is valid only for one short span of time in the long and complex history of the cathedral. Moreover, we are unsure of the specific cultic function of the south transept. To whom was this message of the Last Judgment addressed in this part of the church possessed by bishop and chapter? The old liturgy of the cathedral and the original role of the bishop and the chapter disappeared with the introduction of the Reform in 1525. With this rupture of tradition the Last

Judgment pillar has become enigmatic, precipitating a long series of hypothetical interpretations.[18] Reintegration in the full sense would only be possible if we could reconstruct the religious life of the persons using the medieval monument.

Let us approach our third example. Unhappily, we know almost nothing about the individuals responsible for planning the medieval programs of these churches. It seems improbable that the architects, sculptors, or glass painters had the authority, or even the intellectual experience, to dictate an iconographic program for a cathedral or abbey. We often surmise that the director must have been a member of the chapter, presumably the abbot or even the bishop. We search local texts in the hope of comparing references with certain local images.[19] Often we are unaware of specific historic circumstances, perhaps very short-lived ones, which may have influenced the adoption of a program or caused a shift in content of one already under way. When such a situation can be documented, it becomes of great interest. The north façade of the cathedral of Chartres is such a case. The design of the façade, with three portals surmounted by a rose, offered a frame into which a great many different programs could have been adapted. The decision to focus the program on the Virgin, her descent, virtues, and coronation as Queen of Heaven, seems quite natural given the dedication of the cathedral to the Virgin Mary. This decision could have taken place at any time after the canons' decision to rebuild following the fire of 1194. The ultimate form of the portal, however, could not have been conceived before 1205, the year the program was altered to integrate a newly founded cult. Between October 1204 and April 1205, Catherine, countess of Blois and Chartres, gave the cathedral a relic of the head of Saint Anne that her husband had acquired after the sack of Constantinople in 1204.[20]

The new cult of Saint Anne, the mother of the Virgin, was concentrated at Chartres at an altar which stood near the northeastern pier of the crossing.[21] Images of Saint Anne were added to a program that retained as its core the depiction of the lineage of Christ. A statue of Saint Anne was placed on the trumeau (central pillar) of the central portal, thus making her the most important image of the north façade. A second image of Anne was installed on the inside of the façade in the form of a stained-glass window beneath the rose and centrally located between the great biblical kings, David and Solomon. In both instances the image of the saint recalls an eastern model and makes a visual statement of the oriental provenance of the new relic. We must now ask what conclusions we may draw from the Chartrain events concerning our topic of integration. I see two major themes. First, a program which displays iconographic concepts current in Capetian France since about 1140, underwent dramatic change in order to emphasize a new cult, a new pilgrimage, and ultimately a new source of income for the chapter. The staging of the program is not, as traditional iconographers would have phrased it, an abstract illustration of sacred history, but a visual response to the religious life in the cathedral and its enrichment by new donations. Second, the addition to the program seems to reflect a unified planning embracing the portals and the stained-glass windows above them. We can therefore accept another case of integration.

The glass in the spandrels beneath the rose of the northern transept display the royal arms, the lilies of France and the castles of Castile. It is therefore highly probable that the glazing of the north façade represents a royal donation of Saint Louis and his mother, Blanche of Castile, whose patronage is also discussed by Beat Brenk for the Sainte-Chapelle.[22] Beneath the figure of Saint Anne in the central lancet is a shield with lilies, the arms of France. These details are important for an integrated understanding of the change in program. The images seem to prove that the royal house participated in the new cult of Saint Anne and that the windows encode a political message. The king and the queen mother saw themselves represented via images emphasizing the royal descent of Christ. The Christian rulers of France understood their role as that of ideal successors to the biblical kings. Does this observation concerning a change of program on the north façade of the cathedral manifest a holistic intention? Yes and no – yes, because it shows a unity of planning embracing architecture, sculpture, and stained glass, and it reveals a specific cause for the transformation of the program; no, because it shows that the cathedral of Chartres was not a unity planned from the beginning, but rather an accumulation of cults and images reflecting changing circumstances and agendas. It is only the uniformity of the architectural design which creates for the modern beholder the illusion of a wholeness, which did not exist in quite the way our modern conceptions would have it.

I come to my final example, the cathedral of Naumburg. Like many cathedrals in the Empire, Naumburg had two choirs, one at the east and another at the west. The eastern choir, liturgically the more important one, was dedicated to Saints Peter and Paul, and the western choir to the Virgin. A rebuilding of the cathedral in the first quarter of the thirteenth century began in the east and continued into the nave. The western choir was erected by a new workshop of Gothic training which did not arrive in Naumburg before 1250, and very probably some years later.[23] The choir shows a complete unity of planning and execution. The architecture, the sculpture, and even the furniture were evidently designed in the same moment, probably by the same *magister operis* (master of the works) and created by the same craftsmen. The western choir consists of a square bay and a polygonal apse. The stalls for the canons, executed in stone, stand in the square bay and are technically part of the walls of the choir. It is probable that prayers said in these stalls comprised supplications for the salvation of the souls of the founders and the most prominent donors of the chapter of Our Lady at Naumburg. We may assume that this liturgical function justified the placement of life-sized statues of the most prominent donors above the choir-stalls and in the corners of the eastern polygon. The stained glass presents a heavenly choir of apostles, saints, and virtues triumphing majestically over vices.[24] The heavenly choir radiates into light-filled space, the donors stand fixed in stone, and the flesh-and-blood canons move in the human space of the choir's enclosure. It is a case of total integration of function; the donors are present in effigy, while the canons voice prayers for their salvation. It is also a case of complete technical integration. The statues were erected with the building and are literally a part of it, chiselled from the same blocks as the responds supporting the ribs of the vaults. This then is a case of total integration of architecture, furniture, glass, and sculpture – in technique and in meaning.

But even in Naumburg the original text remains fragmentary. If the choir-stalls are still there, heavily restored, all the altars of the choir have disappeared. We are uninformed about the kinds of masses and prayers said for the donors. The liturgical texts in use before the Reformation at Naumburg, if they still exist, are not published. We question the curious attitudes and gestures of the statues, finding no text to explicate their uniqueness. Therefore, even in the case of Naumburg any holistic approach remains speculative, a point corroborated by the long and often erratic scholarship inspired by the site.[25]

Scattered as these examples are, they encourage some general remarks. If integration is taken to mean that all the parts of a Gothic church and all the images and furniture assembled in it form together a treasure house for different venerations, cults, and customs, there is no reason to deny integration. This integration over time, however, does not lend itself easily to any traditional art-historical approach. It is more a topic of ecclesiastical, religious, or liturgical history. Integration as a unity of planning, design, or style, embracing architecture, sculpture, and stained glass, is a very different problem. Such integration, which interests the art historian, does certainly exist. It is found, however, only in small and chronologically short-lived parts of the vast ensemble of the huge cathedrals. I have singled out some cases where such integration can still be recognized, although always in a fragmentary state of conservation. A holistic approach to the entire ensemble of an Early Gothic church is either a retrospective illusion or a practical impossibility.

NOTES

1 Emile Mâle, *L'art religieux du XIIIe siècle en France* (Paris, 1898; 5th ed., 1923).
2 For the glass, see Evelyn Ruth Staudinger, "Thirteenth-Century Stained Glass in Notre-Dame of Noyon," Master's thesis, Tufts University, 1980; Staudinger reconstructed parts of the glazing program from documents and studied the nine remaining panels from a life of Saint Pantaleon attributed to a local workshop and dated ca. 1220–30. For the architecture, see Charles Seymour, Jr, *La cathédrale de Noyon au XIIe siècle* (Paris, 1975), and Thomas Polk, *Saint-Denis, Noyon, and the Early Gothic Choir* (Frankfurt and Bern, 1982).
3 The most detailed account of the restorations at Laon is found in R. Echt, *Emile Boeswillwald als Denkmalpfleger* (Bonn, 1984), pp. 53–70 and 143–55.
4 Eric Fernie, "La function liturgique des piliers cantonnés dans la nef de la cathédrale de Laon," *Bulletin monumental* 145 (1987), 257 ff.
5 Mâle, *L'art religieux*, pp. 148–53. See also M.L. Thérel, "Etude iconographique du portail de la Vièrge-Mère de la cathédrale de Laon," *Cahiers de civilization médiévale* 15 (1972), 41–51.
6 See A. Bouxin, *La cathédrale Notre-Dame de Laon* (Laon, 1902), pp. 8 and 229–30.
7 For the coronation of the kings of France, see J.P. Bayard, *Sacres et couronnements royaux* (Paris, 1984), with extensive bibliography. See now for the program of the choir at Reims, Willibald Sauerländer, "Observations sur la topographie et l'iconographie de la cathédrale du sacre," *Académie des Inscriptions et Belles-Lettres, Comptes-Rendus* (1992), 463–79.

8 For these windows, see Eva Frodl-Kraft, "Zu den Kirchenschaubildern in den Hochchorfenstern von Reims – Abbildung und Abstraktion," *Wiener Jahrbuch für Kunstgeschichte* 25 (1972), 53–86. For the possible influence of the council held at Saint-Quentin in 1231, see Robert Branner, "Historical Aspects of the Reconstruction of Reims Cathedral, 1210–1241," *Speculum* 35 (1961), 26, note 15.

9 See the chandeliers of Aix-la-Chapelle, Grosskomburg, or Hildesheim and the representation of the Heavenly Jerusalem in the Apocalypse in Trinity College, Cambridge, Ms. R. 16.2.

10 The biblical or French identity of the statues is still under debate. See J.G. von Hohenzollern, *Die Königsgalerie der französischen Kathedrale* (Munich, 1965).

11 For these windows, see Hans Reinhardt, *La cathédrale de Reims* (Paris, 1963), pp. 190–2, and Louis Grodecki and Catherine Brisac, *Le vitrail gothique au XIIIe siècle* (Fribourg, 1984), p. 113 [trans. *Gothic Stained Glass* (Ithaca, 1986)].

12 The most detailed study of these sections of the building remains Etienne Fels, "Le choeur et le transept de la cathédrale de Strasbourg, étude architecturale," *Bulletin de la Société des Amis de la cathédrale de Strasbourg* 2 (1932), 65–96.

13 See Augustine, *Sermo X, Patrologia Latina* 38: 91–7.

14 Bernhard Kerber, "Salomo," *Lexikon der christlichen Ikonographie*, vol. 4 (Freiburg, 1972), col. 22.

15 Julius von Schlosser, *Quellenbuch zur Kunstgeschichte des abendländischen Mittelalters* (Vienna, 1896), p. 131.

16 For this window, see Victor Beyer, Christiane Wild-Block, and Fridtjof Zschokke, *Les vitraux de la cathédrale de Strasbourg. Corpus Vitrearum France*, IX (Paris, 1986), pp. 95–103.

17 See F. Werner, "Christophorus," *Lexikon der christlichen Ikonographie*, vol. 5 (Freiburg, 1975), cols. 497–9.

18 See, for instance, Otto von Simson, "Le programme sculptural du transept méridional de la cathédrale de Strasbourg," *Bulletin de la Société des Amis de la cathédrale de Strasbourg* 10 (1972), 33–50.

19 One example of this tendency must suffice. Half a century ago Adolf Katzenellenbogen suggested that Peter the Venerable might have been the author of the program of the central portal at Vézelay ["The Central Tympanum of Vézelay: Its Encyclopaedic Meaning and Its Relation to the First Crusade," *Art Bulletin* 26 (1944), 141–51]. This opinion has not been supported by later scholars.

20 See E. de Lépinois and L. Merlet, eds., *Cartulaire de Notre-Dame de Chartres*, vol. 3 (Chartres, 1862–5), pp. 898f and 178.

21 Bulteau, *Monographie de la cathédrale de Chartres*, vol. 3 (Chartres, 1901), pp. 83–8.

22 See Grodecki and Brisac, *Le vitrail gothique*, p. 68.

23 The most recent discussion of the Naumburg problem is E. Schubert, "Zur Naumburg-Forschung der letzten Jahrzehnte," *Wiener Jahrbuch für Kunstgeschichte* 35 (1982), 121–38. The chronology of the sculpture and architecture is still an open problem. I continue to believe that the sculptures at Naumburg and Meissen were done shortly after one another by the same workshop. Since Meissen dates from the 1260s, there is good reason to believe that work at Naumburg began after 1250.

24 Louis Grodecki with Catherine Brisac and Claudine Lautier, *Le vitrail roman* (Fribourg, 1977), pp. 249–53, 274.

25 See Willibald Sauerländer, "Die Naumburger Stifterfiguren. Rückblick und Fragen," *Die Zeit der Staufer. Geschichte - Kunst - Kultur*, vol. 5 (Stuttgart, 1977), pp. 169–245. This article should now be read together with the work of Schubert, cited in note 23 above. See also H. Sciurie and F. Möbius, *Der Naumburger Westchor. Figurenzyklus, Architektur, Idee* (Worms, 1989). For a critical historiography of the hypothesized "Naumburg Master," see Kathryn Brush, "The Naumburg Master: A Chapter in the Development of Medieval Art History," *Gazette des Beaux-Arts*, 6th ser. 122 (1993), 109–22. See also Heinz Wiessner and Irene Crusius, "Aneliges Burgstift und Reichskirche. Zu den historischen Voraussetzungen des naumburger Westchores und seiner Stifterfiguren," in Irene Crusius, ed., *Studien zum weltlichen Kollegiatstift in Deutschland* (Göttingen, 1995), pp. 232–58.

11

The Architectural and Glazing Context of Poitiers Cathedral: A Reassessment of Integration

Virginia Chieffo Raguin

Raguin argues that much of what we have accepted as "medieval styles" may be concepts influenced by nineteenth-century restorers and Gothic Revival modes of thinking. She suggests that the overall coherence of Poitiers cathedral does not result from an imposed plan, whether for iconography or for sculpture, but from an organic interplay of a variety of local traditions. The cathedral of Poitiers, under construction from about 1160 to about 1300, affirms its affinity to general Poitevin building and pictorial traditions, and to the specific context of the city of Poitiers itself. The author argues against adherence to self-generating stylistic sequences. Rather, she suggests that, by looking at interrelationships among media over extended periods, we may observe a site-specific coherence, or "integration," of a variety of forms and images within the monument.

The cathedral was probably not ever designed for a fully saturated legendary glazing program, as was believed by the nineteenth-century historians. Rather, it developed an interaction between storied windows, grisaille, and mural painting to provide colour, image, and light. Rather than seeing religious patterns, such as typology, determining meaning, it would seem more reasonable to see the stained glass at Poitiers as visual narratives of individual adventures, much like a contemporaneous romance, such as Parsifal. Whether a window showed the story of the Prodigal Son, of Saint Peter, or of Joseph and his brothers, the primary focus was on the eventful story, formally if not ideologically, parallel to Christ's own dramatic life. Indeed, because medieval objects, such as the Crucifixion window in Poitiers, are not "art" in the way art has evolved in our contemporary world, they convey multivalent meanings of political as well as religious import. Christ is dead but also alive; he is a king but also a felon; he is naked, but clothed in purple. The points of view of the "artists" constantly shifted (as in medieval poem "'The Dream of the Rood'"), as did representations of space and the proportions of figures. One could also conflate separate events into a single spatial plane.

Raguin suggests that we reassess our understanding of the "visual" nature of this period. The Middle Ages defined, communicated, and transformed its traditions via the artificial objects it created. That these objects took their place within certain primary loci, such as cathedrals, not only enduring, but replicating parts of themselves via their impression on the minds of their multiple users, suggests that they sponsored an artistic integration of the most profound and comprehensive sort.

The city and the cathedral of Poitiers offer an unusually rich and accessible field for an analysis of artistic integration as an underlying principle of medieval construction. Integration, which I am here defining as synonymous with coherence, may be used as a guiding principle in our reading of a building and in our definition of design principles that allowed constructions to address their primary audiences, the populations that supported over extended periods of time these foci of communal urban activity.

The city of Poitiers retains to a remarkable degree the physical structure of its Gallo-Roman past, an ideal elevated fortress protected by a steep slope to the east meeting the half-circle passage of the river Le Clain on the west (flowing into the Vienne and then the Loire). Not simply urban topography but the buildings themselves remain accessible to the modern visitor. Of the episcopal group, the baptistry retains much of its primitive form, and the cathedral its original placement. The proximity of the buildings is evident today, clustered at the easternmost extremity of the city. Within two hundred metres of one another are the cathedral (fig. 1), baptistry, the church of Sainte-Radegonde and the ancient site of the monastery of Sainte-Croix. Above, on the arch of the hill, the church of Notre-Dame-la-Grande dominates the market-place and sits on the direct axis of the "Grand'Rue," a few paces from the ducal palace. This remarkable conservatism or, as it is sometimes more pejoratively labelled, resistance to northern French artistic forms in Poitiers can be understood only in the context of a city deeply imbued with a sense of its own past, a sense of past communicated to the inhabitants through their daily contact with these architectural settings. As one studies the many pieces of Poitevin construction – buildings, sculpture, mural painting, or stained glass – one is struck by a recapitulation of similar forms, albeit with considerable variation within these forms. As new houses were built according to the construction principles of their times, but along ancient Roman streets, so one repeated time-honoured massing of recognizable shapes, within which habits of construction and representation could vary. The effect was one of integration and familiarity, linking what to us now appear the far distant and more recent pasts, but which appeared to the medieval world as simply "yesterday."

Re-Evaluation of the Critical Approach to the Buildings and Its Windows

This study will concentrate on the glazing programs of the cathedral (fig. 2) and the architectural issues which relate to them. In order to deal directly with critical re-evaluation, descriptions of the present form of the building and windows, and the chronology of construction campaigns, have been relegated to the commentary following this essay. By addressing the issue of integration, the separate questions of dating, program, style, patronage, and the interrelationship of sculpture, architecture, and stained glass become not ends in themselves but elements contributing to a broader, and one hopes more meaningful, interpretation of the cathedral.

Programmatic Unity and Sequence of Construction

Hitherto we have tended to evaluate buildings according to a stylistic progression and a generally accepted belief that stylistic modes appear in sequential fashion. This does not appear to be a fruitful approach to Poitiers. The building, if judged in this manner, is remarkably *retardataire*. Rather than Gothic manqué, however, we may interpret the building as affirming its relationship to previous buildings, and to previous glazing traditions, justifying its legitimacy in a way analogous to the claims by the aristocracy to inherited rights by virtue of continuity. It is not so much that we have a "local tradition" of craftsmanship, or that stonemasons may have come from the chantiers of Angers, which experienced much rebuilding around

1150, but that "the right thing to do" appeared in this southern region to reaffirm many of the great qualities of what we have come to term the Romanesque heritage.[1] In their evaluations of Saint-Denis, Eric Fernie and William Clark have posited a similar impetus behind Abbot Suger's interest in repeating antique and Merovingian forms in a twelfth-century structure. Peter Draper's discussion of the cohesion of forms at Wells interprets a use of architectural features to create an overall effect with a purposeful sense of decorum. His use of the attitudinal term "coherence" rather than style can be directly applied to provide a more comprehensive and integrated analysis of the context of Poitiers.

Few medieval patrons wrote about their accomplishments; Fernie has analysed Abbot Suger's textualized attitudes concerning Saint-Denis in this volume. Figuring predominantly, and I would argue, standing even behind Suger's text, is the strength of the medieval oral tradition. A reassessment of modes of transmission of a spoken culture allows us to link the issues of the integration of forms achieved within a building to the integrative patterns of the social structure supporting them. Walter Ong comments that oral societies, which include pre-Gutenberg Europe, "lived in a continual present" manipulating memory and preserving equilibrium by retaining or sloughing off memories according to their relevance.[2] Thus the concern of this society was in general to preserve tradition, and the very forms of its buildings became a most effective means of "speaking/singing that tradition." The building stood as an accretion and/or revision of elements that may reflect a continuing tradition. Thus we err profoundly in prioritizing elements of change, or, in the opposite extreme, in seeking fixed states that we feel represent the "original" plan or ideal state of a building.

Our artificial definitions of Romanesque and Gothic thus appear as impediments to an integrated view of a building such as Poitiers.[3] It has been axiomatic for us to accept the "High Gothic" glazing programs of Chartres or the Sainte-Chapelle as representing ideal states. My recent work into the attitudes towards revival styles of the nineteenth and twentieth centuries has revealed that this belief in the high point of glazing as lying between 1150 and 1250 and in the hegemony of French styles is a recent phenomenon.[4] It appears to be very much related to Emile Mâle's work at the turn of the century, but reinforced in the popular imagination by experience of the Gothic Revival. In the United States, the "Gothic" aesthetic was projected by architects such as Ralph Adams Cram, writers such as Henry Adams, and stained glass designers such as Charles Connick and Lawrence Saint.[5] This thinking was, in turn, influenced by the concept of change equated with progress (Darwin, Marx, etc.) that we have generally accepted as being a natural state of societies. Thus we could speak of *retardataire* expressions or provincial art untouched by the innovations of major artistic centres, usually measured by constructs based on observations of the Ile-de-France. Poitiers challenges all of these assumptions.

The Relative Importance of Grisaille and Figural Glass

It has also been taken as axiomatic, probably because of the temporary glazing in grisaille patterns sometimes used in nineteenth- and twentieth-century buildings before the donors of figural windows could be found, that major medieval buildings were meant to have a full complement of medallion windows. Absence of such windows was attributed to a crisis in funding or to destruction by iconoclasts or natural disasters. Applying the same traditional assumption to Poitiers, the absence of a totally saturated program (pot metal glass of figural design) was explained as evidence of loss and destruction. We have, however, been prepared to accept grisaille as a necessary response to the Cistercian ban on imagery. We have also become aware of its importance in smaller buildings, such as the chapels of Saint-Germain-des-Prés or the axial chapel of Auxerre. Grisaille, or tapestry, windows have been recognized as major elements of English and German glazing programs, and yet we have neglected their continued importance in general French building practice.[6] Their use, however, has been cited by a number of recent studies by Madeline Caviness, Naomi Kline, Elizabeth Pastan, and Meredith Lillich.[7] Whatever may be our ultimate conclusions about Poitiers, we cannot now dismiss grisaille or ornamental glass out of hand as inferior to the legendary windows or presume that it was not meant as part of an original plan. Leaving out the three windows of the façade, there are twenty-three openings in the entire cathedral. Eleven windows, fewer than half of the total, now have coloured glass occupying the full extent of the windows (fig. 3).

In a church where the only illumination comes from these twenty-three windows, we might expect to see grisaille windows as part of an original, integrated concept and not as substitutes for lost windows with narrative scenes. We forget, to our peril, that most medieval buildings were painted, and that the present display of naked stone in buildings gives a highly inaccurate impression of the once-rich interiors. The vaults of Poitiers were once russet and the ribs deep blue, echoing the general French aesthetic of blue and red colour schema in the windows. The two transept chapels originally had altars along the east wall, and painted figural decoration along the west and end walls. A grisaille window above the altar would allow light to fall on the images in the lower walls, linking them to the images in the stained glass in the upper areas. Consideration of the total integrated effect of painted wall and painted window encourages a serious reassessment of the importance of grisaille as a possible necessity for the achievement of artistic integration.

In addition, Caviness has pursued issues of glazing patterns at Saint-Remi at Reims by considering the relationship of the medieval ornamental windows to the monks' choir.[8] Applying the same reasoning to Poitiers reveals interesting results. The canons of the cathedral were the primary users of the building, and their line of sight, when seated in the choir, would include the west and outer wall of the transepts, but a grisaille window above the transept altar would not have been visible.

Sequence of Style and Definition of Workshops

The Crucifixion window (fig. 4) has attracted attention from the scholar and the amateur alike.[9] In the past attempts have been made to analyse the "clash" of hieratic and narrative modes in the window, seeing this as an indication of a change in original conception. Thus scholarly energies were expended in trying to determine the original intention of the designers and the alterations made to that original design.[10] Our present inquiry challenges these assumptions.

The heterogeneity of types of images may have less to do with a chronological sequence of development in the windows than with the models underlying each image and their meaning for the inhabitants of Poitiers. Thus, the change of forms was integrative rather than disjunctive. We should recall again the context of the episcopal group and related monuments. The dominant image of the Ascension in the baptistry, a central figure of Christ flanked by an agitated angel on either side, seems quite close to the image dominating the upper portions of the cathedral's axial window. Although a Crucifixion is not an unusual theme in axial windows, the richness of the treatment of the cross and the regal purple cloth worn by Christ transcends generic images to evoke the presence of the Relic of the Holy Cross in the abbey adjacent to the cathedral and the hymns written in the late sixth-century Fortunatus to honour the reception of the relic.[11] The narrative medallion of the martyrdoms of Saints Peter and Paul and the royal donors below honour both the religious and the secular patrons of the cathedral.[12]

An acceptance of the integration of a variety of "stylistic" forms within a single image is supported by current re-evaluation of medieval literature being produced at the time of the building of Poitiers. Scholars have addressed the distinctions between our present view and what appears to have been a medieval view of inconsistency. Whereas the medieval editor respected the integrity of the story as a whole and the demands of its audience, the modern editor has been trained to respect the integrity of the author – that is, a purported individual's view of purpose and structure.[13] The very notion of authorship, however, as an articulate and self-reflective act, has been called into question by scholars assessing the habits of composition in medieval societies.[14] The repetitions and inconsistencies in descriptions of numbers of followers or participants in a battle, in the relationship of characters, even of personality traits (in one episode magnanimous, and in another vindictive) appear to have been quite consonant to a medieval listener with the idea of good storytelling. The possibility that these same concepts may have animated the composer of medieval visual narratives should encourage us to examine our modern concept of purpose and integrated program, especially in a corporate building such as a cathedral.

Grodecki's ground-breaking analysis of patterns of ornament and medallion schema was a turning-point in stained glass studies.[15] His analysis of pattern and style was continued in the study of the region by Jane Hayward, and her study of the style of contemporaneous windows at Angers and the Loire valley further defined the stylistic context of Poitiers.[16] The chronology of the windows originally proposed by Grodecki, however, is not totally supported by a close review of the extant panels. The chevet glass does show an earlier style, close to that of the Le Mans Ascension window.[17] The figures from Le Mans, dated 1140–45, are similar not only in the striking red and blue oppositions but in the boldness of figural delineation, especially the finely drawn parallel lines of the drapery and the sharp patterns of the folds. Although dated some fifty years before the Crucifixion window, the Poitevin manuscript of Sainte-Radegonde shows credible similarities and testifies to the strong influence of tradition.[18] One finds the same insistent outline, use of highly contrasting saturated colours, and emphasis on surface pattern. There is a dynamic integration of frame, ground, and figure, a tendency that appears to be characteristic of this region. The Noah panel now at the Cloisters can be compared to a detail of Christ in Majesty from the summit of the Glorification of the Virgin window from Angers. Above all, the rectilinear face, heavy eyebrows, and overlapping bands of hair remain typical of Angevin and Poitevin work.[19]

The windows that Grodecki has dated to a later campaign, around 1210–15, show a continuation of these conventions of representation. Again, interlocking borders are everywhere evident. The Isaac window contains many of the same stylistic formulas as the chevet windows and the Noah fragments. The painting style softens, becoming more fluid and sophisticated, but the same strength of outline; facial type; and fusion of ground, figure, and frame continue. The panels of the First Joseph window (figs. 5 and 12) show similar large, rounded heads but a more supple handling of the drapery. A number of panels in the window tentatively identified as depicting Saint Blaise (fig. 6) show similar characteristics. One sees the continuity of an atelier that favoured large, rounded, and especially full-jawed heads, a fluid drapery style, and rhythmic motion in the figures. The sleeve shows a particularly distinctive cluster of folds. The Prodigal Son window in the south transept may also be associated with this group. One finds the same thin-bodied figures with large, heavily jawed heads. The nested folds of the drapery, and the alternation of long, rectangular bearded heads with youthful rounded types recall the conventions observed in the Isaac window. In searching for a broader context for this style, I am drawn to a comparison with the Saint Eloi windows from the choir of Angers. Although differing in drapery conventions, this cycle shows the same predilection for larger heads and rounded forms favoured by this "sophisticated" style at Poitiers.

It is problematic whether to treat the group of windows defined by Grodecki as a "later" stylistic development as the result of a chronological sequence or simply as variety within a workshop repertoire. The Blaise window of the north transept contains two kinds of panels; one the "sophisticated" style treated above, the other a sort of "art brut," believed by Grodecki to be a product of a workshop in devolution. Faces, or bodies, have little anatomical verisimilitude; hair radiates from the head, and drapery folds fall, or rather shoot out, in straight lines. The same group of glass painters must have been responsible for the Joshua windows (fig. 7). Comparisons for such a style brings us back to Angers and the Saint Catherine window of about 1180.[20] The exaggerated profiles and energetic drapery encourages us to believe that the origins for the later windows at Poitiers, like the earliest, must be looked for in local soil. We can also compare the Balaam window at Poitiers, in this same group, with a fragment from a panel at Angers. The head shows a similar predilection for wide staring eyes and harsh linearity. The Passion and Infancy windows from Poitiers also belong more to this series than to any other, which cause us to reassess a belief in a chronological development from east to west, since the windows are located in the south choir, a section of the church presumably finished in 1165 and glazed before 1200. Either the windows were glazed in a sequence that did not correspond to the architectural sequence, or this window was transferred to the choir bay during a subsequent restoration.

It is precisely this essay into regional continuity that brings us into the Berry. Grodecki cited the regional affinities between the Angevin and Poitevin styles and the twelfth-century Nativity panels in the cathedral of Bourges.[21] Dated about 1160, the window shows a strong affinity to the style of the Saint Lawrence window in Poitiers. Both emphasize dynamic interaction of dense surface patterns and fully saturated colours. We see a sharp contrast in value as well as hue. It is possible to see the "region" of such a stylistic vocabulary extending far beyond the limits of Poitou, and well across central-southern France. Thus Poitiers and Bourges can be seen as part of the same region and the Bourges twelfth-century panels a product of a local rather than an imported workshop. One might also look at the striking similarities between the Nativity panels from the twelfth-century glass at Clermont-Ferrand and the Lot windows dated by Grodecki to 1210–15.[22] Thus we may even see the windows associated with the Good Samaritan workshop as similarly grounded in local traditions, from a "travelling" workshop from the Poitou. Actually, it is the Bourges New Alliance or "classicizing" workshop that now emerges as the truly alien style. The three-dimensional drapery style and elegant heads appear to derive from northern workshops familiar to us from the Saint Eustache Master of Chartres, windows in the north transept at Dijon, the axial chapel of Troyes, and ultimately the great cycles of Laon and Soissons.[23]

The "Integrated" Architectural Context

The cathedral presents a sense of large, continuous space (fig. 8), perhaps disorienting for visitors already familiar with Ile-de-France architecture of the period. Significantly, most studies have confined themselves to observing differences from section to section in the search for accepted signals of breaks in construction, even though the building is remarkably homogeneous. Most striking to the observer is the uniformity of a consistent spacing of bays, window placement, wall arcade, or even capital form, with only the slightest variation of vault shape and ribbing. Observe, for example, the similarities of the three bays closest to the crossing in the north nave (fig. 9). Even a trained eye labours to decipher changes in foliage patterns in the capitals stretching from chevet to west façade (fig. 10). Clearly novelty of form was not a priority at Poitiers.

Sculptured capitals, like moulding profiles, are often used as touchstones in dating sequences, but at Poitiers such an approach does not yield firm results. The capitals receiving the nave ribs, as well as those of the aisles and window openings, are remarkable for their overall similarity. The chevet at first glance appears to have employed a single multiple-leaf curly-edged variant of a Corinthian prototype. On closer observation, however, the treatment of spine, number of bands, or profile of leaf employed shows considerable variation. While the general outline of the form is identical, the elaboration of the details within the form varies. This principle, albeit with greater variation among foliage patterns, organizes the subsequent array of nave capitals even to the series framing the windows on the inner wall of the façade. At first disconcerting, the consistency of design over quite probably a century and a half reaffirms artistic practices evident elsewhere in the region. Most striking is the pattern of the façade decoration of Notre-Dame-la-Grande, a short distance from the cathedral. Indeed the splendour of that building, despite its small size, may have given some impetus for the construction of the cathedral. The sequences of rounded arches at Notre-Dame appear quite uniform, but within each "form envelope" one is hard pressed to find two patterns that are exactly the same. Even within the individual voussoirs of the archivolts surrounding the portal and central window, the foliate patterns differ slightly in outline and subject. Diversity of detail within homogeneity of form may be the general principle animating Poitevin construction as it was certainly for the integrative design concept for the cathedral.

The concept of diversity within uniformity may allow us to understand the largely ignored (presumably because of its awkward implications) thirteenth-century recutting of windows in choir and nave (figs. 3 and 13). There is no indication that the stained glass of the cathedral suffered major losses during these years. The recutting of openings does not seem to obey imperatives of north–south symmetry. In two cases (bays 1 and 5) the double-lancet Romanesque-style window is retained on the south, although the original glass is now replaced with grisaille, while on the north side of the bay, the opening is recut in later Gothic style. Only in the case of the two westernmost bays of the nave (bay 8) might arguments be raised to support a "stylistic" change owing to a later date of construction, presumably the 1250s, and concern to link the westernmost portion of the church with the façade. In the south choir bay, now with the four Renaissance saints, the tracery pattern is close to that in Saint-Sulpice-de-Favières, dating after 1245.[24] The facing window on the north is even simpler, although with a seven-lobed oculus, as opposed to a cinquefoil on the south. We must conclude that the diversity of fenestration was not considered an aesthetic impediment to the overall integration of the building. In particular, the windows of the western portions of the nave appear to have been completed in the latter part of the thirteenth century. They seem to have been originally planned as double-lancet openings similar to the openings containing the historiated glass of the Moses and Joshua, for the lower portions of the windows, now concealed behind the eighteenth-century balustrade, show the same column bases. The decision to complete the windows in a later Gothic manner, each window somewhat different in form, was not considered disruptive to the overall integration of the building. Indeed, the ability of the multilancet windows to afford additional light to the building appeared to be a desirable innovation, but one acceptable within the consistent development of the mural simplicity of the structure.

The conservative tendencies of the cathedral may also be observed in the baptistry, only 150 metres from the cathedral. The "Romanesque" murals of the baptistry of Saint-Jean affirm that tradition played an extremely strong role in Poitevin decorative concepts.

Although dating from the late eleventh or early twelfth century, the program is Early Christian! Four mounted Early Christian emperors suggesting an *adventus*, an Ascension (the flesh of Christ glorified and integrated into the realm of the heavens), Christ and Saint Maurice flanked by peacocks and dragons, and images of urns and flowers must echo an earlier program and/or similar themes on Early Christian sarcophagi.[25] As discussed earlier, the programs in the baptistry, which functioned as the exclusive site for the sacrament during the period of the cathedral's construction and decoration, may even explain some of the iconographic and stylistic choices in the cathedral windows.

Not simply the decoration, but architectural elements of the building exhibit continuity with the traditions of the area. Resonances among these buildings include examples such as the abbey of Fontevraud, the nave of the cathedral of Angers (1148–53), or the thirteenth-century nave of Sainte-Radegonde two hundred metres distant.[26] The blind arcading of the interior walls, the broad single vessel, or hall church type, repeat the language of the region, a language that bridges our generally accepted framework of a Romanesque or Gothic "style" (fig. 11). We cannot so easily define construction through stylistic changes, nor in a broader perspective should this issue intrude to the exclusion of perhaps more important questions. Spacious ground plans and a lateral, rather than vertical, emphasis seem to be regional priorities and appear in all these buildings (figs. 1, 8, and 11). The question of the sequence of the cathedral's construction may now be addressed with a different set of priorities. André Mussat's traditional east–west sequence does not sufficiently take account of numerous breaks in the stonework or unexpected structural similarities from east to west.[27] More consistent with the evidence would seem a thesis that the building was laid out from east to west in its first campaign – if not every section of the lower levels, at least key elements to define the size of the building. For some sections, the walls up to the springing of the vaults were constructed, and then the vaults themselves. One may then think of the construction of the cathedral in successive layers, not vertical sections. Thus both the glass and its framework reiterate continuity and visual integration of earlier and later periods of construction.[28]

Patronage

Documentation on donations and dedications for the cathedral is virtually non-existent for this period in Poitiers. In the absence of primary written evidence we are forced to use analogies with better-documented buildings, such as those argued here by Peter Kurmann and Brigitte Kurmann-Schwarz for Chartres, Peter Draper for Wells, and Beat Brenk for the Sainte-Chapelle. The first extant text recording the cathedral's patronage dates from the Renaissance and is a citation from a local historian in 1525 that the building was due to the initiative of Henry II in response to "la resqueste de madame Alienor son epouse."[29] The tradition seems plausible, since corroborating arguments include the presence of a royal donor couple at the base of the Crucifixion window and the stylistic evidence of both glass and architecture suggesting a date of around 1160–70. Caviness has suggested that the window may have been offered in expiation for Becket's murder, and may date after 1172, when Henry was reconciled with the church.[30] The episcopate of Jean Belmain, an Anglo-Norman and intimate of the king, extended from 1162 to ca. 1182.[31] Henry had married Eleanor in 1152, assuming her powers as duchess of Poitou in 1154. In 1160, Henry installed his son Richard as count of Poitiers and in 1162 succeeded in placing his candidate on the episcopal seat. Jean Belmain had developed an intimacy with Thomas Becket, then Henry's chancellor, and above all with Roger de Pont l'Eveque, archbishop of York, where Jean had served as cathedral treasurer from 1158 to 1162. Jean was not only an able individual, but one of wide personal experience and knowledge of the most important Anglo-Norman centres of power. It is persuasive to think that the plan for an extremely large and massive building may have originated with this conflux of education and political power, similar to the situation surrounding Abbot Suger's rebuilding of Saint-Denis. It is to be remembered that, in England during the century preceding Jean Belmain's episcopate, the Norman hierarchy had announced routinely its ascendency to the previously Saxon bishoprics by massive building campaigns. Jean Belmain may very well have exerted a personal influence on the selection of styles for the construction of the cathedral of Poitiers. His experience in England would argue that he was familiar with, and appreciative of, several site-specific practices, such as English traditions that favoured grisaille elements as well as medallion windows, and the English use of the flat chevets, specifically the twelfth-century construction of York Minster.

The shift from Poitevin forms to those more closely patterned after

Ile-de-France precedents may also indicate the intervention of a new patron's particular tastes. The precise dating of elements of the façade, towers, window openings, and sculpture is controversial. Willibald Sauerländer suggests on the basis of stylistic affinities that the sculptures date about or shortly after 1250.[32] Mussat suggests that the towers are earlier than the portals and windows, noting that the central rose is patterned after the north transept rose of Notre-Dame in Paris completed about 1255.[33] One might envisage, however, a sculptural program being carved while construction of the cathedral was in process, or that sculptors were working in a style that may have become out of date in "more progressive" northern areas, allowing for the later dates of the last quarter of the thirteenth century, as suggested by Elisa Maillard.[34] Scholars have tried to associate the work of northern trained sculptors with an intervention of a northern patron. Alphonse of Poitiers, brother of Louis IX, who became count of Poitiers in 1241, has sometimes been named, but no concrete evidence connecting his liberality, or even interest in the cathedral, has been forthcoming. For proponents of a later date for the façade, the episcopate of Galterus of Bruges, governing the see from 1278 to 1306, may be significant.

Integration or "Unity" in the Iconographic Program

An analysis of the principle of integration as opposed to unity reveals some of the principles against which new integrative studies of medieval buildings must operate. There does not seem to have been any attempt on the part of the canons, or others, to record the iconography of the windows. A study of the subject-matter of the windows appeared along with the new attitudes towards restoration and Gothic Revival of the nineteenth century. Viollet-le-Duc, Lassus, Didron, and their followers championed a revival of Gothic forms as ideal expressions of Christian purpose as well as natural expressions of unity and harmony as principles of artistic beauty.[35] It became inconceivable to approach a building, or a window, as if there were not an overall plan. If the individual accepted the religious edifice as important and "beautiful," it was presumed that a coherent didactic and formal unity was at its core, certainly a concept still vibrant in Mâle's work at the turn of the century. The task of the researcher was to strip away the confusion, recover the original core, and when possible to re-create the context of the original plan, even to rebuilding missing windows, or extending a truncated or damaged building. This attitude was furthered by the belief that the modern architect and glass painter could achieve works that were not nineteenth century, but a continuation of medieval objects, though produced in the nineteenth century. In the mid-nineteenth century, Abbé Auber therefore analysed all the windows, and made a panel-by-panel description of each scene.[36] Rayon produced a similar manuscript in 1925.[37]

This quest for unity, and the belief that the glass painter could restore and complete windows in an original style was the ethos that supported Steinheil's restoration at the end of the nineteenth century. It was during this restoration that the Noah panels now in the Cloisters Museum were removed and eventually found their way to the art market.[38] I would suggest that it was this ethos that permitted what we now term "theft" on the grounds that the panels were extraneous to the iconographic unity of the hagiographic cycles under repair. It was even a current practice to consider that such disjunctive elements would better serve as workshop models deserving to be integrated into the studio of the glass restorer. This nineteenth-century definition of integration appears to me confining and rigid. I prefer an approach, like the views of Arnold Klukas on Durham, or the analysis of Brigitte Bedos-Rezak, that identifies fluid and ever-changing relationships, seeing the entire cathedral as an organized vocabulary of symbolic lines, colours, and volumes operating in systems similar to those informing contemporary philosophy.

A very great deal of work needs to be done on the Poitiers narratives, and I can only offer a few observations at this juncture. A concept of north/south typological ordinance with Old Testament in the nordic cold, and New Testament scenes associated with the regions of the south and the warmth of God's grace is very much a heritage of Mâle's structuralist views. A typological program was also the Abbé Auber's conclusion in 1848. Poitiers, however, truly does not evidence such a format, for, excluding the three windows of the chevet, ten (including Noah) are of Old Testament subjects as compared with three of the Life of Christ and two of the Parables.[39] Caviness's evaluation of narratives in biblical windows and Wolfgang Kemp's discussion of narrative windows at Chartres and of French and German typological formats, as well as recent work on literature of the twelfth and thirteenth centuries, encourage us to reassess the concept of internal coherence, and above all, the existence of a textual source for windows.[40] I would add my voice to these scholars who suggest that there are generic patterns for narrative sequences, patterns that tap deeper sources than our contemporary distinctions of Old or New Testament, or religious and secular. Above all, the windows must be seen as the products of a predominantly oral culture. Their development took place at the same time as the elaboration of the "secular" romance in literature.

The essential elements of medieval narrative are repetition, dialogue or altercation, and a passage through the story by means of key episodes. Star-crossed lovers are many, but we recognize Tristan and Iseult by the episode of the love potion at the head of the narrative. In Poitiers's First Joseph window (fig. 12), prominently silhouetted at the top are the signature episodes of Joseph's dreams of the wheat sheaves bowing down and of the sun, moon, and eleven stars worshipping him. The repetitive, but reversed compositions showing Joseph in bed in the second register reflect the conventions of verbal narrative by signalling to the listener a turning-point episode by the use of similar introduction and closure passages. The repetition of the dream or vision, moreover, functions as a standard emphatic device. The episodes that follow are generic; they might relate to any story, and indeed, I believe they are meant to strike resonances with all standard confrontation narratives. We see sequences of altercation, first between two individuals, and then of an individual with a group. I believe it is not very productive to try to link any one panel with specific passages in the Vulgate (which are quite complex) between the telling of the dream and the lowering of Joseph into a cistern. The window does not illustrate the Vulgate text; it parallels it.

In this window, three signature episodes appear, artfully distributed at the top, centre, and bottom to organize the narrative. The dream appears at the top, the lowering into the cistern in the centre, and in the lowest register, Joseph led off to Egypt on a camel. The episodes are linked by the standard devices of repetition and altercation. Joseph speaks to his brothers on the left, and possibly to his father Jacob on the right. In the register immediately below, this sequence is reversed: the brothers surround Joseph on the right (who is recognized by his white shift) and Jacob is alone with Joseph on the left.

I suggest that it is fruitful to begin to read the Poitiers windows as visual narratives of individual adventures, much like a contemporaneous romance, such as *Parsifal*. Whether the story of the Prodigal Son, Saint Peter, or Joseph and his brothers, the primary focus was on the dramatic telling of the tale, formally if not ideologically, parallel to Christ's own dramatic life. Recall, for a moment, the structure of the Passion, with the signature episodes of the Kiss of Judas and the Flagellation, linked by the standard confrontation sequences of the altercation of Christ and the High Priest, Christ and Pilate, and Christ and the crowd of Jews. The correspondences are analogous to those that Draper described as the superficial appearance and associations of architectural forms at Wells. Such practices of construction, for both the church and the story, are typical of an oral culture which stores and reinforces cultural information by associative recall. I suggest that is also fruitful to begin to read the entire cathedral as a whole, as a "text" constructed from a vocabulary of symbolic lines, colours, and volumes, storing, receiving, and restating societal presumptions, not simply of its own age, but across time.

The Cathedral in Its Present Form: Descriptive Text

Although much altered by time and by natural and human disasters, a very large amount of glass dating between the mid-twelfth and mid-thirteenth centuries is extant (fig. 2). The cathedral's flat chevet holds its three best-known windows. In the centre is a monumental Crucifixion, with Ascension above and martyrdom of Peter and Paul at the bottom (fig. 4). Medallion windows narrate the legend of Saint Lawrence on the north and Saints Peter and Paul on the south.

The choir contains windows of Abraham and Lot to the north, and the Nativity (?) and Passion (?) to the south. In the north transept are two windows portraying the story of Joseph, the legend of an unknown saint (Blaise?) and the Exodus (?). In the south transept are windows of Lazarus and Dives and the Prodigal Son, and two additional windows, one of which appears to contain scenes relating to Christ's miracles. In the north nave are two windows of the story of Joshua, and opposite them, on the south, a window of the story of Moses and one of Balaam. The windows now stand as completed in 1948 with panels in a modern style by Francis Chigot of Limoges.[41]

The glass is housed in clerestory windows that are the only means of illumination to the interior. The cathedral therefore "works" in a very different manner from the High Gothic of the Ile-de-France, but certainly with great power. Its great openness calls to mind the aesthetic of the German hall church (fig. 8). The choir stresses the high, almost domical, vaults peculiar to the Poitevin-Angevin region in the twelfth century. Even in the transepts and nave, dating to the thirteenth century, the vaulting echoes this earlier disposition and the elevation retains a two-part system of wall and clerestory, very unlike the three-storey elevation of the Gothic north.

The windows had been subjected to a number of restorations previous to Chigot's. In 1884, Steinheil (fig. 13) restored the chevet windows and completed them with panels in an archaizing style.[42] That windows should be reglazed in a period style appears to be a nineteenth-century concept, undoubtedly contingent on the development of the "vitrail archéologique" as a desirable means of repairing or completing a building in a medieval style, and achieving a "modern" sense of integration as uniformity. A century earlier the restorers appeared to have limited their work to cleaning and releading, as well as to necessary repairs. The expertise (evaluation) by Reverad and Descantes in 1775 is meticulous, fortunately, allowing one to decipher a numbering system that segmented the building: south choir and transept, north choir and transept, chevet, north nave, south nave, then west wall (fig. 14). The restorers used the term *verre peint* for the pot metal glass and several terms for the white glass – *grisaille, verre blanc,* and *verre demi-blanc.*

The earlier restorers, such as Frovignault and Robin, who made a detailed expertise in 1562, appear to have cannibalized older, less complete windows (fig. 15). In the 1560s, after what appears to have been major losses of glass effected by Huguenot zealots, glass was moved from the nave to act as stop-gaps for the chevet windows much in the same way that windows in the cathedral of Auxerre were conflated, sometimes resulting in two or even three narrative cycles in a single opening.[43] There is no evidence of an attempt by these sixteenth- or eighteenth-century restorers to complete windows with new panels in either a medieval or a Renaissance style. The figural windows, except those of the transept ends, were provided with an infill of white glass in the lower portions. In 1775 the eastern windows of the transept are described as being *verre blanc; bordure en verre peint.* On inspection, it is clear that the border of pot metal glass comprises fragments of medieval glass of a variety of periods. In several of the panels, stop-gap heads alien to the cathedral's program appear, but they are similar to the fourteenth-century painting styles in the windows of Sainte-Radegonde. The evidence suggests that a studio worked on more than one site, perhaps even concurrently, and used any glass available as stop-gap aid.[44]

After the sixteenth-century restoration, the choir became neatly apportioned, two double-lancet medallion windows between openings in grisaille on the north and south walls and three fully saturated windows in the chevet.[45] It is interesting that in the 1562 expertise the windows were named according to their location within the church, for example, "in the chapel of Saint Andrew" (the name given to the north transept), and not according to their subject-matter.[46] It is interesting that there does not seem to be a difference in prices listed by Frovignault and Robin for repairs to a window in pot metal or in grisaille glass.

Chronology

Mussat has suggested that the cathedral's construction progressed in a predictable east–west sequence: the chevet and first two bays of the choir about 1155–65, the third choir bay and the transept about 1190–1210, the beginning of the nave about 1210, and the final bays of the nave in the last quarter of the thirteenth century.[47] Grodecki's analysis dated the choir glass to the late twelfth century, and that in the nave to the 1240s, which accorded with this building chronology.[48]

Many of the window openings, however, were recut throughout the thirteenth century. Three bays of the late twelfth-century choir show recut stonework dating to about the 1250s. Five of the nave windows also show a varied degree of recutting, so that the exterior view of the cathedral presents a wide variety of window openings. A simple chronological sequence is difficult to construct if we try to base sequences on changes in the foliate capitals and mouldings. The sculpture, like the architecture, demonstrates a highly uniform appearance across the 150 years of the building's construction.[49]

Grodecki's analysis concentrated on the chevet glass and the windows of the north side of the choir and transept. Relying heavily on the photographic documentation of the Steinheil restoration, he assigned the three chevet windows to a single workshop working about 1165–70.[50] Grodecki also posited a travelling workshop centred around the Good Samaritan Master who accomplished the north side of the choir and north transept glass (Lot, Isaac, and First and Second Joseph windows) around 1210–15, travelled to the cathedral of Bourges to execute the windows of the Good Samaritan and others in the ambulatory around 1210–15, and returned to Poitiers to complete the glazing in the 1230s.[51] As with the architecture, the Poitiers glazing shows an underlying continuity, emphasizing bold graphic patterns and a dynamic integration of frame, ground, and figure.

BUILDING OR RESTORATION CAMPAIGNS AND COMMENTARY

1980s	Releading and cleaning of windows.
1981	Publication of Jane Hayward's "The Lost Noah Window from Poitiers," *Gesta* 20/1, 129–39.
1951	Publication of Louis Grodecki's "Les vitraux de la cathédrale de Poitiers," *Congrès archéologique de France* 109, 138–63. First modern assessment of complete program.
1948	Publication of Louis Grodecki's "A Stained Glass "Atelier" of the Thirteenth Century," *Journal of the Warburg and Courtauld Institutes* 11, 87–111. Relationship of workshops producing thirteenth-century windows to contemporary windows of the cathedral of Bourges: The Good Samaritan Master posited.
1938–1948	Francis Chigot, Limoges: Releading of windows. Removal of grisaille panels completing nave and transept windows and replacement with panels in a modern style. Some rearrangement of original panels in windows. Restoration campaign documented with several small-scale photographs of entire windows after work was completed. No photographs of pre-restoration state. (MH Dossier 3146)
1933	Repair of grill work protecting three chevet windows (MH Dossier 3145)
1925	Compilation by Rayon, "Inventaire des vitraux du département de la Vienne" (MH Archives 4 Doc.12)
1920	Windows in grisaille glass damaged by a hurricane and repaired. (MH Dossier 3145)
1910	Repair of glass and masonry of second window of south and first window of north nave in grisaille. (MH Dossier 3145)
1884–1904	Pierre Eugène Guérithault, glass painter, Poitiers: Nov. 1885 "devis" for the restoration of all "vitraux medallions de couleurs," naming each of the extant

windows except the three of the chevet. Continuation of repairs to plain glazed windows, including Leprévost's proposal for the westernmost window of the south nave in 1901. (Archives nationales F19 7821 and 7822; Archives de la Vienne V 5 14)

1872–85   Steinheil and Leprévost: Report by J. de Mérindol, architect, with Steinheil's window-by-window expertise for entire program, 12 October 1872 (Archives nationales F19 7821; MH Dossier 3145). Only three windows of chevet restored. In 1883 detailed photographs taken by Durand of the original condition and post-restoration state (1:4 scale, Series MH 6745–51, 6753, 6754, 6756-61, 6776, 6778–82, 6785–91, 15493, and 15494). Bill for work, including account of extent of restoration in each panel, approved 18 February 1884. Extraneous panels removed; four Renaissance figures placed into "verrières blanches" in 1885 (Archives nationales F19 7821). Some panels enter art market. Panels from a Noah story and that of a bishop saint (Martial?) acquired in 1924 by the Metropolitan Museum of Art [Jane Hayward, "The Lost Noah Window from Poitiers," *Gesta* 20/1 (1981), 129–39]. Virgin and Child panel originally from Sainte-Radegonde and used as stop-gap? [Jules Roussel, *Vitraux du XIIe au XVe siècle*, vol. 2 (Paris, 1913), pl. 16]. Some restoration of the grisaille or plain glazed windows of the cathedral made at the same time by the local glazier Pierre Eugène Guérithault (Archives nationales F19 7821).

1860s   François de Guilhermy: Brief description, mentioning date of 1765 in the western nave window, and a fragment of an Annunciation placed as stop-gap in the Crucifixion window (Paris, Bibliothèque nationale, MS nouv. acq. fr. 6106, fols. 42–4).

1848–9   Publication of Abbé Auber, *Histoire de la cathédrale de Poitiers* [*Mémoires de la Société des Antiquaires de l'Ouest*], 2 vols. Panel by panel description of the windows, in diagrams and text.

1838–44   Brothers Gon: restoration of three windows of façade (Archives nationales F19 7819; Archives de la Vienne V5 3).

1820s	Drawings by Alexandre Gardnier of north transept and by A. Hivonnait of north side of cathedral, detailing fenestration from exterior. (Poitiers, Bibliothèque municipale, MS 547, fols. 323-24; published in Auber, *Histoire*, vol. 1, pls. IV and VII).
1804	Restoration campaign for all windows "devis, l'an 12, 4 ventose." The work presumably was confined to structural needs. Cult officially re-established 1806. (Archives de la Vienne V5 3)
Revolutionary period	No damage reported but use of building for religious purposes interrupted.
1791	Organ by François-Henri Clicquot of Paris installed.
1775–8	The widow Reverad and her son-in-law Descantes, Poitiers: Complete restoration of all windows. Presumably no rearrangement of panels, but possibly renewal of some grisaille and releading (expertise in Archives de la Vienne G191). Expertise by Steinheil, of 1872, mentions white glass with dates: in No. 1 (north nave) the date of 1763, in No. 3 (north nave) date of 1779 (MH 3145 and Architect's report of 12 October 1872 in Archives nationales F19 7821).
1759-87	With election of Bishop Martial-Louis de Beaupoil de Saint Aulaire, large gift from Louis XV for renovation of the cathedral (Auber, *Histoire*, vol. 2, pp. 396-418). Construction of gallery at window level surrounding the interior, the tribune to provide for the planned organ, and the three altars of chevet. Interior probably cleaned of its medieval paintings.
1569	Between 24 July and 7 September, bombardments of the cathedral. The angle of cannon fire from across the river makes it highly unlikely windows could have been damaged, except possibly for the chevet [M. A. Libergé, *Ample discours ... au siège de Poitiers* (Paris, 1569); Auber, *Histoire*, vol. 2, pp. 266–71].
1562	Huguenots enter city and seriously damage the cathedral (Archives de la Vienne G 164; Auber, *Histoire*, vol. 2, pp. 239–58). René Frovignault and Michel Robin, glaziers in Poitiers, produce expertise of damaged windows (Archives de la Vienne G181). Repairs made

	either at this time or following the 1569 damages. White glass placed in lower portions of the figural windows, with the exception of windows of transept ends. Four Renaissance saints, probably originally in westernmost bay of south choir, placed into chevet windows to either side of Crucifixion as a stop-gap measure. Other stop-gaps include Noah panels and a late thirteenth-century Virgin and Child. The state of the windows presumably unchanged when Auber describes them in 1848. (Auber, *Histoire*, vol. 1, pp. 341–8).
c. 1290 ?	Termination of façade.
1280 ?	Construction of westernmost bay of north nave (compare radiating rose pattern in fenestration in nave of Clermont-Ferrand).
1278–1306	Episcopate of Galterus of Bruges.
1250s ?	Recutting of stonework of windows of choir.
1162–82	Episcopate of Jean Belmain, an Englishman. Probable period of the first stages of the construction of the cathedral and the three chevet windows.

NOTES

1 Jacques Mallet, *L'Art roman de l'ancien Anjou* (Paris, 1984), esp. the churches of Angers, pp. 264–74.

2 Walter J. Ong, *Orality and Literacy* (New York, 1982). Brian Stock, *The Implications of Literacy* (Princeton, 1983), and others, have brought new insights into the development of literacy at this time. Yet it seems to me that, until a general written vernacular culture and a means of transmission other than the handwritten text becames current, visual imagery must be viewed as the primary, if not the exclusive, means of preserving the traditions under study.

3 For example, the glazing program at Poitiers is split between the two volumes of Grodecki's study of Romanesque and Gothic glazing traditions, *Le vitrail roman* (Fribourg, 1977) and Louis Grodecki and Catherine Brisac, *Le vitrail gothique au XIIIe siècle* (Fribourg, 1984) [trans. *Gothic Stained Glass* (Ithaca, 1986)]. For the sake of consistency, all the dates cited here are those of the 1977 publication.

4 Virginia C. Raguin, "Revivals, Revivalists, and Architectural Stained Glass," *Journal of the Society of Architectural Historians* 49/3 (1990), 310–29.

5 See Henry Adams, *Mont-Saint-Michel and Chartres* (Boston, 1904), and Ralph Adams Cram, *The Substance of Gothic* (Boston, 1917), among other works. Lawrence Saint provided watercolour illustrations for a text by Hugh Arnold, *Stained Glass of the Middle Ages in England and France* (London, 1913). Unlike almost all earlier publications on the history of glazing, the book dealt exclusively with English and French glazing traditions, establishing a canon of great early buildings, Le Mans, Poitiers, Saint-Denis, Chartres, Canterbury, and York, with Rouen of the fourteenth century and Fairford in the fifteenth century as the rare examples of later programs. The book exerted a profound influence on American attitudes, professional and lay, concerning the "true principles" of stained glass. The impact is still evident in Charles Connick's *Adventures in Light and Color* (New York, 1937).

6 One would more justly describe the German works as tapestry windows. See Erfurt's Franciscan, Dominican, and Augustinian church windows: Erhard Drachenberg, Karl-Joachim Maercher, and Christa Schmidt, *Die mittelalterliche Glasmalerei in den Ordenskirchen und im Angermuseum zu Erfurt, Corpus Vitrearum Medii Aevi, Deutsche Demokratische Republik* 1.1 (Berlin, 1976), pp. 61–4, 120–41, 199–212.

7 Madeline Caviness, *The Sumptuous Arts of the Royal Abbeys of St Remi and Braine* (Princeton, 1990), p. 49, Catalogue D, R.0.1-4; Elizabeth Pastan, "The Early Stained Glass of Troyes Cathedral c. 1200–1240," Dissertation, Brown University, 1986, pp. 98–103; Naomi Kline, "Stained Glass of the Abbey Church of Orbais," Dissertation, Boston University, 1983; Meredith Lillich, "The Band Window: A Theory of Origin and Development," *Gesta* 9/1 (1970), 26–33.

8 Caviness, *Sumptuous Arts*, pp. 45–9.

9 The Crucifixion window intrigued the Gothic Revival glass painters. See N.J.H. Westlake, *A History of Design in Stained and Painted Glass*, vol. 1 (London, 1881), p. 33; Lewis Day, *Windows: A Book about Stained and Painted Glass* (London, 1909), pp. 112–15, figs. 27, 68–70; Charles Connick created a series of watercolour sketches showing how the window was transformed by light at different times of the day (*Adventures in Light and Color*, pp. 178–9, pl. 1C, Morning, Autumn; pl. 2C, Afternoon, Autumn). For the most thorough study and reference to previous authors, see Robert Grinnell, "Iconography and Philosophy in the Crucifixion Window at Poitiers," *Art Bulletin* 28 (1946), 171–96.

10 Grinnell, "Iconography and Philosophy," pp. 171–7; correspondence between Jean Lozinski and Louis Grodecki, Grodecki papers, 1950s; René Crozet, "Vitrail de la Crucifixion de Poitiers," *Gazette des Beaux-Arts* 11 (1934), 218–31. Elisa Maillard, however, did see an intrinsic formal unity:

"Structure géométrique du vitrail de la Crucifixion de la cathédrale Saint-Pierre de Poitiers," *Actes du 87e Congrès National des Sociétés Savantes* (Paris, 1963), pp. 329–37.

11 Especially the *Vexilla regis*, which became a customary part of the liturgy for Good Fridays throughout the Latin church. See Yvonne Labande-Mailfert in *Histoire de l'Abbaye Sainte-Croix de Poitiers. Mémoires de la Société des Antiquaires de l'Ouest*, 4th ser., 19 (1986–7), 25–60. For a shorter discussion of the hymn, see *The Catholic Encyclopedia* (New York, 1911), vol. 15, pp. 396–7.

12 The 1406 inventory of the cathedral's treasury begins with the relic of Saint Peter's skull (Archives de Vienne).

13 Karl Frederick Morrison, *History as a Visual Art in the Twelfth Century Renaissance* (Princeton, 1990), pp. 103–8, also presentation by James Schultz and others in "Coherence in Medieval Art," Dale Kinney, session organizer, 23rd International Congress on Medieval Studies, Kalamazoo, MI, 1988.

14 Eric A. Havelock, *Preface to Plato* (Cambridge, MA, 1963).

15 Louis Grodecki, "A Stained Glass 'Atelier' of the Thirteenth Century," *Journal of the Warburg and Courtauld Institutes* 11 (1948), 87–111.

16 Jane Hayward, "The Angevine Style of Glass Painting," Dissertation, Yale University, 1958, and idem., "The Redemption Windows of the Loire Valley," *Etudes d'art médiéval offertes à Louis Grodecki* (Paris, 1981), pp. 129–38.

17 For the Le Mans glazing, with quality illustrations, see Catherine Brisac in *La cathédrale du Mans*, ed. André Mussat (Paris, 1981), pp. 60–9, 103–26.

18 Poitiers, Bibliothèque municipale, MS 250. The manuscript is generally dated to the late eleventh century. Magdalena E. Carrasco, "Spirituality in Context: The Romanesque Illustrated Life of St. Radegund of Poitiers," *Art Bulletin* 72 (1990), 414–35. See also Grodecki, *Vitrail roman*, fig. 45.

19 Grodecki, *Vitrail roman*, fig. 64; Hayward, "Angevine Style."

20 Grodecki, *Vitrail roman*, fig. 65.

21 Ibid., fig. 69.

22 Raguin, *Stained Glass in Thirteenth-Century Burgundy* (Princeton, 1982), pp. 90–2, figs. 144 and 145.

23 Ibid., pp. 92–6.

24 Louis Grodecki, *Gothic Architecture* (New York, 1985), pp. 112–13, fig. 111.

25 Otto Demus and Max Hirmer, *Romanesque Mural Painting* (New York, 1970), p. 419, pl. p. 29.

26 Mallet, *L'art roman*, p. 112; Grodecki/Brisac, *Vitrail gothique*, pp. 42–4, figs. 40–5.

27 He does note some unusual continuity in form and tentatively suggests that, for the transept area, "peut-être la construction se fait-elle alors par

tranches horizontales" and continues to speculate that the walls of the nave must be considerably earlier than the vaults: André Mussat, *Le style gothique de l'Ouest de la France* (Paris, 1963), pp. 258–9.

28 See similar construction in layers at Saint Martin's church in Landshut, a comparable hall church type. Brigitte Kurmann-Schwarz, in *Sankt Martin zu Landshut* (Landshut, 1985), 53–6, 102–9. I am grateful to Peter Kurmann for calling my attention to this comparison.

29 Jean Bouchet, *Annales d'Aquitaine* (Poitiers, 1644), p. 145 [first ed. 1525, fol. LXII].

30 Caviness, *Sumptuous Arts*, p. 48, note 102.

31 Mussat, *Style gothique de l'Ouest*, pp. 245–6; René Crozet, "Recherches sur la cathédrale et les evêques de Poitiers des origines au commencement du XIIIe siècle," *Bulletin de la Société des Antiquaires de l'Ouest*, 4th ser., 4 (1962), 366–9; P. Boissonnade, "Administrateurs laïques et ecclésiatiques anglo-normands en Poitou à l'époque d'Henri II Plantagenet (1152–1189)," *Bulletin de la Société des Antiquaires de l'Ouest*, 3d ser., 5 (1919–21), 170–3.

32 Willibald Sauerländer, *Gothic Sculpture in France 1140–1270* (New York, 1972), pp. 506–8, pls. 296–9, ill. 109.

33 Mussat, *Style gothique de l'Ouest*, p. 259.

34 Elisa Maillard, *Les sculptures de la cathédrale Saint-Pierre de Poitiers* (Poitiers, 1921), pp. 89–122.

35 See for example Adolphe Napoléon Didron, "harmony is the first and most important law of beauty," *Annales archéologiques* 1 (1844), 152. See also Jean-Michel Leniaud, "Les projets de transformation du Clicquot de la cathédrale de Poitiers au milieu du dix-neuvième siècle," *Bulletin de l'Association François-Henri Clicquot* (1979), 16–26.

36 Iconography described in a running text and in diagrams in Auber, *Histoire*.

37 Manuscript notes, E. Rayon, "Inventaire des vitraux de la Vienne, 1925," Archives de la Commission des Monuments Historiques de la France, Paris.

38 Jane Hayward, "The Lost Noah Window from Poitiers," *Gesta* 20/1 (1981), 129–39.

39 One is tempted to suggest that the unusual choice might have something to do with the erudition of Jean Belmain, noted for his knowledge of Greek and Hebrew as well as Latin. See above, note 31.

40 Caviness, "Biblical Stories in Windows: Were They Bibles for the Poor?" *The Bible in the Middle Ages: Its Influence on Literature and Art*, ed. Bernard S. Levy, pp. 103–47 (Binghamton NY, 1992); Wolfgang Kemp, *Sermo Corporeus: Die Erzählung der mittelalterlichen Glasfenster* (Munich, 1987), esp.

pp. 119–32, and idem., "Parallelismus als Formprinzip. Zum Bibelfenster der Dreikönigskapelle des Kölner Doms," *K–lner Domblatt* (1991), 259–94.

41 Yves-Marie Froidevaux, in *Francis Chigot, Maître Verrier* [exh. cat.] (Limoges, 1980), n.p. See also Louis Grodecki in *Le vitrail français* (Paris, 1958), p. 87, fig. 54. The restoration, praised by Grodecki, was lamentably undocumented with no pre-restoration photographs deposited in the Historical Monuments Commission archives. Panels were added to the lower portions of all the figural windows except those of the chevet and the transept ends. The restorers attempted to continue the iconographic programs identified and even repositioned the original panels.

42 For details of this campaign and others see "Building or Restoration Campaigns and Commentary."

43 Virginia Raguin, *Stained Glass in Burgundy* p. 30; François de Guilhermy, notes of visits of 1854, 1858, 1864, Paris, Bibliothèque nationale MS nouv. acq, fr. 6095.

44 We see the same process in the nineteenth and twentieth centuries, sometimes even an assembling of fragments into a *panneau d'antiquaire* such as the panels with the head of "Abraham" and the "tête Gérente" in the collection of glass from the Burgundian church of Saint-Fargeau now in the Musée d'Art et d'Histoire, Geneva [Virginia Raguin, "The Thirteenth-Century Glazing Program of Saint-Fargeau (Yonne)," *Corpus Vitrearum, United States, Occasional Papers* I (New York, 1985), pp. 72–3.] There have been many instances of reassembled panels discovered by the Corpus Vitrearum, United States Committee, in its survey of stained glass in American collections. For example, one of twelve large panels now in the apse of the Cathedral Church of Saint Paul, Detroit, shows a female saint made up of a face, hands, fragments of drapery, background, and architectural elements telling quite plausibly from a distance [*Stained Glass before 1700 in American Collections: Mid-Western and Western States, Corpus Vitrearum Checklist III, Studies in the History of Art* (Washington, DC, 1989), p. 178].

45 See expertise of Frovignault and Robin, Archives de la Vienne G181. The term *verre blanc ouvré* refers to grisaille glass and *ouvré* to the figural windows of pot metal glass. There are omissions from the list, which I interpret as indicating that if a window was not slated for repair, it was not mentioned by the restorers. The numbering system, however, proceeding counter-clockwise from the west rose allows us to see that the overview was complete.

46 The one exception appears to be the south choir window that now contains Renaissance standing saints. The window is referred to in the expertise as "le vitrail appellé le vitrail de Saint Christophe qui est en plusiers

endroits rompu de verre ouvré." In 1775 this window was not described and or slated for repair, simply noted to be cleaned. I suggest that the four Renaissance figures were once in this window, and that Frovignault and Robin had transferred them to the chevet as a stop-gap measure. The glazing of this window may therefore have been in relatively good condition. There may have been a confusion concerning the identities of these figures since there is no Christopher.

47 Mussat, *Style gothique de l'Ouest*, p. 258.

48 Louis Grodecki, "Les vitraux de la cathédrale de Poitiers," *Congrès archéologique de la France* 109 (1951), 138–63; and later, idem., *Vitrail roman*, esp. ch. III, "Les vitraux de l'Ouest de la France."

49 See also Maillard, *Les sculptures*.

50 See above, notes 47 and 48.

51 Grodecki, "Stained Glass 'Atelier,'" pp. 87–111. See also, for comparison, René Crozet, "Note sur les vitraux du XIIIe siècle de la cathédrale de Poitiers," *Bulletin de la Société des Antiquaires de l'Ouest*, [unnumbered] (1949), 51–4.

12

The Sainte-Chapelle as a Capetian Political Program

Beat Brenk

The Sainte-Chapelle of Paris is one of the most cited yet least analysed of medieval monuments. Brenk addresses the integrative context of the entire monument by including references to the architecture, sculpture, painting, stained glass, and the liturgical/historical context. He builds on the separate studies on architecture by Branner, Hacker-Sück, Bony, and Kimpel and Suckale; stained glass by Grodecki; enamels by Branner; and sculpture by Salet and Sauerländer. He argues, as does Raguin, that the medieval monument is far more compressed and multivalent than equivalent "works of art" in modern society. The medieval object does not operate on a single level, and can comprehend at the same time personal, eschatological, historical, political, and religious issues.

Brenk, with strong documentary evidence, argues for the intentionality of the patron. In this instance, he posits the convergence of the political and religious motivations of both King Louis IX and his mother, Blanche of Castile. The kingship of Louis, the reception of the Crown of Thorns from the emperor Baldwin of Constantinople in response to Capetian aid against the Moslems, and the image of Blanche as queen and as virtuous widow can be read in the monument. In the iconographic program, Brenk sees both conventional themes of sacred history and specific references to Louis as the good king and to the contemporary biography of the queen-mother and her son. Emphasizing the integration between structure and its specific users and functions, Brenk also argues that the particularly insistent heraldic signatures in windows of Esther on the south wall and its northern counterpart from the Book of Numbers relate to the liturgical/ceremonial positions of the king and his mother within the edifice.

Hardly any other medieval monument presents so ideally an opportunity to explore issues of ideological, material, and formal integration as does the Sainte-Chapelle in Paris (figs 1 and 2). Architecture,
stained glass, sculpture, enamel work, and liturgical vessels have
been preserved to such an extent that it would seem we cannot but
accept the challenge of simultaneous analysis. In the past, however,
scholars specializing in architecture devoted themselves exclusively
to the art of construction and building, those specializing in painting
dealt only with painting, and so on. This approach, I feel, has hin-
dered a deeper and more comprehensive understanding of meaning.
Despite the limits of so short an essay, I will endeavour to develop
new lines of inquiry and to integrate the often disparate conclusions
of previous studies separated by medium.

We can rely upon the architectural studies by Robert Branner,[1] Inge
Hacker-Sück,[2] Jean Bony,[3] and Dieter Kimpel and Robert Suckale.[4]
Louis Grodecki[5] published the stained glass in the first volume of the
Corpus Vitrearum of France. Branner[6] interpreted the enamelled *tondi*,
while Francis Salet[7] and Willibald Sauerländer[8] have analysed the
style of the Apostle statues. The historical situation and the liturgical
furnishings have been examined and interpreted by Jean Guerot,[9]
and Henri Stein,[10] and more recently by Sauerländer.[11]

Several historical facts are essential. The construction of the Sainte-
Chapelle was begun after 1239, the consecration taking place in 1248.
It replaced the older palace chapel of Saint Nicholas and was erected
as a shrine to house Christ's Crown of Thorns, a relic received by
Louis IX in 1239 from the grateful emperor of Constantinople. To
meet the needs of a palace chapel, a two-storeyed design was chosen,
similar to that of the Camara Santa in Oviedo[12] and to the Cappella
Palatina in Palermo.[13] The low ground floor housed an altar dedicated to Mary and served to raise the upper floor to the level of the
royal apartments. Direct access was provided from the chapel to the
apartments by a walkway - the so-called *belle étage* - that extended
along the whole upper floor of the palace.

The Sainte-Chapelle is noteworthy not only because of its impressive dimensions but also because it supported an unprecedented out-
burst of luxury in stained glass, sculpture, and enamelled *tondi*. The
Crown of Thorns was exhibited on an altar-like platform;[14] the reliquary enshrining it was shaped like a chalice, surmounted by a lily-
crowned circlet (fig. 3). This fusion of palace chapel with the housing,
on a monumental scale, of a major relic reflected a new politico-reli-

gious idea. For the first time a king claimed a prominent relic of Christ for a palace chapel, accessible to him alone and to the people closest to him. The official chronicler, Gauthier Cornut, justified the king's possession of the relic by claiming that it extended to the realm itself. The relic had become a source of joy (*causa laetitiae*) for the Gallican Church (*Ecclesia Gallicana*) and for all French people (*tota gens Francorum*).

Cornut was the archbishop of Sens and an intimate of the king. His history of the reception of the relic, written in 1239, outlined a Capetian-centred story of universal salvation. He was explicit: "Just as Our Lord Jesus Christ singled out Israel as the country to demonstrate his redemption, he singled out France to demonstrate the triumph of his Passion."[15] I would argue that this statement elucidates the entire program of the Sainte-Chapelle; the Capetian presence is framed by the story of salvation.

The program of the Sainte-Chapelle glass (fig. 2) has never been subjected to a comprehensive interpretation. Most telling is the fact that only the three apsidal windows behind the altar illustrate the New Testament while all other windows portray the Old Testament. A superficial reading of the program indicates that it was not intended to be a mere chronological illustration of Old Testament history. The cycle begins with Genesis in the first bay on the north. The second window depicts Exodus, the third Numbers, the fourth Deuteronomy, and the fifth Judges. There the chronological order stops. The five choir windows reveal an independent program; the Passion of Christ is flanked by the lives of both John the Evangelist and John the Baptist, as well as by the four prophets Isaiah, Daniel, Ezekiel, and Jeremiah. The Passion window, in the axial bay, is the only window that portrays Christ.

Thus, in the Sainte-Chapelle, Christ is wholly understood through his relationship to the Old Testament. He is surrounded by his immediate predecessor, John the Baptist, and the four major prophets. This arrangement, however, did not aim at total symmetry, since Isaiah appears to the left of the central window, while Daniel, Ezekiel, and Jeremiah are positioned to the right. Along the south the program continues with Tobias, Judith, Job, Esther, and Kings, towards the westernmost window, dedicated to the story of Louis's Reception of the Crown of Thorns.

This arrangement makes sense in so far as we notice parallels between events. Facing Genesis, which marks the beginning of the story of salvation, we confront the present, Louis's acquisition of Christ's Crown of Thorns. Thus salvation through Christ, and the king, is equated with God's creation of the world. This concept is further strengthened by the presence in the west rose of the Apocalypse, that is, the culmination of the story of salvation. Despite the total reconfiguration of the window in the fifteenth century, the theme appears to have been a part of the original program.[16]

Thus approached, the program of the Sainte-Chapelle reveals a hitherto ignored meaning. If the two windows located in the first bay along the north and south walls correspond to the beginning and continuation into the present of the story of salvation, perhaps the Exodus window also is to be understood as corresponding to the window illustrating the Book of Kings. The political possibilities of the program may, at the juncture, be important to explore.

In various places and differing in size and quantity, the chapel's windows display the coats of arms of the Capetians and of the kings of Castile. The coats of arms represent realms, not persons, and therefore do not function as legal representations, as do seals. On the north the third window (fig. 3), illustrating the Book of Numbers (M), displays both arms, outsized and incontrovertible. Special importance must be attached to this window since it alludes to both the Old Testament story of salvation and to the contemporary history of the Capetians. The Esther window opposite (C) is dominated by equally prominent Castilian castles, not only in the smaller medallions but in the larger quatrefoils as well. Only these two windows display such an abundance of large armorial devices. The composer of the program obviously wished to paraphrase the kingship of the Old Testament as well as the kingship of the Capetians.

The program is also distinguished by the unusual subjects depicted in the uppermost central medallions. The Genesis window (O) depicts the story of Jacob (although the central image is modern).[17] The uppermost subject of the Exodus window (N) presents the wedding of Joseph[18] and the centre of the medallion in the Deuteronomy window presents once more a wedding scene with stories from the Book of Ruth.[19] Uncontestably the wedding is that of Boaz and Ruth, despite its absence in the Scriptures (Ruth 4: 13). In the top medallions of the choir windows (K, J, I, H, G, F, E), the prophets, angels, God the Father, and David are enthroned.[20] The centre field of the upper medallion in window D shows Job's descendants during a banquet, Job himself presiding at the head of the table over this gathering.[21] Beneath the central picture we recognize another banquet scene of Job's descendants.

We can summarize by stating that the central parts of the upper-most medallions describe two weddings (Joseph, Boaz and Ruth) and a banquet (Job's descendants). There is much to suggest that the remaining central areas were equally adorned with kings and queens ceremoniously enthroned. Leaving aside the separate subjects of the choir windows (K–E), we are confronted with a program of enthroned kings, prophets, and angels headed by God enthroned. By having himself also portrayed with royal pomp,[22] Louis IX revealed his belief concerning his own kingship, that is, his authority rooted in the Old Testament story of salvation.

Such an elaboration of wedding scenes would suggest a very personal meaning for the donors. The chronological evidence suggests that it can hardly have been the wedding of Louis IX with Marguerite de Provence, celebrated in 1234.[23] At their wedding Louis presented his wife, Marguerite, with a ring elaborated with braided lilies and daisies inscribed "Hors cet annel pourrion-nou trouver amor."[24] The armorial badges of the Sainte-Chapelle clearly do not present Louis and Marguerite as the patrons, nor Louis and Blanche, but the fusion of the two kingdoms of France and Castile. The wedding and banquet scenes crowning the windows were designed, most likely, to represent kingship as an hereditary institution, responsible for continued prosperity and power. Royalty celebrates its splendour with a banquet.[25]

Up to this point, we have investigated the meaning of the large and numerous coats of arms in the windows of Numbers and Esther. Only when contemplating the two windows in their architectural context, however, does the message become obvious. Each window is located above a roomy niche (fig. 4), resembling an alcove embedded in the wall. This alcove has been ignored by nearly all scholars in spite of its distinctive decoration (restored in the nineteenth century - and possibly altered as well). It is an architectural context deserving serious consideration none the less.[26] In the sculptural program along the segmental arch of these alcoves, at the top Christ is portrayed above clouds, holding a globe. Two kneeling angels, their hands covered, are offering crowns to him. More angels are kneeling to the left and right swinging vessels of incense. In the left spandrel of the arch, another half-figure of a censing angel appears above the clouds, while in the spandrel on the right an angel above clouds holds a crown in both hands. It is risky to make a conclusive decision about the authenticity of these reliefs. The half-figure of Christ holding the globe seems of doubtful authenticity and I suspect that the head has been restored.[27]

What is the meaning of the angels holding and offering two crowns? The crown-offering motif was adopted by Christianity from the pagan Roman rites of the golden crown (*aurum coronarium*) and from the fifth century onwards influenced various pictorial displays.[28] The pagan personifications of victory were changed to angels, but Christ was always the crown's recipient.

The crown as a ruler's attribute is mentioned quite frequently in the Old and New Testaments, most impressively in Revelation (4: 10–11), "The four and twenty elders fall down before him who is seated on the throne, and worship him who lives for ever and ever; they cast their crowns before the throne, singing, Worthy art thou, our Lord and God, to receive glory and honour and power ..." Thus, the crown-offering act "from the hands of angels" is simultaneously characterized as a political and liturgical act, the crowns symbolizing glory, honour, and power.[29]

Precedents from Carolingian and Ottonian times may even have been known to Louis. The ivory throne probably presented to the Pope by Charles the Bald to mark his coronation as emperor showed for the first time the half-figure of an emperor holding a globe in his left hand and two angels offering crowns with covered hands.[30] This iconography is a typical Carolingian creation. The implication was not simply the coronation of the emperor, for *one* crown would have sufficed. It indicated liturgical as well as political homage. In this scene of homage and glorification, two additional angels were depicted, one carrying a palm branch, the other a book. Angels in immediate proximity to the ruler were also evident in the illuminated manuscripts of Charles the Bald. In the portrait of the emperor in the Codex Aureus of Saint Emmeran, A.D. 870, he is flanked by two angels carrying ceremonial staffs.[31] The ivory carving in the Castello Sforzesco depicts the Emperor Otto II venerated by two angels with draped hands. Covered hands are gestures of submission required at the appearance of a ruler or deity.[32]

Monuments representing emperors venerated by angels are not nearly as numerous as representations of the venerated Christ flanked by angels. The pinnacle of the Calixtus portal of the cathedral in Reims offers a version of the enthroned Christ, blessing and holding a book, while two kneeling angels offer crowns with covered hands.[33] This type of representation is closely related to the little scene depicted on the segmental arch of the alcoves in the Sainte-Chapelle. I also cite the shrine of the Three Kings in Cologne, where the enthroned Lord is presented in the gable flanked by two angels, one carrying a chalice and paten, the other carrying a crown.[34]

The issue is complex. Are we viewing Christ himself, or Christ's power as incorporated in his representative, the king? The four-lancet window above the north alcove exhibits twenty coronations of Israelite rulers (fig. 2). It follows, logically, that Louis IX was the focus of the entire program, for he most likely attended the service from this alcove. Such a hypothesis remains undocumented, but it is suggested by the existence of analogous alcoves in private chapels, for example, that of the chapel of Jacques Coeur in Bourges.[35] The elaborately illustrated *Life of Louis IX* by Guillaume de Saint-Pathus from the fourteenth century (fig. 5) contains a picture presenting Louis as a participant during a Mass in the Sainte-Chapelle.[36] In this picture Louis kneels in a low alcove, accompanying Mass by reading in his own missal. The priest and his attendants stand before an altar with crucifix, and clearly outside the alcove.

Let us return briefly to the glazing program. Louis Grodecki suggested that the many apocryphal coronation scenes of the Israelite princes reiterated the themes of kingship present throughout the entire program.[37] He did not, however, develop the implications of these specific representations.[38] The coronations, as Grodecki stated, are quite uniform, even monotonous. Often the same cartoon is used. The king is always placed frontally on his throne, his right hand lifted, while holding a sceptre in his left. The person crowning him does this by placing the crown upon his head with an extended arm. The other extended arm barely touches the body of the enthroned. All the figures are clad in tunic and *pallium*.

Similarly stiff and formal gestures appear in the coronation of David in the Glazier Psalter, an English work of the early thirteenth century.[39] In the Sainte-Chapelle, however, insignia and status symbols are absent. The persons performing the coronation are not dressed like bishops, and the emphasis is obviously placed upon the liturgical ceremonial act of coronation itself. In the four-lancet window the coronation scenes are framed by a mosaic ground of yellow lilies on a blue backdrop, a heraldic field into which, in turn, large medallions are embedded, emblazoned with the castles of Castile. We see again, quite clearly, the Capetian story of salvation. The princes mentioned in the book of Numbers (1: 5–16 and 3: 17–37) are documented by inscriptions:

N ... ASO (Nahshon?)

E ... IZACH (Eliasaph?)

S ... MEON ... ICE (Simeon?)

AL ... MU (Ammihud?)

AMIS ... AR ... PRI(NCE) (Ammishad'dai)

JUDA

ELITSAPHAN (Elizaphan?)

TSURIELIS (Zuriel?)

The biblical text does not describe the coronations; the designer of the glazing program alone was responsible for this idea. He seized upon the long list of names in the book of Numbers as an opportunity to construct a mythical genealogy of the royal house of Capet. At the beginning of Numbers (1: 2–4), God asks Moses to "Take a census of all the congregation of the people of Israel" and to name an elder to head the families of the tribe. This is a conscription-like examination of the fit and able. But to the designer of the chapel's program the test meant something else, the origin not only of kingship but also the initiation of the coronation rites in the Old Testament. It was *this* venerable tradition that Louis IX wished to have depicted. The designer therefore connected the liturgical act of the Capetian coronation back to the times of Moses and Aaron, hence acquiring a highly respected instrument for the legitimization of kingship. Only after having recognized the designer's considerable – and in my opinion decisive – development of the pictorial narrative does one realize that the glazing program and the sculptural one in the alcove beneath it form a conceptual whole. This, in turn, implies that the architect of the Sainte-Chapelle, the stonemasons, and the glass painters engaged in cooperative interaction. The logical consequence of this diagnosis should encourage art historians to undertake a simultaneous analysis of architecture, sculpture, stained glass, and liturgical accessories instead of wrestling with sterile problems of media categories and classification.

The narrative of Moses further justifies this interpretation. We notice at once that four scenes grouped together are of purely sacramental character, Moses and Aaron anoint the altar, the Israelites carry the Ark of the Covenant, God commands the installation of lamps in the temple, and the Ark of the Covenant is lifted by soldiers.[40] In the Book of Numbers (1: 50), the tribe of Levi is appointed to minister the tabernacle and all its vessels. In the glass, however, Moses and Aaron anoint the altar (see Numbers 7: 1, which mentions only Moses). The second picture demonstrates the transporting of the Ark of the Covenant (Numbers 17, 21, 33), the third the installation of lamps (Numbers 8: 2), and the last one the lifting of the tabernacle by the Israelites. In no way, though, do these four renditions illustrate biblical events in their chronological order, but, instead, the designer's obvious intent to present Moses and Aaron as models for Louis IX as sponsor and founder of churches. Considering the many choices from Numbers available to the designer, I argue that this selection is highly specific to the program's theme. The tabernacle paraphrases the reliquary housing the Crown of Thorns, for which Louis IX erected the Sainte-Chapelle. The four scenes function as an "introductory text," after which a fairly chronological illustration of the book of Numbers is observed.

The sculpture of what I have identified as the "king's alcove" (third bay on the north) and the glazing of the window above suggest that the whole program is related to the kingship of Louis IX. The corresponding alcove on the south presents a similar sculptural program. We might suppose that the Esther window (C) would also present a royal message.[41] The Esther window C (fig. 6) lacks the Capetian tapestry of arms of its northern counterpart, but, as if trying to make up for this, the arms emblazoned with the Castles of Castile have not only multiplied but also gained monumental proportions.[42] The arms appear in vertically arranged smaller medallions and in larger quatrilobes. As the book of Esther is one of the shortest in the Old Testament, the elaboration of 120 scenes presented a certain challenge to the designer. The cycle begins at bottom left, covering the first four fields with a banquet given by King Ahasuerus for the people (Esther 1: 5–8).[43] Interestingly enough the designer then omits the story of Vashti's repudiation and jumps ahead to the second chapter: Mordecai presenting the beautiful Esther to Ahasuerus (Esther 2: 8).[44] The narration proceeds directly to Esther's coronation by Ahasuerus (Esther 2: 17),[45] depicted in the second register.

The biblical text (Esther 2: 19–23) briefly describes the conspiracy discovered by Mordecai and reported by Esther to the king. Esther prevents the king's murder, which was planned by two of his officials.[46] They are hanged for their crime. This hardly enjoyable episode has been depicted in sixteen (originally probably eighteen) images.[47] We note continual contemporary references. The Scriptures state that both officials were hanged on a tree (Esther 2: 23), whereas the stained glass shows gallows, thus bringing the death penalty up to date, that is, to the thirteenth century. I suggest, also, that the designer was not as concerned with promoting Louis IX, as he was in depicting justice itself. Ahasuerus applied the death penalty not for an actually committed crime but for its mere intent. In addition the designer exhibited the queen's role as the king's counsellor. Joinville, also, recorded that Louis benefited from "the good instructions he received from his mother."[48]

Esther's role as counsellor is demonstrated repeatedly. To illuminate the dialogue between Esther and Ahasuerus the designer allotted five images.[49] The content of dialogue cannot be presented, but its outward appearance can; the queen appearing before the king - once standing, once seated. The next five scenes are taken up with the banquet given by Esther for the king and Haman (fig. 6).[50] The second banquet (7: 1–6) arranged by Esther is shown in at least two renditions.[51] At a later date Esther is received one more time by Ahasuerus (8: 3–8).[52] Hence, it becomes evident that by illustrating the story of Esther the designer most likely intended a depiction of Blanche of Castile's life at the court of Louis IX. Here the story of salvation is no longer the main objective. The designer has phrased the story of Esther as a model for a queen's *vita* par excellence. Blanche was the mother of Louis IX, not his wife, so that we may not interpret Esther and Ahasuerus as biblical predecessors of Louis IX and Blanche. This was a generic, behavioural model: "Before he (Louis IX) went to bed, the king used to send for his children and tell them of the deeds of good kings and emperors, at the time pointing out that they should take such men as example."[53] Louis appears to have used religious texts in the same way. "He made them learn the hours of Our Lady, and repeat to him the hours of each day."[54]

From the argument above, I contend that the alcove beneath the Esther window was reserved for Blanche of Castile to use during liturgical services. But it was not necessarily her idea to place the Castilian arms in the foreground or to remodel the life history of

Esther into a queen's *vita*. The designer combined in a revealing way the queen's alcove with an exemplary *vita* of an Old Testament queen and the arms of Castile.

Esther, however, is not the only woman of the Old Testament honoured by a pictorial sequence in the Sainte-Chapelle. One bay farther east represents the story of Judith (D) in forty scenes.[55] It is difficult to decide whether or not to relate this window to Blanche. The Castilian arms are absent, and the story of Judith culminates in the murder of Holofernes. The window is unusual in that it offers a number of old French inscriptions, the most precious one reading "Ci Bainie Judi" a commentary on a unique scene of the naked Judith taking a bath in a tub.[56] I am tempted, however, to accept the Judith cycle as representing another phase of Blanche's life, that of a virtuous widow.[57] In any case, we are not dealing here with the story of salvation exclusively, but with exemplary female Old Testament biography as well. Judith combing her hair and taking a bath does not represent a type reserved for biblical and theological realms, but to more generic models of female behaviour. Such a model was also described by Guillaume de Lorris in his *Roman de la rose*, a work written in the years around 1225–40:

Ne suefre sor toi nule ordure;
Lave tes mains, tes denz escure;
S'en tes ongles pert point de noir,
Ne l'i laisse pas remenoir.
Couds tes manches, tes cheveux pigne,

(Do not permit for yourself any uncleanliness.
Wash your hands and scour your teeth.
If your nails have an edge of black
Do not allow the blemish to remain.
Lace your sleeves; comb your hair)

These verses were cited by Gérard Sivéry in order to illustrate a tempting hypothesis of R. Lejeune. According to Lejeune, the poet of the *Roman de la rose*, Guillaume de Lorris, had the young queen Marquerite of Provence in mind when he described the rosebud, and Sivéry adds: "Courtoisie also gives Guillaume de Lorris advice on elegance and hygiene. At least for the French court these were novel ideas."[58]

I contend that the program of the Sainte-Chapelle operates on at least two levels: a religious/typological sphere, and one presenting sociological models. The story of salvation is omnipresent in the Sainte-Chapelle, but at the same time we see exemplary social behaviour, demonstrated in isolated situations, but well within the story of salvation's framework. Under these circumstances it is not possible to associate the Esther window exclusively with Blanche or the Judith window exclusively with Marguerite de Provence. Both windows present the courtly life of Old Testament queens. The program of the Sainte-Chapelle is not the only one where exemplary events are juxtaposed with the story of salvation. The Old Testament picture book of the Pierpont Morgan Library (fig. 7) must be mentioned here; a manuscript for reasons of size alone executed for a king – most likely for Louis IX.[59] Grodecki believed one of the illustrators of this manuscript to be responsible for the design of the Judith and Esther windows in the Sainte-Chapelle. But more important is the fact that the Morgan Old Testament also sets the story of salvation next to worldly examples. For instance, the illustrator seized upon any imaginable opportunity to display a raging battle, even when the biblical text offered only slight provocation.[60] Moreover, wherever possible, the artist represented a king sitting isolated on his throne. The designer of the Morgan Bible arbitrarily presented the renovation of Saul's kingship at Gilgal as an anointment of someone already crowned.[61] The Morgan Bible contains a set of pictures without text, which is why later owners had explanations added. By using images as the exclusive narrative force, the Morgan Bible is closely related to the Sainte-Chapelle and on this basis must have originated in the same artistic context as the windows.

Let us return now to the chapel's program, in particular to the window relating the story of Louis IX's acquisition of the relics of the Passion. This is the first window to the right of the entrance. Few original panels have survived, but I would argue that the iconography is substantially intact. Three separate historical events differing not only in their subject but in their time frame have been combined. In the lower field we see Saint Helena discovering the True Cross and its subsequent capture by the Persian king Chosroes.[62] Then follows the Byzantine emperor Heraclius's victory over the Persian army near Nineveh and the return of the Cross to Jerusalem. To these stories from the fourth and seventh centuries we find associated Louis IX's acquisition of the Crown of Thorns, events depicted in the upper part of the window. Most medallions date from the mid-nineteenth-century restoration, but are typical. The relics are carried in the Ark of the Covenant and subsequently presented to King Louis IX.[63] The king and Robert d'Artois jointly carry the litter with the Crown of Thorns.[64] Next the Crown of Thorns is ceremoniously displayed.[65] A bishop, the king, and the queen are standing behind a balustrade upon which the Crown of Thorns is exhibited. Several ceremonious processions follow and, finally, we see Louis IX personally carrying the cross.[66] Represented at the top of the window is the veneration of the Passion relics by courtiers and others in the king's presence.

This window has not yet received the scholarly attention it deserves, especially since in its iconography contemporary history is connected to the story of salvation. In the window Louis IX operates on the same level as Empress Helena and Emperor Heraclius, as all three acquire, and venerate, the relics of Christ's Passion. The window designer actually showed Louis IX with his brother Robert d'Artois carrying the relics together. The window not only exhibits the story of salvation - as phrased by the Capetian ideology - but constructs a line of ancestors (Helena, Heraclius, Louis IX) to fit the context of the Passion relics: Helena discovered them, Heraclius recaptured them from the infidel, and Louis acquired them for the Christian West. Once again we are confronted with the insistence upon a model. Helena and Heraclius are models of Christian rulers, rewarded for their labours on behalf of the relics of our Lord, and thus they inspire Louis's actions.

If the acquisition of the Passion relics was such an important event for Louis IX as to be exhibited in a window in the Sainte-Chapelle, should we not ask if he commemorated the event in other media as well? The earlier-mentioned Morgan Bible offers an extensive illustration of the first book of Samuel. It is striking that the first miniatures in Samuel repeatedly display the Ark of the Covenant, ten times altogether. For half these times the depiction has no basis in the Scriptures. It must have been the designer's idea to present the Ark of the Covenant as a reliquary set on a base, surrounded by people praying.[67] In the battle of the Israelites against the Philistines (fig. 7) the Ark of the Covenant alone occupies the stage.[68] Omitting the Israelites' first defeat, the designer moved on immediately to a jubilant image (1 Samuel 4: 5): "And when the ark of the covenant of the Lord came into the camp, all Israel shouted with a great shout." Nothing, however, of the camp and of the shouting is seen in the miniature.

The designer represented this scene as an impressive transfer of relics, heralded by a group of knights clad in full armour and accompanied by trombone-playing musicians. I suggest that the Ark of the Covenant represents the reliquary of the Crown of Thorns acquired by Louis IX and that the illustration of 1 Samuel 4: 5 paraphrases the ceremonial transfer of the relic to Paris. One is further tempted to equate Hophni and Phinehas, the two bearers of the ark, with Louis IX and his brother Robert d'Artois.

A second prominent manuscript may also contain a veiled reference linking the Old Testament Ark of the Covenant to the relic of the Crown of Thorns – namely, the Psalter of Saint Louis (fig. 8). The psalter's calendar entries refer to the Sainte-Chapelle and to the royal family. Like the Morgan Bible, the psalter illustrates chapters four and five of the first book of Samuel. An image shows the Philistines (fig. 8) offering the captured ark to the idol Dagon. The golden chest is topped by a most unusual decoration: a crown fashioned of leaves. The appearance of this Ark of the Covenant is so noticeably different from traditional representations that we can assume that the illuminator had a specific model in mind. I suggest that he alluded to the shape of the reliquary (fig. 3) enshrining the Crown of Thorns.[69]

The designer for Louis IX and Blanche of Castile conceived of the Sainte-Chapelle as a shrine for the Passion relics, as a palace chapel, and as a monument to the Capetian ideology of kingship. Such a conclusion does not rest on the presence and distribution of armorial devices alone but is supported by the choice of Old Testament scenes and cycles and by the text of Gauthier Cornut, recording the transfer of the Crown of Thorns.[70] His report of 1239 must have inspired the designer of the Sainte-Chapelle. Cornut had stressed that thanks to the attentive care of the king and his pious mother, Blanche, the realm of France was thought worthy to crown itself with Christ's Crown of Thorns. In a bull of 1244, Pope Innocent IV said that the Lord had crowned Louis with his Crown of Thorns; the Pope "implied an equation of the Crown of Thorns with the crown of France."[71] The idea of using Old Testament figures as generic behavioural models appears earlier on the Solomon portal of the north transept of the cathedral of Chartres.[72] I perceive a growing trend in the thirteenth century where Old Testament literature such as the books of Tobias, Judith, Job, Samson, and Esther, depicted at Chartres, are mined for their ability to reference contemporary royalty. The program of the Sainte-Chapelle thus continues, and amplifies, a tradition whose common theme was the validation and depiction of royal presence through Old Testament metaphor.

NOTES

I thank Mrs Annelies Weil and Virginia Raguin for the translation of this text from German into English. I am obliged also to Philippe Büttner for sharing his knowledge of Capetian heraldry with me.

1 Robert Branner, *Saint Louis and the Court Style in Gothic Architecture* (London, 1985), pp. 56–84.

2 Inge Hacker-Sück, "La Sainte-Chapelle de Paris et les chapelles palatines du moyen-âge en France," *Cahiers archéologiques* 13 (1962), 217–57.

3 Jean Bony, *French Gothic Architecture of the 12th and 13th Centuries* (Berkeley, 1983), pp. 388–91, 400–1.

4 Dieter Kimpel and Robert Suckale, *Die gotische Architektur in Frankreich 1130–1270* (Munich, 1985), pp. 400–5 [*L'Architecture gothique en France 1130–1270*, trans. Françoise Neu (Paris, 1990)].

5 Louis Grodecki in Marcel Aubert, Jean Lafond, and Jean Verrier, *Les vitraux de Notre-Dame et de la Sainte-Chapelle de Paris. Corpus Vitrearum France*, I (Paris, 1959), pp. 71–349; Virginia Raguin, *Stained Glass in Thirteenth-Century Burgundy* (Princeton, 1982), pp. 83–8; Madeline Caviness and Louis Grodecki, "Les vitraux de la Sainte-Chapelle," *Revue de l'art* 1–2 (1968), 9–16; Madeline Caviness in *Stained Glass before 1700 in American Collections: Mid-Atlantic and Southeastern Seaboard States. Corpus Vitrearum Checklist II. Studies in the History of Art* (National Gallery of Art, Washington, DC, 1987), pp. 148–9; Jean-Michel Leniaud and Françoise Perrot, *La Sainte-Chapelle* (Paris, 1991).

6 Robert Branner, "The Painted Medallions in the Sainte-Chapelle in Paris," *Transactions of the American Philosophical Society* 58/2 (1968), 5–42.

7 Francis Salet, "Les statues d'apôtres de la Sainte-Chapelle," *Bulletin monumental* 109 (1951), 135–56, and 112; (1954), 357–63.

8 Willibald Sauerländer, *Gotische Skulptur in Frankreich 1140–1270* (Munich, 1970), pp. 152–3, figs. 184 and 185 [*Gothic Sculpture in France 1140–1270*, trans. Janet Sandheimer (New York, 1972), pp. 471–2, figs. 184 and 185]; Helmut Bauer, "'Der Apostelzyklus der Sainte-Chapelle,'" Dissertation, University of Munich, 1983.

9 J. Geurot, "Le palais de la Cité, des origines à 1417," *Essai topographique et archéologique. Fédération des sociétés historiques et archéologiques de Paris et de l'Ile-de-France, Mémoires* I (1949), pp. 57–212; II (1950), pp. 21–204; III (1951), pp. 7–101.

10 H. Stein, *Le palais de justice et la Sainte-Chapelle* (Paris, 1912).

11 Willibald Sauerländer, "Die Sainte-Chapelle du Palais Ludwigs des Heiligen," *Jahrbuch der Bayerischen Akademie der Wissenschaften*, 1977, 1–24.

12 Jacques Fontaine, *L'art préroman hispanique* (La Pierre-Qui-Vire, Yonne,
1973), pp. 271–2, 275–6, figs. 100 and 103, pls. 95 and 96; E. Dyggve, "Le
type architectural de la Camara Santa d'Oviedo et l'architecture asturi-
enne," *Cahiers archéologiques* 6 (1952), 125–33.

13 G. di Stefano, *Monumenti della Sicilia normanna*, 2d ed. a cura di W. Krönig
(Palermo, 1979), pp. 37–40, pl. LII–LVIII.

14 Louis Grodecki, *La Sainte-Chapelle* [Paris, Caisse Nationale des Monuments historiques et des sites], 2d ed. (1975), pls. on pp. 2 and 13 (after S. J.
Morand, *Histoire de la Sainte-Chapelle Royale du Palais* [Paris, 1790]).

15 "Sicut igitur Dominus Jesus Christus ad Suae redemptionis exhibenda
mysteria terram promissionis elegit, sic ad passionis sua triumphum
devotius venerandum nostram Galliam videtur et creditur specialiter
elegisse." *Opusculum Galteri Cornuti, de susceptione coronae spineae Jesu
Christi*, in *Recueil des historiens des Gaules et de la France*, vol. 22 (Paris,
1865), pp. 26–32; Hans Belting, "Die Reaktion der Kunst des 13. Jahrhunderts auf den Import von Reliquien und Ikonen," in *Il medio oriente e l'occidente nell'arte del XIII secolo. Atti del 24 congresso internazionale di storia
dell'arte* (Bologna, 1982), p. 37.

16 Grodecki, *Vitraux de Notre-Dame et de la Sainte-Chapelle*, pp. 310–28.

17 Ibid., pp. 94–106.

18 Ibid., pp. 107–24, pls. 20 and 21.

19 Ibid., pp. 142–58, pls. 32 and 33.

20 Ibid., pls. 38, 39, 46, 47, 50, 51, 54, 55, 58, 59, 62, and 63.

21 Ibid., pls. 66 and 67.

22 Ibid., pls. 84 and 85.

23 E. Boutaric, "Marguerite de Provence, son caractère, son rôle politique,"
Revue des questions historiques 3 (1867), 417–18, 420; H. Wallon, *Saint Louis
et son temps*, vol. 1 (Paris, 1875), pp. 40–1; Gérard Sivéry, *Marguerite de
Provence. Une reine au temps des cathédrales* (Paris, 1987), p. 67.

24 *Saint Louis roi de France (Le Mémorial des Siècles) présenté par le duc de Lévis
Mirepoix* (Paris, 1970), p. 64; Sivéry, *Marguerite de Provence*, p. 269, note 36.

25 On Capetian heraldry see Hervé Pinoteau and Claude le Gallo,
"L'Héraldique de saint Louis et ses compagnons," *Cahiers nobles* 27 (1966),
6–10; Hervé Pinoteau, "La date de la cassette de Saint Louis: été 1236?"
Cahiers d'héraldique du C.N.R.S. 4 (1983), 97–130.

26 Kimpel and Suckale, *Gotische Architektur*, p. 404, "Gebetsnische," figs. 392
and 421; Sauerländer, "Die Sainte-Chapelle du Palais Ludwigs des Heiligen," p. 19.

27 Concerning Lassus's restoration see J.-M. Leniaud, *Jean-Baptiste Lassus (1807–1857) ou le temps retrouvé des cathédrales* (Geneva, 1980), pp. 84–9, 104–6, 109–13, 191–4. A restoration of "Les deux réduits, place du roi et de sa mère" took place in 1845 (p. 193). I thank Peter Kurmann for this reference.

28 Theodor Klauser, "Aurum Coronarium," *Römische Mitteilungen* 59 (1944), 122 ff; J. Engemann, "Herrscherbild," *Reallexikon für Antike und Christentum* (1988), pp. 966–1047; T. Hölscher, *Victoria Romana* (Mainz, 1967); Wolfgang F. Volbach, *Elfenbeinarbeiten der Spätantike und des frühen Mittelalters*, 3d ed. (Mainz, 1976), pl. 26, notes 48–50; pl. 66, notes 125 and 126; pl. 69, note 132.

29 Ernst Kantorowicz, *Kaiser Friedrich II*, Ergänzungsband (Berlin, 1931), p. 72; idem., *Laudes Regiae* (Berkeley, 1946), pp. 65–111.

30 "La cattedra lignea di S. Pietro in Vaticano," *Atti della Pontificia Accademia Romana di Archeologia, Memorie*, vol. 10 (1971), pp. 226–7, pls. XXXVI and XXXVII (Kurt Weitzmann); pp. 277–8, 293 (Percy E. Schramm); pp. 198–9 (P. Romanelli).

31 Percy E. Schramm and Florentine Mütherich, *Denkmale der deutschen Könige und Kaiser* (Munich, 1962), pp. 134–5, fig. 52.

32 Ibid., pp. 144–5, fig. 75; Franz Cumont, "L'adoration des mages et l'art triomphal de Rome," *Atti della Pontificia Accademia Romana di Archeologia. Memorie*, vol. 3 (1932), p. 93.

33 Sauerländer, *Gotische Skulptur*, pl. 245; see also pl. 199 (Chartres) and pl. 278 (Amiens).

34 Schramm and Mütherich, *Denkmale der deutschen Könige und Kaiser*, pp. 187–8, fig. 192.

35 A. Gandilhon and R. Gauchery, "L'Hôtel Jacques Coeur," *Congrès archéologique de France* 94 (1932), 83, plan II, pp. 93–6; U. Albrecht, *Von der Burg zum Schloss. Französische Schlossbaukunst in Spätmittelalter* (Worms, 1986), pp. 85–91.

36 Paris, Bibl. Nat. ms. fr. 5716; Guillaume de Saint-Pathus, *Vie de Saint-Louis*, ed. H. F. Delaborde (Paris, 1899).

37 Grodecki, *Vitraux de Notre-Dame et de la Sainte-Chapelle*, p. 126.

38 Ibid., pp. 83–4; Karen Gould, "The sequences 'de sanctis reliquiis' as Sainte-Chapelle Inventories," *Mediaeval Studies* 43 (1981), 334–5.

39 John Plummer, *The Glazier Collection of Illuminated Manuscripts* (New York, 1968), pp. 22–3, pl. I; Meyer Schapiro, "An Illuminated English Psalter of the Early Thirteenth Century," *Journal of the Warburg and Courtauld Institutes* 23 (1960), 179–89; Rosemary Muir Wright, "A Image Fit for a King: The Glazier Psalter Reconsidered," *Journal of Medieval History* 19 (1993), 69–124.

40 Grodecki, *Vitraux de Notre-Dame et de la Sainte-Chapelle*, p. 130, panels M-124, M-125, M-126, and M-127, pl. II.

41 Ibid., p. 259.

42 Ibid., pls. 72 and 74.

43 Ibid., p. 261, C-204, pl. 74.

44 Ibid., p. 261, C-193, pl. 74.

45 Ibid., p. 261, C-195, pl. 74.

46 Ibid., p. 262, C-182, C-183.

47 Ibid., pp. 261–2, C-173–96, pl. 74.

48 Jean, Sire de Joinville, *The Life of Saint Louis*, in J. Joinville and G. Villehardouin, *Chronicles of the Crusades*, trans. M.R.B. Shaw (Baltimore, 1963), p. 182.

49 As in note 40, pp. 269–70, C-137–9, C-120, C-121, pl. 75.

50 Ibid., p. 270, C-123–7, pl. 75 (C-123).

51 Ibid., p. 271, C-88, C-89, pl. 72.

52 Ibid., p. 272, C-65, C-66, pl. 72.

53 Joinville, *The Life of Saint Louis*, p. 336.

54 Ibid., pp. 336–7.

55 Grodecki, *Vitraux de Notre-Dame et de la Sainte-Chapelle*, pp. 241–57.

56 Ibid., pp. 241–57, pl. VI.

57 According to Paulinus of Nola, the women's section in the narthex of Saint Felix in Cimitile was decorated with the stories of Judith and Esther, while the men's section was painted with cycles of Job and Tobit: *Paulinus Natalicium S. Felicis*, X: 15 (*Patrologia Latina*, 61: 663); A. Weis; "Die Verteilung der Bilderzyklen des Paulinus von Nola in den Kirchen von Cimitile (Campanien)," *Römische Quartalschrift für christliche Altertumskunde* 52 (1957), 137.

58 Sivéry, *Marguerite de Provence*, pp. 65–7; R. Lejeune, "La courtoisie et la littérature au temps de Blanche de Castile et de Louis IX," *Le siècle de Saint Louis*, ed. R. Pernoud (Paris, 1970), pp. 191–6.

59 Sydney C. Cockerell, with a preface by John Plummer, *Old Testament Miniatures* (New York, 1969); Harvey Stahl, "Old Testament Illustration during the Reign of St. Louis: The Morgan Picture Book and the New Biblical Cycles," *Il medio oriente e l'occidente nell'arte del XIII secolo. Atti del 24 congresso internazionale di storia dell'arte* (Bologna, 1982), pp. 79–91; J.M. Plotzek, *Die Handschriften der Sammlung Ludwig*, vol. 1 (Cologne, 1979), pp. 72–9.

60 Cockerell, *Old Testament Miniatures*, p. 104, fol. 20v (bottom) [1 Samuel 4: 11–17].

61 Ibid., p. 116, fol. 23v (bottom) [1 Samuel 11: 15].

62 Grodecki, *Vitraux de Notre-Dame et de la Sainte-Chapelle*, pp. 295–309, pls. 86 and 87.

63 Ibid., p. 306. A-96, pl. 88; colour pl. III.

64 Ibid., p. 307, A-84.

65 Ibid., p. 307, A-71.

66 Ibid., p. 308, A-44.

67 Cockerell, *Old Testament Miniatures*, p. 98, fol. 19r (bottom); p. 100, fol. 19v (top); p. 102, fol. 20r (top); p. 104, fol. 20v (bottom).

68 Ibid., p. 104, fol. 20v (bottom) [1 Samuel 4].

69 *Der Psalter Ludwigs des Heiligen*, introduction by M. Thomas (Graz, 1985), pl. 70, fol. 70. I owe this important observation to Philippe Büttner, who is preparing a dissertation on Capetian royal imagery in thirteenth-century manuscripts.

70 *Opusculum Galterii Cornuti, de susceptionem coronae spineae Jesu Christi* in *Receuil des Historiens des Gaules et de la France*, vol. 22 (Paris, 1865), p. 27.

71 Gould, "The sequences," p. 334.

72 Beat Brenk, "Der Concepteur und sein Adressat oder: Von der Verhüllung der Botschaft," *Modernes Mittelalter. Neue Bilder einer populären Epoche* (Frankfort a/M, 1994), pp. 431–50.

13

Artistic Integration Inside the Cathedral Precinct: Social Consensus Outside?

Barbara Abou-El-Haj

This essay, like the one following, addresses issues beyond the building itself. Abou-El-Haj assesses the ways in which major cathedral campaigns may have interacted with the broader historical and social conditions of the many constituencies in medieval society. She is particularly careful to counteract any implied consensus of meaning based simply on the visual coherence of the building itself. The corporate entity of the cathedral had an ever-changing, at times contradictory, relation to its setting. Between those who built and decorated cathedrals, and the local audience, was a dialectic space occupied by individuals and groups whose ambiguities and tensions shifted over time. Abou-El-Haj explores a variety of texts in her analysis of social and political countermovements criticizing luxurious edifices. The responses of the cathedral builders to modify, postpone, or abandon projects demonstrate the degree to which such monuments were "integrated" into the social and economic structures of their communities.

Abou-El-Haj, like Reynolds and Klukas, is concerned with the use of buildings. These other authors, however, confine their analyses to the perspective of those "benefiting" from the building, and do not consider those excluded or co-opted from the centres of power, as does Abou-El-Haj.

Integrating the fragmented categories (almost subdisciplines) under which Gothic building is conventionally discussed advances the analysis of concrete monuments and the physical space they occupy. However, we work not only on concrete monuments, but also within discursive and historiographical paradigms. Embedded in this project lurks an old art-historical disciplinary paradigm, one which speaks almost entirely for the builders and presumes for them a sphere of imaginative extravagance unconstrained by the social and material world in which these huge churches were erected and decorated. Taken on its own terms, artistic integration is in danger of becoming the aesthetic counterpoint to a very successful paradigm which made these churches into integrative spiritual, even integrative economic, enterprises.[1] Within these terms, artistic integration inside cathedral precincts carries with it an implicit corollary, social consensus outside.

Yet at a series of building sites, construction of key churches was brought to a halt by communal insurgencies. These discordant histories have been very often ignored; their centre-pieces and catalysts are generally discussed in entirely the same terms as churches built in relatively peaceful environments, such as Saint-Denis, discussed in this volume by Eric Fernie and William Clark; Wells, by Peter Draper; Poitiers, by Virginia Raguin; and the Sainte-Chapelle, by Beat Brenk.[2] Scholars seem to succumb to the cohesive world of integrative spaces, designs, and images built into twelfth- and thirteenth-century churches which frequently concealed a factional social environment, a dialectical space occupied by individuals and groups whose tensions and loyalties shifted over time. Gothic churches, whether they were built in quiescent or contentious environments, were challenged, even attacked, during the later eras of Reformation and Revolution, and restored and meticulously documented in the modern era.[3] If we can approach this social space of consensus, ambivalence, and tension from the bottom up and from the outside in, we can avoid reproducing the clergy's version of itself, visualized in its hegemonic monuments and images.

This essay will suggest that the considerable resources required to build and decorate on this scale and technical level had the potential to generate quite spectacular disturbances within a political structure whose prerogatives were undergoing a prolonged and systemic challenge within the communal movement. It will also suggest, briefly, how builders may have responded in their architectural designs and decoration to the world outside their ecclesiastic precincts.

Gothic cathedrals – like the Romanesque monastery churches before them – were enabled and at the same time constrained by economic expansion and social transformations, which were, however, asymmetric in their distribution and provoked repeated struggles over seigneurial prerogatives exercised by the landlord clergy in towns whose topography was dwarfed by the new churches they built. The communal movement was particularly violent where the landlords were clerical, whether they shared jurisdictions with a secular lord or held both ecclesiastical and secular lordship.[4] Fierce disputes frequently erupted and sometimes halted extravagant building ventures.

At Vézelay, clashes accompanied significant building phases of the twelfth-century church: the initiating abbot, Artaud, was assassinated two years into building (1106); a new wave of unrest had to be arbitrated in 1137 as the church was rebuilt after a catastrophic fire in 1120; the worst violence, the commune of 1152–5, followed the completion of the west portal. In each instance town and abbot battled over taxation and costly octaves of hospitality that burghers were obliged to provide for huge numbers of pilgrims gathered for the Magdalene and Easter feasts (1,020 died in the fire of 1120).

Stephen Murray has observed that, in the following century at Beauvais, "it is no coincidence that the tenures of the two most enthusiastic building bishops of the thirteenth century, Miles de Nanteuil and Guillaume de Grez, were accompanied by violent urban uprisings," in contrast to Troyes discussed below.[6] At Reims, when funds from a series of quests and rapidly expanding papal indulgences ran short, the archbishop cancelled burgher out-of-town loans and rents on the grounds that the town was his seigneurial possession. His interference catalysed an unresolved, century-old communal struggle into an uprising which halted cathedral construction and drove the clergy from the town for more than two years at a time.[7] Where the social order was structured by spiritual claims, and where power relations were supported by spiritual authority, this authority and those claims were an open arena for reciprocal demands and confrontations. Thus heretics were pursued in towns with communal ambitions; Jacques de Vitry denounced communards and heretics almost in a single breath, and court procedures were developed to link usurers and heretics. At Reims, the chronicle of Saint Nicaise states that the burghers feared to be accused of usury when they attacked the canons, forcing them into exile for more than two years.[8]

None the less, these struggles, no matter how violent, affected neither the initiation nor the realization of these vast churches, but what can be called the negotiated outcome, decisions about size, scale, design, and decoration. This negotiated outcome, however difficult to locate at first glance, is nevertheless discernible in the integrated spaces and public images of consensus so persuasively crafted by the clergy. In the sculpture and glass of Gothic churches, narratives of Christian history and eschatology increasingly offered reassurance rather than threats. Compare, for example, the terrorizing judgment on the Romanesque west façade of Saint-Lazare at Autun set by Bishop Stephen Bagé before the restless audiences of a town divided between his jurisdictions and those of the Duke of Burgundy (who possessed the merchants' quarter) with the virtually contemporary human and reassuring judge on Saint-Denis's west façade set by Abbot Suger before his free peasants, town, and pilgrim visitors in the Ile-de-France. Yet, even Suger felt compelled to provide his church with defensive capacity, as Kimpel and Suckale noted: "We also committed ourselves richly to elaborate the tower[s] and the upper crenelations of the front, both for the beauty of the church and, should circumstances require it, for practical purposes."[9]

Funding Sources and Unrest

Ambition clashed with constraints when there was a sudden need for funds to build on a new monumental scale. Yet, since all these churches, regardless of their local material or social conditions, were in fact built, resources were apparently not only available, but also sufficient. Thus, despite the instances cited above, there would appear to be no essential link between increased demands on resources for church building, on the one hand, and urban violence, on the other. Evidence for linking economic and artistic, social, and spiritual spheres of activity must be sought in circumstantial rather than direct testimony, and in the distinction between resources per se and their social distribution.

Accordingly, the *resource question*, which entails sources and levels of labour and materials, has to be distinguished from the *political question*, the distribution of resources. The political question is fundamental to any discussion of a world of unequal exchange, where one group had the power to absorb resources asymmetrically and sought to coerce consensus by spiritual authority backed by a monopoly over arms. Yet, most efforts to address this issue have examined resources rather than political structures.

A debate on precisely the issue of resources was engaged in the

1950s between Robert Lopez, who suggested huge churches may have "immobilized surplus in stone" and "killed developing economies in under-developed towns," and Otto von Simson, who argued that profits from the pilgrimage industry at Chartres prompted the town and chapter to rebuild the burned cathedral together, and that building produced rather than consumed surplus.[10] Von Simson's contention presumed a model of social balance, even cooperation in building and decoration.[11] Without belabouring an old dispute that has been aired elsewhere, we can ask why, of these two models, von Simson's was the uncontested winner. As important as the substance of the debate may be, we must also address the reception and reproduction of one paradigm and the virtual obliteration of the other.[12] Whether Lopez was right or wrong, the historiographical reception has pre-empted discussion until recently.[13] It set the limits of inquiry even more firmly than the absence of fabric rolls which makes it so difficult to assess the sources and levels of funds for twelfth- and thirteenth-century churches.[14]

Detailed evidence of funding sources for monumental building is virtually absent prior to the fourteenth-century records of the scope of Troyes. At Troyes revenue sources crossed a spectrum from quests to anonymous collection boxes, from portions of regular income collected by the canons for spiritual services to money raised by lay confraternities, and to occasional large gifts.[15] In the twelfth and thirteenth centuries, Chédeville and Murray suggest revenues came from a narrower spectrum of sources, principally from agricultural rather than from urban jurisdictions.[16] Since the countryside has been portrayed as more peaceful than towns prior to widespread uprisings in the fourteenth century, this would seem to separate urban unrest from church building.[17] Yet relative peace in the countryside may be overstated.

There is evidence of rural communes organized by peasants crushed in the twelfth and thirteenth centuries. At Laon, where Bishop Gaudry was assassinated in 1112 in a town that clashed with his successors throughout the century, Bishop Roger de Rozoy had to send knights to put down the Laonnais commune of 1177. The commune had been encouraged by Louis VII during an episcopal vacancy that followed the tenure of Bishop Gautier de Mortagne (1155–74). Gautier had increased rents, according to William W. Clark, in order to develop episcopal vineyards and houses, restore the episcopal palace, and perhaps to support the new cathedral initiated by the chapter at the beginning or just prior to Gautier's episcopate.[18]

In the middle of the thirteenth century, the canons of Notre-Dame in Paris imprisoned a number of their serfs who had rioted against repeated *tailles*, characterized by Marc Bloch as the most arbitrary and onerous of seigneurial levies. The *tailles* had been used for ancillary building and to pay various debts or charges when normal revenues proved inadequate. In the twelfth century, only two *tailles* are recorded, the first between 1148 and 1163, the second in 1178. *Tailles* were imposed with increasing frequency in the first half of the thirteenth century during the early years of construction: in 1212, when the chapter began building in the cloister, another between 1198 and 1216 (for Innocent III's levy on French churches), another for canons' houses in 1219, and yet another two years later, in 1221, to purchase a *dîme*. A *taille* in 1232 is unspecified, and another in 1247 was to liquidate an unspecified debt incurred by the chapter.[19] Even if Laon and Paris are atypical, the supposed peace on agricultural estates prior to the fourteenth century compared with urban jurisdictions may reveal only that peasants were more successfully subordinated than were their urban counterparts.

At Chartres and Reims there is ample evidence that a systematic effort to mobilize resources in the towns provoked violent resistance. Chartres's principal episcopal income may have come from large grain fields and vineyards, but the bishops endeavoured to expand revenues from their urban jurisdictions on a variety of fronts, from appropriating urban tradesmen and serfs from comtal jurisdiction into their own *familia* to provide goods and services they would otherwise have had to purchase, to expanding profits from the money changers and mint, previously the domain of the count and countess of Chartres.[20] At Reims, the archbishop, who was also count, seized control of the town's money supply as the new cathedral reached the more costly building stages as noted by Robert Branner.[21]

Even the supposed voluntary donations listed for Troyes in the fourteenth century may be misleading, since these gifts spring from the same sources as seigneurial taxes – in other words, appropriation and extraction on a wider and more diffuse scale, which created the surplus wealth donated to the fabric. Since many gifts were not local, indeed they may not have created friction. As for the diocesan quests, we might at least ask what can be considered "voluntary" within seigneurial relations, aside from the anonymous contributions to collection boxes, which in Murray's words "did not account for much of the income (relic-boxes)" or made up "pitifully small" income (boxes placed in Troyes's churches). According to Murray, burghers built parish churches, while the "faithful of the diocese of Troyes" – in other words, those under the seigneurial jurisdiction of the bishop or the chapter – contributed significantly to the cathedral.[22] In the end, whether from quiescent rural or resistant urban sources, we can imagine that extraction provided funds, especially extraordinary funds, where the clergy exercised seigneurial rights.[23]

More important than distinctions between rural and urban sources are the economic and political prerogatives of the builders in each instance: whether they were sweeping, as at Reims; divided, as at Chartres; or limited by a commune, as at Amiens. Chartres and Reims, where revenues were secured from rural as well as urban sources, appear in the centre of dense ecclesiastical construction in the map drawn up by John James to represent the uneven distribution of significant building projects in this region. Amiens's bishop and chapter, which held very few urban properties in the commune and derived their principal revenues from agricultural estates, are virtually isolated. James's map suggests that an episcopal chapter that rebuilt its cathedral competitively in a communal town with funds from rural estates was less capable of supporting multiple building projects. At Reims, by contrast, Saint-Remi was finished just before the cathedral burned, and Saint-Nicaise was begun shortly after, with expenditures amounting to £28,000 between 1231 and 1258.[24]

Resources cannot be assessed in absolute terms, even if we had the numbers, but only proportionate to local labour and materials. Nevertheless a remarkable model for calculating construction cost was offered by H. Thomas Johnson, an economic historian, who responded to Lopez, using the unusual Westminster accounts of 1252–74.[25] Having already absorbed von Simson's model, but unaware of Chédeville's critique, Johnson questioned Lopez's assessment of the burden on local economies by calculating the number of wage-labourers against the cubic volume of the churches they built – ignoring the labour intensive production of glass, sculpture, wall surfaces, and vaulting.[26] Similarly, John James ventured to "cost" Chartres by using equivalents in modern construction materials and labour, making no distinction between medieval and modern wage-labour, nor between seigneurial and capitalist resources and production.[27]

Within this debate, only von Simson had considered the social arena. Here he argued for two components of consensus, spiritual and economic, based upon the town's self-interest in the pilgrimage trade. To support the huge enterprise to rebuild the whole of the burned cathedral of Chartres behind its twelfth-century façade, he projected a market value in pilgrimage fairs and feasts commensurate with the more modest project for Saint-Denis in the mid-twelfth century. Chédeville, on the other hand, doubted the value of Chartres's four pilgrimage fairs that had to compete with the year-round fairs of Champagne and the commercial quarter in Paris expanded by Philip Augustus.[28] One might add that there is little evidence that pilgrimage profits were shared to the satisfaction of burghers, even within the more valuable twelfth-century system of intermittent and local feasts and fairs. Burghers at the two premier supra-regional shrines in Europe, Vézelay and Santiago, which experienced repeated communal riots, complained that rents for their stalls were too high and that competing ecclesiastical stalls curtailed their profits.[29]

Financial records like Westminster's are rare. Henry III bankrupted his treasury in order to rebuild the abbey on a lavish scale. The records of Troyes, which represent broader revenue sources, date from 1296, and become significantly detailed in the latter part of the fourteenth century, considerably later than the churches under discussion here. In the twelfth and thirteenth centuries, we have fewer records, and these often list gross expenditures. We are left to imagine indirectly from the partisan accounts of builders the nature and levels of resources and labour.[30] I use here only the most familiar and frequently excerpted sources. First among them is the expanding rhetorical curve in the clergy's accounts of material provision and voluntary labour, conducted in penitential silence, called "the cult of carts" from its accounts of volunteers harnessing themselves to carts pulling stone and other materials to building sites. These stories circulated quickly from builder to builder, and each time they were repeated, their components were embellished.[31] They simultaneously reveal and conceal the level of resources and the nature of social consensus or subordination which had to be mobilized or imposed at building sites because, in underdeveloped economies, resource weakness in labour, material, and transport could be made up with political strengths and ideological strategies.

Second are the miracle stories and factual accounts of revenue raising among the construction reports that accompanied the new wave of monumental building beginning in the late eleventh century and continuing into the thirteenth. When Laon cathedral had to be repaired after the bishop had been assassinated and the town burned in 1112, an ox miraculously appeared to replace one of a team too weary to go on dragging stones to the cathedral site.[32] It is not hard to see here a scarcity of heavy draught animals. Scarce funds were only partly remedied by three quests undertaken in the same years. Funds collected throughout France by August 1112 ran out in six months, and another journey had to be undertaken in March 1113. Like the canons of Chartres one hundred years later, those of Laon had to travel all the way to England seeking funds.[33] A century later, Laon's bishop strenuously protested for forty years at the papal curia against his metropolitan's right to send funding quests into the diocese to build Reims's new cathedral, while Laon's new cathedral remained unfinished. In response, Henri de Braine excommunicated the bishop and the chapter's dean, among others in the diocese. In the middle of the twelfth century, Suger worried how far he would have to transport very large stones and wooden beams needed to remodel Saint-Denis until he discovered huge monoliths in the nearby quarry at Pontoise and in his forest at Chevreuse. He then relates how the faithful hauled stones gratis at the quarry, and a miracle that, on one rainy day, a few weak and disabled men and boys miraculously lifted what normally required nearly ten times their number. Suger, it is clear, solved his difficulties because he could mobilize resources and labour from his own seigneurial estates.[34]

One hundred fifty years earlier, the "considerable quantity of gold" discovered where the foundations for the new cathedral of Orléans were to be laid, as Duby wryly observed, was no miracle; it certainly came from the church treasure.[35] Where funds were secured by other means – for example, from the bishop's mint at Santiago at the beginning of the twelfth century – there was no cult of carts, as Stokstad observed, and no miracles. According to the *Pilgrim's Guide*, pilgrims carried blocks of lime for mortar. Funds were also raised through Gelmírez's seigneurial jurisdictions, so intensively that he was nearly assassinated by members of the town and a faction of his own canons dissatisfied with their prebends.[36]

From the miracle stories and from more conventional documents directed at different audiences, we can imagine how narrow was the surplus and how heavy the squeeze upon it. This does not appear to have changed dramatically with the ever more lavish churches in the following century. According to Williams, Bishop Renaud's expenditures and generosities "changed to dangerous avarice" after Chartres burned in 1194, and Bishop Gauthier (1219–1234) died debt-ridden. Murray quotes Bishop Milo of Beauvais as "obligated with innumerable debts."[37] Such accounts multiply in the complaints of insolvency assembled by Martin Warnke, not surprising since bishops frequently initiated building by setting aside no more than three to five years' partial income.[38] At least in two familiar cases, Chartres and Amiens, the canons restored to themselves the portion of revenues they had temporarily donated to the fabric, perhaps before the first walls were erected.[39] How did they expect to make up the inevitable shortfalls as building progressed? This is not a resource question, but rather a political question.

Political Structure and the Distribution of Resources

The issue, then, is not whether there were resources, but who had power over them, and in what structural circumstances. Peter Kurmann and Brigitte Kurmann-Schwarz have cited one condition for relating resources to building advanced by Chédeville and Esch: churches were built when the financial situation of the builders had been consolidated. But even when the economic situation may have been resolved in favour of the landlord, the political one was not in many instances. And since the capacity to make up resources was political, backed by spiritual authority, the buildings came to be sites of power struggles not only about spiritual authority but about all those other authorities and monopolies under assault by the communal movement. Within these struggles, churches of discrepant size were both catalysts and responses, excessive yet built of necessity, since spiritual authority was no mere superstructural ideology, but rather functional and dialectic. Churches provided ever more dramatic settings for the clergy at a time when local audiences could no longer be guaranteed, when they were no longer docile or submissive, when there were powerful competitors: Capetian kings in the royal arena, mendicants in the local, and energetic censors within and without the church who drew upon a long tradition for criticizing the size, scale, and decoration of monumental ecclesiastical building.

The earliest critics responded not only to Constantine's churches, but also to a parallel literature of marvellous description of lavish churches sponsored by pious rulers based on the Old Testament model of Solomon's temple, which interfaced so well with imperial building traditions. The critique of luxury drew on the New rather than the Old Testament, on apostolic poverty rather than pious, royal largess. For every panegyrist there was a critic: for Eusebius, Jerome; for Procopius in his official biography, indirectly, Procopius in his secret history; for Suger on his additions to Saint-Denis, Bernard of Clairvaux.[40] In the ninth century, the first period of economic and architectural expansion since Late Roman times, Jerome was quoted by Louis the Pious in his admonition to Abbot Eigil of Fulda to "reduce to a minimum ... immense building projects and unnecessary undertakings which tire the servants outside the monastery as well as the monks within."[41] Bernard of Clairvaux used Jerome in his well-known attack on monastic luxury in 1125, and was in turn quoted for the censure of lavish episcopal building by Alexander Neckham and Peter the Chanter of Paris towards the end of the twelfth century.[42]

Each tradition relied on explicit rhetorical conventions, often on the same phrases. Eric Fernie observes in this volume that Suger described the early medieval church of Saint-Denis in the same language he used for his own dramatically different additions: shining "with inestimable splendor," and that around 1080, Goscelin of Saint-Bertin, writing in England, described churches not at all like Paris, Chartres, Reims, or Amiens, as "most lofty, most spacious, filled with light, and most beautiful." Part of the documentary spectrum, then, is discursive, part of a calculated debate. The texts are partisan and rhetorical, based on their own traditions and ambitions. But they are also realistic and descriptive, in so far as they aimed at promoting or curtailing extravagant building and decoration in their own time. They suggest that builders had to prevail not only in the social and spiritual, but also in the intellectual and literary arena, as well as in the public space articulated by their decorated churches and the liturgies they celebrated within.

Responses to the Social Arena in Design and Decoration

Internal and external challenges were answered by judicial and spiritual as well as artistic strategies. When the economic and political jurisdictions that underlay spiritual power were challenged, the spiritual environment was a fundamental arena of response. The finished and decorated basilicas can be understood as negotiated outcomes. In their integrated designs, sculpture, and glass, the clergy represented itself, while simultaneously it addressed a volatile social world outside the cathedral precinct. Grand churches provided dramatic stages for archbishops, bishops and canons, abbots, and monks to enact their spiritual authority, processionally and liturgically. As Roger Reynolds observes in this volume, liturgy possessed not only a spiritual but also a social function. At Reims the competing insurgents and canons possessed and repossessed the urban topography: liturgical processions mandated in the twelfth- and thirteenth-century ordinals gave way to the communards with their banners, bowmen, and barricades. When the commune was put down, the urban setting and the cathedral precinct became the stage for the canons to impose humiliating penitential processions upon the town.

Within the new architecture, in Brigitte Bedos-Rezak's compelling description, Gothic design articulated spatial and spiritual unity in a social world increasingly divided into a multiplicity of groups, whose tensions crossed the political, social, economic, and cultural spectrum. On the occasions when these groups were assembled, the integrated spaces of Gothic designs set up an order – enacted in liturgy, in offerings, in taxes, in reparations ceremonially delivered on specified feast days – that naturalized hierarchy while it subsumed divisions, in a setting which was both a space of unity and an instrument of coercion.

The new Gothic designs not only created huge and imposing integrated interior spaces, but shifted the division of space allocated to clergy and laity in favour of increasingly larger clerical communities. At Laon the new cathedral was finished in a hostile environment with a rather modest choir of a type common to the preceding generation of churches. Thirty years later, the choir was dismantled and replaced with one of a size and proportion in keeping with the newer Gothic designs: a liturgical decision, an artistic decision, but likely also a social decision. These new choirs provided imposing settings, concealed by screens, for the expanding clergy (eighty canons at Laon, whose liturgical space extended into the eastern bays of the nave). It was also a resource decision, not possible at Laon until 1204, when the chapter had at its disposal the gift of an entire quarry. Even so, a large number of original stones had to be reused.[43]

Recently scholars have begun to disentangle the levels on which seemingly transparent images in glass and sculpture responded to – or sidestepped – local tensions in a few prominent towns in the twelfth and thirteenth centuries. Vézelay's central narthex lintel has been examined as an appeal to civil consensus in the tense decades following the assassination of Abbot Artaud (1106), who had initiated building. On the lintel the abbey's tithers approach from the left, delivering tokens of the taxes they had violently resisted, while pilgrims approach from the right, invoking the hospitality demanded from the town over the octaves of the Magdalen and Easter feasts. Everything withheld in the riot of 1106, the conspiracy of the 1130s, and the commune of 1152–5 is freely offered in a liturgical procession derived from late antique homage scenes, quintessential images of political and economic subordination. In this arrangement, resistant peasants under the ecclesiastical and seigneurial jurisdiction of the abbey, whose economic monopolies were confirmed in liturgy, are assimilated to the pilgrim visitors, who came voluntarily with their offerings and experienced the same liturgy as spectacle.[44]

At Chartres, from the mid-twelfth century and throughout the years that the new cathedral was built and decorated, the bishop and chapter engaged in a "permanent state of war,"[45] with the count and countess over serfs (who were tradesmen) whom the clergy incorporated into their *familia*, removing them from the countess's taxable jurisdictions. Serfs were snatched back and forth, and occasionally imprisoned and executed by the countess's men. Williams shows that precisely these disputed trades were selectively depicted throughout the cathedral windows. Those she examined in detail – bread, wine, and money lending – served simultaneously as commercial commodities, sacramental offerings, and obligatory contributions. At Chartres, then, where agents of the count and countess provoked a riot in the cloister in 1210, and where the bishop and chapter were driven from the town for four years (1253–7), the clergy created a stained-glass vision of unity, devotion, and labour dedicated to the Virgin on the part of all social groups.

At Reims, the canons retrofit their processional entrance in the north with unmatched portals that carry threatening, eschatological, and authoritarian images highlighting episcopal spiritual monopolies, coordinated with the economic and spiritual subordination of the town after two insurgencies forced the chapter into exile (1234–6 and 1238–40).[46] Archbishop Henri de Braine (1227–40) had himself portrayed in the centre of the high choir glass with all the signs, real and imaginary, of the spiritual office he had been unable to exercise in four of the previous six years. The Virgin and Christ appear above Reims's cathedral and archbishop; Apostles and Evangelists above their successors, Reims's suffragan bishops, who also appear together with their diocesan cathedrals in two ensembles coordinated laterally and vertically. Their cathedrals are given topographical precision in details that compare with built churches, though not necessarily the same ones.[47] Among their conspicuous features, a variety of rose windows can be found on built churches, making them persuasive and perhaps reassuring, at least to Henri and his successors. Their distinctive portals invoke spiritual metaphors that equated church thresholds with the door into heaven (Revelation 4: 1) and Christ with the door (John 10: 9).[48] Through apostolic succession, the clergy who possessed these churches mediated between heaven and earth, the sole access to salvation (John 11: 44, Matt. 16: 19), a doctrine ignored by the excommunicated communards and all the more insistent in the glass. The events of 1234–6 and of 1238–40 were thus erased in a fantasy of metropolitan order that encompassed not only the insurgent burghers but also Henri's subordinate bishops, whom the exiled archbishop could not unite behind his decision to interdict Louis IX's domains within the province in order to elicit from the king an armed response to the commune.

In the late twelfth and in the thirteenth centuries, then, the design and decoration of grand churches offered reassuring imaginary panoramas of universal harmony. Between the two distinct images of Judgment offered to a restless urban audience in Burgundy and a mixed audience of free locals and pilgrims in the Ile-de-France, not Autun, but Saint-Denis prevailed.

NOTES

1 Otto von Simson, *The Gothic Cathedral* (New York, 1956; rev. ed., New York, 1962). See also von Simson's retrospective review of his work in the *Frankfurter Allgemeine Zeitung* (27 Jan. 1988), pp. 35–6.

2 These embodied social and political, as well as spiritual and artistic meaning. Brenk, in this volume, discusses social and political strategies associated with Louis and his mother, Blanche of Castile, informing the program of the Sainte-Chapelle. I suggest that one might see this miniature cathedral, and in Branner's words "giant reliquary" [Robert Branner, *St Louis and the Court Style in Gothic Architecture* (London, 1965, repr. 1985), p. 57] as a sacred setting for this "most Christian king" to handle relics of Christ's Passion as he pursued heretics at home and as a substitute for his failure to secure the Holy Sepulchre abroad.

3 See Paul Frankl, *The Gothic: Literary Sources and Interpretations Through*

Eight Centuries (Princeton, 1960), and Tom Cummins, "The Trumeau Figure of the South Central Portal of Chartres," Master's thesis, UCLA, 1980. In this volume, see also Kathryn Brush, Willibald Sauerländer, and Madeline Caviness.

4 These instances do not contradict the arguments by several authors that seigneurs also granted franchises in their own political and economic interests, as Suger did for the town and new villages of Saint-Denis. See *La charte de Beaumont et les franchises municipales entre Loir et Rhin. Actes du colloque organisé par l'institut régionale de l'Université de Nancy II* [Nancy, 22–5 Sept. 1982] (Nancy, 1988). This charter was granted by Archbishop William of Reims in 1182 to Beaumont-en-Argonne. Another was given to Reims some fifteen years after a rebellion against the tyrannical Archbishop Henri de France. It was, however, soon withdrawn. This unresolved dispute underlies the communal rebellions at Reims in the thirteenth century, discussed below.

5 See Barbara Abou-El-Haj, "The Audiences for the Medieval Cult of Saints," *Gesta* 30 (1991), 3–15, esp. pp. 7–9, using J. Scott, and J. Ward, *Hugh of Poitiers. The Vézelay Chronicle* (Binghamton, NY, 1992); Rosalind K. Berlow, "The Case of the Disappearing Abbot," *Studia Monastica* 23 (1981), 325–38, and "The Rebels of Vézelay," in J.A.S. Evans and R.W. Unger, eds., *Studies in Medieval and Renaissance History* 9 (1987), 137–63; and J.S. Feldman, "The Narthex Portal at Vézelay: Art and Monastic Self-Image," Dissertation, University of Texas, Austin, 1986.

6 See Stephen Murray, *Building Troyes Cathedral* (Bloomington, 1987), p. 233, note 14. See also idem, *Beauvais Cathedral: Architecture of Transcendence* (Princeton, 1989). In some cases local feuds were embedded in the extension of royal prerogatives against episcopal monopolies, particularly over certain courts, as at Beauvais and Reims. At Beauvais, Murray observed that "certain elements of the bourgeoisie were angry at the Bishop's excessive financial exactions," which fuelled the commune's riot, embroiled in a struggle with Louis IX and Blanche of Castile over the extension of royal justice. See Murray, "The Choir of the Church of St.-Pierre, Cathedral of Beauvais: A Study of Gothic Architectural Planning and Constructional Chronology in its Historical Context," *Art Bulletin* 62 (1980), 536. At Reims, the king restored the clergy only after he expanded royal justice in the town by securing control over temporal pleas involving clergy. See Pierre Desportes, *Reims et les Rémois au XIIIe et XIVe siècles* (Paris, 1979), p. 164. For Beauvais, Murray concluded ("Choir of Beauvais," p. 551) that misalignment of the choir and the 1284 collapse of the vaults resulted from a funding and personnel crisis

precipitated by the struggle between the count-bishop, the commune, and the monarchy.

7 See Desportes, *Reims et les Rémois*, pp. 159–69, and Barbara Abou-El-Haj, "The Urban Setting for Late Medieval Church Building: Reims and Its Cathedral between 1210 and 1240," *Art History* 11 (1988), 17–41, esp. pp. 20–3.

8 "In this year ... many citizens of the archbishop's ban and of the chapter's ban, fearing an inquisition into usury would be made against them, made a conspiracy against the chapter." See Desportes, *Reims et les Rémois*, p. 161, note 32, citing Pierre Varin, *Archives Administratives de la Ville de Reims* (Documents inédits sur l'histoire de France), 5 vols. (Paris, 1839–48), vol. 1, pp. 566–7; *Monumenta Germaniae Historica Scriptores*, vol. 13, pp. 85 and 87; and *Receuil des historiens des Gaules et de la France*, vol. 18, p. 699.

9 On Autun, see Otto-Karl Werckmeister, "Die Auferstehung der Toten am Westportal von St. Lazare in Autun," *Frühmittelalterliche Studien* 16 (1982), 208–36, esp. pp. 225–8, 236, with literature. See also Willibald Sauerländer, "Über die Komposition des Weltgerichts-Tympanons in Autun," *Zeitschrift für Kunstgeschichte* 29 (1966), 261–94; Don Denny, "The Last Judgment Tympanum at Autun: Its Sources and Meaning," *Speculum* 57/3 (1982), 532–47; and Hélène Setlak-Garrison, "The Capitals of Saint Lazare at Autun: Their Relationship to the Last Judgment Portal," Dissertation, UCLA, 1984. On Saint-Denis, see Sumner McKnight Crosby, *The Royal Abbey of Saint-Denis from Its Beginnings to the Death of Suger, 475–1151* (New Haven, 1987), esp. pp. 182–7; Sumner McKnight Crosby, Jane Hayward, Charles T. Little, and William D. Wixom, *The Royal Abbey of Saint-Denis in the Time of Abbot Suger (1122–1151)* (New York, 1981), esp. Little, "Monumental Sculpture at Saint-Denis under the Patronage of Abbot Suger: The West Facade and the Cloister," pp. 25–31; Conrad Rudolph, *Artistic Change at St-Denis: Abbot Suger's Program and the Early Twelfth-Century Controversy over Art* (Princeton, 1990); and Pamela Z. Blum, *Early Gothic Saint-Denis: Restorations and Survivals* (Berkeley, 1992). On Suger's defensive measures, see Dieter Kimpel and Robert Suckale *Die gotische Architektur in Frankreich 1130–1270* (Munich, 1985), [trans. by Françoise Neu, *L'architecture gothique en France 1130–1270* (Paris, 1990)], esp. p. 78. For Suger's text, see *Abbot Suger: On the Abbey Church of St.-Denis and Its Art Treasures*, ed. Erwin Panofsky. (Princeton, 1946, 2d ed. by Gerda Panofsky-Soergel, Princeton, 1979), pp. 46–7.

10 Robert Lopez, "Economie et architecture mediévales. Cela aurait-il tué

ceci?" *Annales. Economies. Sociétés. Civilisations* (1952), 433–8, esp. pp. 434, 436–8, and von Simson, *Gothic Cathedral*, p. 169.

11 Constructed both by the medieval builders and by the nineteenth-century project to restore medieval churches along with the Catholic church as a model for social balance in post-Revolutionary France. See Cummins's discussion in "The Trumeau Figure of the South Central Portal of Chartres," ch.1. For the early phases of the Monuments Historiques projects to reconstruct French medieval churches, see F. Bercé, *Les premiers travaux de la Commission des Monuments historiques 1837–1848. Procès-verbaux et relevés d'architectes* (Paris, 1979).

12 Von Simson offered reassurance about a world of social and artistic integration, while incorporating economic incentive into the medieval accounts of cooperation. He was quoted in the immediate response to Lopez's essay (see below). Only Robert Branner, in "Historical Aspects of the Reconstruction of Reims Cathedral, 1210–1241," *Speculum* 36 (1961), 23–37, note 20, and Louis Grodecki, in his introduction to *Gothic Architecture* (Milan, 1978; New York, 1985), p. 16, briefly considered Lopez's observations. According to A. Chédeville they did not apply to a town like Chartres, but rather to towns where cloth, merchants, or money played a major role and where the bourgeoisie possessed power: *Chartres et ses campagnes (XI-XIIIe siècles)* (Paris, 1973), p. 520.

13 Among recent contributions, aside from histories of the building trades, and the notable contribution by Branner (see note 12), see M. Warnke, *Bau und Überbau. Soziologie der mittelalterlichen Architektur nach den Schriftquellen* (Frankfurt am Main, 1976); Henry Kraus, *Gold Was the Mortar* (London, 1979), reviewed by S. Murray, *Art Bulletin* 63 (1981), 152–4; Kraus's reply was published in no. 64 (1982), 164–5; W.H. Vroom, *De financiering von de kathedraalbouw in de middeleewven in het bijzonder van de dom von Utrecht* (Maarsen, 1981); William W. Clark, and R. King, *Laon Cathedral* [Courtauld Institute Illustration Archives], Companion Text, 1 (London, 1983), esp. pp. 14–22; Kimpel and Suckale, *Die gotische Architektur*; Murray, *Troyes*; Abou-El-Haj, "Urban Setting"; Jane Welch Williams, *Bread, Wine, & Money: The Windows of the Trades at Chartres Cathedral* (Chicago, 1993).

14 Even where there was unusual evidence, the organization of resources has been ignored. Erwin Panofsky, in his edition *Abbot Suger*, dropped chapters 2–23, Suger's account of his economic reorganization and funding methods, from his otherwise complete translation of *De administratione*. On gross expenditures, see Kimpel and Suckale, *Die gotische Architektur*, note 9, pp. 221–2.

15 Published by Stephen Murray, *Troyes*, appendix C, pp. 209–15.

16 See Chédeville *Chartres et ses campagnes*, pp. 521, 525, and Murray's review of Kraus, above note 13. Clark suggests the greater part of Laon's funding came from the chapter domains, but describes along the way the difficulty in augmenting normal sources with extraordinary means, like quests. See Clark and King, *Laon*, Arch. vol. 1, p. 22.

17 On peasant unrest in Europe, see Rodney Hilton, *Bond Men Made Free: Medieval Peasant Movements and the English Rising of 1381* (London, 1973), esp. pp. 80–5 on peasant communes in France.

18 Clark observes, however, that it was the chapter that organized cathedral construction and it did not participate in the communal dispute, Clark and King, *Laon*, vol. 1, p. 18. See also pp. 14–15 on the communal riot of 1111–12, as well as Guibert of Nogent's famous account in *Self and Society in Medieval France: The Memoirs of Abbot Guibert of Nogent*, ed. John Benton (New York, 1970), pp. 167–82.

19 Villages found these taxes so burdensome they offered to buy the right of the chapter to levy arbitrary *tailles* for £2,000 in addition to an annual rent of £100, likely lent by Parisian burghers, recorded in an inquest conducted in 1252. Marc Bloch, "Blanche de Castille et les serfs du Chapitre de Paris," *Mémoires de la Société de l'histoire de Paris et de l'Ile-de-France* 38 (1911), 224–72, reprinted in Marc Bloch, *Mélanges historiques*, vol. 1 (Paris, 1963), pp. 463–90, esp. pp. 471–6. The dates of the *tailles* correspond with those of building campaigns: see Kimpel and Suckale, *Die gotische Architektur*, p. 527.

20 Williams, in *Windows of the Trades*, pp. 25–6, has linked funding and peak building periods to urban violence, particularly the 1210 cloister riot, set within a communal struggle which pre-dated the 1194 fire and continued beyond the building period. Chédeville, in *Chartres et ses campagnes*, makes the same observation (p. 524). For his discussion of the mint, see p. 435. See also the essay on Chartres by Peter Kurmann and Brigitte Kurmann-Schwarz in this volume.

21 Archbishop Henri de Braine demanded his tenth for loans to Auxerre and Troyes and annulled a contract to sell rents to Arras, as the town was his feudal possession and not a corporate entity. See Desportes, *Reims et les Rémois*, p. 159; Branner, "Historical Aspects," pp. 30–1; and Abou-El-Haj, "Urban Setting," pp. 20–3.

22 See Murray's summary of funding, *Troyes*, pp. 21–7, esp. p. 22, for his comments on spiritual expectations that might have prompted "voluntary" contributions. For his discussion of the fabric accounts, see pp. 111, 209–10.

23 The meagre evidence for burgher contributions to thirteenth-century churches has been surveyed in Murray's review of Kraus, above, note 13.

24 See John James, "An Investigation into the Uneven Distribution of Early Gothic Churches in the Paris Basin 1140–1240," *Art Bulletin* 66 (1984), 15–46, Map I, p. 17. On the bishop's and chapter's holdings in Amiens, see Jean Massiet de Biest, *La carte et le plan considerés comme instruments de la recherche historique. Etudes sur les fiefs et censives et sur la condition des tenures urbaines à Amiens. XIe – XVIIe siècles* (Tours, 1954). For recent studies of the town and cathedral with literature, see Kraus, *Gold Was the Mortar*, pp. 39–59; Kimpel and Suckale, *Die gotische Architektur*, pp. 10–64; and Barbara Abou-El-Haj, "Building and Decorating at Reims and Amiens," *Europäische Skulptur im 12./13. Jahrhundert*, ed. H. Beck and K. Hengevoss-Dürkop (Frankfurt a/M, 1994), pp. 763–76, 508–19. For Saint-Nicaise, see Kimpel and Suckale, p. 222, citing Victor Mortet and Paul Deschamps, *Receuil de textes relatifs à l'histoire de l'architecture et à la condition des archi-tectes en France au moyen âge* (Paris, 1929), p. 242.

25 For Westminster's thirty-two consecutive weeks of accounts in 1253, see Richard Morris, *Cathedrals and Abbeys of England and Wales* (New York, 1979), pp. 214–17, with literature.

26 For Chédeville "sur le plan purement économique, la cathédrale couta beaucoup plus à la région qu'elle ne rapporta à la ville," *Chartres et ses campagnes*, pp. 523–4. For responses to Lopez, see H. Thomas Johnson, *Explorations in Entrepreneurial History*, 2d ser. 4 (1967), 191–210, disputed by B.W.E. Alford and M. Q. Smith, *Explorations in Entrepreneurial History* 6 (1969), 158–69. These commentaries were followed by rejoinders by Johnson, pp. 170–4, and by Alford and Smith, pp. 329–32, in the same volume.

27 See John James, "What Price the Cathedrals?," *Transactions of the Ancient Monuments Society* 14 (1972), 47–65. Chédeville quotes a nineteenth-century estimate by the architect Lassus of 125 million francs at 1840 value, *Chartres et ses campagnes*, p. 520.

28 Chédeville, *Chartres et ses campagnes*, pp. 523–4. On the economic expansion of Paris, see John W. Baldwin, *The Government of Philip Augustus: Foundations of French Royal Power in the Middle Ages* (Berkeley, 1986), pp. 345–9.

29 See Abou-El-Haj, "Audiences for the Cult of Saints," esp. p. 8 with literature, or idem., *The Medieval Cult of Saints: Formations and Transformations* (Cambridge, 1994), pp. 19–25. For struggles over pilgrimage profits from selling badges and souvenirs well into the thirteenth century and later, see Esther Cohen, "In the Name of God and Profit: The Pilgrimage

Industry in Southern France in the Late Middle Ages," Dissertation, Brown University, 1976, pp. 39, 47–8, 151–2, 176–7. Still, she argues that towns "derived a large portion of their livelihood from the pilgrimage trade" (p. 140).

30 See Kimpel and Suckale, *Die gotische Architektur*, pp. 221–2.

31 Compare the letter circulated by the Archbishop of Rouen with the almost contemporary version by Abbot Haimon in Mortet and Deschamps, *Recueil de textes*, pp. 63–7, trans. Teresa Frisch, *Gothic Art 1140– c.1450: Sources and Documents* (Englewood Cliffs, NJ, 1971; repr. Toronto, 1987), pp. 25–6. I have discussed these briefly in "Urban Setting," pp. 18–19.

32 See Benton, ed., *Guibert of Nogent*, p. 197.

33 See Clark and King, *Laon*, vol. 1, p. 22.

34 For Reims and Laon, see Branner, "Historical Aspects," p. 31, note 37. For Saint-Denis, see Panofsky, ed., *Abbot Suger*, pp. 90–7.

35 See Georges Duby, *The Early Growth of the European Economy: Warriors and Peasants from the Seventh to the Twelfth Century* (Ithaca, 1974), p. 161.

36 See Marilyn Stokstad, *Santiago de Compostela in the Age of the Great Pilgrimages* (Norman, OK, 1978), p. 103, and pp. 69–78 for the communal insurgency at Santiago; L. Vázquez de Parga, "La Revolución Comunal de Compostela en los Años 1116 y 1117," *Anuarió de historia del Derecho Español* 16 (1945), 685–703; and on Gelmírez's lordship, R. Pastor de Togneri, "Diego Gelmírez: une mentalité à la page. A propos du rôle de certaines élites de pouvoir," *Mélanges René Crozet*, vol. 1 (Poitiers, 1966), 597–608, and R.A. Fletcher, *Saint James's Catapult: The Life and Times of Diego Gelmírez of Santiago de Compostela* (Oxford, 1984). See also my *Medieval Cult of Saints*, pp. 19–22.

37 "The income of the bishops seems to have been more than adequate before the rebuilding of the cathedral ..., and less than adequate toward the end of reconstruction": Williams, *Windows of the Trades*, pp. 32–3, and Murray, "Choir of Beauvais," p. 550, note 63.

38 See Warnke, *Bau und Überbau*, and Branner, "Historical Aspects," pp. 30–3. At Beauvais, compounded by the struggle over the king's seizure of episcopal revenues in his effort to extend royal justice, and the bishop's interdict over his diocese, even ten years was insufficient. See Murray, "Choir of Beauvais," pp. 535–6.

39 In 1233 the chapter of Amiens increased its distributions to itself, taking back revenues awarded to initiate building. See Georges Durand, *Monographie de l'église Notre Dame, cathédrale d'Amiens*, 3 vols. (Amiens-Paris, 1901–3), vol. 1, p. 19., and J. Roux and A. Soyez, *Cartulaire du chapitre de la cathédrale d'Amiens* [Mémoires de la Société des Antiquaires de Picardie,

14 and 18. Documents inédits concernant la Province], 2 vols. (Amiens-Paris, 1905, 1912), vol. 1, p. 293.

40 For excerpts from Eusebius and Procopius, see Cyril Mango, *The Art of the Byzantine Empire 312–1453* (Englewood Cliffs, NJ, 1972), pp. 4–7, 10–14, 72–8, and for Procopius's *Secret History*, see the translation by Richard Atwater (Ann Arbor, 1963). For Jerome and Bernard, see Caecilia Davis-Weyer, *Early Medieval Art 300–1150* (repr. Toronto, 1986), pp. 38–40, 168–70. For Suger, see Frisch, *Gothic Art*, pp. 5–13, and Panofsky, ed., *Abbot Suger*. For Bernard, see also Conrad Rudolph, *The "Things of Greater Importance": Bernard of Clairvaux's Apologia and the Medieval Attitude Toward Art* (Philadelphia, 1990), and idem., *Artistic Change at St-Denis*.

41 In order to build an immense church under what must have been proportionately similar constraints at ninth-century Fulda, Eigil's predecessor, Abbot Ratgar, conscripted every monk, every novice, and every fugitive lured to sanctuary in the monastery until the monks walked out and the abbot was deposed. When Louis the Pious addressed the new abbot, he quoted Jerome: "I admonish you not to waste [monastic possessions] in a reckless and imprudent fashion, nor to give unjust orders and rules as if you had unlimited powers. Jerome teaches you ... not to squander what belongs to the poor." Apparently, Abbot Eigil had wide enough powers to continue the enterprise. See Davis-Weyer, *Early Medieval Art*, pp. 104–5. See also Richard Krautheimer, "The Carolingian Revival of Early Christian Architecture," reprinted in *Studies in Early Christian, Medieval, and Renaissance Art* (New York, 1969), pp. 203–56, esp. 209, where he quotes the monks' petition to Charlemagne to stop Ratgar's "enormous and superfluous buildings and all that other nonsense (*inutilia opera*) by which the brethren are unduly tired and the serfs are ruined ... everything should be done within limits (*iuxta mensuram et discretionem*) and the brethren should be allowed, according to the rule, to read at times and to work at other times."

42 See the excerpts in Frisch, *Gothic Art*, pp. 31–3; the full discussion by Conrad Rudolph, *Things of Greater Importance*, and Mortet and Deschamps, *Recueil de textes*, pp. 156–8, 179–80. On Peter the Chanter, see also John Baldwin, *Masters, Princes and Merchants: The Social Views of Peter the Chanter and His Circle* (Princeton, 1970).

43 At major churches, the clergy occupied the crossing and often the eastern section of the nave, according to Eric Fernie, who located Laon's choir screen two bays into the nave between sets of *piliers cantonnés*. See Fernie, "La fonction liturgique des piliers cantonnés dans la nef de la cathédrale de Laon," *Bulletin monumental* 145 (1987), 257–67, esp. pp. 260, 265. I am

grateful to Peter Draper for this reference. For rebuilding the choir, see Clark and King, *Laon*, text vol. 1, p. 48 and text vol. 2, p. 61.

44 According to J.S. Feldman, "the monks immortalized ceremonies which expressed public consensus of the abbey's power and authority": "Narthex Portal," pp. 51–68. See also Peter Diemer, "Das Pfingstportal von Vézelay – Wege, Umwege und Abwege einer Diskussion," *Jahrbuch des Zentralinstituts für Kunstgeschichte* 1 (1985), 77–114. See also Abou-El-Haj, "Audiences," pp. 7–9, or *Medieval Cult of Saints*, pp. 22–5.

45 Williams, *Windows of the Trades*, p. 21, citing Lucien Merlet, and pp. 21–30, for the following.

46 For the urban history of Reims, see Desportes, *Reims et les Rémois*, esp. pp. 155–69.

47 See L'Abbé V. Tourneur, *Histoire et description des vitraux et des statues de l'intérieur de la cathédrale de Reims* (Reims, 1857); Hans Reinhardt, *La cathédrale de Reims. Son histoire, son architecture, sa sculpture, ses vitraux* (Paris, 1963, repr. Marseille, 1983), pp. 183–9; Eva Frodl-Kraft, "Zu den Kirchenschaubildern in den Hochchorfenstern von Reims - Abbildung und Abstraktion," *Wiener Jahrbuch für Kunstgeschichte* 25 (1972), 53–86; *Les vitraux de Champagne-Ardenne. Corpus Vitrearum France, Recensement 4* (Paris, 1992), pp. 383–91, with literature. See also Abou-El-Haj, "Urban Setting," pp. 28–31, and idem., "Program and Power in the Glass of Reims" *Kunstgeschichte: Richtung radikale Historizität? Eine Zwischenbilanz. Festschrift für Karl Werckmeister*, ed. Joan Weinstein and Wolfgang Kersten (in preparation).

48 Laon displays a majesty in the choir glass that corresponds with the west façade of the built church. See Frodl-Kraft, "Hochchorfenstern," p. 67.

14

Form as Social Process

Brigitte Bedos-Rezak

Bedos-Rezak's essay is grounded in historical methodology. She suggests an open approach that identifies fluid and ever-changing relationships between the cathedrals and their circumstances. She posits our viewing the entire cathedral as an organic vocabulary of symbolic lines, colours, and volumes exhibiting the growth and development of forms in accordance with contemporary philosophy. Thus she incorporates references to developments that took place contemporaneously in law and literature. Most significantly she sees the cathedral not simply as an illustration of society, but at the very centre of the social order. She, like Reynolds, Brenk, Klukas, and Abou-El-Haj, does not simply note the place of the powerful building set in prime urban space, but also emphasizes its clearly demarcated interior spaces. Areas were reserved for the clergy alone, and in the laity's space subdivisions reflected ranks and distinctions, thus substantiating the hierarchical social order.

She assesses, and ultimately rejects, the issue of authorial intention by artist or by patron, as retrievable to subsequent inquiry. She suggests, rather, the importance of viewing the cathedral as evolving materially, socially, and ideologically, with meaning and intentionality residing principally in use and social acceptance, rather than in a master design. The variety of solutions of continuity, revival, and survival demonstrated at Poitiers and Saint-Denis in this volume, as well as Bedos-Rezak's interpretation of contemporaneous writings by Saint Thomas Aquinas (1226–1274), support this conclusion.

In this essay, I propose to be "emblematic of society", and of history.[1]

The normative technique of my craft dictates that in reconstructing the past I use its vestiges – among which we may count Gothic cathedrals – for their documentary content rather than for their physical and aesthetic appearance. While positing the form–content dyad as an inseparable entity, I consider its elements, one signifying, the other meaning, as having independent histories and contingent modes of interaction. An exclusive focus on morphology might imply that the cathedral was intended as an end in itself, instead of being a by-product of other activities. Such a focus could also lead to the assumption that appearances principally document the results of people's conscious designs.[2] Indeed the very notion of design compels a return to the consideration of intentionality. Drawing on my viewpoint as a social historian, I would like to consider the Gothic cathedral as an event, which happened to, and with the participation of, its surrounding society, and which derived its meaning from use and interpretation rather than from initial intention.[3] This approach does not seek to establish an absolute identity between the cathedral and the social structure informing its meaning, to see the cathedral as an empty shell awaiting the collective intention to fill it.[4] A cathedral may preferably be seen as a system of signs articulated in stone, glass, and paint, with its own processes of signifying, though it performs this semiotic function within the context of a larger sociocultural code of semantics.[5]

One element in this process of signifying has been identified in the present volume under a variety of terms, such as order, coherence, unification, integration, continuity, and "holism."[6] These and related notions are thematic constituents of the architectural strategy of meaning. Here I propose to consider art and society from the perspective of order and integration.[7] In doing so I will attempt to trace the larger system of principles which enabled these very concepts of order and integration to determine the shape, and the intelligible significance of the Gothic cathedral in twelfth- and thirteenth-century Western Europe.

Seeking integration in the appearance of a given cathedral entails an examination of the interaction of architecture, stained glass, and sculpture within that edifice. But perhaps this methodology is best applied without reference to a presumed overall plan, for the idea of such a plan presents several problems.[8] First, the assumption of an overall design obscures those solutions of continuity, revival, and survival which have been demonstrated for Saint-Denis, Poitiers, and Durham and thus tends to undermine the very idea of integration as a dynamic, rather than programmatic, process. Second, the notion of integral design implies that the construction of a Gothic cathedral is necessarily the product of situated intention. And this implication engenders a debate already classic within literary criticism: whether the reconstruction of authorial intention is ever an appropriate goal in interpreting a work of art, and whether such intention can ever be recovered.[9] The *post hoc* descriptive writings of Abbot Suger or of Gervase of Canterbury offer representations of their thinking about their monuments,[10] but not accounts of their intentions, which are most likely irretrievable. Aquinas stated that "a craftsman, as such, is commendable not because of his intentions, but because of the work he produces",[11] thus providing a release from the conundrum of intentionality by denying status to intended meaning as a psychological category.[12] Aquinas emphasizes the concept, also present in the holistic approach to Gothic art, that the mechanics of art generates its meaning.[13] According to this concept, the locus of intentionality is shifted from the author to the crafted work, and this work therefore may be seen as the objective autonomous transmitter of a meaning from which initial design may be phenomenologically recovered. It is no longer what the patron – or architect – of a cathedral meant, but what the cathedral form means and reveals of its author's conception.[14]

However, even this view involves an assumption that meaning is intrinsic to the object, in this case the cathedral. I believe we should reject this assumption in favour of a more open approach that would aim at identifying relationships between the cathedrals and their circumstances. Why did cathedrals assume their particular shape at this specific historical moment,[15] and how did they come to take the form they did?[16] Is it relevant to this enquiry that medieval theories of art are invariably theories of formal composition, not of feeling and expression, and that art therefore appears as a construction, as an operation aiming at a specific result?[17] Questions about form therefore lead to the issue of how style is expressive of meaning, not a meaning intrinsic to the cathedral, but one deriving from the monument's own processes of producing meaning, and from the conventions of meanings shared by a society, that is, those rules of thought and sensitivity which underlie the formal realization of Gothic architecture.[18]

The builders of cathedrals reckoned with their audience's capacities – to see and to touch with understanding. Though the senses are innate, understanding of the impressions they transmit is made possible only by the experience of living in the midst of specific things to look at, to think about. To paraphrase Clifford Geertz, "cathedrals and the equipment to grasp them are made in the same shop."[19] No cathedrals without their audiences, which implies that meaning and intentionality reside principally in use and social acceptance, rather than in a master design or in the numerous complex and elusive chains of causation which brought these edifices into being.[20] An inquiry into the medieval perception of, and the circumstances surrounding, the Gothic manner of building introduces a welcome sense of context larger than that of patrons and artists. An understanding of this context requires identification of the fundamental structure of cultural products, as well as of the relationship between these products and their circumstances.[21]

In considering this relationship, we are again brought back to the problem of intentionality, which is so closely linked to the notion of holistic planning. For in locating intention in the design, the holistic theory implies a dialectical link between authorial intention and monumental form and function. That such purposefulness may best be associated with the cathedrals rather than with their designing patrons has already been discussed;[22] it remains for us to assess whether the cathedral's purposefulness or function can be used as a valid narrative of what went on in the mind of the designer. For functions, unlike intentions, are retrievable in so far as they may be inferred from the relation of the monuments to identifiable circumstances.[23] Here again, the testimony of Aquinas is relevant, for he states that "every craftsman aims to produce the best work that he can, not in a simple manner, but by reference to the end."[24] Beauty is to be seen in terms of the relationship of adequacy to scope. In this context it is worth remembering that there was no medieval manufacture of objects whose primary function was to be enjoyed aesthetically.[25] Rather, the desired outcome of medieval craftsmanship was the production of a functional object. In most of the essays in this book there is evidence for the functional purposes of cathedrals – liturgical, didactic, and political. I am especially struck by the large role that rivalries and competitions seem to have played in the building and stylistic programs of most churches. The functionalist view allows dialectical causality between purpose, the form it elicits, and the planning it implies; but, along with Baxandall, I believe that what appear to us now as voluntary causes may well have been implicit in formulas or behaviours unreflectively enacted by medieval patrons.[26]

After reviewing the theoretical possibilities for a hypothesis of holistic design in Gothic cathedrals, the time has come to consider the archaeological evidence directly. None of the essays in this book, it seems to me, makes a compelling case that any given monument resulted from holistic planning. In fact, a contrary impression emerges of ongoing differences between concept and execution, of changes of programs, and of partial transformations or reconstructions. There is evidence that in some buildings details were routinely worked out during construction;[27] in others, specific architectural contingencies dictated pragmatic solutions. In yet others, competition dictated a change of direction. The work planned for the portal of Reims by Jean Le Loup, for instance, was rearranged by Maître Gaucher so that the Reims portal might be more grandiose than that of Amiens. In Reims, too, the original plan for a porch provided by the master mason Jean d'Orbais is known to have been modified so that the patron saints of the cathedral, originally expected to occupy a central position, were made to give way to the Virgin.[28] So the Gothic cathedral seems to have remained mutable throughout its construction, a process giving form to liturgical, doctrinal, or political ideas, and therefore susceptible to transmutation by such ideas and by their audience. Donors, whether guilds or noble lineages, insisted on having their own stained-glass windows.[29] The members of each guild saw to it that the techniques of their specific craft were accurately represented, and the members of each lineage that they were properly identified by means of their heraldic emblems. Such donations were even denounced as sins of pride masquerading as public exhibition of generosity.

This sensitivity of the architectural process created its true medium – namely, the capacity of the medieval audience to see meaning in the cathedral's visual representations. Virginia Raguin, in this volume, has connected the pictorial composition of the Poitiers stained glass to narrative forms in predominantly oral societies. I would go a step further and see the entire cathedral as an organic vocabulary of symbolic lines, colours, and volumes exhibiting the growth and development of forms in accordance with contemporary rules of interpretation. Indeed, as Hans Belting has posited, art works must be studied concomitantly with language in order to illuminate the historical systems of symbolic communication inherent in the forms of the art work themselves.[30] And, going beyond a consideration of forms as means of communication, an effective study of the Gothic cathedral should move towards a consideration of these forms as modes of thought.[31]

In fact, the emergence of a Gothic architecture has been compared with what took place contemporaneously in law and literature.[32] The written word, which up to then had merely recorded, now governed the principles of coherence and inner meaning, while the Gothic cathedral achieved an integration of the visual with this same idea of logical order.[33] Though this evocation of logical order might appear to support the notion of an overall conscious plan, the case for such a plan is weak; the archaeological evidence clearly points towards a Gothic cathedral that maintained narrative and structural flexibility. So the cathedral comprises both logical order and flexible structure, and it is as if the structure had generated a referent, logical order, that subverted the very flexibility to which it owed its constitution.[34]

For there seems to be some consensus, both medieval and contemporary, that principles of order did characterize the Gothic church whose unity was celebrated as a sum of discrete elements,[35] and whose language was that of clarity, light, and logic.[36] This holistic outcome did not result from a "wholeness of intention," nor necessarily from an array of parts, but may best be seen as a larger cultural principle for the generation of parts. There are multiple lines of evidence for the existence of such a principle. Though its validity has been questioned, Panofsky has suggested an analogy between the scholastic *summa* and the Gothic cathedral, both of which aspired to a totality achieved by the twin processes of homology and divisibility.[37] Then, too, the contemporary theology that influenced the process of Gothic creation derived in part from the Pseudo-Dionysian tradition studied by Suger. One basic principle of this tradition is that God is light, but even more relevant to the present discussion is that these texts envision the universe as a structure whose elements are disposed in a precise hierarchical gradation.[38]

The contemporaneous growth of written culture imposed new divisions of time and space upon experience, for example, organizing books into chapters, rubrics, and paragraphs, which extended the intellectual partitioning of the subject-matter to the visual layout of the written page.[39] In written history, the chronicle tradition increasingly took precedence over the annals format, an evolution which occurred principally at Saint-Denis. Significantly, the abbey developed as the most important centre of historical studies under the direction of Abbot Suger.[40] In contrast to annals, which consist only of a list of events arranged in chronological sequence, the chronicles aspire to a narrative in which events are revealed as possessing a structure, an order of meaning that they do not possess as mere sequence.[41] This ability to envision a set of events, or a set of any particular articulation/division, as belonging to the same order of meaning – the story, the book, the cosmos, the cathedral – requires the capacity to transform parts (events) into a discourse about the parts considered as a totality, and marks the desire for an integrated order.[42] This concept of integration, which I have described earlier as a cultural principle for the generation of parts, appears to have controlled medieval culture between roughly 1150 and 1250, a period in which value systems were related to one another by mutual implication.[43]

The holistic cathedral, or Gothic as an integrated order, is at the very centre, and not simply illustrative, of this era's social order. A late twelfth-century copy of Gilbert of Limerick's *De Statu Ecclesiae* represents his description of society in the form of early Gothic tracery.[44] His diagram makes a significant analogy between the social and architectural structures of the period. Moreover, Gilbert's description of society, as simply divided into the three traditional orders of those who pray, those who fight, and those who toil, is gainsaid by the diagram, which consists of multiple triangles and arcs within a single integrated tracery design. This diagram displays vividly how Gothic order functioned as both a subverted and an enforcing principle. Gothic art displays a propositional language claiming a structural order functioning holistically, when in fact it simultaneously supports a continually evolving pattern whose functioning defies linear causality. As such, Gothic holism is directly about order and diversification, about control and organization within society. It is of course ideationally, not mechanically, connected to society.

To a certain extent, the twelfth century, which commenced with the settlement of the Investiture controversy, witnessed a redistribution of powers and a destabilization of the traditional order. The paradigm of a tripartite society was no longer adequate to integrate the multiplying social groups and activities. As a result, many traditional categories seem to have experienced fractures, which in turn produced a tense multiplicity of relationships. Within the Church, heresies challenged doctrinal positions, and bishops and their schools gained ascendancy over the monks with their centres of learning. Within the lay orders, the nobility faced the strictures of a growing royal power from above, while also having to tolerate the entry from below of the rising group of knights, formerly mere military retainers. The growth of cities and urban franchises highlighted the dichotomy between town and country, and the increased circulation of money ultimately resulted in a redefinition of the forms of social interdependence.

This diversification of the social fabric generated an accrued concern for assuring order, an order which, given its failure to prevent the segmentation and growing complexity of society, might at least integrate those divisions into a workable system. The new order drew effectiveness and force from, and therefore generated, validating forms of representation. As seals for documentary authentication spread throughout society, they displayed an iconographic and heraldic grammar which identified and situated the individual in relation to his family, to his land, and to his social function. Beyond its utility as a device for documentary validation, the seal also served to validate its representational system, which conceptualized the complementarity of functional orders.[45]

Three other modes emerged, which projected as natural, rationalized, and spiritualized societal order. Naturalization was achieved by the use of bodily images to describe the social organism, as, for instance, John of Salisbury did in the *Policraticus* (1159);[46] this corporeo-social image naturalized order in biology.[47] The rationalization of societal order emerged from the growth of written records in which the principles of coherence gave shape to a social vocabulary that established structure by defining specific titles of status. Indeed such rationalization correlates with the scholastic mental habit of assuming that systematic division must lead to synthesis and totality. Finally, a spiritualization or divine validation of the social order was achieved in the cathedral, both in its configuration, as indicated by the diagram of Gilbert of Limerick, and in its space.

Remarkably, the Gothic cathedral acted as a symbol of Christian unity, while playing a divisive role as an instrument of social control.[48] Built with the new wealth derived from trade and agricultural clearings, the cathedral gave sanction to the new currency, money. Built within the city, it ratified the significance of urban space, and of episcopal hegemony. It celebrated dogma against heretic propositions, and proclaimed royal power. Cathedrals also demarcated interior spaces; some parts were reserved for the clergy alone, and in the laity's space, subdivisions reflected ranks and distinctions, and substantiated a hierarchical order with seats given over to the powerful who did not wish to stand and could afford particular proximity to the holy. Special chapels served select groups, and pictorial representations, by privileging certain groups and implicitly rejecting others, contributed to the cathedral's role in organizing, enacting, and publicizing a hierarchy of social differentiation.[49] True to the dialectical principle of integration inherent in its form, the cathedral was also a locus for contacts and interactions between pilgrims and locals, gentry, rustics and bourgeois, laity and clergy, images and human eyes, forms and sensory perceptions, logic and the supernatural. The result of these encounters was a propositional social order, which had its place in the architectural order, and through it in the order of Creation.

In conclusion, holism as a concept of integrated order had great symbolic value at the time of Early Gothic constructions and was a way of experiencing a specific social structure. Whether this entailed an initial holistic planning phase for cathedrals cannot, I think, be ascertained; but it surely involved a process of elaboration which resulted in an holistic appearance of organization. A narrative in stone, the cathedral cast its spell by an ability to subsume all within an order that had the form of truth.

NOTES

1 In the words of Natalie Zemon Davis, in "Art and Society in the Gifts of Montaigne," in *Representations* 12 (1985), 24.

2 Michael Baxandall, *Patterns of Intention: On the Historical Explanation of Pictures* (New Haven and London, 1985), pp. 13–14.

3 On this conception of meaning, see William Ray, *Literary Meaning: From Phenomenology to Deconstruction* (Oxford, 1984), pp. 154, 161.

4 Ibid., p. 162

5 Michael Ann Holly, *Panofsky and the Foundations of Art History* (Ithaca and London, 1984), pp. 160–3, 180–3.

6 See also the emphasis on the impression of architectural unity given by Gothic cathedrals in Charles M. Radding and William W. Clark, "Abélard et le bâtisseur de Saint-Denis. Etudes parallèles d'histoire des disciplines," *Annales* ESC 6 (1988), 1263–90, 1272–3.

7 Despite Baxandall's claim that "'Art' and 'Society' are unhomologous systematic constructions put upon interpenetrating subject matters," in "Art, Society and the Bouguer Principle," *Representations* 12 (1985), 42.

8 This program was outlined by Richard Schneider in his original proposal for the conference "Artistic Integration in Early Gothic Churches" held at York University (Toronto) in April 1989. Thanks are due to Prof. Schneider for his conception, planning, and management of the entire enterprise.

9 On the collaboration between art historians and literary critics, see *The Language of Images*, ed. W.J. Thomas Mitchell (Chicago and London, 1980), pp. 1–2.

10 In the words of Baxandall, in *Patterns of Intention*, p. 5. Compare the essay by Eric Fernie in this volume.

11 Saint Thomas Aquinas, *Summa Theologiae* Ia–IIae.57.3, ed. and trans W.D. Hugues (London, 1969), 23: 46–7: "Non enim pertinet ad laudem artificis, inquantum artifex est, qua voluntate opus faciat, sed quale sit." See a discussion of this passage in Umberto Eco, *Art and Beauty in the Middle Ages*, trans. Hugh Bredin (New Haven and London, 1986), pp. 80–1.

12 As recommended by Ernst H. Gombrich, in *Symbolic Images: Studies in the Art of the Renaissance* (London, 1972), p. 17.

13 See background for, and criticism of, this idea in Clifford Geertz, *Local Knowledge. Further Essays in Interpretive Anthropology* (New York, 1983), 118.

14 For a good presentation of phenomenology see Ray, *Literary Meaning*, pp. 8–59.

15 Baxandall, *Patterns of Intention*, p. 26; Holly, *Panofsky*, p. 185; Barbara Abou-El-Haj, "The Urban Setting for Late Medieval Church Building: Reims and Its Cathedral between 1210 and 1240," *Art History* 1 (1988), 18.

16 Baxandall, *Patterns of Intention*, p. 29.

17 Eco, *Art and Beauty in the Middle Ages*, pp. 41, 93.

18 Holly, *Panofsky*, pp. 166–7, 184–6, 188; Ray, *Literary Meaning*, pp. 161–2.

19 Geertz, *Local Knowledge*, p. 118.

20 Gombrich, *Symbolic Images*, p. 17.

21 Holly, *Panofsky*, p. 181.

22 See especially the essays by Willibald Sauerländer, Virginia Raguin, and Peter Kurmann and Brigitte Kurmann-Schwarz in this volume, and above, pp. 237–8, in this essay.

23 Baxandall, *Patterns of Intention*, p. 109.

24 Saint Thomas Aquinas, *Summa Theologiae* Ia.91.3, ed. and trans. Edmund Hill (London, 1964), 13: 24–6: "Quilibet autem artifex intendit suo operi dispositionem optimam inducere, non simpliciter, sed per comparationem ad finem." See a discussion of this passage in Eco, *Art and Beauty in the Middle Ages*, p. 78.

25 Eco, *Art and Beauty in the Middle Ages*, p. 97; Madeline Caviness, "Broad-
    ening the Definitions of 'Art': The Reception of Medieval Works in the
    Context of Post-Impressionist Movements," in *Hermeneutics and Medieval
    Culture*, ed. Patrick J. Gallacher and Helen Damico (Albany, 1989), p. 275.
    Geertz, in *Local Knowledge*, p. 119, argues that commonality among the arts
    is not fostered by an appeal to a universal sense of beauty, but that the
    commonality is based upon the fact that certain activities everywhere
    seem specifically designed to demonstrate that ideas are visible, audible,
    tactile.

26 Baxandall, *Patterns of Intention*, p. 42. Note that we discount Suger's own
    account of his architectural enterprise, which describes the intentional
    object as Merovingian, when it was in fact Carolingian. Suger's text,
    inconsistent with archaeological data, may be rejected as a reliable
    account of the object's intentionality, but not as an exposition of Suger's
    ideology. Compare the views expressed by Eric Fernie and William Clark
    in this volume.

27 Paul Crossley, "English Gothic Architecture," in *The Age of Chivalry: Art in
    Plantagenet England 1200–1400*, ed. J.J.G. Alexander and P. Binski [exh. cat.,
    Royal Academy of Arts] (London, 1987), p. 68.

28 Georges Duby, *History of Medieval Art, 980–1440*, 3 vols. (New York, 1986),
    vol. 2, pp. 120, 141; Peter Kurmann, *La façade de la cathédrale de Reims* (Paris
    and Lausanne, 1987).

29 On donors, see André Scobeltzine, *L'art féodal et son enjeu social* (Paris,
    1973), p. 302; Duby, *History of Medieval Art*, vol. 2, pp. 37, 129, 166; T.A.
    Heslop, "Attitudes to the Visual Arts: The Evidence from Written
    Sources," in *Age of Chivalry*, p. 30; Michael Camille, "The Language of
    Images in Medieval England, 1200–1400," in *Age of Chivalry*, p. 40. There is
    a debate surrounding the relationship between the depictions of specific
    artisanal corporations in the windows of Chartres, and the role of these
    corporations in giving or ordering these windows. On this debate, see the
    remarks by Madeline Caviness in her review of Jean-Paul Deremble and
    Colette Manhes, *Les vitraux légendaires de Chartres: Des récits en images*
    (Paris, 1988), and Wolfgang Kemp, *Sermo Corporeus: Die Erzählung der mit-
    telalterlichen Glasfenster* (Munich, 1987), *Speculum* 65/4 (1990), 974, where
    she also mentions the doctoral dissertation by Jane Welch Williams and
    her thesis "that artisanal corporations did not give, or direct, the windows
    in which they were imaged." Williams's dissertation has been published
    as *Bread, Wine, & Money: The Windows of the Trades at Chartres Cathedral*
    (Chicago, 1993). I want to thank Richard Schneider for bringing this dis-
    sertation to my attention.

30 See review of Hans Belting, *The End of the History of Art?*, trans. Christopher S. Wood (Chicago and London, 1987), in *American Historical Review* 93 (1988), 1296.

31 Geertz, *Local Knowledge*, p. 120.

32 See the state of the question and additional bibliography in Radding and Clark, "Abélard et le bâtisseur de Saint-Denis," pp. 1263–90.

33 Brian Stock, *The Implications of Literacy: Written Language and Models of Interpretation in the Eleventh and Twelfth Centuries* (Princeton, 1983), p. 82.

34 This is an application of Paul de Man's deconstruction as presented in Ray, *Literary Meaning*, p. 200.

35 *Opus Oxoniense* IV, d.11, q.3, note 46. See a discussion of Duns Scotus's notion that unity depends upon a natural subordination of partial forms to the ultimate form in Eco, *Art and Beauty in the Middle Ages*, pp. 86–7, and in Efrem Bettoni, *Duns Scotus: The Basic Principles of his Philosophy*, trans. and ed. Bernardine Bonansea (Washington, DC, 1961), pp. 70–3.

36 Scobeltzine, *L'art féodal et son enjeu social*, pp. 261, 281–2; Duby, *History of Medieval Art*, vol. 2, pp. 40, 68, 105 (on Grosseteste's views); Crossley, "English Architecture," p. 69; Peter Draper, "Architecture and Liturgy," in *Age of Chivalry*, pp. 88, 91; Eco, *Art and Beauty in the Middle Ages*, p. 110. The surviving notebooks of Villard de Honnecourt show his gift for envisaging schematically the overall effect of an edifice: see Duby, *History of Medieval Art*, vol. 2, p. 105.

37 Erwin Panofsky, *Gothic Architecture and Scholasticism* (New York, 1976), passim. See discussions of Panofsky's analogy in Holly, *Panofsky and the Foundations of Art History*, p. 162 and passim; Walter Horn, "Survival, Revival, Transformation," in *Renaissance and Renewal in the Twelfth Century*, ed. Robert L. Benson and Giles Constable (Cambridge, 1982), p. 715; Scobeltzine, *L'art féodal et son enjeu social*, pp. 242, 258, 261, 271.

38 Duby, *History of Medieval Art*, vol. 2, p. 14; also Grover A. Zinn, in "Suger, Theology and the Pseudo-Dionysian Tradition," in *Abbot Suger and Saint Denis*, ed. Paula Lieber Gerson, pp. 33–40 (New York, 1986), assesses (pp. 33, 37) Panofsky's identification of the Dionysian elements in Suger's thought (Erwin Panofsky, ed., *Abbot Suger on the Abbey Church of St.-Denis and Its Art Treasure* [1946; 2d ed. by Gerda Panofsky-Sorgel, Princeton, 1979], pp. 18–25). See also Conrad Rudolph, *Artistic Change at St-Denis* (Princeton, 1990), and Peter Kidson, "Panofsky, Suger and St Denis," *Journal of the Warburg and Courtauld Institutes* 50 (1987), 1–17.

39 Stock, *The Implications of Literacy*, p. 82; Panofsky, *Gothic Architecture and Scholasticism*, pp. 38–9.

40 Gabrielle Spiegel, *The Chronicle Tradition of St. Denis: A Survey* (Brookline, MA, and Leyden, 1978), p. 40.

41 Hayden White, *The Content of the Form: Narrative Discourse and Historical Representation* (Baltimore, 1987), p. 5.

42. Ibid., pp. 15–16.

43 Eco, *Art and Beauty in the Middle Ages*, p. 15.

44 See a discussion of this diagram in Michael Camille, "The Book of Signs: Writing and Visual Difference in Gothic Manuscript Illumination," *Word and Image* 1 (1985), 136–7.

45 Brigitte Bedos-Rezak, "The Social Implications of the Art of Chivalry: The Sigillographic Evidence (France, 1050–1250)," in *The Medieval Court in Europe*, ed. Edward R. Haymes, *Houston German Studies* 6 (1986), 142–75, pl.; revised and reprinted in idem., *Form and Order: Essays in Social and Quantitative Sigillography* (London, 1993), IV; idem., "Medieval Seals and the Structure of Chivalric Society," in *The Study of Chivalry*, ed. Howell Chickering and Thomas H. Seiler (Kalamazoo, MI, 1988), pp. 313–72; idem., "Women, Seals, and Power in Medieval France, 1150–1350," in *Women and Power in the Middle Ages*, ed. Mary Erler and Maryanne Kowaleski (Athens and London, 1988), pp. 61–82, reprinted in *Form and Order*, IX; idem., "Medieval Women in French Sigillographic Sources," in *Medieval Women and the Sources of Medieval History*, ed. Joel T. Rosenthal (Athens and London, 1990), pp. 1–36, reprinted in *Form and Order*, X; idem., "Towns and Seals: Representation and Signification in Medieval France," *Bulletin of the John Rylands University Library of Manchester* 72 (1990), pp. 35–48, reprinted in *Form and Order*, XII.

46 John of Salisbury, *Policraticus* 5.2, ed. Clement C.J. Webb (Oxford, 1909), pp. 282–4. See discussions and interpretations of the uses of the body metaphor in Georges Duby, *The Three Orders: Feudal Society Imagined*, trans. Arthur Goldhammer (Chicago and London, 1980), pp. 264–5; Scobeltzine, *L'art féodal et son enjeu social*, p. 257; Jacques Le Goff, "Head or Heart? The Political Use of Body Metaphors in the Middle Ages," in Zone 5: *Fragments for a History of the Human Body*. Part 3, ed. Michel Feher (New York, 1989), pp. 13–26. See also the remarks of Eco, *Art and Beauty in the Middle Ages*, p. 64.

47 I borrow the expression from Michael Camille, "Tres ordines in imagines." I wish to thank Professor Camille for sending me a draft of this essay, which was read as a discussion paper at Johns Hopkins University on 19 April 1988.

48 See Camille who does not recognize a unifying symbolism in the Gothic cathedral in his "Tres ordines in imagines," pp. 4 and 47.

49 On this see ibid., pp. 4–5, 47, and Scobeltzine, *L'art féodal et son enjeu social*, pp. 252, 261, 275, 299–301.

Artistic Integration in Gothic Buildings:
A Post-Modern Construct?

Madeline H. Caviness

Caviness examines the themes of this volume by considering the separate concepts encoded in the title of this volume through a retrospective recon-struction of meanings. She first addresses the possible reception of such terms as "artistic," "integration," and "Gothic" by a learned audience in Paris around 1200. She plays out for us suppositions of the reaction such an inquiry would have elicited from scholars such as Peter of Celle (d. 1183) and Stephen Langton (d. 1228) or a poet such as Geoffrey de Vinsauf. Second, like Sauerländer, Brush, and Bedos-Rezak, she addresses the climate of the scholarly world around 1900, the time of Mâle and other structuralist art historians. This world had developed a consensus that assumed an ability to "read" the past and discern authorial intention, unvarying meanings inher-ent in text and image, and a coherent agenda shared by a cohesive society.

She suggests that to examine the same title around 1960, at the height of Modernism, would be to discern yet another shift in meaning. The existence of Art could then have been taken for granted because of the long-current idea of "art for art's sake." The term "artistic" would have achieved the reso-nance of aesthetic quality, and the scholar would find it easy to project a self-conscious desire on the part of the persons responsible for the form of these works, invariably seen as the sculptors, painters, and architects, to search for an aesthetic expression. In the Post-Modern climate of the 1990s, however, we witness a critique of the historicism of the past. She stresses the ineluc-table impact of context on the formulation of scholarly ideas, as we look out over urban landscapes in the process of re(de?)construction through colour-ful forms from a variety of historic pasts. She observes that, unlike prior revival movements such as the Neoclassical or the Gothic Revival, our Post-Modern revivalism is without an historic focus or label, which may make it easier for the contemporary scholar to look at an assemblage that came into being sporadically over time as if it were a coherent, purposeful creation.

The theme of this volume, or more specifically the concepts of "artistic integration" and of "Gothic," have their own histories in our discipline. To assist in examining our own definitions I will attempt to look back, albeit schematically, at some prior moments to see whether or how these concepts were formulated at different times. It seems fitting to begin in the Middle Ages, even though I can provide little more than a fanciful digression in dealing with some of our terms.

Would the title of this volume have meant anything to a learned audience at the University of Paris around 1200?[1] A diligent sermon writer, such as Peter of Celle (d. 1183) or Stephen Langton (d. 1228), would have proceeded term by term to find the multivalent meanings of the whole. *Artistic* (vernacular): approximating Latin *formosa*, and also *ornatus, nitidus, splendens, sumptuosus* as suggested by Peter Draper, or, related to the *artes*, either mechanical or liberal. For instance, some of these terms might apply to the mechanical arts or crafts, such as metalwork, stained glass, or manuscript illumination described by "Theophilus" in his treatise *De diversis artibus*, but these decorations are generally regarded as more varied than integrated, except in so far as all contribute to the sumptuousness of God's house.[2] Among the liberal arts, geometry and music may be *integrated*, as in plain chant. *Convenientia et cohaerentia*: approximating concordance and harmony, or integration, commensuration, and coherence, as suggested in this volume by Virginia Raguin, and as used by Abbot Suger to characterize the columnar supports of the choir of Saint-Denis that he added to the earlier nave.[3]

Integration may connote deliberation or intention, a point I will return to in a later context. One medieval voice that speaks to this question is that of Geoffrey de Vinsauf, who is oddly at variance with the passage from Aquinas quoted by Brigitte Bedos-Rezak in her essay "Form as Social Process." In his treatise on poetry, the thirteenth-century author enlarged on the conceptualization and planning that must precede the execution of a building:

If a man has a house to build, his impetuous hand does not rush into action. The measuring line of his mind first lays out the work, and he mentally outlines the successive steps in a definite order. The mind's hand shapes the entire house before the body's hand builds it. Its mode of being is archetypal before it is actual. Poetic art may see in this analogy the law to be given to poets: let the poet's hand not be swift to take up the pen, nor his tongue be impatient to speak: trust neither hand nor tongue to the guidance of fortune. To ensure greater success for the work, let the discriminating mind, as a prelude to action, defer the operation of hand and tongue, and ponder long on the subject matter. Let the mind's interior compass first circle the whole extent of the material. Let a definite order chart in advance at what point the pen will take up its course, or where it will fix its Cadiz. As a prudent workman, construct the whole fabric within the mind's citadel; let it exist in the mind before it is on the lips.[4]

The doctrine effortlessly mirrors the Joannine concept of the primacy of the idea: "In the beginning was the Word; and the Word became Flesh" (John 1: 1, 14). It also reflects the concept of "seeing with the inner eye" that was propagated by the Victorines.[5] The emphasis on "definite order," however, and on the dependence of the realized work on the ideal plan, bespeak a will to integrate the parts. Geoffrey goes on to stress the importance of even execution throughout the work, and this is where art (again we would say craft) comes into play, with the concomitant risk of imperfections:

When due order has arranged the material in the hidden chamber of the mind, let poetic art come forward to clothe the matter with words. Since poetry comes to serve, however, let it make due preparation for attendance upon its mistress. Let it take heed lest a head with tousled locks, or a body in rumpled garments, or any final details prove displeasing, and lest in adorning one part it should in some way disfigure another. If any part is ill-groomed, the work as a whole incurs censure from that one part. A touch of gall makes all the honey bitter; a single blemish disfigures the entire face. Give careful thought to the material, therefore, that there may be no possible grounds for reproach.

The process of writing poetry advocated by Geoffrey de Vinsauf does seem to approximate that of "artistic integration," in that the wholeness or unity of the work depends on its coherent plan and on the consistent quality of its parts. His use of architectonic metaphor underscores the connection between order and architecture, but the shift to clothing as a metaphor for finishing the work departs from what we might have wished; would that he had continued the building metaphor to describe the integration of sculpture and painting!

Another poet who used the metaphor of architectonic order for his creation was the twelfth-century troubadour Marcabru:

E segon trobar naturau
Port la peir'e l'esc e'l fozill,
Mas menut trobador bergau
Entrebesquill,
Mi tornon mon chant en badau
En fant gratill.

(And according to natural [or vernacular] composition,
I bring the stone and the mortar and the file,
but destructive minor troubadours
mix it up,
turning my song into mockery,
doing just as they please with it.)[6]

In this case, blemishes are not the result of poor finish, but arise later from misuse in other edifices, or, one might say, are attributable to the deficiencies of the reader.

Our imaginary Parisian scholar would have had insurmountable difficulties, however, with "Gothic buildings." *Gothic* (*goticus*??) might well have had no appropriate resonance in Latin around 1200, since by then little attention was paid to the historic Germanic tribes. By an etymological leap, our preacher might have suggested *Golgotha* as a stem: Calvary, the ancient burial place of Adam where Christ was later crucified to rescue him from the tomb, and where later pilgrims could visit a basilica erected by Constantine to mark the spot. Churches (*ecclesiae*) would be primarily thought of as institutional, as in the seven churches of the Apocalyptic vision, the churches of Rome, or of the eastern patriarch; secondarily, they might be thought of as buildings. Yet the term for buildings as we use it would have been *aedificia*, or in a more restricted sense, with the connotation of sacred space, *aediculae*. Thus, in Paris about 1200, our *titulus* might have seemed to speak of the consonance and coherence of the liturgy (combining the arts of music and poetry) in the martyria on Calvary, or (closer to our meaning) of the coherent planning and execution of the ancient churches of Golgotha.

Gothic, of course, was not applied to an architectural style until the sixteenth century.[7] And in the eighteenth, unity rather than integration was the cry. Meanwhile the hierarchies of the fine and applied arts prevailed; sculpture and painting were decorations added to architecture, not necessarily integrated with it.[8] But, by 1831, Victor Hugo used the metaphor of symphonic music to suggest how polarities were resolved in the Parisian cathedral of Notre-Dame, which he saw as "a vast symphony in stone ... the colossal work of a man and of a nation, combining unity with complexity ... a sort of human Creation, in short, mighty and prolific as the Divine creation, of which it seems to have caught the double character, variety and eternity."[9] The resolution of binary polarities, this time opposing mechanical forces, also dominated Eugène Emmanuel Viollet-le-Duc's thinking about Gothic cathedrals.[10]

Around 1900, in a general academic climate that favoured structuralism, Emile Mâle proposed that the decoration of the French cathedrals of the thirteenth century – by then known as Gothic – tended to adhere to normative iconographic programs. On the south side, through which natural light flooded, were represented the saints of the New Testament and Christ himself, whereas the Old Testament was a predawn era restricted to the north side, and the verbal connection between west and dying (*occidens*) made it the locus for the Last Judgment.[11] The many exceptions to Mâle's normative program suggest that he formed its idea(l) as a distillation from existing varieties, much as Viollet-le-Duc had figured a composite cathedral as the ideal of Gothic half a century earlier.[12] The very suggestion that programs existed introduced the problem of intention.[13] Now, from the vantage point of the New Historicism, we would have to ask: where such rules seem to be in evidence, were they part of a preconceived plan, or, as more eloquently argued by Brigitte Bedos-Rezak in this collection, an unconscious application of cultural norms?[14] Mâle was inclined to adduce evidence from texts to suggest authors for such programs, implying authorial intention.[15] The coherence he perceived was conceptual rather than artistic, in Geoffrey's terms the result of "pondering long on the subject matter" rather than "clothing the matter." Somewhat later, Panofsky skirted the issue of intentionality by another structuralist device which proposed analogous patterns for scholastic thought and architectonic order in the Gothic era.[16] The abstraction represented by this idea did not hold up well to the evidence from archaeological and sociological facts adduced over subsequent decades.[17]

Meanwhile, in 1948, Hans Sedlmayr had introduced the concept of *Gesamtkunstwerk*, defining the Gothic cathedral as the "composite task in which all the arts were employed," and decrying the loss of this principle in the modern period as a result of the rigid separation of the arts.[18] This is not the place to discuss the repercussions of his ideas in any depth, but it may be noted that his term is still in use.[19] In opposition, many modern critics argued for the pristine separation or "purity" of the different plastic arts of painting, sculpture, and architecture.

As a consequence, the title of this volume would have had very different associations for an art historian in Paris (or Toronto) about 1960, at the height of Modernism. The existence of *Art* could then be taken for granted, because of the long-established idea of art for art's sake, even if its definition was constantly enlarged by artists and critics.[20] Artistic had the resonance of aesthetic quality, and Meyer Schapiro had argued for a conscious, textualized, Romanesque aesthetic, albeit one that preferred variety over regularity, whereas Focillon had argued for the virtue of the formal unity of Gothic architecture.[21] Integration was also a term with newly enriched associations about 1960, especially racial (in America); it meant everyone being treated alike within social institutions such as schools. By analogy, all the parts of a building, even those formerly discriminated against as "decoration," were ideally integrated into the larger whole, and treated equally as part of the canon. Robert Sowers's last book presents this ideal, and traces the history of such formal integration.[22] Around 1960 Gothic still had a fairly clear definition in architecture (Suger's Saint-Denis being accepted as the first monument), whether argued from structural innovation or from "style," and the history of the term had been traced back to the High Renaissance;[23] sculpture and painting were being worried over, carrying the search for the origins of the Gothic style back to a transitional period.[24] Older art, like Modern art, was pure form; in addition to the separations between the arts, there was a new binary polarity, that of form and content.[25] History was the pursuit of pure truth.[26] The historian was also pure, in other words, not subject to the ideologies of his or her own culture, except of course if he or she were writing the propagandist version.

Finally, how are we to read this title from a current perspective? Clearly, it has given each author more or less trouble, and several have wanted to modify it. More radically, concern with historiography has led to a perception that all histories are constructions; the canon, judgments as to its merits, period labels, and notions of development are all matters of labelling, agreement, and convention.[27] "Gothic" is quintessentially one of these modern constructs, even though some still argue their cases as if there was a real Gothic existing in the past, to be uncovered and properly described.[28] Others argue that the label is imperfect and that it has narrowed the canon and our diachronic analyses.[29]

A shift towards the synchronic, a wish to look at all periods of fabric that make up a building and see them as interrelated, is a logical departure from old developmental ways of thinking.[30] It still begs the question of intentionality; is the integration we perceive the result of a strategy on the part of those who successively added to a given structure, or did it stem from underlying continuities, such as those of the cult of relics and the liturgy? One answer to the dilemma of intentionality is to shift emphasis from intention, as unknown and unprovable, and to concentrate instead on perceptions of the work.[31] Yet even freeing interpretive acts from supposed acts of creation, concentrating on reception rather than on the dynamics of genesis, raises another equally important question; through whose eyes is a modern audience to see the work? The historian may attempt to see through the eyes of the medieval audiences, whether of the patron, clerics, and artisans whose intentions became inseparable from the effects of the finished work; or of the later frequenters of the buildings, of various literate and illiterate classes.[32] Such a process is as much reconstructive as the study of creation; indeed, all the groups I have mentioned are arguably modern constructs.

The alternative is to abandon historicism, and see through our Post-Modern eyes, as literary critics have not been afraid to do until recently. In 1988, Kendrick related the destabilization of textual readings to "a change in the dominant idea of order in modern Western society [whereby] under the impetus of scientific discoveries and technological progress, as well as political, economic, social, and moral changes, our notion of order has become more and more acentric."[33] The very need that many of us feel to break down the boundaries between chronological layers may stem from – or at least is in concert with – the new eclecticism in architectural forms, as Sowers suggests.[34] As I wrote a book in which I examined a church that had accumulated elements from the ninth through the twelfth century, I looked out on a Boston that was rapidly dispensing with unadorned concrete and marble modernity to take on the new look of colourful forms from a variety of historic pasts, frequently building onto or around a nineteenth-century core.[35] And I was teaching students for whom past centuries did not present a "perspective" (as they have for my generation), but rather a flat backdrop. [36] Our particular American brand of historicism in Post-Modern architecture blocks traditional historicity. Unlike prior revival movements, such as the Neoclassical or the Gothic Revival, ours is revivalism without an historical focus or label, and that makes it easier to look at an assemblage that came into being sporadically over time as if it were a coherent, purposeful creation. It might also be argued that any group of artefacts from a distant past, even randomly assembled, might represent for us the unity of that culture, broadly viewed.

In addition to defying older notions of historicism, Post-Modern architecture is often without deliberate symbolism and iconography, so that the form becomes content, accruing meanings by its associations. Yet gallery art is no longer pure form; not only have the boundaries between disciplines been broken down by mixed-media work, installations, and performance art, but the most noticed works are pure politics.[37] Likewise, many of its analysts are overtly engaged by ideologies, whether reactionary, conservative, socialist, or feminist.[38] Whereas the academic discourses of the Modern period covertly reinforced existing power structures, Post-Modern constructs are often (mis)represented as deliberately subversive.[39] On the other hand, the notion of an "artistic integration in Gothic churches" seems to rest in the structuralist and formalist past; where it emerges into the recent decade it does so by a symbiosis with Post-Modern architecture, multimedia works, and performance art, rather than by more profound ties to Post-Modern theory such as might have induced a paradigm shift.[40]

NOTES

1 Paris is the obvious choice because modern architectural historians have supposed it was at the centre of Gothic development. For a critique of the tyranny of that claim see, most recently, Marvin Trachtenberg, "Gothic/

Italian 'Gothic': Toward a Redefinition," *Journal of the Society of Architectural Historians* 50 (1991), 22–37.

2 Theophilus, *De Diversis Artibus: The Various Arts*, ed. and trans. C.R. Dodwell (London, 1961), p. 37. In the three prefaces *artes* most often means skills, and the emphasis is on process rather than on the functions of the finished work.

3 Erwin Panofsky, ed. and trans., *Abbot Suger on the Abbey Church of St.-Denis and Its Art Treasures*, 2d ed. (Princeton, 1979), pp. 90–1; the phrase was taken in the sense of the geometric layout of the choir by Sumner McKnight Crosby, in "Crypt and Choir Plans at Saint-Denis," *Gesta* 5 (1966), 4–6, and in the sense of consistent style and proportion by Madeline H. Caviness, in "'De convenientia et cohaerentia antiqui et novi operis": Medieval Conservation, Restoration, Pastiche and Forgery," in *Intuition und Kunstwissenschaft: Festschrift Hanns Swarzenski*, ed. Peter Bloch, Tilmann Buddensieg, and Alfred Müller (Berlin, 1973), pp. 205–21, and William Clark, in the present collection, who claims the ideological importance of the columns, without dealing with this term.

4 Geoffrey de Vinsauf, *Poetria nova*, trans. Margaret Nims (Toronto, 1967), pp. 16–17.

5 For instance, Hugh of Saint-Victor, *De Vanitate Mundi, Patrologia Latina*, 176: 703, and Richard of Saint Victor, *In Apocalypsim Joannis, Patrologia Latina*, 196: 686–7. See also Grover A. Zinn, Jr, "De Gradibus Ascensionum: The Stages of Contemplative Ascent in Two Treatises on Noah's Ark by Hugh of St. Victor," *Studies in Medieval Culture* 5 (1975), 61–79.

6 As quoted by Laura Kendrick, in *The Game of Love: Troubadour Wordplay* (Berkeley, 1988), p. 17. One might prefer to translate *fozill* as chisel in the context of working stone.

7 E.S. de Beer, "Gothic, Origin and Diffusion of the Term: The Idea of Style in Architecture," *Journal of the Warburg and Courtauld Institutes* 11 (1948), 143–62; Wayne Dynes, "Concept of Gothic," *Dictionary of the History of Ideas*, ed. P.P. Wiener (New York, 1973), vol. 2, pp. 366–74.

8 In a recent book on the integration of the different branches of the visual arts, a contemporary stained glass artist has pointed out how rarely the collaboration of artists is anything more than a myth in the post-medieval era: Robert Sowers, *Rethinking the Forms of Visual Expression* (Berkeley, 1990), pp. 91–102.

9 Quoted in translation from Victor Hugo, *Notre-Dame*, vol. 1 (Boston, 1888), p. 154.

10 As remarked by Pol Abraham, *Viollet-le-Duc et le rationalisme médiéval* (Paris, 1934). The theory of red and blue as opposing forces in stained glass

has been examined by James Rosser Johnson, in "The Stained Glass Theories of Viollet-le-Duc," *The Radiance of Chartres* (New York, 1965), pp. 26–52.

11. Emile Mâle, *L'art religieux du XIIIe siècle en France* (1898; repr. Paris, 1958), pp. 6–7.

12 Thus, although he admits exceptions exist, Mâle notes the examples that conform, including the sculpture of Chartres – but without mentioning the glass, which is far from consistent.

13 For an excellent discussion of the recent debates over intentionality, see Annabel Patterson, "Intention," *Critical Terms for Literary Analysis*, ed. Frank Lentricchia and Thomas McLaughlin (Chicago, 1990), pp. 135–46. The discussion of W.K. Wimstatt and M.C. Beardsley's questioning of our ability to reconstruct intention is cogent in their 1946 article, "The Intentional Fallacy," reprinted in W.K. Wimstatt, Jr, and Monroe C. Beardsley, *The Verbal Icon: Studies in the Meaning of Poetry* (Lexington, KY, 1954), pp. 3–18; but I find it hard to think of E.D. Hirsch's response in *Validity in Interpretation* as "a major exercise in literary theory ... transitional in more ways than one between Modernist and postmodernist views of critical method"; see E.D. Hirsch, Jr, *Validity in Interpretation* (New Haven, 1967), p. 143.

14 A provocative critique of the symbiotic relationship between notions of cultural norms and programmatic intention in relation to the "Carolingian Renaissance" is given by Lawrence Nees, in "The Plan of St. Gall and the Theory of the Program of Carolingian Art," *Gesta* 25 (1986), esp. pp. 5–6.

15 For instance, repeating in 1922 material originally published in an article in 1914, he credited Suger with the "invention" of the Jesse Tree; Mâle, *L'art religieux du XIIe siècle en France* pp. 168–75.

16 Erwin Panofsky, *Gothic Architecture and Scholasticism* (Latrobe, PA, 1951).

17 For instance, Lon R. Shelby, "The Geometrical Knowledge of Medieval Master Masons," *Speculum* 47 (1972), 395–421. See also references by Brigitte Bedos-Rezak in this volume.

18 Hans Sedlmayr, *Verlust der Mitte: Die bildende Kunst des 19. und 20. Jahrhunderts als Symptom und Symbol der Zeit* (Salzburg, 1948), p. 16: "es ist *die* Gesamtaufgabe für alle Künste"; see further, pp. 16–91; and Brian Battershaw, trans., *Art in Crisis: The Lost Centre* (Chicago, 1958), pp. 10–93.

19 As for instance by Kimpel and Suckale; the French translation of their work gives "oeuvre de synthèse à laquelle participaient tous les arts," which is closer, in its abstraction, to the original than the English rendering given above which avoids the question of intentionality on the part of the makers [Dieter Kimpel and Robert Suckale, *L'architecture gothique en France 1130–1270*, trans. Françoise Neu (Paris, 1990), p. 431].

20 Madeline H. Caviness, "Erweiterung des 'Kunst'-Begriffs: Die Rezeption mittelalterlicher Werke im Kontext nachimpressionistischer Bewegungen," *Oesterreichische Zeitschrift für Kunst und Denkmalpflege (Festschrift für Eva Frodl-Kraft)* 40 (1986), 204–15, and "Broadening the Definitions of 'Art': The Reception of Medieval Works in the Context of Post-Impressionist Movements," in *Hermeneutics and Medieval Culture*, ed. P.J. Gallacher and H. Damico, pp. 259–82 (Albany, 1989). For the continuing process, see Leo Steinberg, *Other Criteria: Confrontations with Twentieth-Century Art* (New York, 1972), esp. pp. 61–6.

21 Henri Focillon, *La vie des formes en art* (Paris, 1934); trans. as *The Life of Forms in Art* (1948), p. 8: "But there are other arts whose component parts also possess a truly fundamental value. One of these is Gothic art. It might well be said that the rib vault contains Gothic art in its entirety, composes it, and controls the derivation of all its parts." Meyer Schapiro, "On the Aesthetic Attitude in Romanesque Art" [1947, repr. in *Selected Papers: Romanesque Art* (New York, 1977), pp. 1–27]. The debate continued between Focillon's student Jurgis Baltrušaitis and Schapiro.

22 Sowers, in *Rethinking the Forms*, esp. pp. 9–72, deftly analysed the cathedral of Chartres from a perceptual (as opposed to intentional) point of view. He explains later failures of collaboration by the tyrannies of the easel painting and of the individual artist (pp. 73–82).

23 Otto G. von Simson, "The Birth of Gothic," *Measure* 1 (Chicago, 1950), p. 279; Kenneth John Conant, *Carolingian and Romanesque Architecture 800 to 1200* (Baltimore, 1959), pp. 291–93; Paul Frankl, *Gothic Architecture* (Baltimore, 1962), pp. 1–34; de Beer, "Gothic, Origin and Diffusion of the Term."

24 For example, Louis Grodecki, "Les problèmes de la peinture gothique," *Critique* 98 (1955), p. 611, and many of his subsequent articles which articulated a proto-Gothic phase or "style 1200."

25 This was largely the legacy of Heinrich Wölfflin, *Principles of Art History: The Problem of the Development of Style in Later Art*, trans. M.D. Hottinger (New York, 1932), originally published as *Kunstgeschichtliche Grundbegriffe: Das Problem der Stilentwicklung in der neueren Kunst* in 1915, which had significant impact on the teaching of art history, especially in the United States. Henri Focillon's students, such as Louis Grodecki, perpetuated the tradition in France. For Clement Greenberg's role in modern criticism, see Fred Orton and Griselda Pollock, "Avant-Gardes and Partisans Reviewed," in *Pollock and After: The Critical Debate*, ed. Francis Frascina (New York, 1985), pp. 178–9.

26 Historical records were also viewed as truthful: Hayden White, *The Con-*

tent of the Form: Narrative Discourse and Historical Representation (Baltimore, 1987); Nancy F. Partner, "Making Up Lost Time: Writing on the Writing of History," *Speculum* 61 (1986), 90–117; and the essays by Gabrielle M. Spiegel and Lee Patterson in *The New Philology*, ed. Stephen G. Nichols, a dedicated issue of *Speculum* 65/1 (1990), pp. 59–108.

27 A useful model in art history is A. Potts, "Winckelmann's Construction of History," *Art History* 5 (1982), 377–407.

28 For a critique of this kind of approach, see Richard Rorty, *Philosophy and the Mirror of Nature* (Princeton, 1979), esp. pp. 333–79.

29 Trachtenberg, "Gothic/Italian 'Gothic'"; Caviness, "'The Simple Perception of Matter' in Representations c. 1180–1280: Narrative Mode or Gothic Style?" *Gesta* 30 (1991), 48–64.

30 As suggested in my paper "A Diachronical Approach to Medieval Art," in a symposium on the historical synthesis of medieval art, organized by O.K. Werckmeister at Northwestern University, May 1988. A similar approach was proposed by Virginia Raguin in the session "The Middle Ages and the Renaissance in Northern Europe: The Physical Context," 77th Annual Meeting of the College Art Association of America, San Francisco, February 1989.

31 As by Hans Belting, *Das Bild und sein Publikum im Mittelalter* (Berlin, 1981), trans. Mark Bartusis and Raymond Meyer, *The Image and Its Public in the Middle Ages: Form and Function of Early Paintings of the Passion* (New Rochelle, NY, 1990).

32 A systematic study of medieval audiences has been begun by Linda Seidel, Robert Nelson, and Michael Camille.

33 Kendrick, *Game of Love*, p. 23. Cf. the "New Historicism;" a useful review is that of Lee Patterson in Lentricchia and McLaughlin, *Terms*, pp. 250–62.

34 Sowers, *Rethinking the Forms*, pp. 2, 126–7; he condemns Modernism, and especially Clement Greenberg, for the prior separation of the arts.

35 Caviness, *The Sumptuous Arts of the Royal Abbeys in Reims and Braine* (Princeton, 1990), written in 1983–8.

36 Peter Brown, in *The World of Late Antiquity AD 150–750* (London, 1971), p. 176, vividly describes a similar phenomenon in the late sixth century in the west, as the ancient world receded: "For Isidore of Seville (570–636), classical culture stood like a row of blue hills on the horizon: there was no telling how far apart the peaks were – Cicero and Augustine, Vergil and Jerome, pagan and Christian alike were revered by the seventh-century bishop, as the "masters" of a long-dead past."

37 W.J.T. Mitchell, "The Violence of Public Art: Do the Right Thing," *Critical Inquiry* 16/4 (Summer, 1990), 880–99.

38 This became increasingly clear during 1989–90, when the appropriations for the Endowments for the Arts and Humanities were under congressional scrutiny; funding was cut off from the Southeastern Center for Contemporary Art because of a controversial show of Andres Serrano, and from the Institute of Contemporary Art in Philadelphia because of the travelling exhibition it generated: see Janet Kardon, *Robert Mapplethorpe: The Perfect Moment* (Philadelphia, 1988). Supporters of the Jesse Helmes amendment "to prohibit the use of appropriated funds for the dissemination, promotion, or production of obscene or indecent materials" were battled by organizations such as the College Art Association of America in their pamphlet *Urgent – Call for Action* (Washington, 15 Aug. 1989), and in two recent issues of the *Art Journal*, 50/3 and 50/4 (1991), dedicated to censorship. Calls for a paradigm shift had destabilized Modernist art history, as recounted by Griselda Pollock, in *Vision and Difference: Femininity, Feminism and Histories of Art* (London and New York, 1988), p. 2.

39 The American Association of University Professors has responded to these charges in two issues of its bulletin *Academe*: "Censorship and the Arts" 76/4 (July-Aug. 1990), and "Statement on the "Political Correctness" Controversy" 77/5 (Sept.-Oct. 1991), 48.

40 This is not intended as a criticism of any of the papers in this collection, several of which wrestle with the title. I have deliberately avoided reference to all but a few overlapping points contained in them, in the hope that a reading of them will none the less be enriched by an awareness of some of the questions formulated here.

Towards a Cultural Biography of the Gothic Cathedral: Reflections on History and Art History

Brigitte Bedos-Rezak

Bedos-Rezak examines scholarly issues in the current debate concerning the self-definitions of history and art history. The principal theme of this book, Gothic integration, emerged from just such questions as to the role of the separate studies of categories of art, and also from the larger question of what role the study of liturgy, religion, or social and diplomatic history may play in the assessment of the meaning of the Gothic church. Taking the standpoint of the historian, she comments on the natures of history and art history, on their modes of interaction, and the implications of an interdisciplinary approach to the study of Gothic building. In this process of self-examination, she observes that historians have appeared to challenge the very conceptual foundations of their discipline: time, facts, past, reality, text, and objectivity. Although sensitive to the multidisciplinary nature of much contemporary scholarship in art history, she suggests that the form of the art work remains the principal focus of art-historical study. She also assesses the art-historical division of connoisseurship and the issues of visual skills as they intersect with interpretative skills of historical inquiry.

In this compelling essay she suggests that an approach that art history might contribute afresh is an inquiry into art as an agent of opposition in history. It is the tension between art and life which imprints its form upon the art work. Thus produced, the art form sustains a multifaceted dialogue with reality; with the reality that grounds its modes of figuration. Both art and history are concepts, and their relationship to each other, and to the artefact itself, must involve the recognition that they spring from two different categorizations of human experience: art as being, and history as becoming.

"What else are such cathedrals
but a stone-embodied "Nevertheless"
against the world in the world."
Franz Rosenzweig[1]

When, in the nineteenth century, the architect Viollet-le-Duc and his colleagues undertook to restore French Gothic cathedrals, they were inspired by a specific mythic conception of the cathedral and of the circumstances of its creation. Swept by the powerful vision of Victor Hugo's *The Hunchback of Notre Dame* (*Notre-Dame de Paris*, 1831), they saw the cathedral as the monument of the people, a vibrant manifestation of popular creative power and spirituality. They also conceived of an ideal original state of the cathedral. In nineteenth-century thought, this ideal cathedral was seen as an intended edifice of thirteenth-century people, however imperfectly achieved as a result of intrusive circumstances. As a result, many cathedrals were consciously restored to a state in which they had never actually existed.[2]

While art-historical constructs usually remain in the realm of cognition and speculation, they often proceed from a conception of the monument in which its structure as object, a retrievable presence, functions as a sign referring to elements beyond that structure itself, such as authorial intention and design, use and purpose, culture and society, as the essays in this volume demonstrate. The cathedral's form, construed as a metastructural referent, also grounds interpretation of the cathedral per se. There are two implications of such a methodology. First, a focus on the cathedral-as-object and as work-of-art conceptually empties the cathedral of culture which, instead of being its constitutive fabric, becomes merely its point of reference. Second, the assimilation of the cathedral-object with the cathedral-referent destroys the autonomy and the recoverability of the cathedral-object. Furthermore, in this process, the reality of the cathedral in art-historical discourse is created by substituting a concept, form, for the referents which it allegedly described: structure, liturgical or ideological function, social and religious practices.

With this statement, more declarative than critical, I wish to engage the principal theme of this book, Gothic integration. This theme was approached from a variety of perspectives, and integration was seen as achieved, or impeded, by disciplinary practice and hermeneutics, style and design, use and function, meaning and ideology, and social process, whether medieval or modern. The essays thus point to a per-

ception of the Gothic monument as a meaningful, that is a constituted, object, rather than as an object per se, one which is found and
not constituted. Such essays thus contribute substantially to the continuing epistemological debate in art history about viewing, reading,
and interpreting. More specifically, they also raise such issues as the
ontologically distinct nature of art work, the role of texts and contexts
as interpretive categories for art works, and the medieval reception of
visual art.

Taking the standpoint of the historian, I propose here to comment
and to theorize on the respective epistemic natures of history and art
history, on their modes of interaction, and on the modalities and
implications of an interdisciplinary approach to the Gothic cathedral.
Particular questions arise for a historian confronted with the evidential nature of art work. What information may be uniquely extracted
from visual evidence? How do art works signify and produce meaning? How does their system of signification relate to that of texts, and
is there any degree of commensurability between the two? Does Art
have a History? Such questions suggest that, in interpreting the
cathedral, both historians and art historians work with, and create,
codifications that relate primarily to the discursive formulations of
their respective disciplines. As a corollary, the only perceivable
Gothic cathedral may be that which peeps out from within the discursive practices forming the fields of enquiry.

The agenda for a pluridisciplinary integration, as advocated and/
or applied in this volume's essays, involves the following disciplines
within art history: architecture, sculpture, stained glass, as well as
disciplines outside of art history, such as liturgy, theology, history. I
will limit my present remarks to history and art history. The crisis of
identity experienced by both disciplines manifests itself in a large
production of theoretical works with apocalyptic overtones which
reflect upon their aims, mean(ing)s, and presumably imminent end.[3]
Recourse to theory often articulates a sense of rupture and alienation
from past practices, and of marginalization from other disciplines
such as literary criticism, linguistics, semiotics, and cultural anthropology. These latter fields are perceived as having generated an ines-
capable agenda for sustaining epistemological relevance and validity,
as it provides compelling formulations and tools for the consideration of admittedly critical questions of meaning and signification.
Resistance to this agenda, which is considered by some to be alien,
splits the fields of history and art history along deeply carved herme-

neutic lines. At stake for each is the integrity of the discipline as a single coherent field with defined boundaries (critical tradition and canon) and directionality, when both fields are now also perceived as inscribed within the troubling circle of heterogeneity and epistemological relativism.

In their current process of self-examination, historians have appeared to challenge the very conceptual foundations of their discipline: time, facts, past, reality, text, context, objectivity. If history is both a contingent sequence of facts – a matter of empirical knowledge – and the code for understanding them –a matter of speculation – then the historian may appear to equate cognitive/empirical action with the speculative process by which facts are constructed into religious, social, and political forms. For such forms, documented facts can offer neither proof nor disproof. This view, while challenging the objectivity of analytical effort and the conviction that one can make sense of history, still accepts that facts are entities, to be found rather than constructed. But though facts seem to exist independently of interpretive gesture, they have already received the interpretation that they are to be perceived as facts. Contexts thus play an important role as enabling analytical frameworks, but historians tend to endow past contexts with a concreteness and objectivity that obscures their provisional and arbitrary status. Of the present contexts in which their own interpretive production takes place, historians tend to be somewhat oblivious, inclined to introduce within their interpretations of the past those principles underlying their own apprehension of the object under study. The problematization of the context is paralleled by that of the text, both having been affected by Post-Modern theories concerning the operation and contingency of language. Historical records, once assumed to contain fixed and accessible meanings are, when processed through a linguistic grid, atomized into multiple representative possibilities. This not only tends to render unlikely the recovery of a stable and determinable past, it also altogether undermines the capacity of language to refer to a reality external to itself. The historian's traditional narrative discourse, long supposed to describe objectively real, rather than fictional, events, has been declared as simply another interpretive operation, linguistically reordering actual events into a coherent and significant sequence possible only for imaginary events. Referential reality and truth thus become redefined as simulated values – particular truths and realities – produced by textual strategies, and history is reconceived as a representational practice that, in the absence of extra-linguistic reference, can perhaps no longer be distinguished from fictional narration. In settling (as I do) for history as a documentary, procedural, interpretive, and perspectival practice for the production of knowledge about things past, I believe that the historian needs to formulate a linguistic model for the relationship between language and the material and mental worlds.

Art history, like history, presupposes a conception of temporal reality in order to constitute its disciplinary program; art works are conceived as historical events of, and in, their times. Yet analysis of the nature and modalities of the interactions between works of art and the circumstances of their production and signification has remained secondary to the examination of forms. This in turn has lead to periodization, and a conception of autonomously evolving styles, with art work seen as having a history of its own, even operating as an agency independent of meaning and social function. Acceptance of the general historical paradigm necessarily takes the discipline of art history beyond this system of artistic phenomena, challenging the notion of autonomous and ontologically distinct art objects which are to be read uniquely from formal and internal criteria. The notion of style thus loses its central status as both the purpose and the framework of art-historical analysis. The artefact, in becoming conceptually more complex, has required newer interpretive models. None to date seems to have achieved the comprehensiveness and general acceptance offered by the stylistic canon; hence the crisis in the discipline.

Connoisseurship draws upon the observer's visual skills for the discernment, delineation, and recognition of forms and of their operating principles. It assumes, and thereby demonstrates, that the artefact's presence of real being inheres in its position within a reified sequence of types, and derives meaning as a referential signpost within the larger class of art works. Such works have been conceived as autonomous, stable, entities having a determinate significance of their own grounded in form and authorial intention, and retrievable by the specialized analyst. Yet, how does the Gothic formulation explain the Gothic cathedral? Can a cathedral be understood simply in terms of its style? What is a cathedral outside its stylistic framework? In mapping a history of forms, art historians have only partially addressed the task of making the visible legible. That attention to content which has been addressed independently of considerations of form has further tended to rob the art work of its historical substance. When looked at, the cathedral projects a material unity, but, when thought of, it becomes a phenomenon of relatedness, which means through its own laws of signification, in relation to the agents of its production and consumption, and thus demands interpretation. From being contemplated, the art object becomes interpreted along the lines of production, reception, signification, and function, which involves reference to the world as embodied in these different points of perspective. All these perspectives consequently entail reliance on specific interpretive frameworks and theorization about the relationship between the artefact and its context. The art object thus considered testifies to man rather to art. Art historians may be concerned that the centrality of the object will be lost when art form is also conceived as articulating the experience of reality. Like the historical fact, however, the nature of an artefact that has not already been interpreted by its author, and by its beholders, past and present, remains elusive.

The form of the art work remains the principal focus of art-historical study. Such analysis now takes into consideration the determinants of the art form, and the world to which it refers and of/in which its speaks symbolically. Yet art historians are apprehensive about the integrity of their technique and discipline at the point when they find that they need to act as social historians or linguists. A key issue is how the art historian is to process the specificity of visual evidence which encompasses signifying modalities and practices, and agency in the formation and codification of past beliefs, ideas, and experiences. Professional connoisseurship scarcely addresses these issues in outlining the temporal development of art, and though this method still fills a necessary function, it seems to be approaching exhaustion as an end in itself. Just as the discipline of history has had to reassess its conceptual tools – facts, truth, objectivity, reality, past – so has art history its own concepts of form, style, and aesthetic autonomy. Both disciplines have become aware that they themselves are practising representation as they engage in the study of vehicles of representation such as texts, images, and artefacts.

Grounding the order of causes and relationships, of diachronic differences and synchronic concordances, history plays a central role in the creation of art as an object of knowledge. Conversely, within the discipline of history, as in many other humanistic fields, greater attention is now given to the social production of meaning, and to media as symbolic languages of communication. Art is seen as one of these media, as one among the many systems for representing the world. That blurring of the boundaries between art and society, between the epistemologies of art history and history, which has been experienced by both disciplines as a crisis, also raises the question: is there any interdisciplinary approach to a work of art, here the Gothic cathedral, that would not be redundant?

Even as historians arbitrarily appropriate works from the past and inscribe them with periodization, directionality, and legibility, art historians insist on the unique profile of these as also ahistorical and ineffable works, endowed with a continuous reality. Art historians establish a repertoire of art forms and deal with their aesthetic integrity; historians attend to art as forms of statements about something else. By both disciplines, as exemplified in this volume, artefacts are interpreted as elements in an actual pattern of life, and not exclusively, if even at all, in the formal, thematic, or functional relationships they bear one to another. This approach implies a vision of art as instrumental in the creation of the world in which humans live, and hence as co-optable by power. Perhaps an approach that art history might contribute afresh is an enquiry into art as an agent of opposition in history. It is the tension between art and life which imprints its form upon the art work. Thus produced, art form sustains a multifaceted dialogue with reality: with the reality that grounds its modes of figuration, with the reality it itself articulates, with the reality it conditions, and with the reality it transcends through continuity. Art form in this layered substance is not factual. The art work's material reality resides in its technique and subject-matter. Both art and history are concepts, and their relationship to one another, and to the artefact itself, must involve recognition that they spring from two different categorizations of human experience: art as being, and history as becoming.

Art historians and historians talk about one another, more rarely to one another. Their fields of knowledge have predetermined spaces of significations. How do the apparatus of these fields provide their practitioners with a conceptually distinctive object of study? A partial answer may emerge from a consideration of how the contributors to this volume have treated the cathedral as source.

In positing the monument as their primary source, art historians saw it as an object and as a meaningful object. Using the category "Gothic style," they have revealed a mode of monumental being even while questioning the extent to which this "style" was an informing principle of construction. Consideration of the cathedral as object, as art, and as artefact, led to several avenues of inquiry, but despite the insistence placed upon the centrality of the monument as source, little meaning was derived from the monument per se. Virtually all essays analysed the work through its structure, its architecture, its form, and the modalities of its internal relationships. Such analysis often led to an attempted recovery of the cathedral's relationship to authorial intention, to a thought or to an experience. This approach, however, seems in turn to have displaced the centrality of the work itself in favour of an imaginary conception of its general setting, the condition of the space and of the time in which it was created, and within which it continues to unfold. The construction of context seems to have displaced monumental analysis, while little theoretical understanding was offered of what the context and the monument actually are, or of the ways in which they interact. Rather, such interactions were simply assumed to be revelation, reflection, articulation, representation, or communication. An alternative approach here might be an inquiry into what the art work designates, since its materiality, though distinct from the immateriality of the imagined context, seems actually to require this external component to achieve significance beyond the structural, the formal, and the normative. The Gothic cathedral continues to exist in the absence of its initial referent, and of any determinate signification. Its analysis as a sign and a medium, that is, within the context of other monuments, or of the circumstances of its own production, seems to me to avoid the issue of real being, and also to allocate meaning "elsewhere," an elsewhere that remains just there, elsewhere. In this volume, the paradigm of artistic integration tends to assign meaning, either to an intentional planning which did not necessarily result in an integrated building, or to a perception of an integrated functional or symbolic whole not necessarily the result of such planning. Intention and perception imply authors or audience, which forces us again to a consideration of context. In this volume, art historians have not chosen to address the materiality of the sign-monument specifically enough to avoid the need for substantiating evidence of intentionality, function, meaning, and signification from extra-monumental sources. Contexts, though themselves anecdotal and fragmentary, have been reified throughout, and accepted as valid interpretive frameworks. Historians face a similar problem whenever they bring extra-textual elements to bear upon the reading of documentary evidence. Incommensurability exists between text or monument, and their context, when the framework which supplies meaning to the materially extant component has remained speculative. This interrelation introduces uncertainty about the integrity of both elements and presents a classical hazard of circular reasoning. Essays in this volume often assume rather than critically investigate the many different contexts to which the cathedral may be referred. In so doing they leave unresolved and unchallenged the notion of a unified, concrete, and accessible context. Historians need to explore more fully the dialogic implications of different contexts. They must question how this contextual multiplicity contributes to, or detracts from, recognition of the constitutive essence of the cathedral in, and of, its normative material being. Where an identity between the artefact and its informing structure of meaning is postulated, then art historians should investigate the art work's formal properties not only from the viewpoint of style, but also from that of the strategies by which signs create representations of the natural order they are supposed to reflect, and which is thus posited as pre-existent and as having an existence outside of them. A source, whether monumental or textual, both bears and subverts the terms of its contextualization.

The issue of visual versus textual evidence is addressed in several of this volume's essays (Fernie, Clark, Draper, Kurmann and Kurmann-Schwarz). Whether these types of evidence are complementary and should be thus used, and how much may be inferred from one form of evidence in the interpretation of the other, is at the heart of the commensurability debate outlined above. Both texts and social experiences are articulated through language. Visual art, on the other hand, utilizes a signifying practice that has peculiar procedures and dimensions (i.e., aesthetics) and hence possesses a faculty for articulation no other medium can match. Texts and artefacts are different modes of communication which, though interdependent because both operate within a common frame of experience, do not directly influence the form the other takes.

In this volume, the cathedral is primarily conceived as product, as produced meaning. Form signifies, content is signified. Both are in fact fused into a stable entity with determinable significance which serves as a passive vehicle for the transmission of various forces such as design and intention, function and ideology. The cathedral is constructed both as a nexus of relationships with ties to the entire sociocultural system, and as a medium between authors/designers and audience/users. In fitting the cathedral to particular tasks, and in studying relevant circumstances, the contributors to this volume have expanded the conception of art as social practice. They have emphasized the dynamic by which social pressures bore upon a monument conceived as an effect of culture.

The pressures that the monument itself exerts on sociocultural practice, its potency and its modalities for the production of social meaning, should also be taken into consideration. By treating sociological and cultural processes on equal terms, rather than as interchangeable backgrounds and foregrounds, a way may be found out of the dilemma in which art is treated either as a sequence of formal transformations or as a passive commentary on processes external to art. Shaped by the encounter between life and a specific concept of visual structures, the Gothic cathedral articulates both life and concept through its form, which is itself the materialization, definition, and interpretation of a content. From a semiological perspective, the cathedral in its formal continuity names its own form(s) and processes of meaning production, and thus makes these processes its own subject-matter, its own ideological content. An important issue for both historians and art historians is an understanding of the cultural system in which Gothic signification is to be retrieved. How much belongs to medieval culture, how much to the critic's circumstances? By accepting that meaning is relational, inscribed in both a chronological and systematic time, and in both the past and the present, the analyst is compelled to question the evidential nature of the monument. Gothic cathedrals translated, and continue to translate, practical acts (building, praying, depicting, gathering, proselytizing, politicking), and objects (stones, stained glass, statues, images, liturgical apparatus), and their related themes, into an encompassing interpretive structure. The Gothic cathedral established frameworks of legibility and thus contributed to the comprehensibility of medieval experience, by imposing meaning upon it. In attempting to grasp the relational modes between medieval meaning and experience, it may be necessary to posit that art forms work most successfully, as the Gothic cathedral did, when they reorganize those semantic formations that underlie their own legibility, reordering dyads of signifiers and their referents, and thus pointing to renegotiated idea(l)s of sociocultural organization. In this respect, the art form sits at the junction of the visible, the legible, and the phatic.

Historians must query the social construct by which certain objects are designated as works of art and, distinguished from worked-upon objects, are considered worthy of preservation in essentially constant form. Thus formulated, this query implies that the "aesthetic" is located in community reception, not in authorial intention or in intrinsic formal qualities of the work itself.

Focusing on the work or fact of art, historians would want to understand how such work articulates an experience of reality, and what kind of reality is articulated. In analysing the art work, they may consider whether the meaning of human experience should be equated with the way it is represented, and whether, or how, the production of meaning through art served to validate practical activities. Conversely, the aestheticization of social practices raises questions about the very nature of such operations: were these negotiations, neutralizations?

Social, economic, technical, functional, ideological, aesthetical biographies of the Gothic cathedral are all legitimate studies of its life history. Historians must, however, avoid using visual evidence as a mere complement to their texts. Visual discourse reveals information about its referents that is different and of a kind that may be told only by means of this discourse.

The pressures of history, as conditions both of the Gothic cathedral and of its twentieth-century critique, form that paradoxically transhistorical frame in which both the cathedral and its interpreter achieve interdependent signification.

NOTES

1 Unpublished letter to Margrit Rosenstock, 11 November 1918, quoted in Stephan Meinecke, "A Life of Contradiction: The Philosopher Franz Rosenzweig and His Relationship to History and Politics," *Leo Baeck Institute Yearbook* 36 (1991), 482.

2 Alain Erlande-Brandenburg, *La cathédrale* (Paris, 1989), pp. 13–39; *Viollet-le-Duc* [exh. cat., Galeries nationales du Grand Palais, 19 February – 5 May 1980] (Paris, 1980).

3 Peter Novack, in his *That Noble Dream*, claims that the "discipline of history had ceased to exist by the 1980s," quoted in *The American Historical Review* 96/3 (1991), 689. Hans Belting titled his recent book *The End of the History of Art* and Donald Preziosi devotes chapter 6 of his book *Rethinking Art History* to "The End(s) of Art History" (see full citations in Selected Bibliography below).

SELECTED BIBLIOGRAPHY

The following readings have been valuable in my conception and development of the arguments for this essay.

"AHR Forum: Peter Novick's *That Noble Dream*: The Objectivity Question and the Future of the Historical Profession." *The American Historical Review* 96/3 (1991), 675–708.

Alpers, Svetlana. "Is Art History?" *Daedalus* 106/3 (1977), 1–13.

Appadurai, Arjun, ed. *The Social Life of Things*. Cambridge, 1986.

"Art and Society: Must We Choose?" *Representations* 12 (1985), 1–43.

Barthes, Roland. *The Responsibility of Forms*. New York, 1985.

Baudrillard, Jean. *Le système des objets*. Paris, 1968.

Belting, Hans. *The End of the History of Art?* Chicago and London, 1987.

Bourdieu, Pierre. *Distinction: A Social Critique of the Judgement of Taste*. Cambridge, MA, 1984.

– *Outline of a Theory of Practice*. Cambridge, London, New York, 1985.

Camille, Michael. *The Gothic Idol: Ideology and Image-Making in Medieval Art*. Cambridge, New York, 1989.

Fleischman, Suzanne. "Philology, Linguistics, and the Discourse of the Medieval Text." *Speculum* 65/1 (1990), 19–37.

Foucault, Michel. *The Archeology of Knowledge*. New York, 1972.

Geertz, Clifford. *The Interpretation of Culture*. New York, 1973.

– *Local Knowledge*. New York, 1983.

Norris, Christopher. *What's Wrong with Postmodernism: Critical Theory and the Ends of Philosophy*. Baltimore, 1990.

Partner, Nancy F. "Making Up Lost Time: Writing on the Writing of History." *Speculum* 61/1 (1986), 90–117.

Porter, Carolyn. "Are We Being Historical Yet?" *The South Atlantic Quarterly* 87/4 (1988), 743–86.

Preziosi, Donald. *Rethinking Art History: Meditations on a Coy Science*. New Haven and London, 1989; see a thorough review by Whitney Davis in *Art Bulletin* 72 (1990), 156–66.

Ray, William. *Literary Meaning: From Phenomenology to Deconstruction*. Oxford, 1984.

Scott, Joan Wallach. "History in Crisis? The Others" Side of the Story." *The American Historical Review* 94/3 (1989), 680–92.

Shoaf, R.A. "Medieval Studies after Derrida after Heidegger." In *Sign, Sentence, Discourse: Language in Medieval Thought and Literature*, ed. Julian N. Wasserman and Lois Roney, pp. 9–30. Syracuse, 1989.

Spiegel, Gabrielle M. "History, Historicism, and the Social Logic of the Text in the Middle Ages." *Speculum* 65/1 (1990), 59–86.

Toews, John E. "Intellectual History after the Linguistic Turn: The Autonomy of Meaning and the Irreducibility of Experience." *The American Historical Review* 92/4 (1987), 879–907.

White, Hayden. *The Content of the Form: Narrative Discourse and Historical Representation*. Baltimore and London, 1987.

– "Historiography and Historiophoty." *The American Historical Review* 93/5 (1988), 1193–9.

Notes on Contributors

Barbara Abou-El-Haj: PhD University of California, Los Angeles, 1975. Faculty appointments at the University of Southern California and the University of California, Los Angeles; Associate Professor of Art History at the State University of New York, Binghamton. Editor for *Review*; member of the Board of Directors of the Fernand Braudel Center for the Study of Economies, Historical Systems, and Civilizations. Publications include articles on the cult of the saints in *Art Bulletin*, *Art History*, *Gesta*, and *Kritische Berichte* and on the social impact of large-scale building in the thirteenth century: "The Urban Setting for Late Medieval Church Building: Reims and Its Cathedral Between 1210 and 1240," *Art History* 11 (1988), 17–41, and "Building and Decorating at Reims and Amiens," *Europäische Skulptur im 12./13. Jahrhundert*, ed. H. Beck and K. Hengevoss-Dürkop (Frankfurt a/M, 1994), pp. 763–76, 508–19. She has published recently *The Medieval Cult Saints: Formations and Transformations* (Cambridge, 1994).

Brigitte Bedos-Rezak: License ès Lettres, Université de Paris, Sorbonne, 1977; Archiviste-Paléographe, Ecole nationale de Chartes (Paris) 1977. Head curator, Central Department of Seals, Archives nationales, Paris; Fellow, Metropolitan Museum of Art; Professor, University of Maryland at College Park, Department of History. Publications include *Histoire de Montmorency: Le Moyen Age* (Paris, 1979); *Corpus des sceaux français du Moyen Age*. Tome 1er: *Les sceaux des villes* (Paris, 1980), *Le châtellenie de Montmorency des origines à 1368* (Pontoise, 1980); *Anne de Montmorency, seigneur de la Renaissance* (Paris, 1990); *Form and Order: Essays in Social and Quantitative Sigillography*

(London, 1993); editor and contributor "Polity and Place: Regionalism in Medieval France," special issue of *Historical Reflections/ Réflections historiques* 19 (1993), 151–278. Articles include "Ritual in the Royal Chancery: Text, Image and the Representation of Kingship in Medieval French Diplomas (700–1200)," in *European Monarchy: Its Evolution and Practice from Roman Antiquity to Modern Times*, eds. Heinz Duchhardt, Richard Jackson, and David Sturdy, pp. 27–40 (Stuttgart, 1992); "The Confrontation of Orality and Textuality: Jewish and Christian Literacy in Eleventh- and Twelfth-Century Northern France," *Rashi, 1040–1900*, ed. Gabrielle Sed-Rajna, pp. 541–58 (Paris, 1993).

Beat Brenk: PhD University of Basel, 1960. Professor and Chair of the Department of Art History, University of Basel. Author of numerous publications on Early Christian, Byzantine, and medieval art, and organizer of symposia on Assisi (1980), Medieval Book Illumination (1983), Konrad Witz (1987), the Cult of the Martyrs (1989), and Innovation in Late Antiquity (1994). Books include *Tradition und Neuerung in der christlichen Kunst des ersten Jahrtausends. Studien zur Geschichte des Weltgerichtsbildes* (Vienna, 1966); *Die frühchristlichen Mosaiken von S. Maria Maggiore zu Rom* (Wiesbaden, 1975), *Spätantike und frühes Christentum* (Berlin, 1977), *Codex Benedictus Cod. Vat. Lat. 1202* (Stuttgart, 1981), *Das Lektionar des Desiderius von Montecassino* (Zurich, 1987). See, most recently, "Bildprogrammatik und Geschichtsverständnis der Kapetinger im Querhaus der Kathedrale von Chartres," *Arte medievale*, 2d series 5/2 (1991), 71–96.

Kathryn Brush: PhD Brown University, 1987. Associate Professor, Department of Visual Arts, University of Western Ontario; Andrew W. Mellon Faculty Fellow, Harvard University 1991–2. Publications include "The *Recepta jocalium* in the Wardrobe Book of William de Norwell, 12 July 1338 to 27 May 1340," *Journal of Medieval History* 10 (1984), 249–70; "Power, Politics and Demonstration in Thirteenth-Century Mainz: The Tomb Slab of Archbishop Siegfried III von Eppstein (+1249)," *RACAR: Revue d'art canadienne/ Canadian art review* 17/2 (1991), 119–26; "The Naumburg Master: A Chapter in the Development of Medieval Art History," *Gazette des Beaux-Arts*, 6th ser. 122 (1993), 109–22; "Wilhelm Vöge and the Role of Human Agency in the Making of Medieval Sculpture: Reflections on an Art Historical Pioneer," *Konsthistorisk Tidskrift* 62 (1993), 69–83, and *The Shaping of Art History: Wilhelm Vöge, Adolph Goldschmidt, and the Study of Medieval Art* (New York, 1995).

Madeline H. Caviness: PhD Harvard University, 1970. Mary Richardson Pro-

fessor and Professor of Art History, Tufts University; President Corpus Vitrearum, International Board 1987–1995; President Medieval Academy of
America, 1993–4. Publications include articles on architecture, manuscripts,
stained glass, and medievalism in *Art Bulletin, Gesta, Journal of the Warburg
and Courtauld Institutes, Antiquaries Journal, La revue de l'art, Speculum, Walpole
Society Publications*. Books include *The Early Stained Glass of Canterbury Cathedral ca. 1175–1220* (Princeton, 1977); *The Windows of Christ Church Cathedral,
Corpus Vitrearum Medii Aevi. Great Britain* II (London, 1981); *Sumptuous Arts at
the Royal Abbeys in Reims and Braine: Ornatus Elegantiae, Varietate Stupendes*
(Princeton, 1990); editor and contributor to *Checklist of Stained Glass before
1700 in America Collections I–IV. Studies in the History of Art* (Washington, DC:
National Gallery of Art, 1985, 1986, 1989, 1990).

William W. Clark: PhD Columbia University, 1970. Professor of Art, Queens
College and The Graduate Center, City University of New York. Editor of
Gesta (International Center of Medieval Art) from 1988 to 1991. Publications
include articles on medieval architecture and sculpture in *Gesta, Journal of the
Society of Architectural Historians, Art Bulletin, Scientific American, Annales,
ESC, Journal d'histoire de l'architecture*; "The Early Capitals of Notre-Dame in
Paris," in *Tribute to Lotte Brand Philip, Art Historian and Detective*, ed. B. Lane
et al., pp. 34–42 (New York, 1985); "Suger's Church at Saint-Denis: The State
of Research," *Abbot Suger and Saint-Denis*, ed. P. Gerson, pp. 105–30 (New
York, 1986); *Laon Cathedral* [Courtauld Institute Illustration Archives: Com-
panion Text], 2 vols. (London, 1983 and 1987); and, with Charles M. Radding,
*Medieval Architecture, Medieval Learning: Builders and Masters in the Age of
Romanesque and Gothic* (New Haven, 1992).

Peter Draper: Postgraduate Diploma, University of London, Courtauld Insti-
tute, 1966. Lecturer and Chair Department of Art History, Birkbeck College,
University of London. Editor from 1978 to 1982 of the *Transactions of the Annual
Medieval Conferences* organized by the British Archaeological Association. Editor since 1985 of *Architectural History*, the journal of the Society of Architectural
Historians of Great Britain. Publications include: "William of Sens and the
Original Design for the Choir Termination of Canterbury Cathedral," *Journal of
the Society of Architectural Historians* 42 (1983), 238–48; "Architecture and Liturgy," in *The Age of Chivalry* [exh. cat. Royal Academy of Arts] (London, 1987),
pp. 83–91; "The Architectural Setting of Gothic Art," in *The Age of Chivalry*
(London, 1992), pp. 60–75; "The Retrochoir of Winchester Cathedral: Evidence
and Interpretation," *Journal of the British Archaeological Association* 139 (1986),
68–74; "'Seeing that it was done in all the noble Churches of England,'" in

Medieval Architecture and its Intellectual Context: Studies in Honour of Peter Kidson, ed. P. Crossley and E. Fernie, pp. 137–42 (London, 1990).

Eric C. Fernie Degree, University of London, Courtauld Institute, 1963. Faculty appointments at the University of Witwatersrand and University of East Anglia. Watson Gordon Professor of Fine Art and Dean of the Faculty of Arts, University of Edinburgh. Publications include articles on Anglo-Saxon, Romanesque, and Gothic architecture in *Gesta, Art History, Art Bulletin, Journal of the British Archeological Association, The Antiquaries Journal, Archaeologia, Bulletin monumental* as well as many contributions to books, such as "Reconstructing Edward's Abbey at Westminster," in *Romanesque and Gothic: Essays for George Zarnecki*, pp. 63–7 (Woodbridge, 1987). Books include *The Architecture of the Anglo-Saxons* (London, 1983), *Medieval Architecture and Its Intellectual Context: Studies in Honour of Peter Kidson*, ed., with P. Crossley (London, 1990), and *An Architectural History of Norwich Cathedral* (Oxford, 1992).

Arnold Klukas: MSD Yale Divinity School, 1972; PhD University of Pittsburgh, 1978. Faculty appointments at Oberlin College, Emory University, Smith College. Lecturer and Acting Director of Architectural Studies, University of Pittsburgh. Ecclesiastical appointment to Saint Paul's Episcopal Church, Pittsburgh. Dissertation title: "*Altaria Superiora*: The Function and Significance of the Tribune-Chapel in Anglo-Norman Architecture. A Problem in the Relationship of Liturgical Requirements and Architectural Form." Publications include "The *Liber Ruber* and the Rebuilding of the East End at Wells," *Wells and Glastonbury* [British Archaeological Association Conference at Wells, 1975] (London, 1981), pp. 30–5; "Winchester, Ely, Canterbury, and the Continuity of Anglo-Saxon Tradition in Post-Conquest England," in *Spicilegium Beccense II: Actes du Colloque International du CNRS: Etudes Anselmiennes IV Session* (1984), pp. 111–24.

Peter Kurmann: PhD University of Basel, 1967. Faculty appointments at the University of Basel, University of Regensburg, Free University of Berlin, and School of Architecture and Faculty of Letters of the University of Geneva. Currently Professor and Chair of the Division of the History of Medieval Art at the University of Fribourg, Switzerland. Publications primarily on architecture and sculpture north of the Alps and on restoration of medieval architecture. Numerous articles in periodicals and collective works, including *Congrès archéologiques de France, Münchner Jahrbuch der bildenden Kunst, Zeitschrift für schweizerische Archäologie und Kunstgeschichte*, and *Kunstchronik*. Books include *La cathédrale Saint-Etienne de Meaux. Etude architecturale*

(Geneva, 1971) and *La façade de la cathédrale de Reims* (Paris and Lausanne, 1987).

Brigitte Kurmann-Schwarz PhD University of Bern, 1984. Research Associate for the Fonds National Suisse de la Recherche Scientifique. Publications include "Les peintures du porche de l'église abbatiale de Saint-Savin. Étude iconographique," *Bulletin monumental* 140 (1982), 273–304; "Hauptwerke der mittelalterlichen Ausstattung," in *Sankt Martin zu Landshut* (Landshut, 1985), pp. 53–98, 102–9; with Peter Kurmann, "Das mittlere und südliche Westportal der Kathedrale von Meaux. Repräsentanten der Pariser Plastik aus dem zweiten Viertel des 14. Jahrhunderts und ihr politischer Hintergrund," *Zeitschrift für Schweizerische Archäologie und Kunstgeschichte* 43 (1986), 37–57, *Französische Glasmalereien um 1450, Ein Atelier in Bourges und Riom* (Bern, 1988), and *Die Glasmalereier im Berne Münster des 15.–18. Jahrhunderts. Corpus Vitrearum Switzerland IV* (forthcoming). Currently producing volume four of the Corpus Vitrearum series for Switzerland, *Les vitraux de l'ancienne collègiale de Berne (XVe et XVIe siècles)*.

Bernard McGinn: PhD Brandeis University, 1970. Naomi Shenstone Donnelley Professor, Divinity School, University of Chicago. Editor-in-Chief, Classics of Western Spirituality Series (Paulist Press); publications include articles on mysticism, medieval theology, Cistercian studies, and the history of religion in *Criterion, Citeaux, Church History, Analecta Cisterciensia, Journal of Religion, Mediaeval Studies, The Thomist,* and *Monastic Studies.* Numerous books authored and edited include *Visions of the End: Apocalyptic Traditions in the Middle Ages* (New York, 1979), *Mystical Union and Monotheistic Faith: An Ecumenical Dialogue,* ed. with Moshe Idel (New York, 1989), *Foundations of Mysticism: Origins to the Fifth Century,* vol. 1 of *The Presence of God: A History of Western Christian Mysticism* (New York, 1991), and *Antichrist through the Ages: Two Thousand Years of the Human Fascination with Evil* (San Francisco, 1994).

Virginia Chieffo Raguin: PhD Yale University, 1974. Professor of Art History, College of the Holy Cross, Worcester, Massachusetts. Member, Corpus Vitrearum, American Committee. Director, The Census of Stained Glass Windows in America. Publications on stained glass, medieval art, and historicism include articles and reviews in *Gesta, Art Bulletin, Stained Glass, Journal of Glass Studies, Speculum, Journal of the Worcester Art Museum;* "Revivals, Revivalists, and Architectural Stained Glass," *The Journal of the Society of Architectural Historians,* 49 (1990), 310–39; and contributions to *Checklist of Stained Glass before 1700 in America Collections I–IV. Studies in the History of Art* (Washington, DC: National Gallery of Art, 1985, 1986, 1989). Books and catalogues include *Stained Glass in Thirteenth-Century Burgundy* (Princeton, 1982) and *Northern Renaissance Stained Glass: Continuity and Transformations* (Worcester, 1987).

Roger E. Reynolds: PhD Harvard University, 1969; Senior Fellow and Professor, Pontifical Institute of Mediaeval Studies. Publications include articles on medieval liturgy, law, and iconography in numerous journals, including "Image and Text: A Carolingian Illustration of Modification in the Early Roman Eucharistic Ordines," *Viator* 14 (1983), 59–82, and "Image and Text: The Liturgy of Clerical Ordination in Early Medieval Art," *Gesta* 22 (1983), 27–38. Books and contributions to books include *The Ordinals of Christ from Their Origins to the Twelfth Century*, Beiträge zur Geschichte und Quellenkunde des Mittelalters 7, ed. H. Fuhrmann, (Berlin and New York, 1978); "Law, Canon, before Gratian," *Dictionary of the Middle Ages*, vol. 7, ed. J.R. Strayer, pp. 395–413 (New York, 1986) "Rites and Signs of Conciliar Decisions in the Early Middle Ages," *Segni e riti nella chiesa altomedievale occidentale XXXIII: Settimane di Studio del Centro Italiano di Studi sull'Alto Medioevo, Spoleto, 11–17 Aprile 1985* (Spoleto, 1987), pp. 207–49.

Willibald Sauerländer: PhD University of Munich, 1953. Academic appointments at the University of Freiburg, 1966–70, and University of Munich, 1970, and Director of the Zentralinstitut für Kunstgeschichte, Munich, 1970–89. Guest-professorships include the University of Paris (Sorbonne), Collège de France, New York University, and Harvard University. Numerous articles and reviews in journals such as *Architectural History, Art Bulletin, Arte medievale, Art History, The Burlington Magazine, Gesta, Jahrbuch der Bayerischen Akademie der Wissenschaften, Revue de l'art, Zeitschrift für Kunstgeschichte*. Books include *Die Skulptur des Mittelalters* (Frankfurt, 1963), *Von Sens bis Strassburg. Ein Beitrag zur kunstgeschichtlichen Stellung der Strassburger Querhausskulpturen* (Berlin, 1966), *Gotische Skulptur in Frankreich 1140–1270* (Munich, 1970); trans. *Gothic Sculpture in France 1140–1270* (London, 1972), and *Die Zeit der grossen Kathedralen* (Munich, 1990).

Michael M. Sheehan (deceased): MSD Pontifical Institute of Mediaeval Studies. Institute Professor, Pontifical Institute of Mediaeval Studies. Publications include books and articles on social and legal history of medieval Europe, and medieval art and architecture, including *The Will in Medieval*

England (Toronto, 1965); *Family and Marriage in Medieval Europe: A Working Bibliography* (Vancouver, 1976); editor and contributor, *Aging and the Aged in Medieval Europe* (Vancouver, 1990); "Religious Life and Monastic Alahan," in *Alahan, an Early Christian Monastery in Southern Turkey*, ed. Mary Gough, pp. 197–220 (Toronto, 1985); "Theory and Practice: Marriage of the Unfree and the Poor in Medieval Society," *Mediaeval Studies* 50 (1988), 457–87; "Sexuality, Marriage, and the Family in Central and Northern Italy: Christian Legal and Moral Guides in the Early Middle Ages," in *The Family in Italy from Antiquity to the Present*, ed. D. Kertzer and R. Saller, pp. 168–83 (New Haven, 1991).

Illustrations

Fig. 1 Durham cathedral, interior of Galilee chapel to east

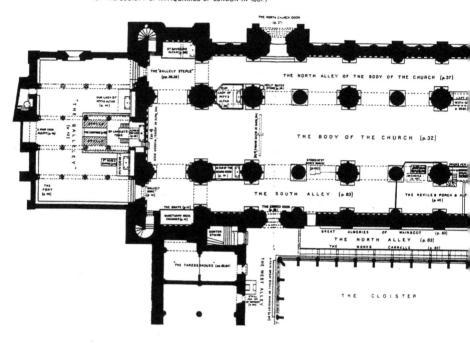

Fig. 2 Durham cathedral, liturgical plan for *Rites of Durham* as reconstructed by St John Hope

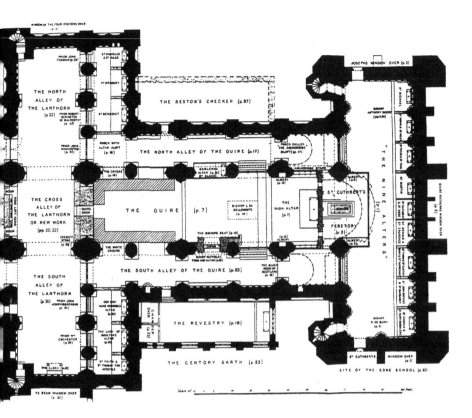

Fig. 3 Durham cathedral, interior of nave to east

Fig. 4 Saint Albans cathedral, nave screen from west.
From Aymer Vallance, *Greater English Church Screens*
(London, 1947), fig. 89

Fig. 5 Ely cathedral, Bishop Alcock's chantry chapel from west

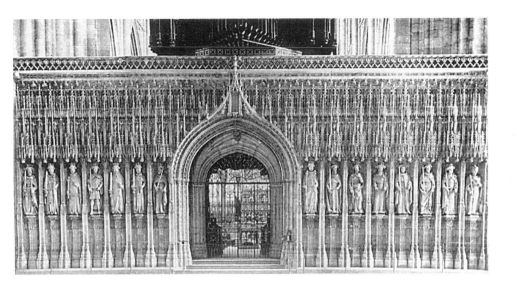

Fig. 6 York Minster, *pulpitum* from west.
From Aymer Vallance, *Greater English Church Screens*
(London, 1947), fig. 14

Fig. 7 Durham cathedral, Neville screen from west

Fig. 8 William Burgess, reconstruction of the medieval appearance of the setting of Edward the Confessor's shrine at Westminister Abbey, watercolour. Collection of the British Architectural Library, Arc. IV/2. Photo courtesy of the Royal Institute of British Architects, London

Fig. 9 Saint Albans cathedral, interior of feretory and watching chamber

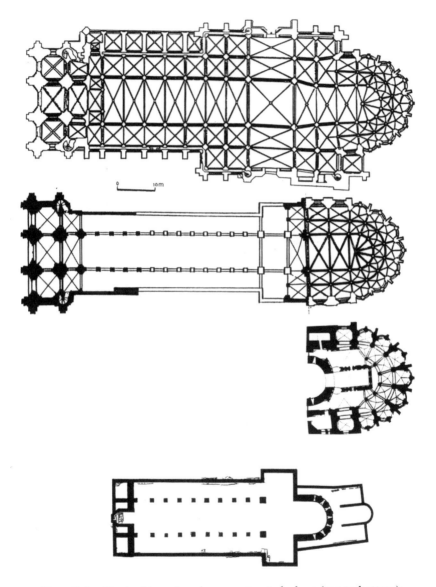

Fig. 1 Saint-Denis abbey church, reconstructed plans (top to bottom):
the present church (Crosby); the church ca. 1150 (Clark); the crypt
ca. 1150 (Clark); and the church ca. 775 with Hilduin's crypt ca. 835
(modified, after Crosby)

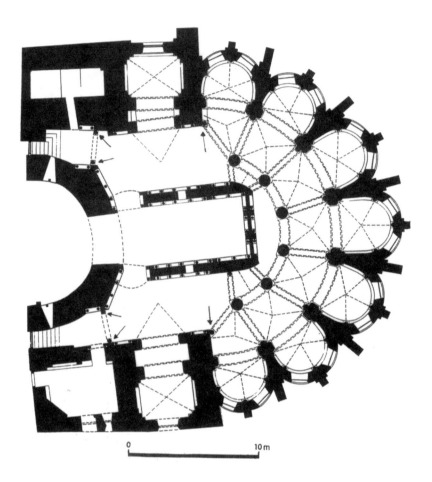

Fig. 2 Saint-Denis, abbey church, reconstructed plan of the crypt with arrows indicating the placement of the Merovingian columns

Fig. 3 Saint-Denis, abbey church, interior of the crypt.
Photo courtesy of Sumner McKnight Crosby

Fig. 4 Saint-Denis, abbey church,
Merovingian marble column in the crypt

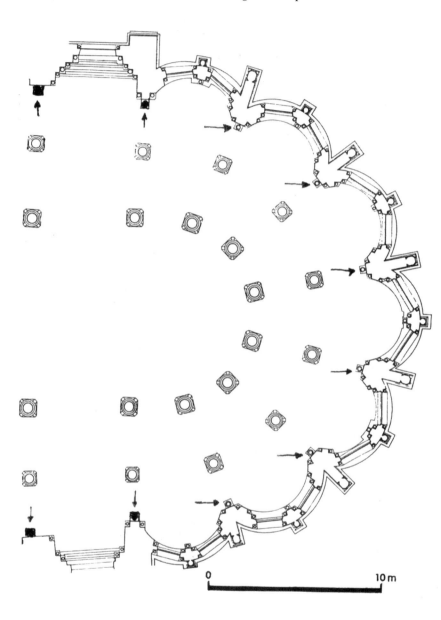

Fig. 5 Saint-Denis, abbey church, reconstructed plan of the upper chevet
with arrows indicating the placement of the six marble columns and the
four missing limestone columns (in black)

Fig. 6 Saint-Denis, abbey church, interior of upper chevet.
Photo courtesy of Joel Herschman

Fig. 7 Saint-Denis, abbey church, interior of the west centre bay

Fig. 8 Saint-Denis, abbey church, capital of the west centre bay, north side

Fig. 9 Saint-Denis, abbey church, Merovingian marble capital, Paris, Musée
National du Moyen Age

Fig. 1 Wells cathedral, interior looking east

Fig. 2 Glastonbury abbey, Lady chapel, south side.
Photo courtesy of Christopher Wilson

Fig. 3 Glastonbury abbey, Lady chapel, interior looking west.
Photo courtesy of the Conway Library, Courtauld Institute of Art,
University of London

Fig. 4 Glastonbury abbey, Lady chapel, detail of interior. Photo courtesy of
the Conway Library, Courtauld Institute of Art, University of London

Fig. 5 Glastonbury abbey, transepts, elevation of east wall. Photo courtesy of the Conway Library, Courtauld Institute of Art, University of London

Fig. 6 Wells cathedral

Fig. 7 Wells cathedral.
Photo courtesy of the Conway Library, Courtauld Institute of Art,
University of London

Fig. 8 Wells cathedral

Fig. 9 Temple church, London, west door.
Photo courtesy of the Conway Library, Courtauld Institute of Art,
University of London

Fig. 10 Temple church, London, nave.
Photo courtesy of the Conway Library, Courtauld Institute of Art,
University of London

Fig. 1 Chartres cathedral, view from the east.
Photo courtesy of Markus Hilbich

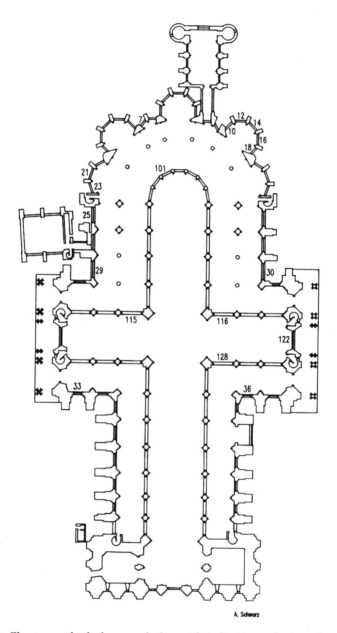

Fig. 2 Chartres cathedral, ground plan with indications of selected stained-glass windows. Courtesy of Andrea Schwarz

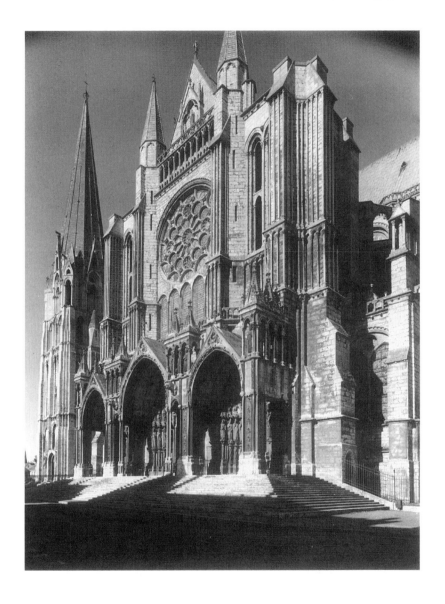

Fig. 3 Chartres cathedral, south transept, façade.
Photo courtesy of Markus Hilbich

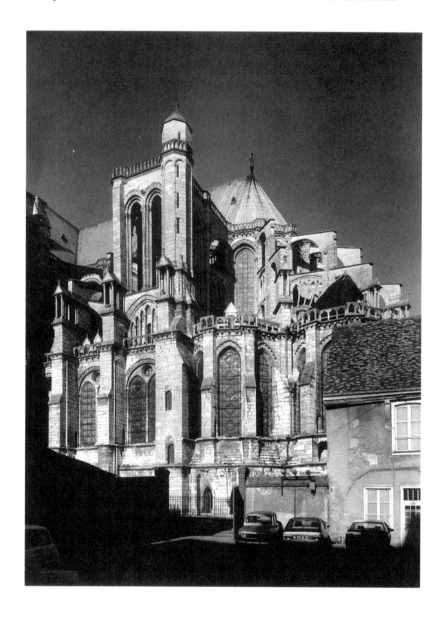

Fig. 4 Chartres cathedral, view from the south.
Photo courtesy of Markus Hilbich

Fig. 5 Chartres cathedral, Saint Lawrence window (25), detail, martyrdom

Fig. 6 Chartres cathedral, Saint Apollinaris legend (36), detail.
Photo courtesy of Markus Hilbich

Fig. 7 Chartres cathedral, upper choir (101), censing angel.
Photo courtesy of Markus Hilbich

Fig. 8 Chartres cathedral, windows of south transept (122), prophets carrying the evangelists on their shoulders. Photo courtesy of Markus Hilbich

Fig. 9 Chartres cathedral, south façade, left portal, Saint Theodore.
Photo courtesy of Markus Hilbich

Fig. 10 Chartres cathedral, window of south transept, east wall (116),
Saint Denis transfers the Oriflamme to Clement of Metz.
Photo courtesy of Markus Hilbich

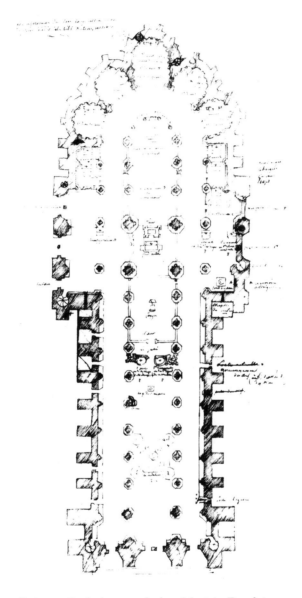

Fig. 1 Reims cathedral, ground plan, Mortain-Daudet, 1722, Reims,
Bibliothèque municipale.
Photo courtesy of the Zentralinstitut für Kunstgeschichte, Munich

Fig. 2 Coronation ceremonies in Reims cathedral showing King enthroned
on choir screen, engraving.
Photo courtesy of the Zentralinstitut für Kunstgeschichte, Munich

Fig. 3 Tabernacle with statue of angel, choir buttress, Reims cathedral. Photo courtesy of the Zentralinstitut für Kunstgeschichte, Munich

Fig. 1 Cathedral of Poitiers, ca. 1165–1300, ensemble, view from northeast.
Photo © ARCH. PHOTO PARIS/S.P.A.D.E.M.

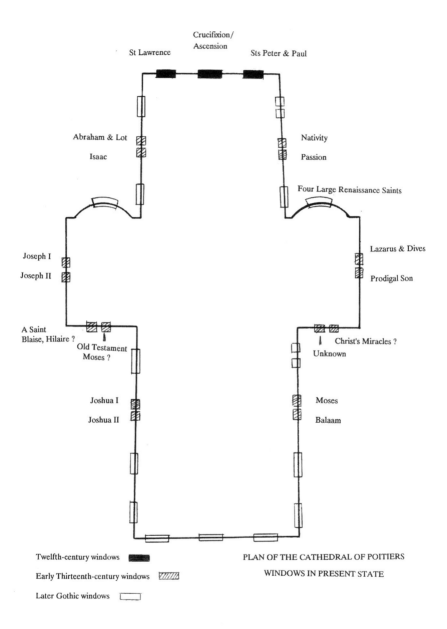

Crucifixion/
Ascension

St Lawrence

Sts Peter & Paul

Abraham & Lot

Isaac

Nativity

Passion

Four Large Renaissance Saints

Joseph I

Joseph II

Lazarus & Dives

Prodigal Son

A Saint
Blaise, Hilaire ?

Old Testament
Moses ?

Christ's Miracles ?

Unknown

Joshua I

Joshua II

Moses

Balaam

Twelfth-century windows

Early Thirteenth-century windows

Later Gothic windows

PLAN OF THE CATHEDRAL OF POITIERS

WINDOWS IN PRESENT STATE

Fig. 2 Cathedral of Poitiers, plan showing location of historiated windows

DIAGRAM OF ORIGINAL AND RECUT CLERESTORY OPENINGS
IN THE CATHEDRAL OF POITIERS

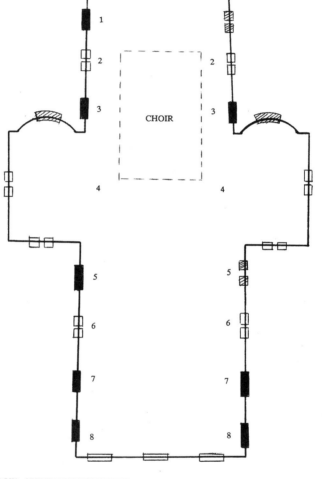

WINDOW OPENINGS RECUT IN THE LATE THIRTEENTH CENTURY (now grisaille glass) ▰▰▰

ORIGINAL OPENINGS (now with grisaille glass) ▨▨▨

Fig. 3 Cathedral of Poitiers, plan of original and recut clerestory openings

Fig. 4 Cathedral of Poitiers, Crucifixion window, ca. 1165–70.
Photo © ARCH. PHOTO PARIS/S.P.A.D.E.M.

Fig. 5 Cathedral of Poitiers, First Joseph window, detail, ca. 1210–15.
Photo © ARCH. PHOTO PARIS/S.P.A.D.E.M.

Fig. 6 Cathedral of Poitiers, Saint Blaise window, detail, ca. 1210–15.
Photo © ARCH. PHOTO PARIS/S.P.A.D.E.M.

Fig. 7 Cathedral of Poitiers, Joshua window, detail, 1225?
Photo © ARCH. PHOTO PARIS/S.P.A.D.E.M.

Fig. 8 Cathedral of Poitiers, interior, view from south aisle of nave.
Photo © ARCH. PHOTO PARIS/S.P.A.D.E.M.

Fig. 9 Cathedral of Poitiers,
renderings of three bays of the north nave to the west of the crossing, 1225?
Photo © ARCH. PHOTO PARIS/S.P.A.D.E.M.

Fig. 10 Cathedral of Poitiers, vaults and capitals, south nave, ca. 1240?
Photo © ARCH. PHOTO PARIS/S.P.A.D.E.M.

Fig. 11 Cathedral of Poitiers, north aisle of nave and choir.
Photo © ARCH. PHOTO PARIS/S.P.A.D.E.M.

Fig. 12 Cathedral of Poitiers,
First Joseph window, ca. 1210–15,
narrative schema

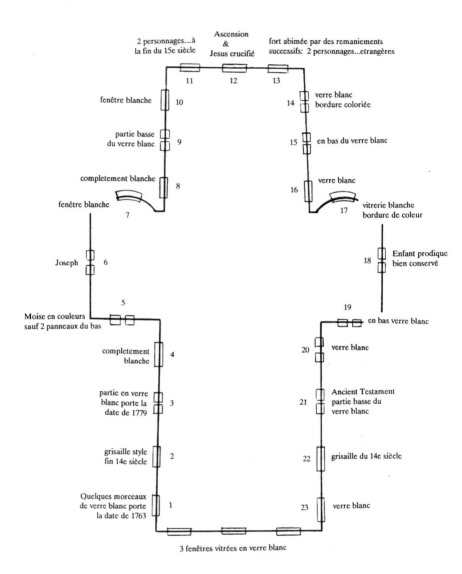

Fig. 13 Cathedral of Poitiers,
plan of windows as expertised by Steinheil in 1872

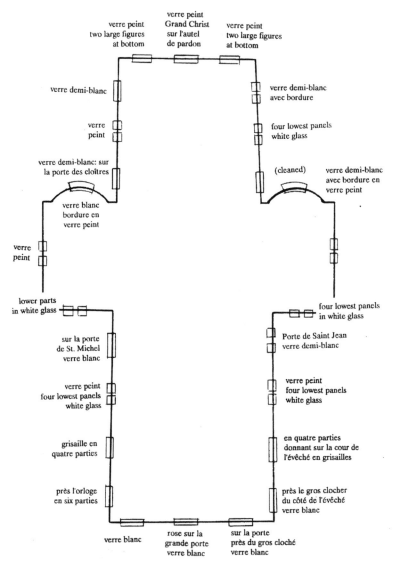

verre peint
Grand Christ
sur l'autel
de pardon

verre peint
two large figures
at bottom

verre peint
two large figures
at bottom

verre demi-blanc

verre demi-blanc
avec bordure

verre
peint

four lowest panels
white glass

verre demi-blanc: sur
la porte des cloîtres

(cleaned)

verre demi-blanc
avec bordure en
verre peint

verre blanc
bordure en
verre peint

verre
peint

lower parts
in white glass

four lowest panels
in white glass

sur la porte
de St. Michel
verre blanc

Porte de Saint Jean
verre demi-blanc

verre peint
four lowest panels
white glass

verre peint
four lowest panels
white glass

grisaille en
quatre parties

en quatre parties
donnant sur la cour de
l'évêché en grisailles

près l'orloge
en six parties

près le gros clocher
du côté de l'évêché
verre blanc

verre blanc

rose sur la
grande porte
verre blanc

sur la porte
près du gros cloché
verre blanc

1775: EXPERTISE BY REVERAD AND DESCANTES

Fig. 14 Cathedral of Poitiers,
plan of windows as expertised by Reverad and Descantes in 1775

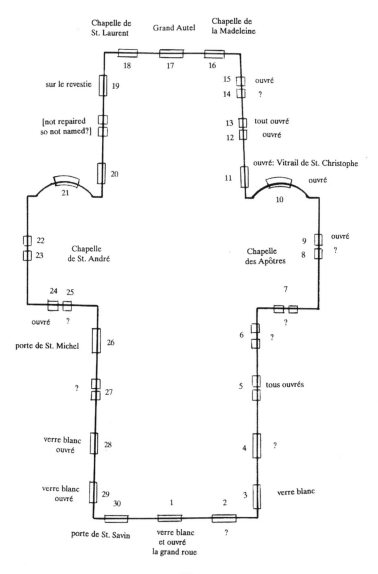

Chapelle de
St. Laurent

Grand Autel

Chapelle de
la Madeleine

18   17   16

sur le revestie   19

15   ouvré
14   ?

[not repaired
so not named?]

13   tout ouvré
12   ouvré

ouvré: Vitrail de St. Christophe

20

11   ouvré

21

10

22

9   ouvré
8   ?

23   Chapelle
de St. André

Chapelle
des Apôtres   7

24   25

7

ouvré   ?

?

porte de St. Michel   26

6   ?

?   27

5   tous ouvrés

verre blanc
ouvré   28

4   ?

verre blanc
ouvré   29
30   1   2   3   verre blanc

porte de St. Savin   verre blanc
et ouvré
la grand roue   ?

1562: EXPERTISE BY FROVIGNAULT AND ROBIN

Fig. 15 Cathedral of Poitiers, plan of windows as expertised by Frovignault
and Robin in 1562

Fig. 1 Paris, Sainte-Chapelle, interior.
Photo © ARCH. PHOTO PARIS/S.P.A.D.E.M.

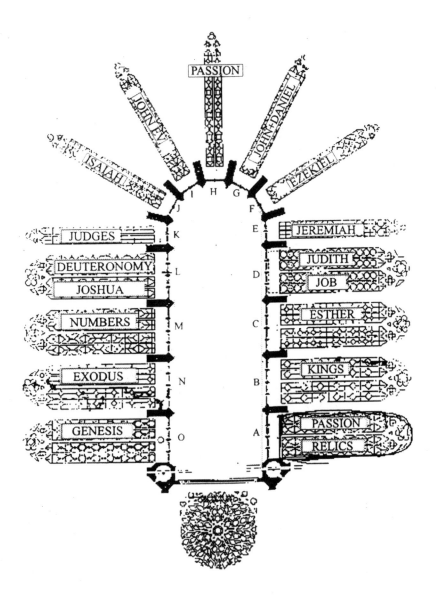

Fig. 2 Paris, Sainte-Chapelle, plan and program of the windows.
After Grodecki

Fig. 3 The relics, Paris, Sainte-Chapelle. From S.J. Morand,
Histoire de la Sainte Chapelle Royale du Palais (Paris, 1790)

Fig. 4 Paris, Sainte-Chapelle, bay M, north alcove.
Photo courtesy of Hirmer, Munich

Fig. 5 Louis at prayer, from *Life of Louis IX* by Guillaume de Saint-Pathus, Paris, Bibliothèque Nationale, ms. fr. 5716, fol. 24v

Fig. 6 Paris, Sainte-Chapelle, bay C: Esther led to banquet.
Photo © ARCH. PHOTO PARIS/S.P.A.D.E.M.

Fig. 7 Israelites battle the Philistines, Morgan Bible, c. 1245, New York,
The Pierpont Morgan Library, ms. 638, fol. 20v

Fig. 8 Sketch of the captured ark offered to the idol Dagon, *Psalter of Saint Louis*, after 1255, Paris, Bibliothèque Nationale, ms. lat. 10525, fol. 70. Courtesy of V. Raguin